池本幹雄

Boruto is serialized in *Weekly Shonen Jump*, but is a special case, appearing only once a month. A weekly series is usually 19 pages per chapter, so monthly would be four times that, or about 76 pages. However, *Boruto* is 45 to 47 pages, only 60 percent of that.

Still, it takes me about a week to produce the thumbnails, about 20 days to draw the final pages and then the rest of the time is spent on coloring and other tasks... So I end up using pretty much a whole month.

It's not something I asked for, and I have no idea whose decision it was, but I sure am glad *Boruto* is a monthly...

–Mikio Ikemoto, 2016

小太刀右京

This era that we live in experiences daily change. When I was a kid, each house only had one phone, and it was not cordless. Video game consoles consisted of Famicom (NES), and the world was waging a mysterious "battle" called the Cold War.

Today, the smartphone is commonplace and the internet is as ubiquitous as air. However, this too will likely become nostalgic history quite quickly. Boruto and his friends are striving in a world that is similarly evolving. Please enjoy their adventures!

–Ukyo Kodachi, 2016

BORUTO
-NARUTO NEXT GENERATIONS-

VOLUME 2

SHONEN JUMP MANGA EDITION

Creator/Supervisor MASASHI KISHIMOTO
Art by MIKIO IKEMOTO
Script by UKYO KODACHI

Translation: Mari Morimoto
Touch-up Art & Lettering: Snir Aharon
Design: Alice Lewis
Editor: Alexis Kirsch

First published in Japan in 2016 by SHUEISHA Inc., Tokyo.
English translation rights arranged by SHUEISHA Inc.

Printed in the U.S.A.

Published by VIZ Media, LLC
P.O. Box 77010
San Francisco, CA 94107

10 9 8 7 6 5 4 3 2 1
First printing, September 2017

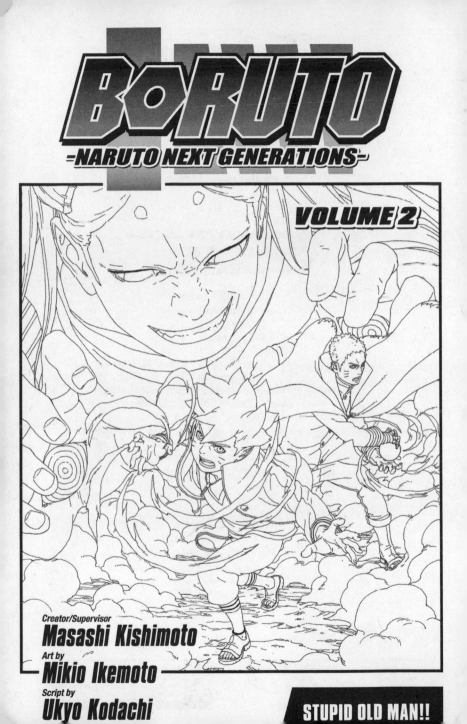

BORUTO
=NARUTO NEXT GENERATIONS=

VOLUME 2

Creator/Supervisor
Masashi Kishimoto

Art by
Mikio Ikemoto

Script by
Ukyo Kodachi

STUPID OLD MAN!!

BORUTO -NARUTO NEXT GENERATIONS- CHARACTERS

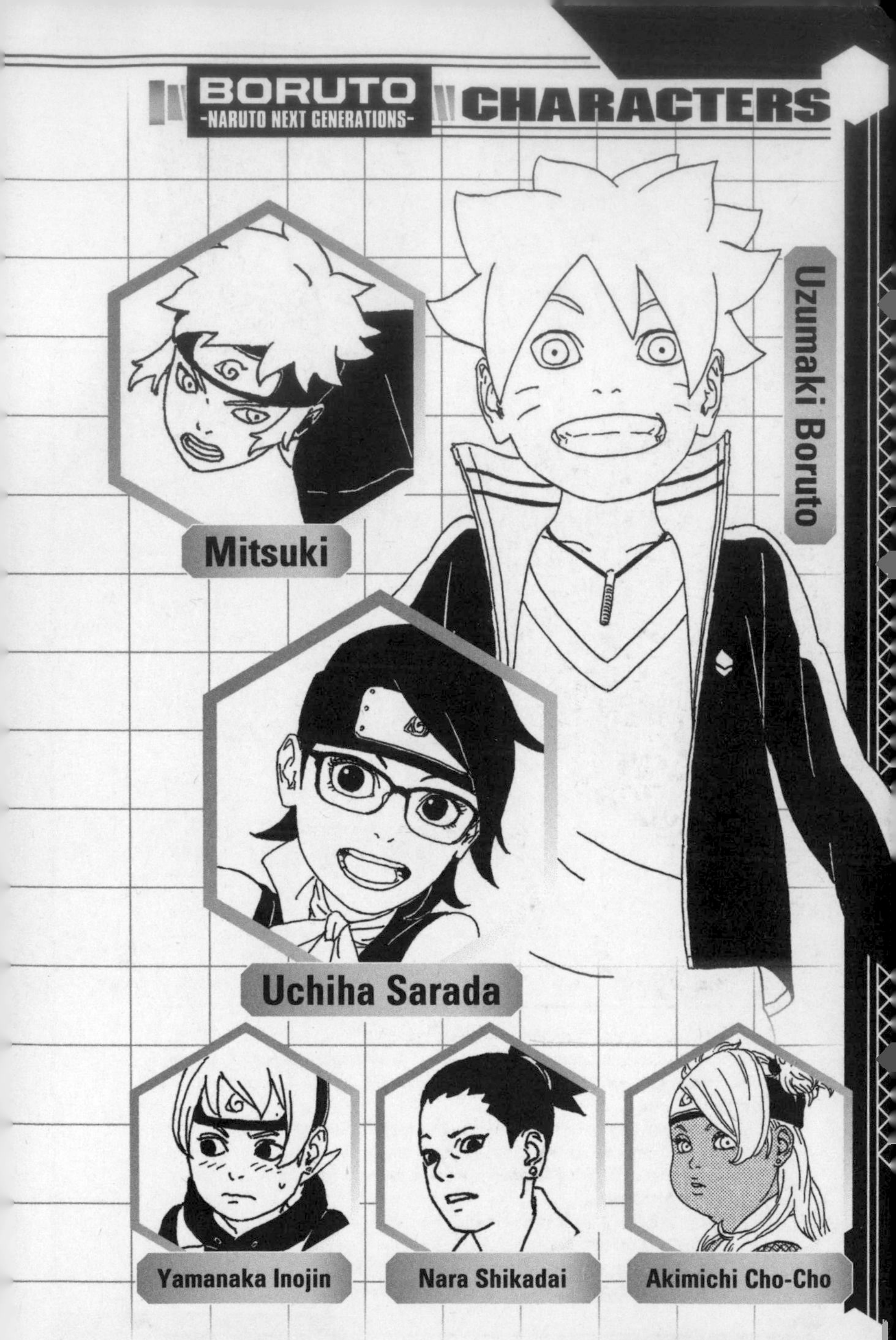
Uzumaki Boruto
Mitsuki
Uchiha Sarada
Yamanaka Inojin
Nara Shikadai
Akimichi Cho-Cho

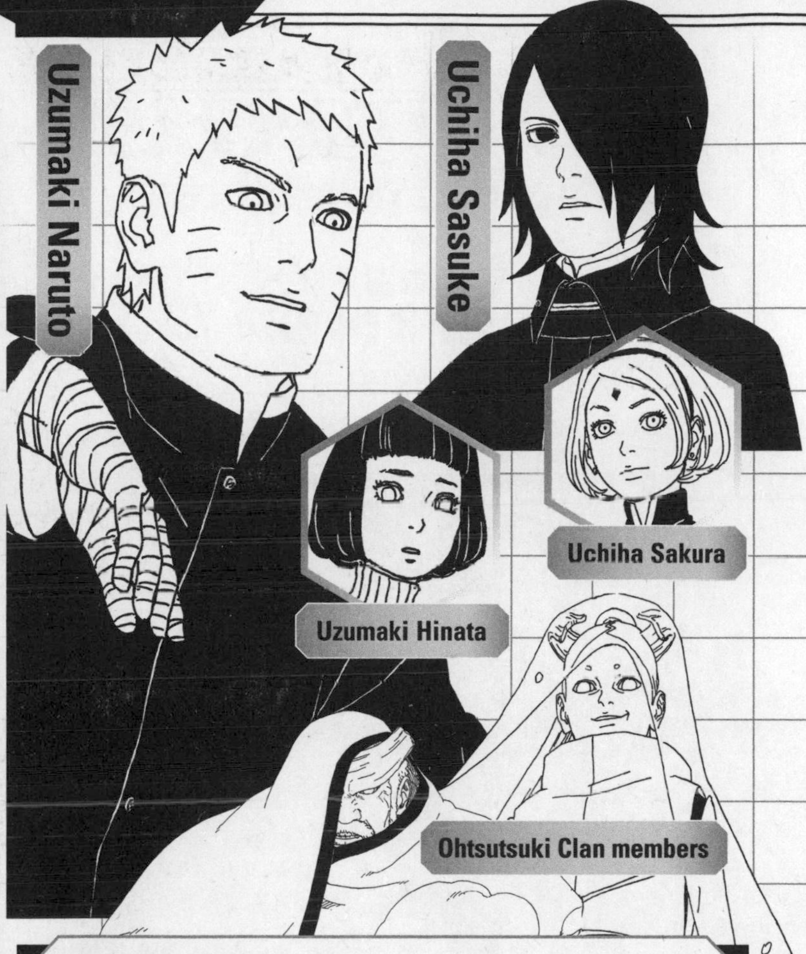
Uzumaki Naruto
Uchiha Sasuke
Uchiha Sakura
Uzumaki Hinata
Ohtsutsuki Clan members

STORY

The Great Ninja War that shook the world and shed much blood is now history. Naruto has become the Seventh Hokage, and the people of Konohagakure Village are enjoying peace. Yet Naruto's son Uzumaki Boruto has a glum life, perhaps due to his father's too-great influence.

Rebelling against Naruto while simultaneously craving his praise, Boruto decides to enter the Chunin Exam along with his teammates Sarada and Mitsuki. In preparation, Boruto becomes the student of Sarada's father and Naruto's former rival, Sasuke, and begins honing his ninjutsu.

However, the exam is more intense than Boruto imagined, and he ends up secretly using a prohibited Scientific Ninja Tool...

And from somewhere beyond their notice, a new threat stealthily approaches... The children of ninja legends are stepping forth onto a new shinobi path!

BORUTO

-NARUTO NEXT GENERATIONS-

VOLUME 2
STUPID OLD MAN!!

CONTENTS

Number 4: Stupid Old Man!!

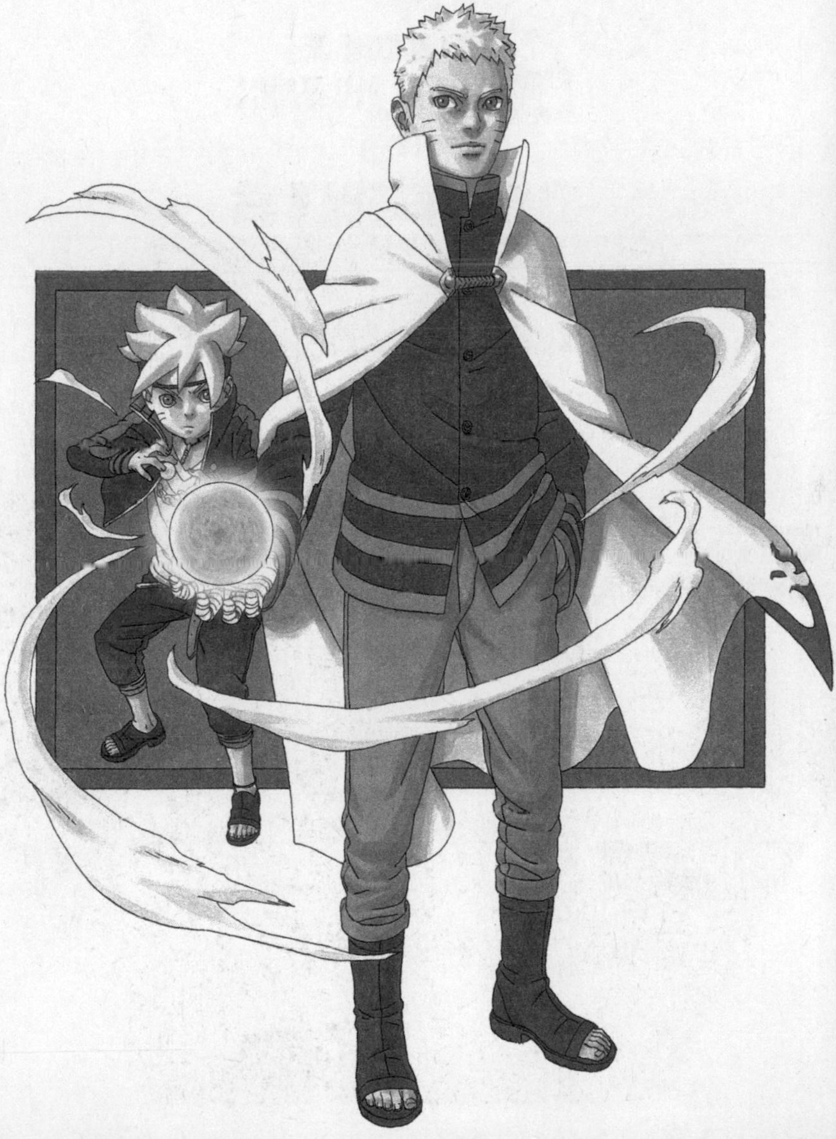

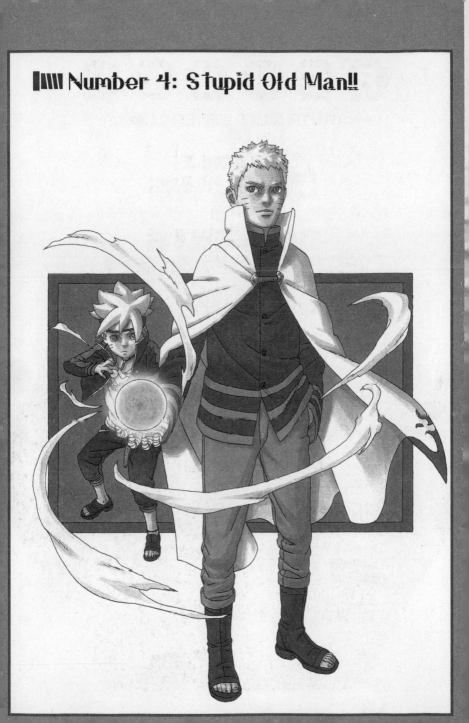

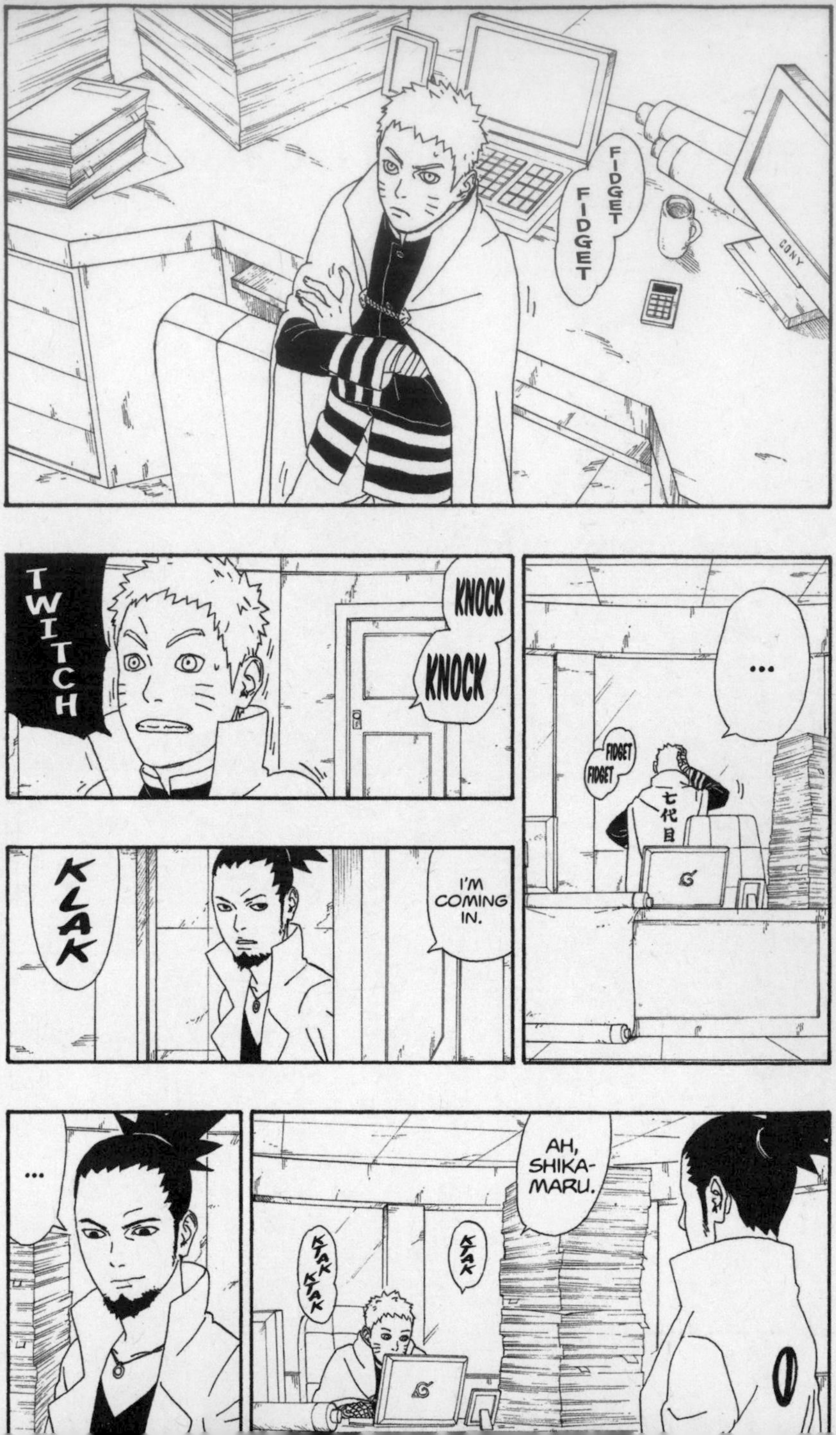
FIDGET
FIDGET
...
FIDGET
FIDGET
七代目
KNOCK
KNOCK
TWITCH
I'M COMING IN.
KLAK
AH, SHIKA-MARU.
KTAK
KTAK
KTAK
...

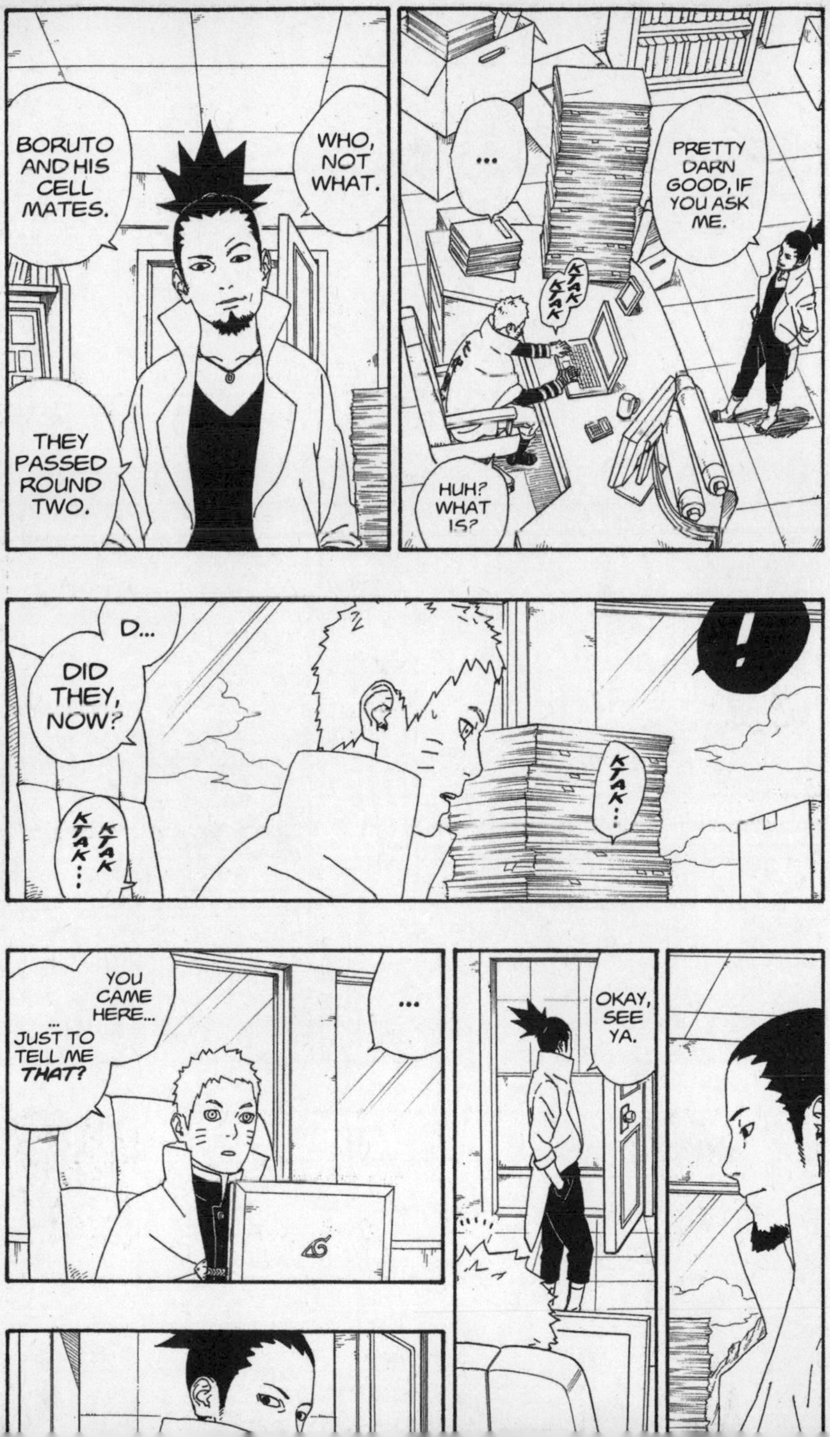
PRETTY DARN GOOD, IF YOU ASK ME.
...
KTAK KTAK
HUH? WHAT IS?
WHO, NOT WHAT.
BORUTO AND HIS CELL MATES.
THEY PASSED ROUND TWO.
!
KTAK...
D...
DID THEY, NOW?
KTAK KTAK...
OKAY, SEE YA.
...
YOU CAME HERE...
... JUST TO TELL ME *THAT?*

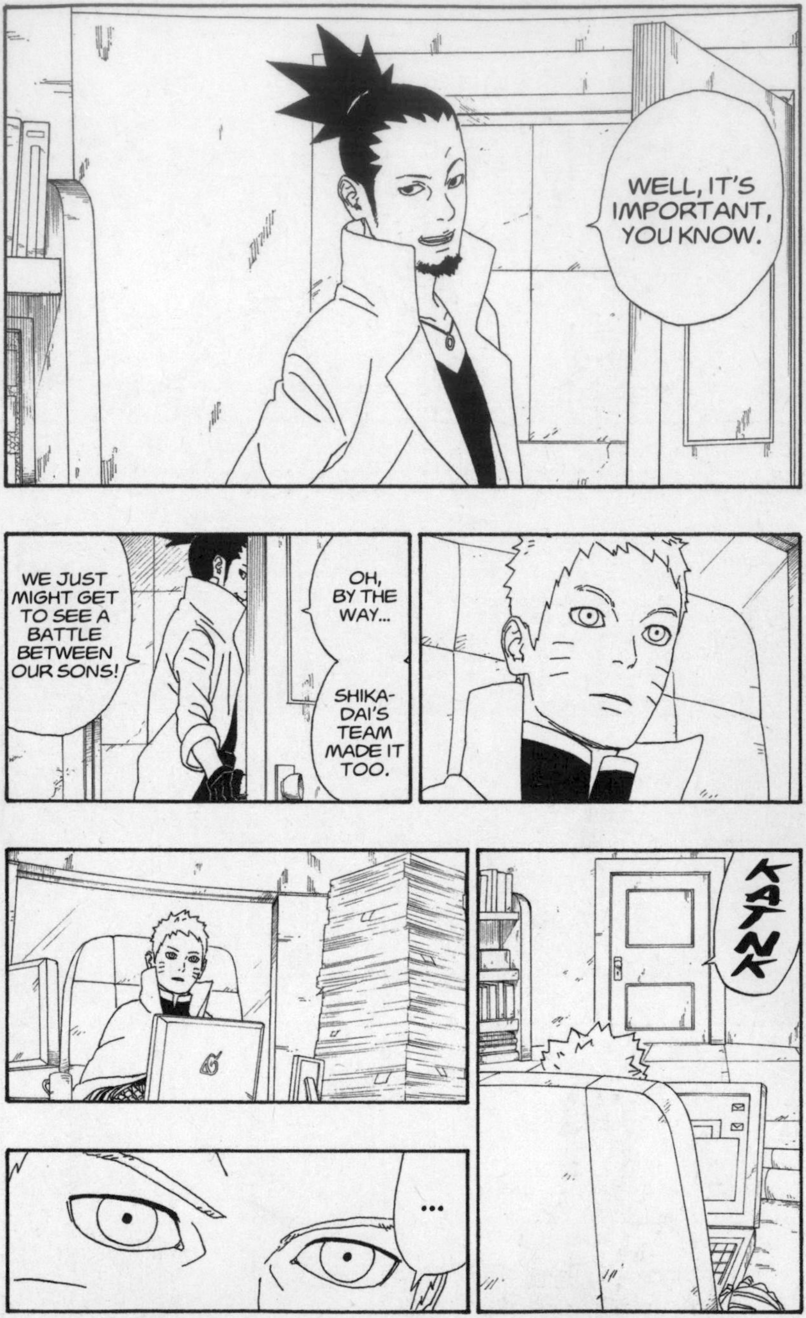
WELL, IT'S IMPORTANT, YOU KNOW.
OH, BY THE WAY... SHIKA-DAI'S TEAM MADE IT TOO.
WE JUST MIGHT GET TO SEE A BATTLE BETWEEN OUR SONS!
KATNK
...

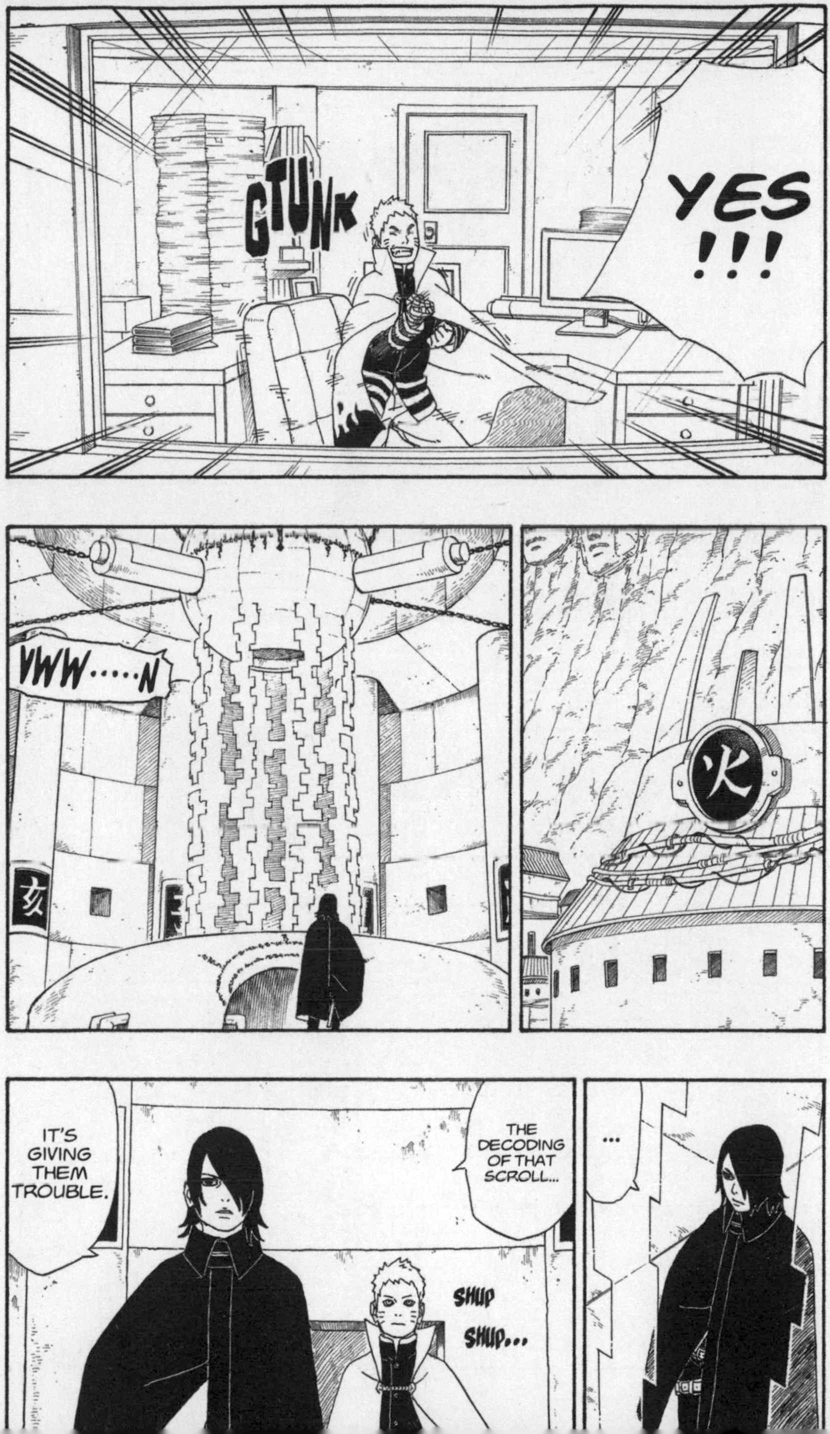
YES!!!
GTUNK
火
VWW.....N
亥
...
THE DECODING OF THAT SCROLL...
IT'S GIVING THEM TROUBLE.
SHUP
SHUP...

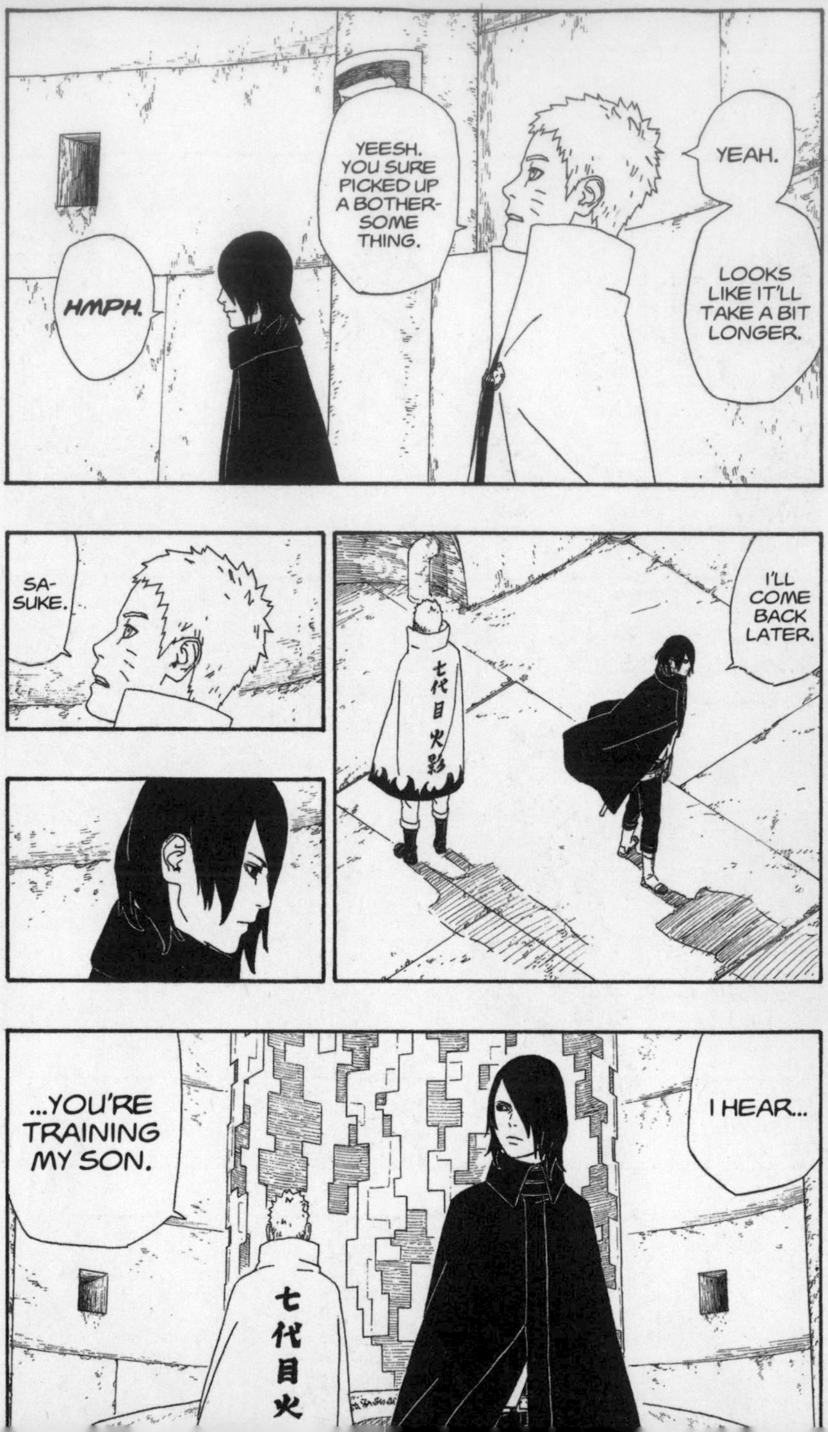
YEAH.
LOOKS LIKE IT'LL TAKE A BIT LONGER.
YEESH. YOU SURE PICKED UP A BOTHER-SOME THING.
HMPH.
I'LL COME BACK LATER.
七代目火影
SA-SUKE.
I HEAR...
...YOU'RE TRAINING MY SON.
七代目火

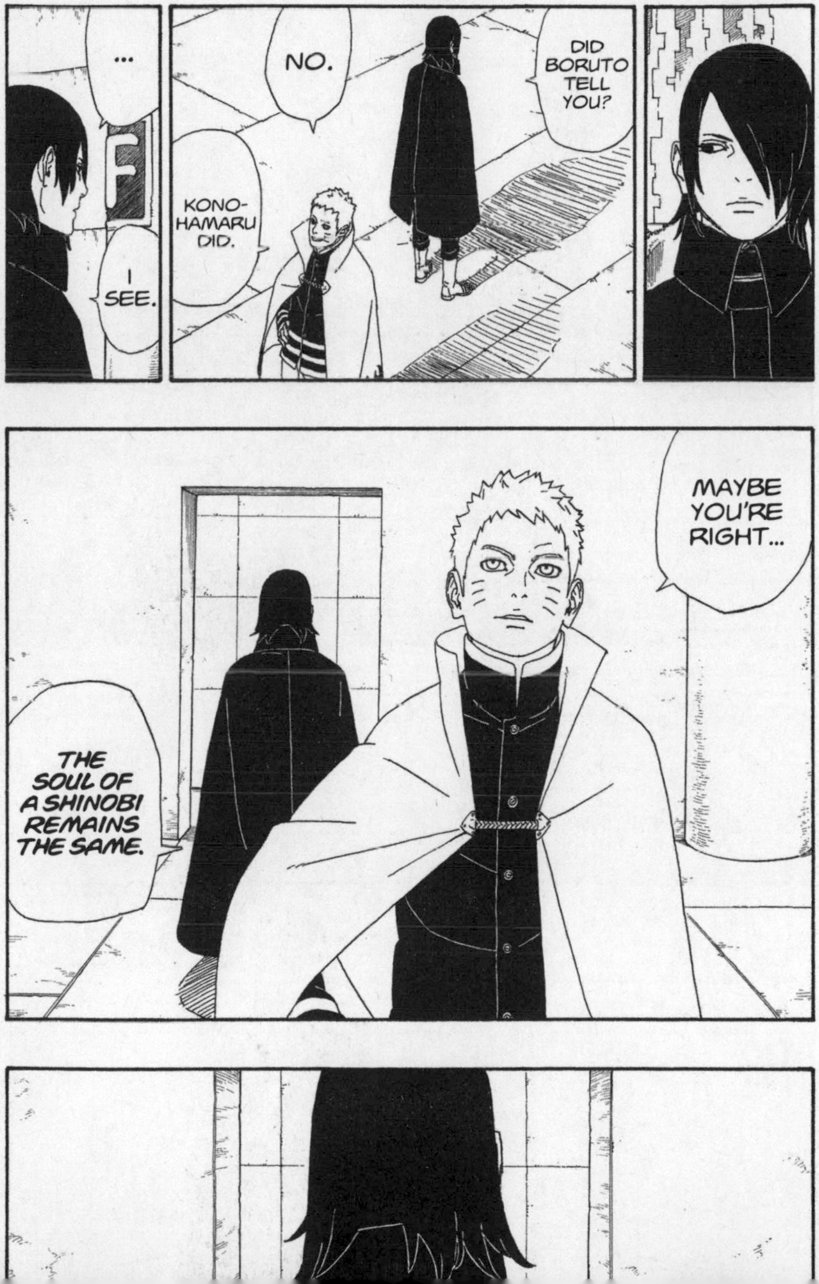
DID BORUTO TELL YOU?
NO.
KONO-HAMARU DID.
...
I SEE.
MAYBE YOU'RE RIGHT...
THE SOUL OF A SHINOBI REMAINS THE SAME.

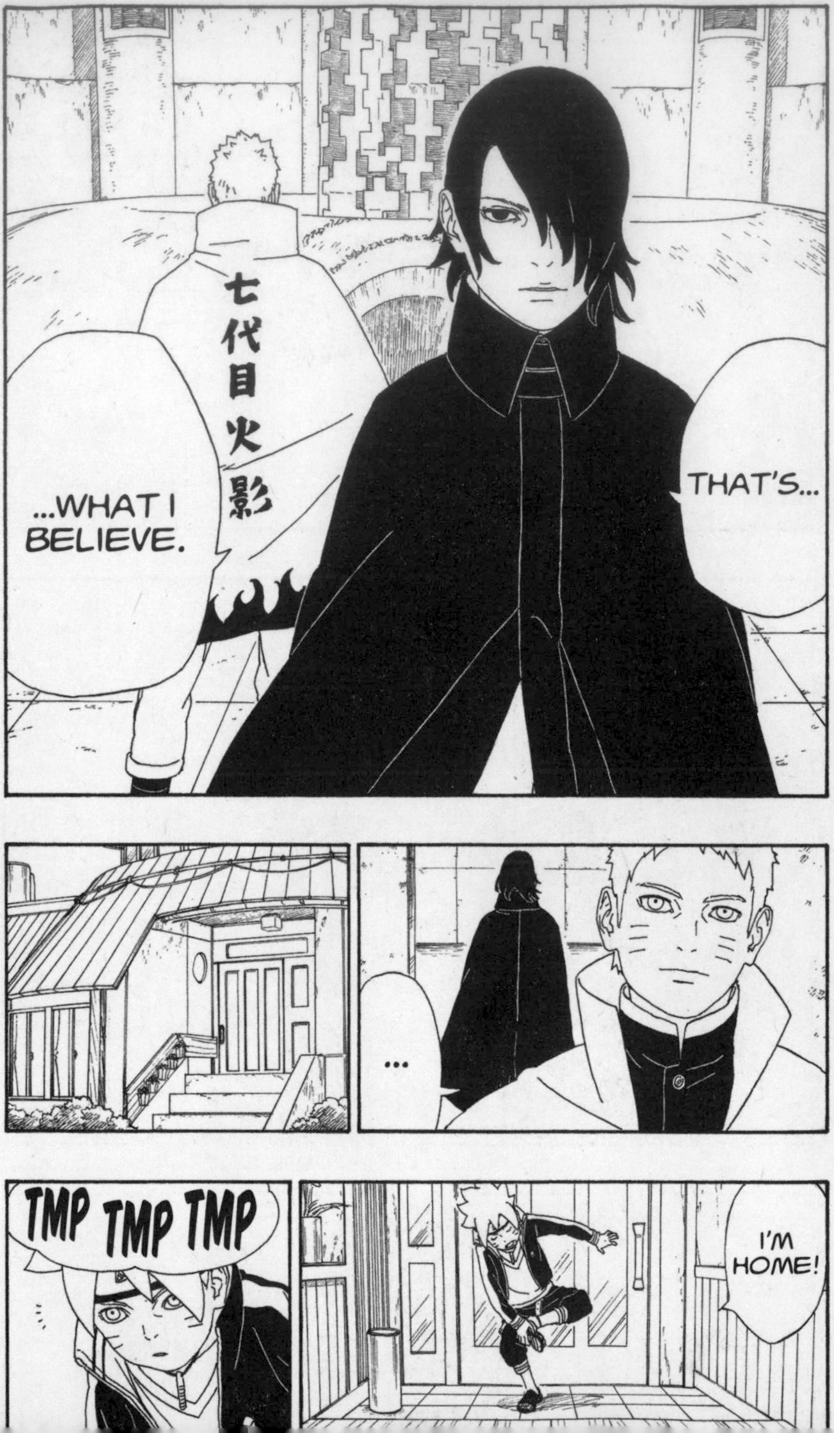
THAT'S...
七代目火影
...WHAT I BELIEVE.
...
I'M HOME!
TMP TMP TMP

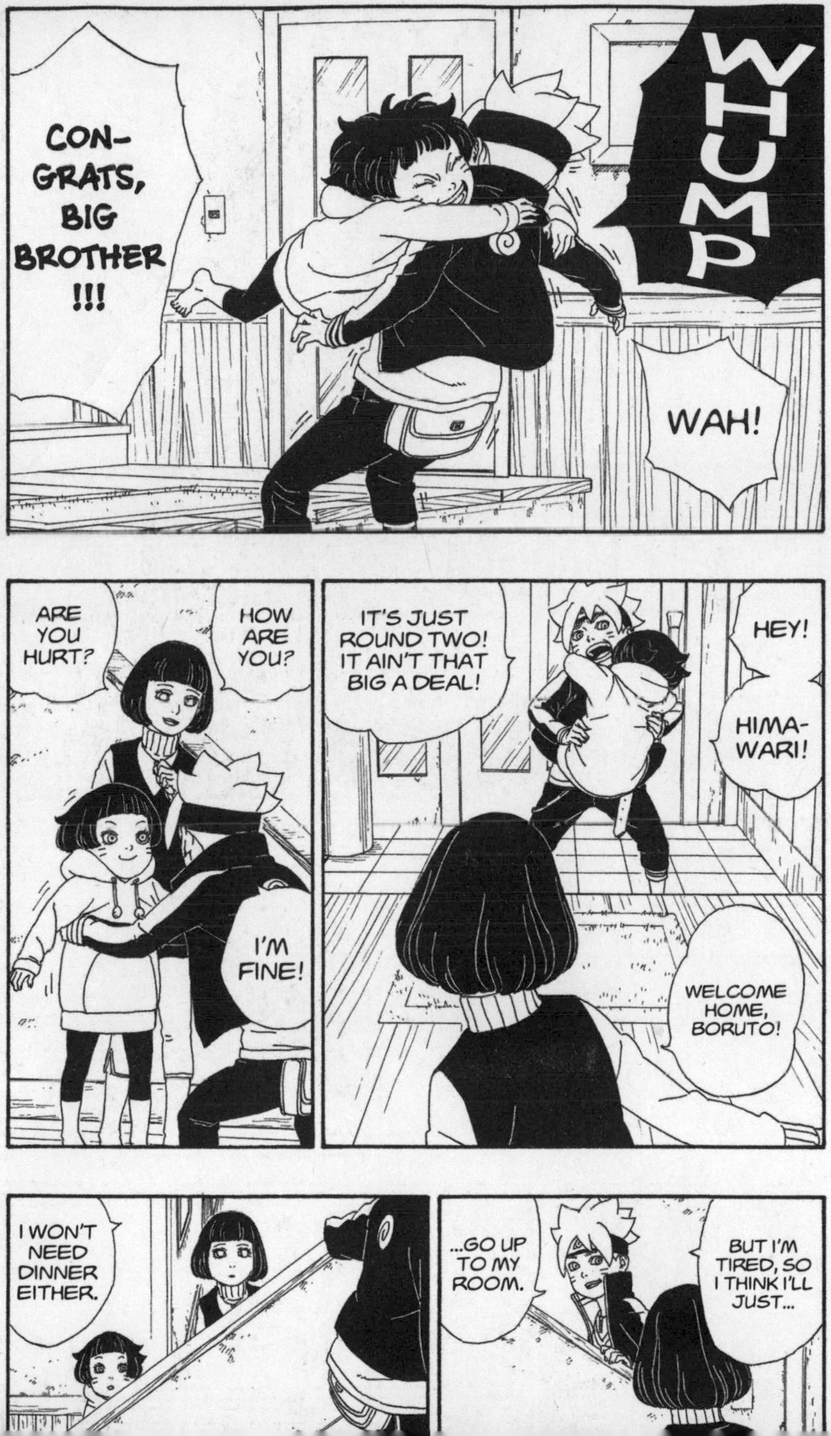
WHUMP
CON-GRATS, BIG BROTHER!!!
WAH!
HEY!
HIMA-WARI!
IT'S JUST ROUND TWO! IT AIN'T THAT BIG A DEAL!
WELCOME HOME, BORUTO!
HOW ARE YOU?
ARE YOU HURT?
I'M FINE!
BUT I'M TIRED, SO I THINK I'LL JUST...
...GO UP TO MY ROOM.
I WON'T NEED DINNER EITHER.

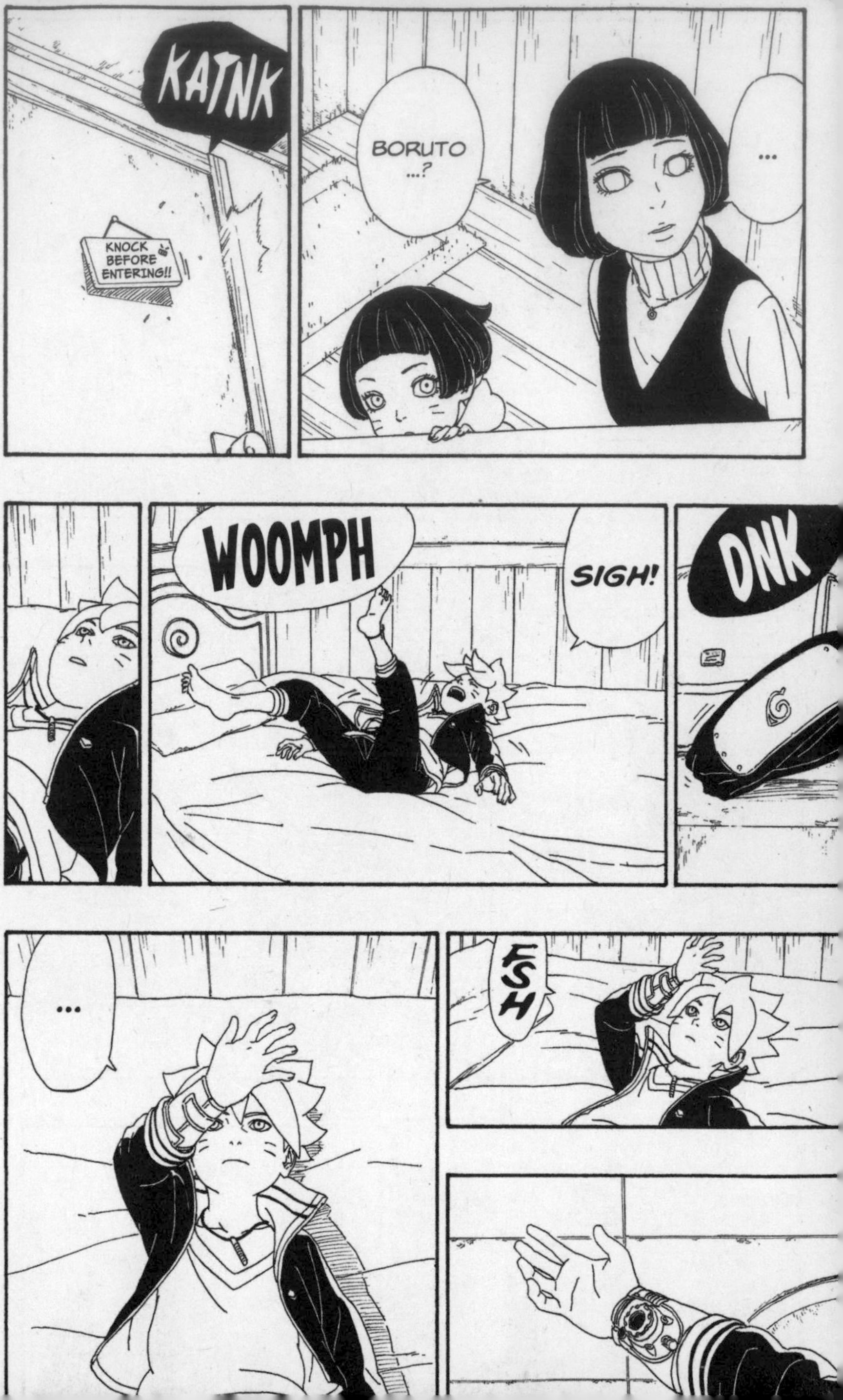
...
BORUTO ...?
KATNK
KNOCK BEFORE ENTERING!!
DNK
SIGH!
WOOMPH
FSH
...

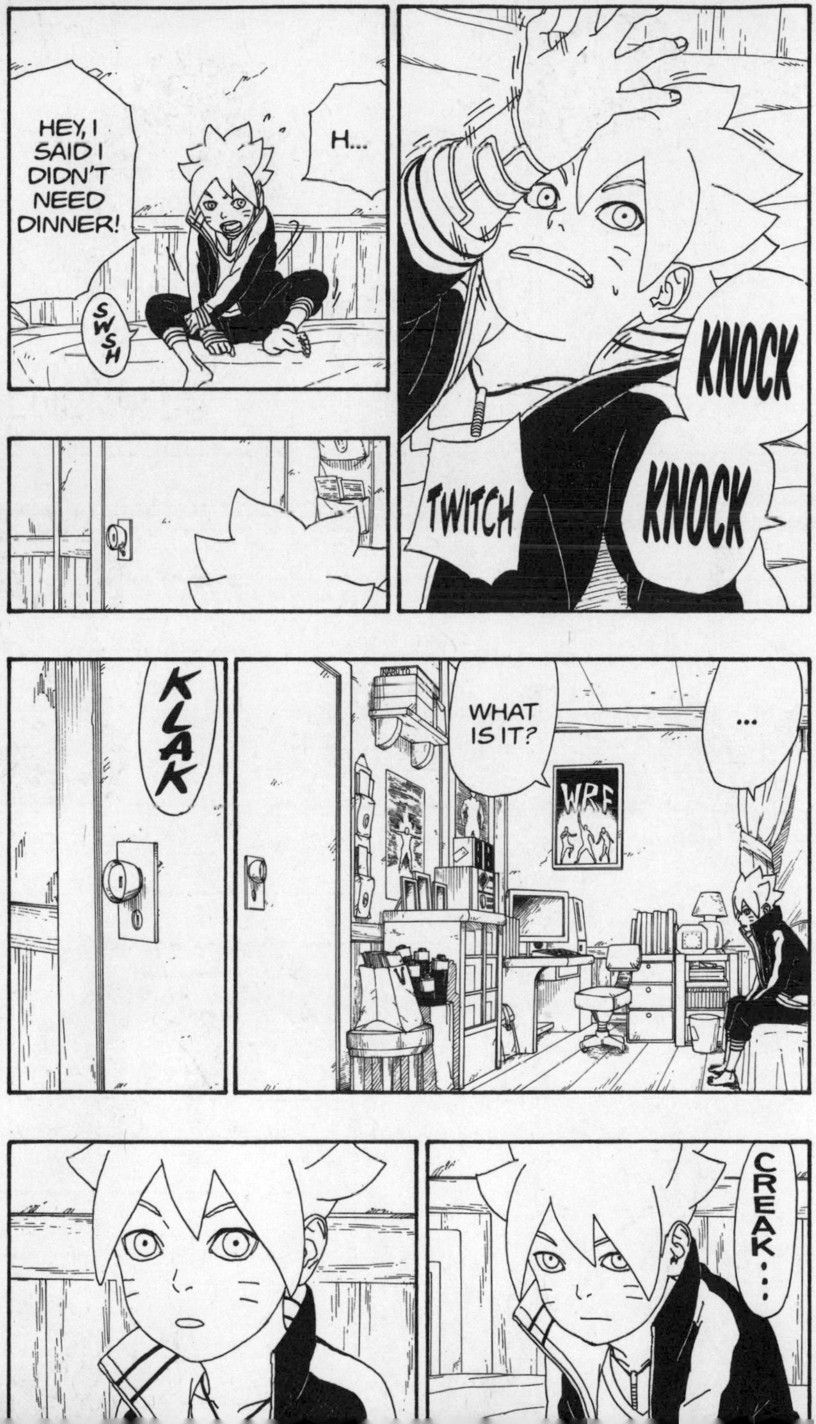
KNOCK
KNOCK
TWITCH
H...
HEY, I SAID I DIDN'T NEED DINNER!
SWSH
...
WHAT IS IT?
WRF
NARUTO
KLAK
CREAK...

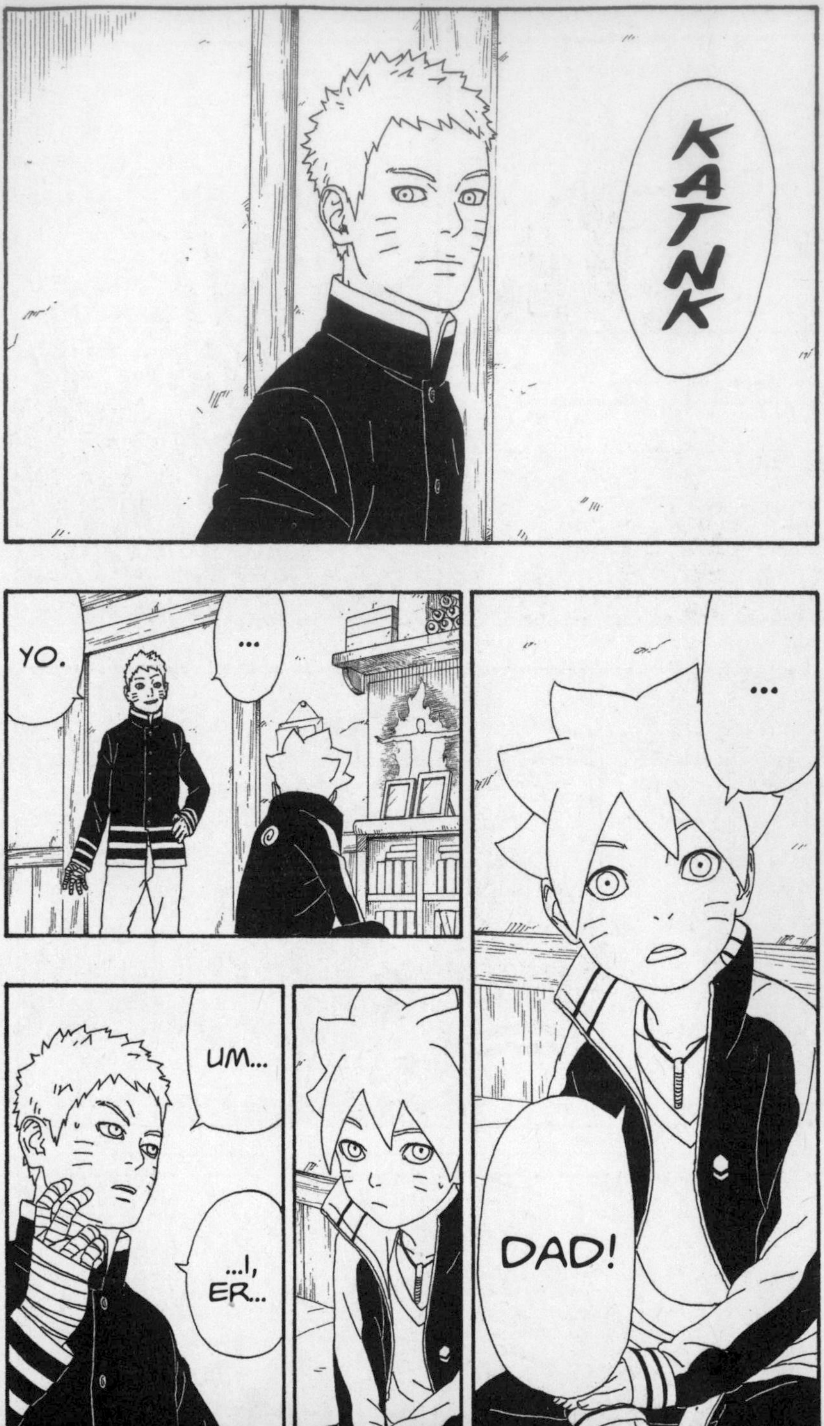
KATNK
...
DAD!
YO.
...
UM...
...I,
ER...

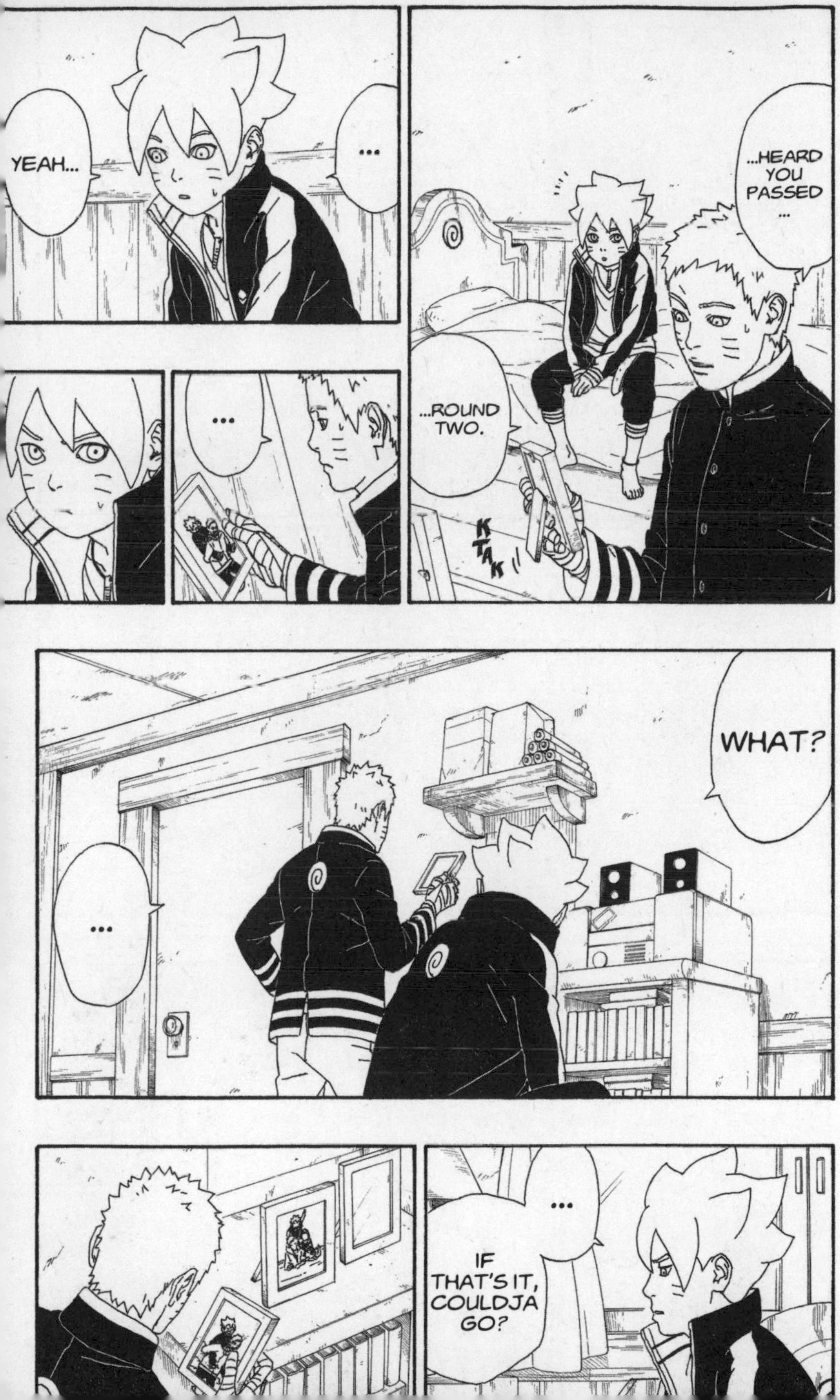
...HEARD YOU PASSED ...
...ROUND TWO.
KTAK
...
YEAH...
...
WHAT?
...
...
IF THAT'S IT, COULDJA GO?

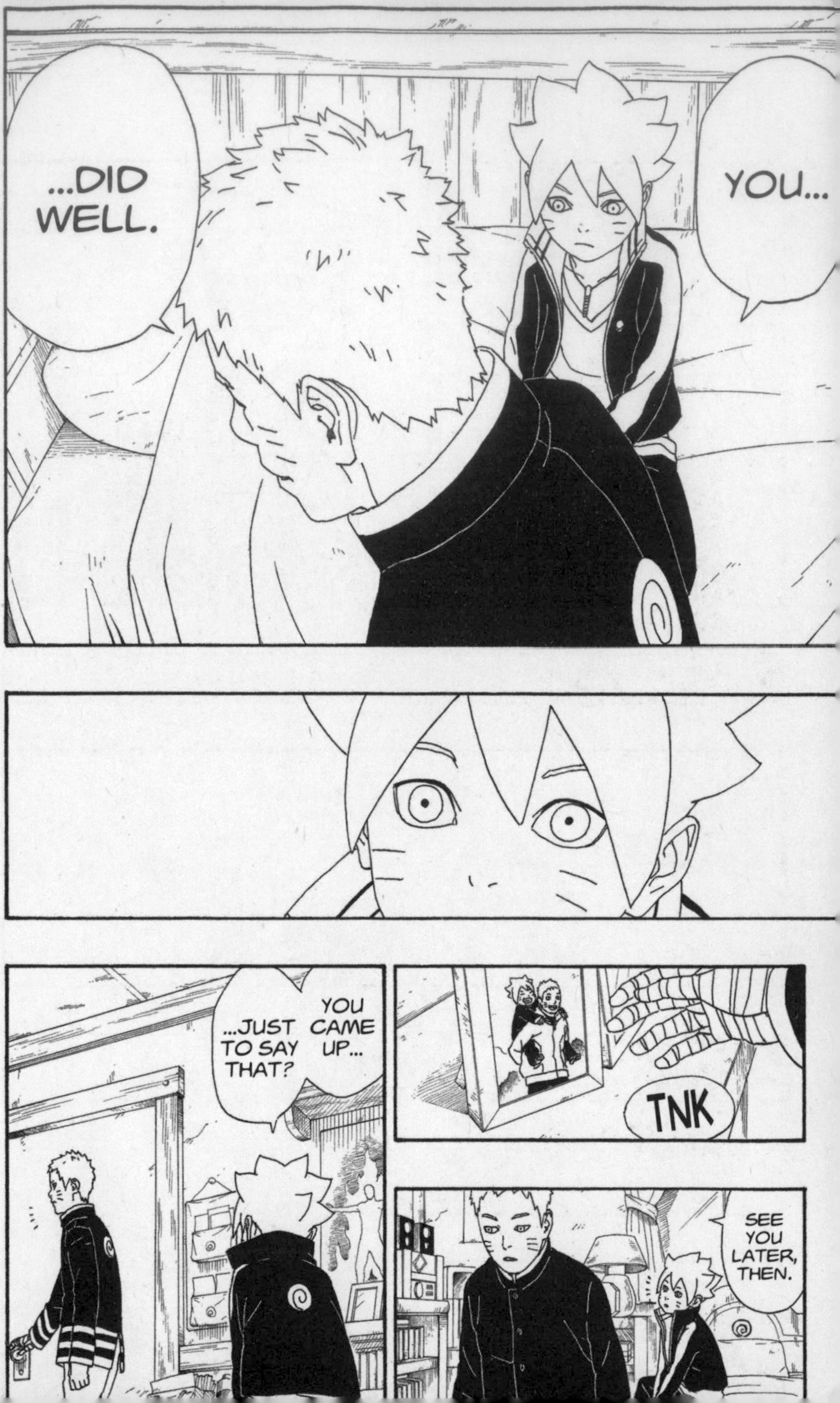
YOU...
...DID WELL.
TNK
SEE YOU LATER, THEN.
YOU CAME UP... ...JUST TO SAY THAT?

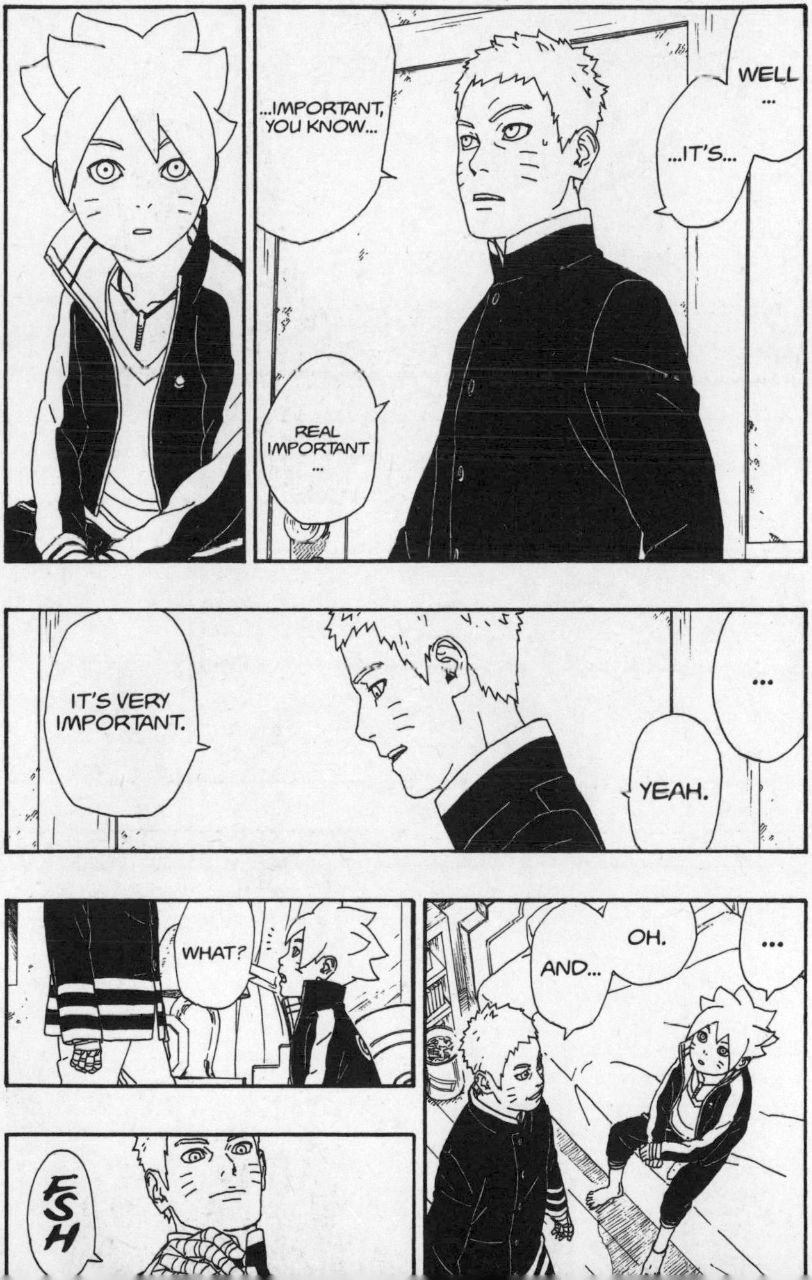
WELL ...
...IT'S...
...IMPORTANT, YOU KNOW...
REAL IMPORTANT ...
...
YEAH.
IT'S VERY IMPORTANT.
...
OH.
AND...
WHAT?
FSH

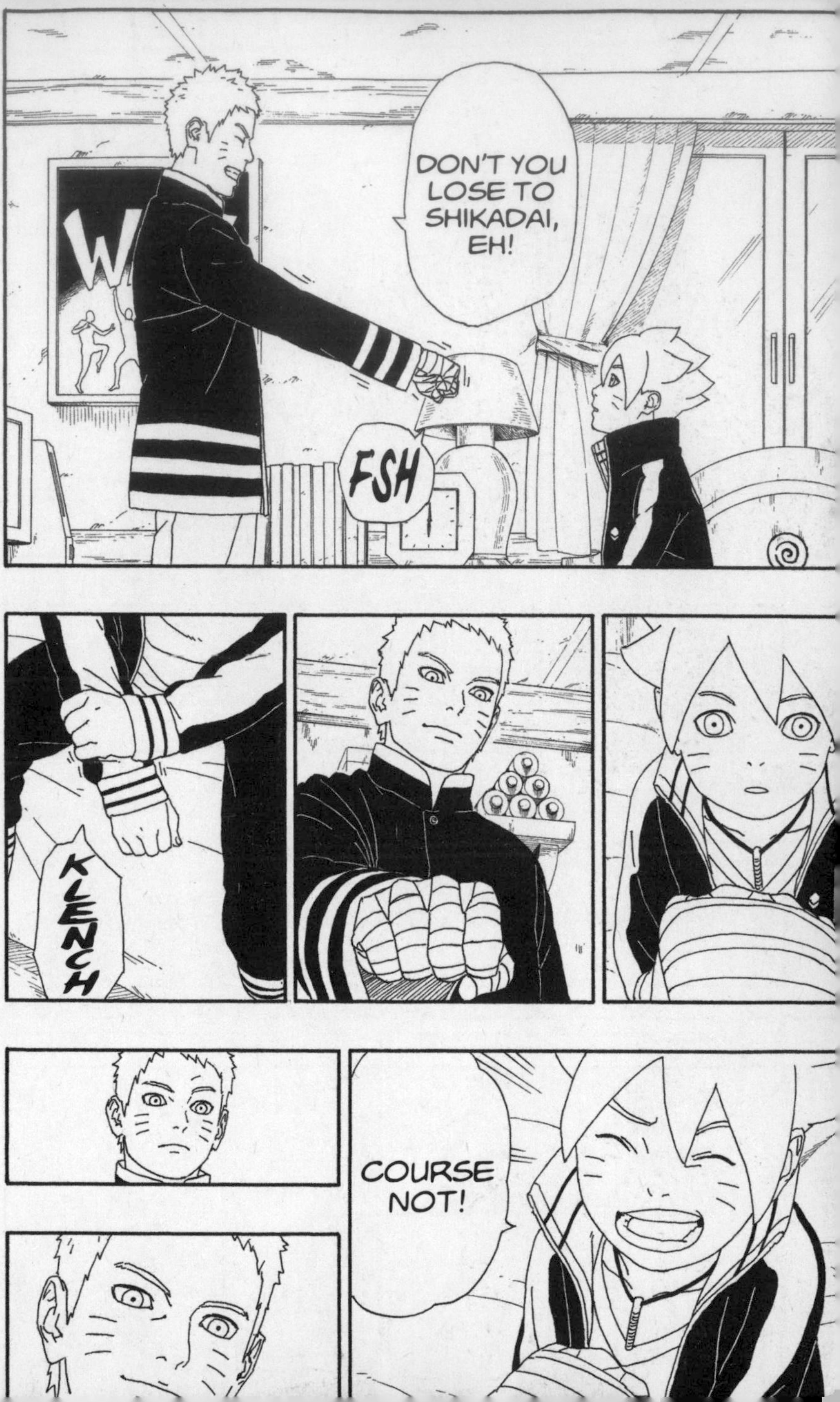
DON'T YOU LOSE TO SHIKADAI, EH!
FSH
KLENCH
COURSE NOT!

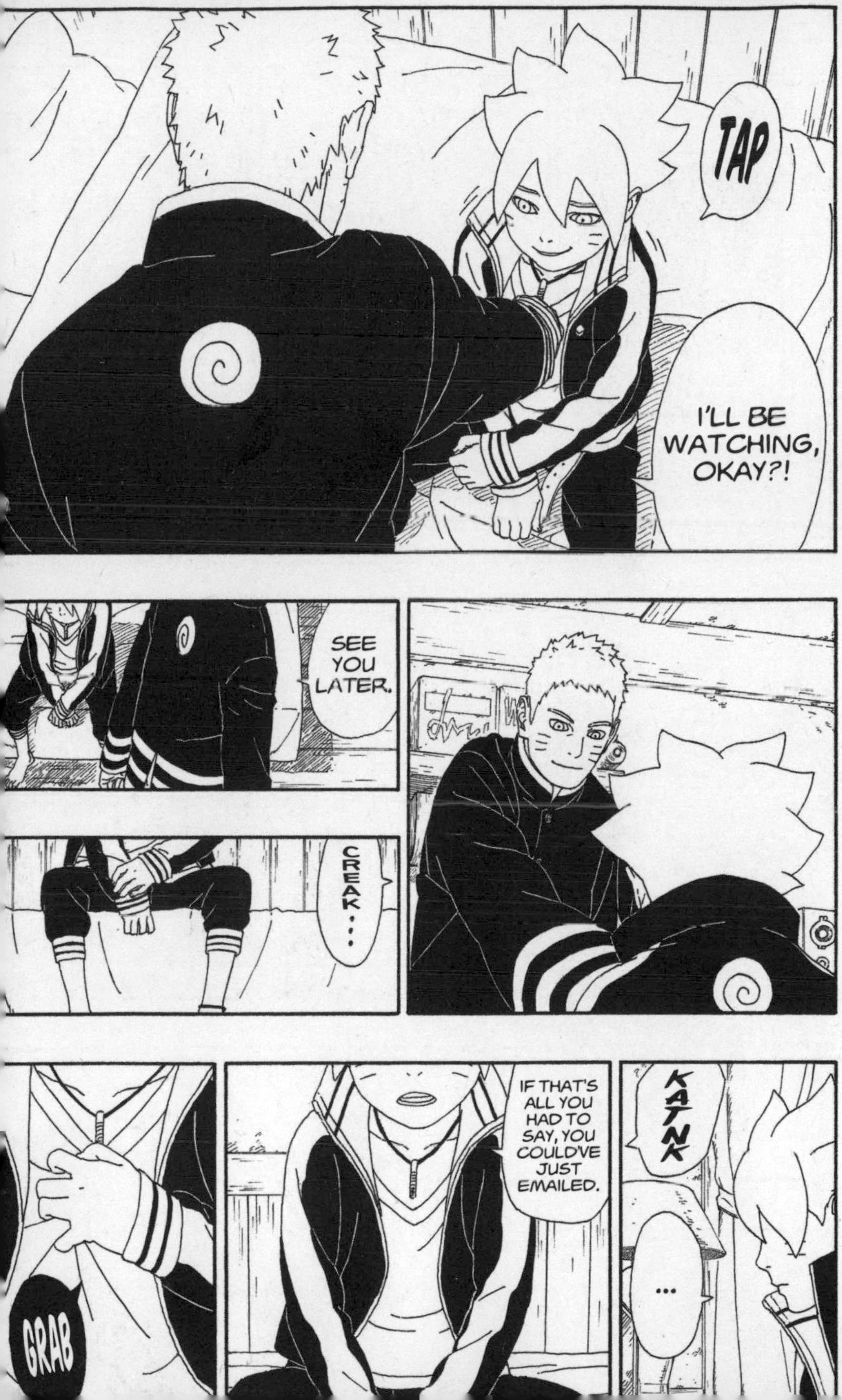
TAP
I'LL BE WATCHING, OKAY?!
SEE YOU LATER.
CREAK...
KATNK
...
IF THAT'S ALL YOU HAD TO SAY, YOU COULD'VE JUST EMAILED.
GRAB

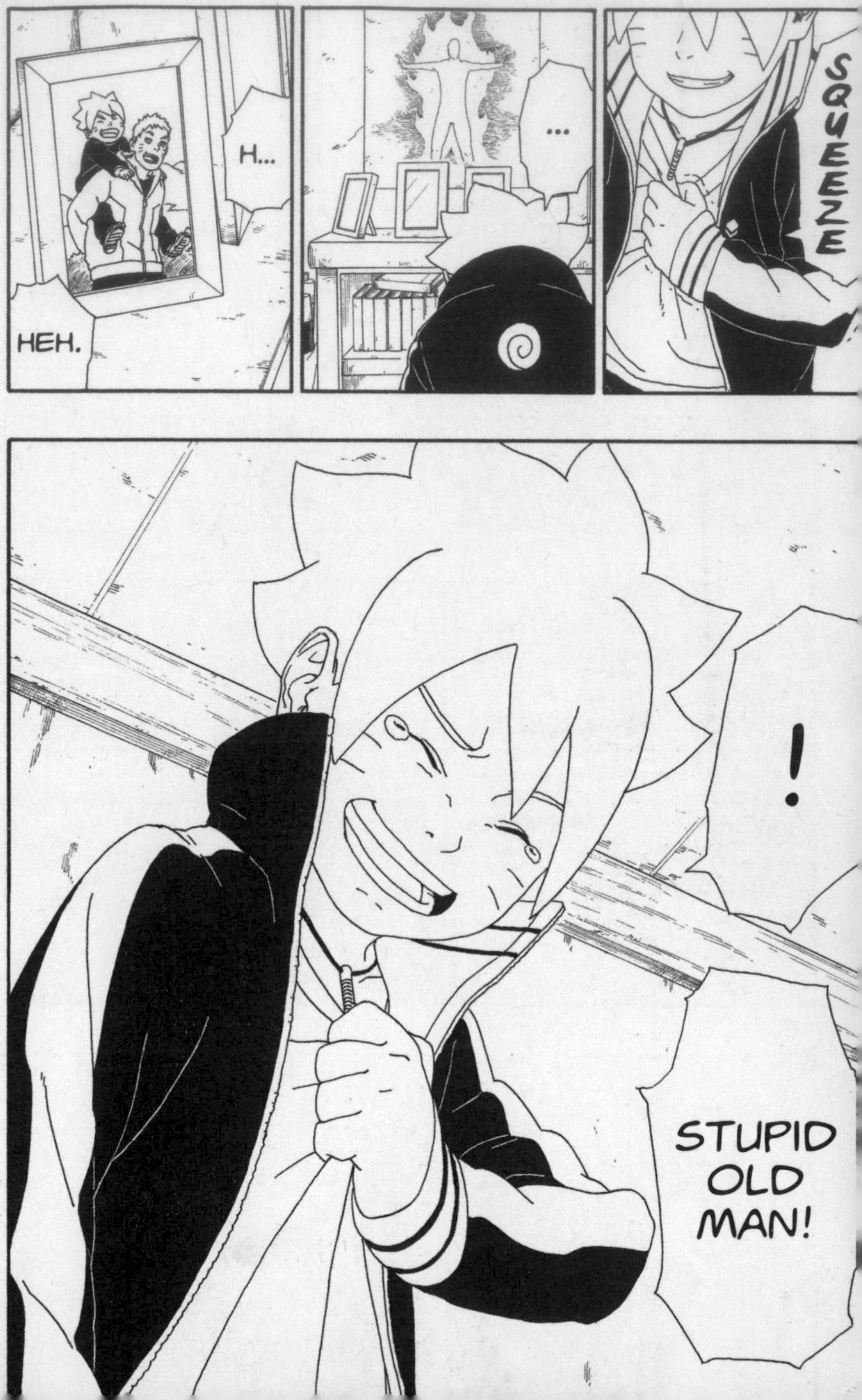
SQUEEZE
...
H...
HEH.
!
STUPID OLD MAN!

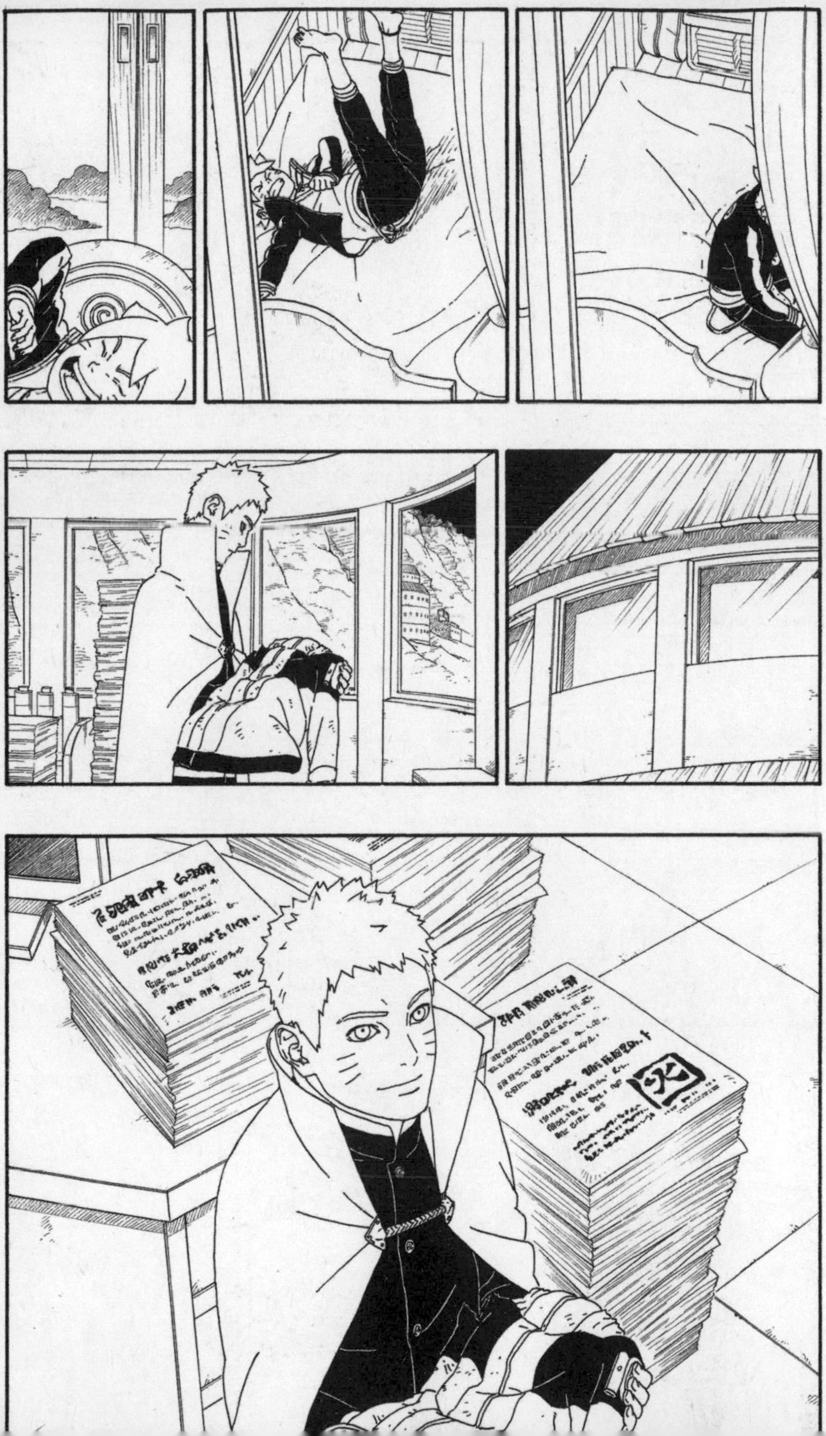
火

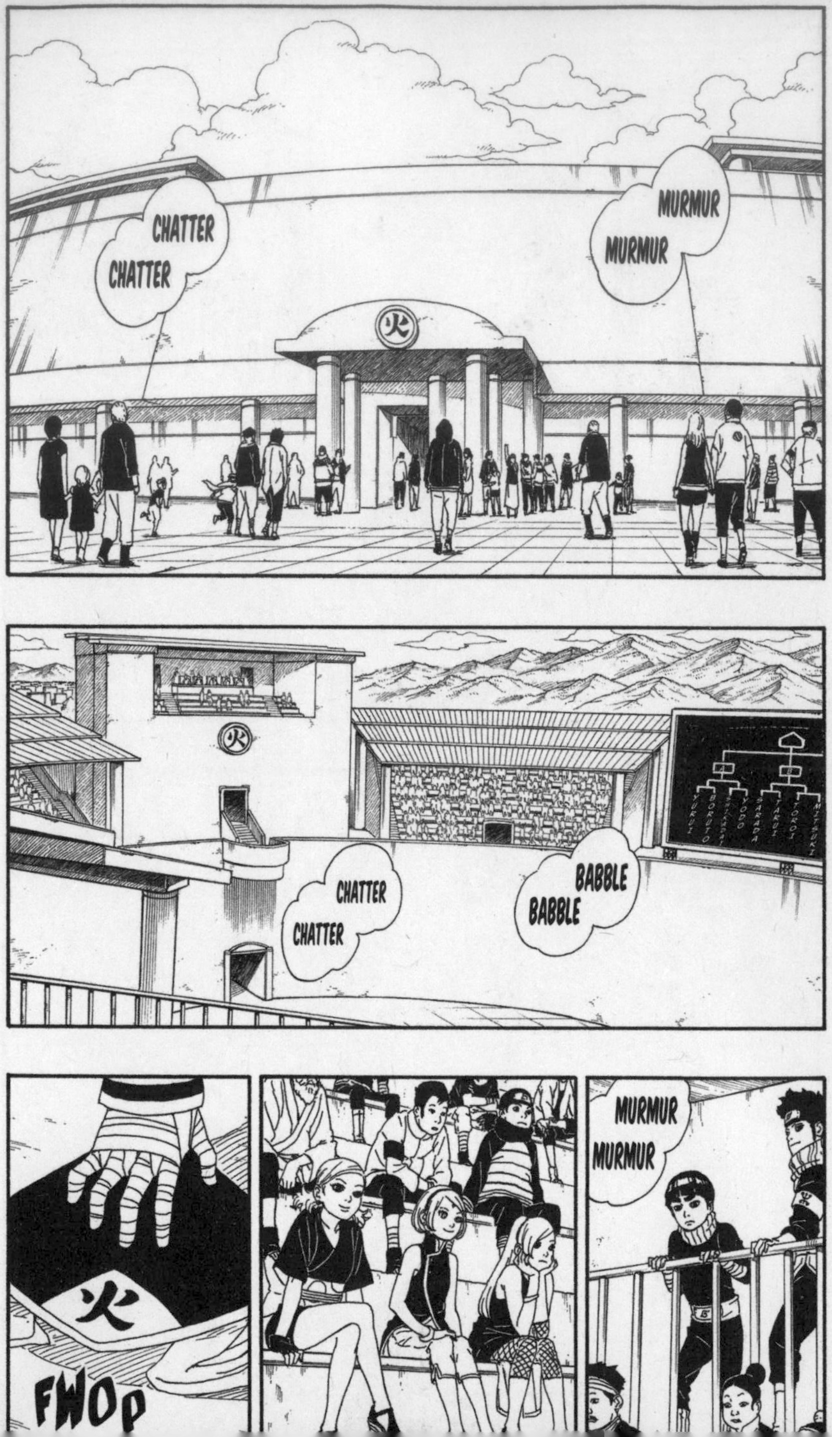
MURMUR
MURMUR
CHATTER
CHATTER
YURUI BORUTO SHIKADAI YODO SARADA TARUI TOROI MITSUKI
BABBLE
BABBLE
CHATTER
CHATTER
MURMUR
MURMUR
FWOP

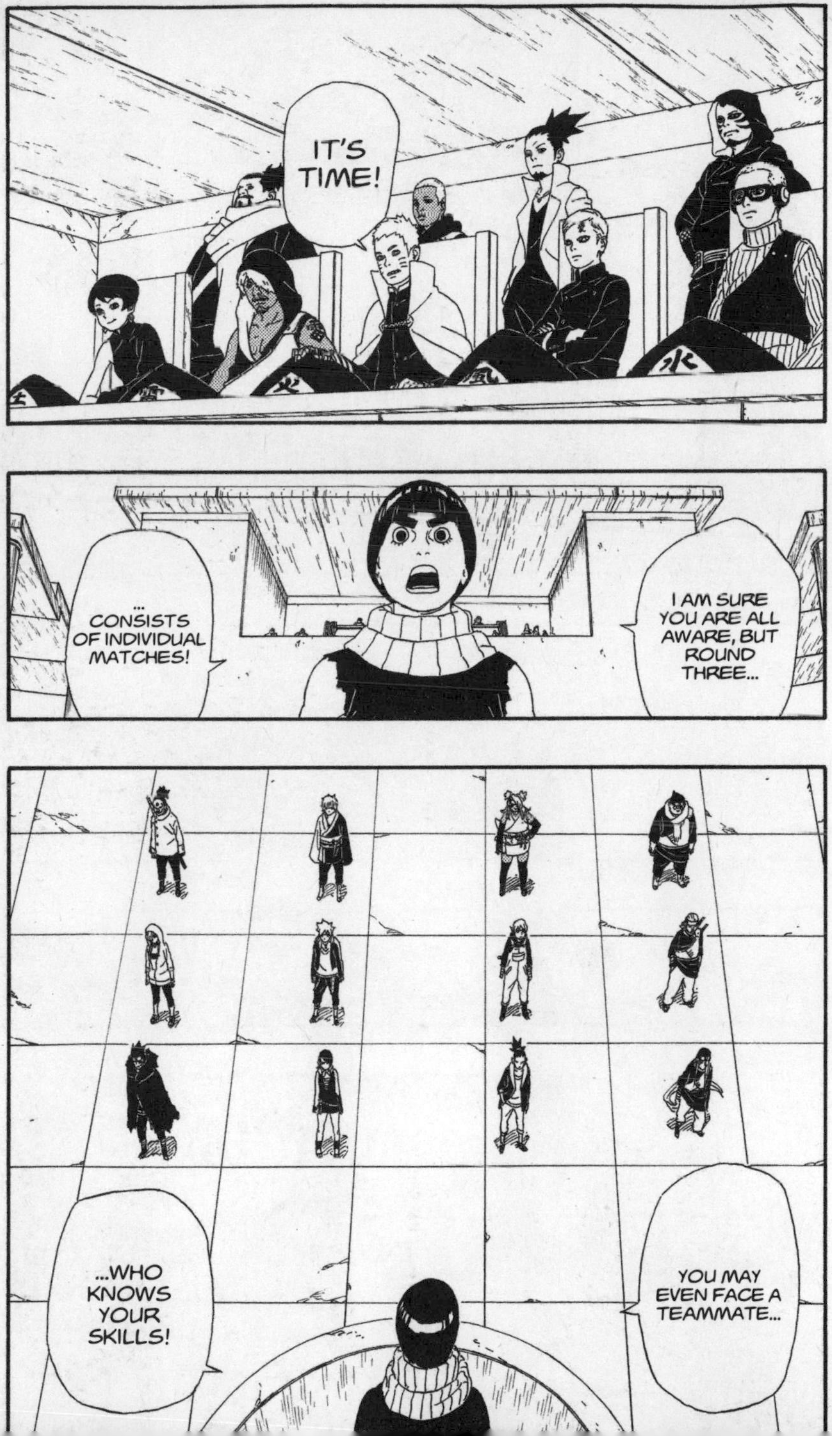
IT'S TIME!
I AM SURE YOU ARE ALL AWARE, BUT ROUND THREE...
...CONSISTS OF INDIVIDUAL MATCHES!
YOU MAY EVEN FACE A TEAMMATE...
...WHO KNOWS YOUR SKILLS!

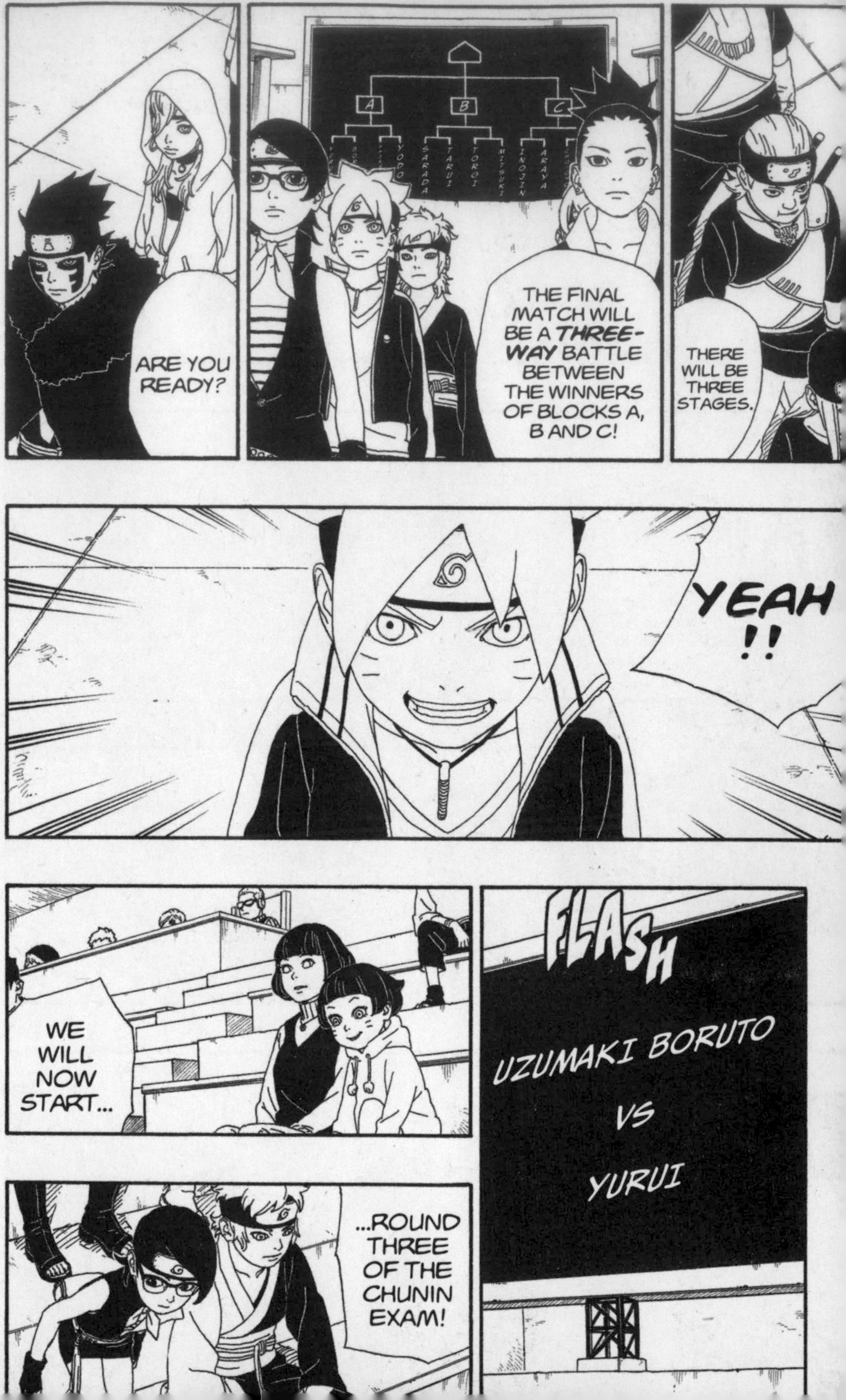
THERE WILL BE THREE STAGES.
A
B
C
YODO
SARADA
TARUI
TOROI
MITSUKI
INOJIN
ARAYA
THE FINAL MATCH WILL BE A THREE-WAY BATTLE BETWEEN THE WINNERS OF BLOCKS A, B AND C!
ARE YOU READY?
YEAH!!
FLASH
UZUMAKI BORUTO
VS
YURUI
WE WILL NOW START...
...ROUND THREE OF THE CHUNIN EXAM!

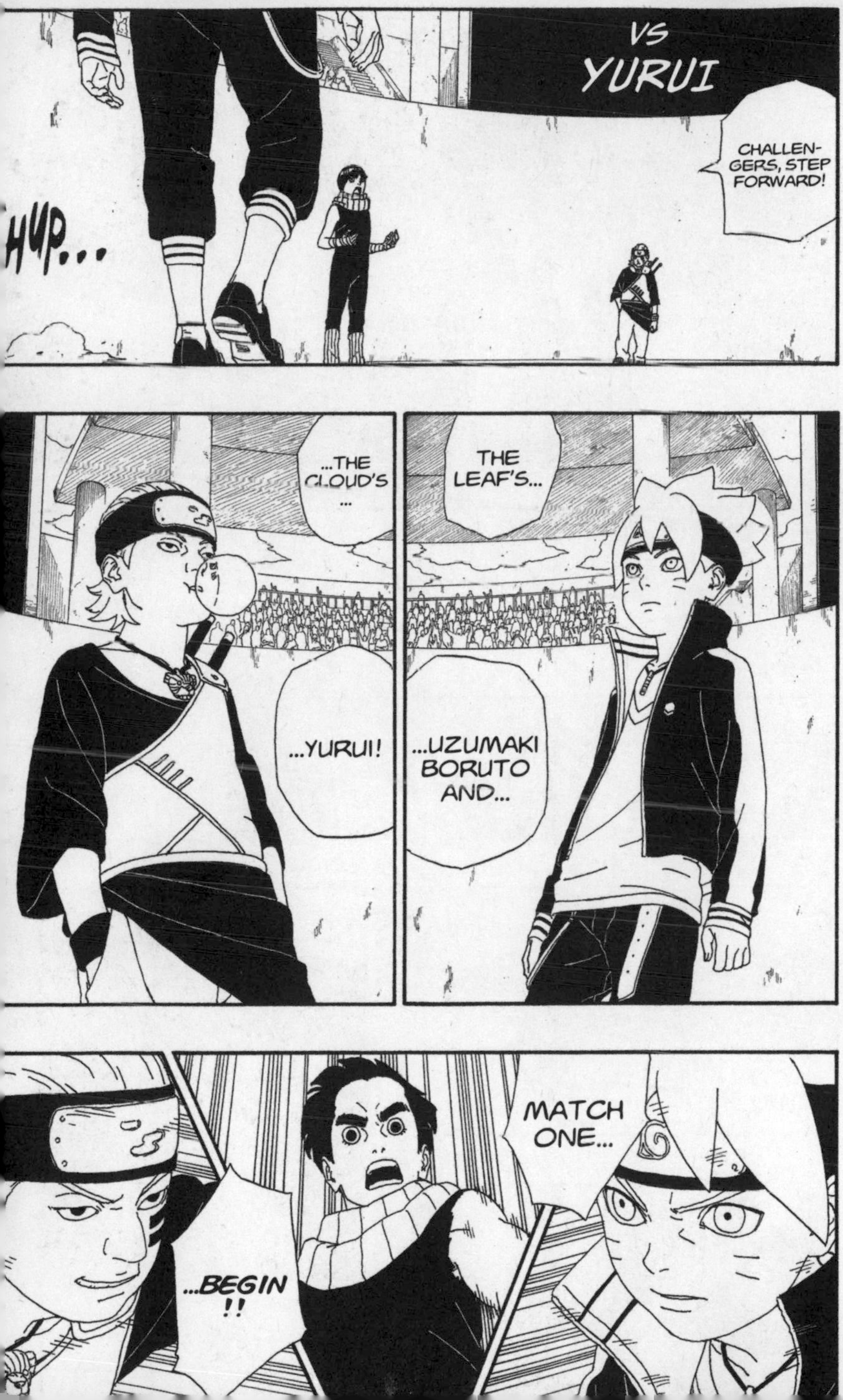
VS YURUI
CHALLENGERS, STEP FORWARD!
HUP...
THE LEAF'S...
...UZUMAKI BORUTO AND...
...THE CLOUD'S ...
...YURUI!
MATCH ONE...
...BEGIN!!

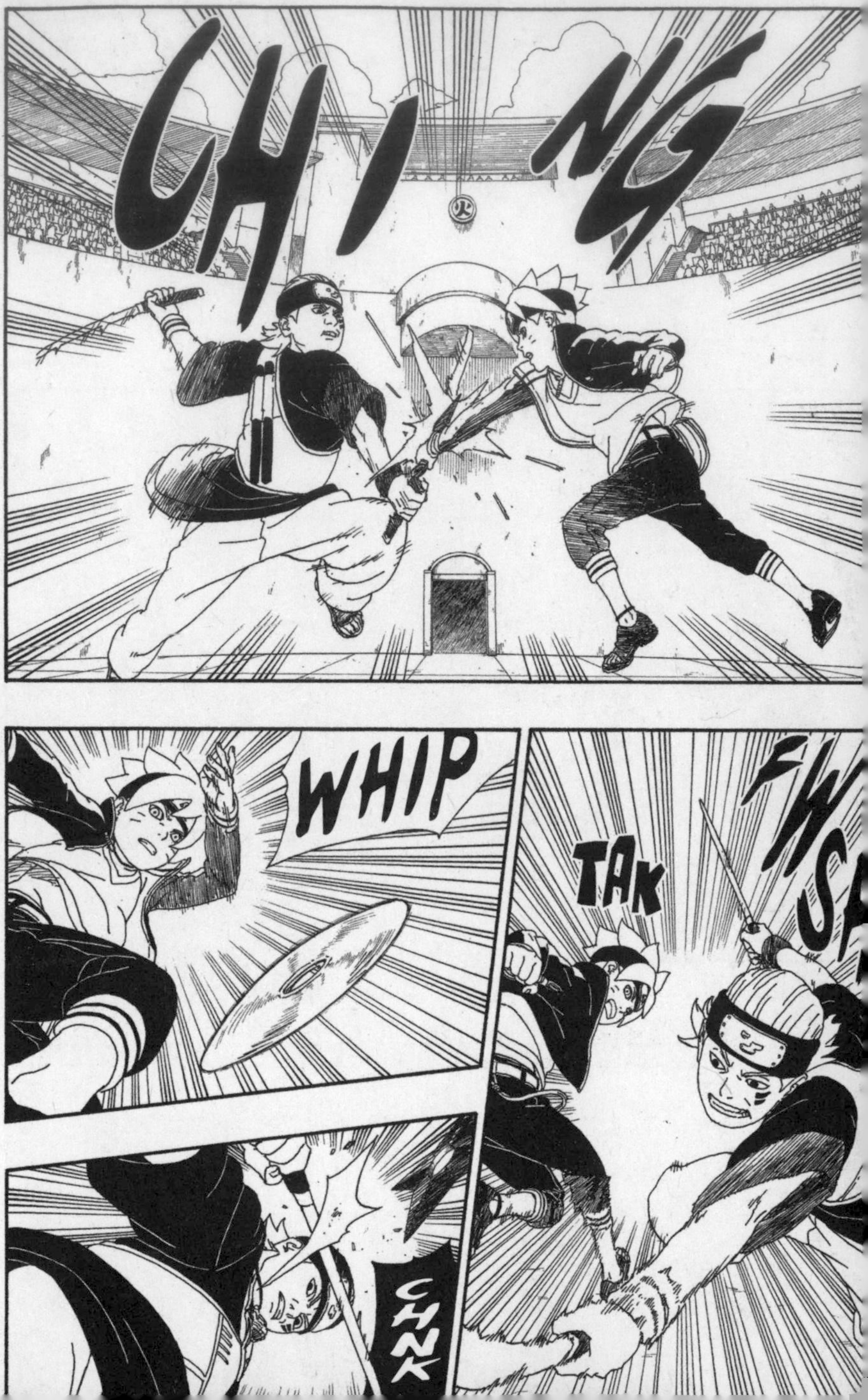
CHING
FWSA
TAK
WHIP
CHNK

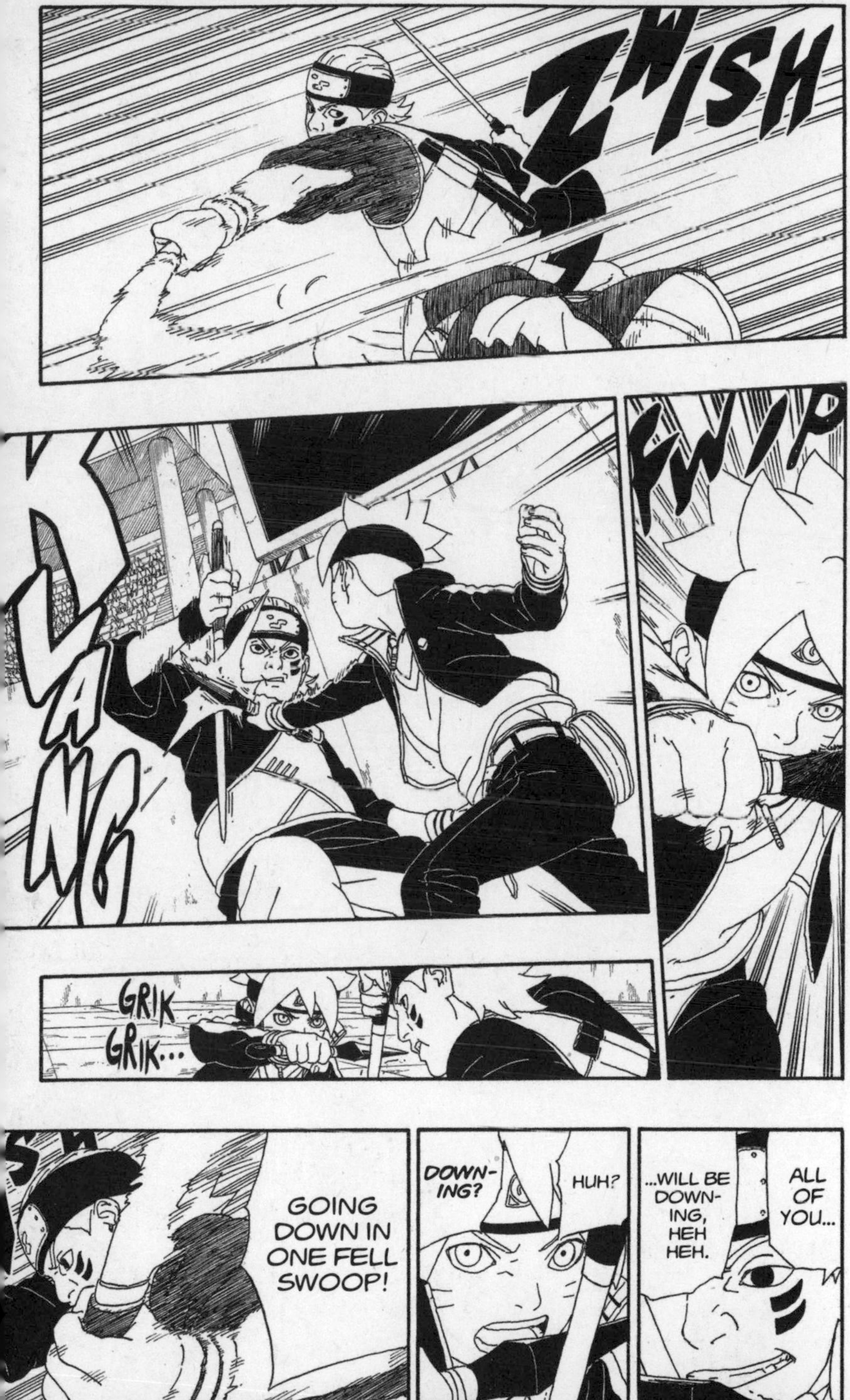
ZWISH
FWIP
CLANG
GRIK GRIK...
ALL OF YOU...
...WILL BE DOWNING, HEH HEH.
HUH?
DOWNING?
GOING DOWN IN ONE FELL SWOOP!

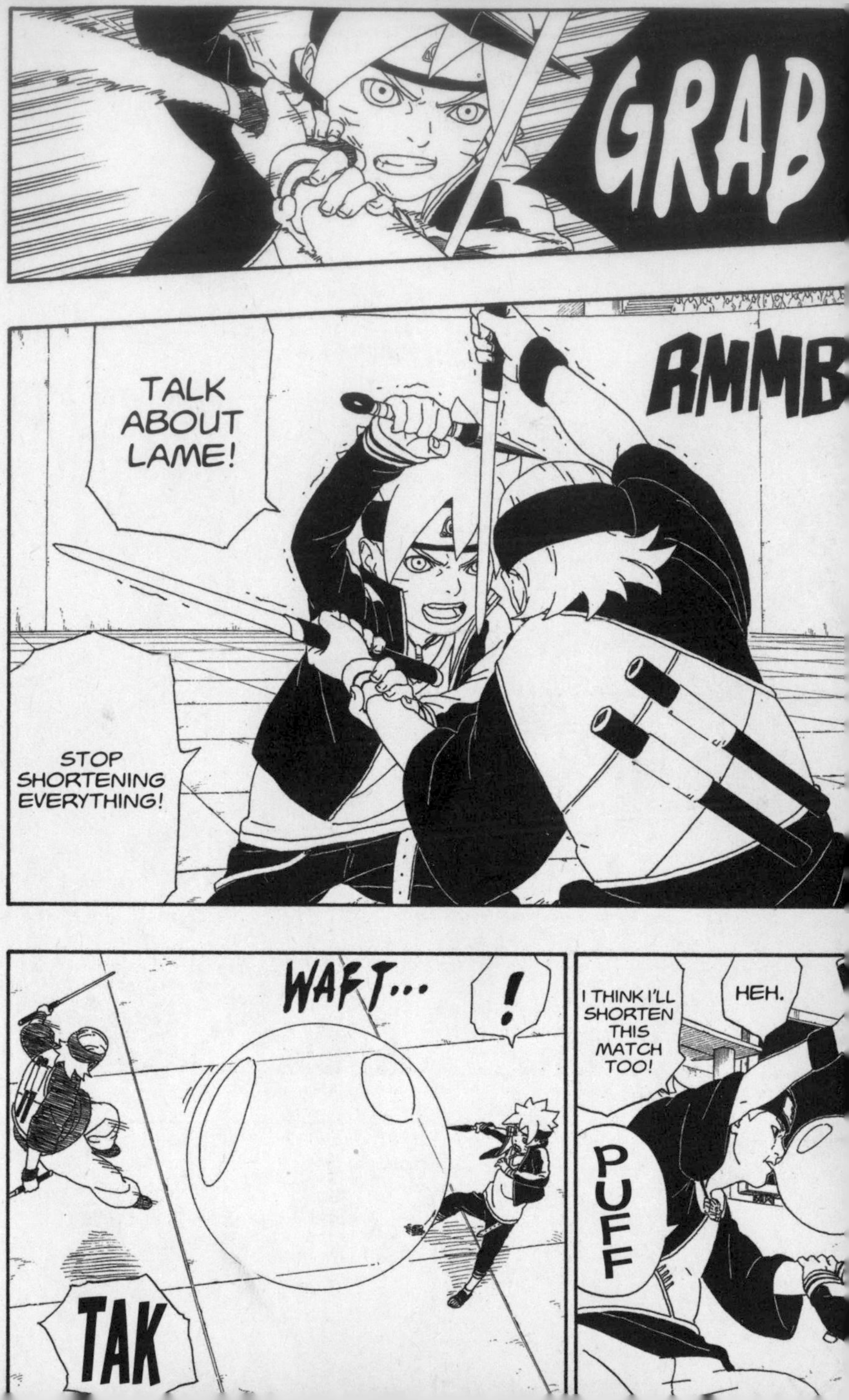
GRAB
RMMB
TALK ABOUT LAME!
STOP SHORTENING EVERYTHING!
HEH.
I THINK I'LL SHORTEN THIS MATCH TOO!
PUFF
!
WAFT...
TAK

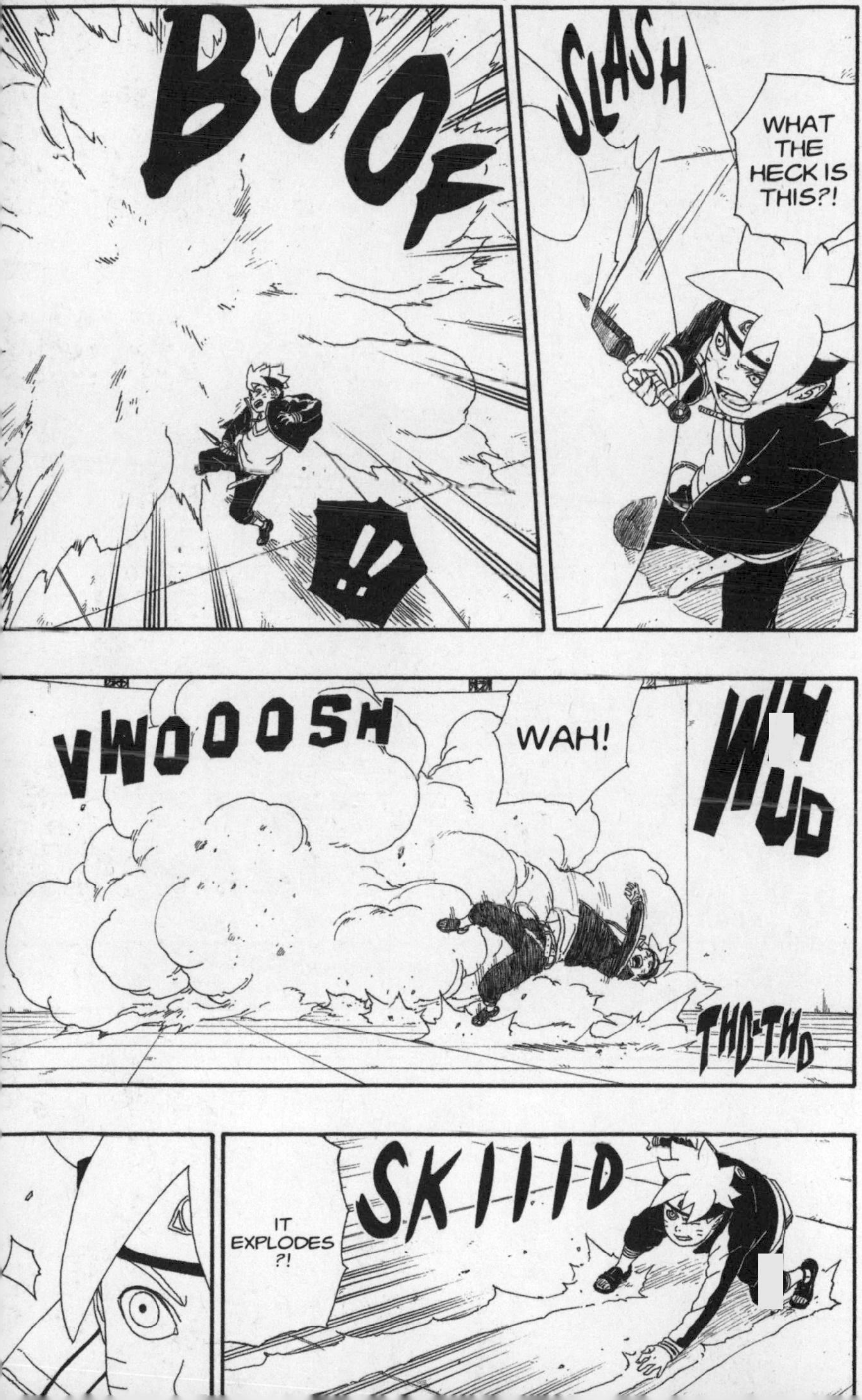
SLASH
WHAT THE HECK IS THIS?!
BOOF
!!
WHUD
WAH!
THD-THD
VWOOOSH
SKIIID
IT EXPLODES ?!

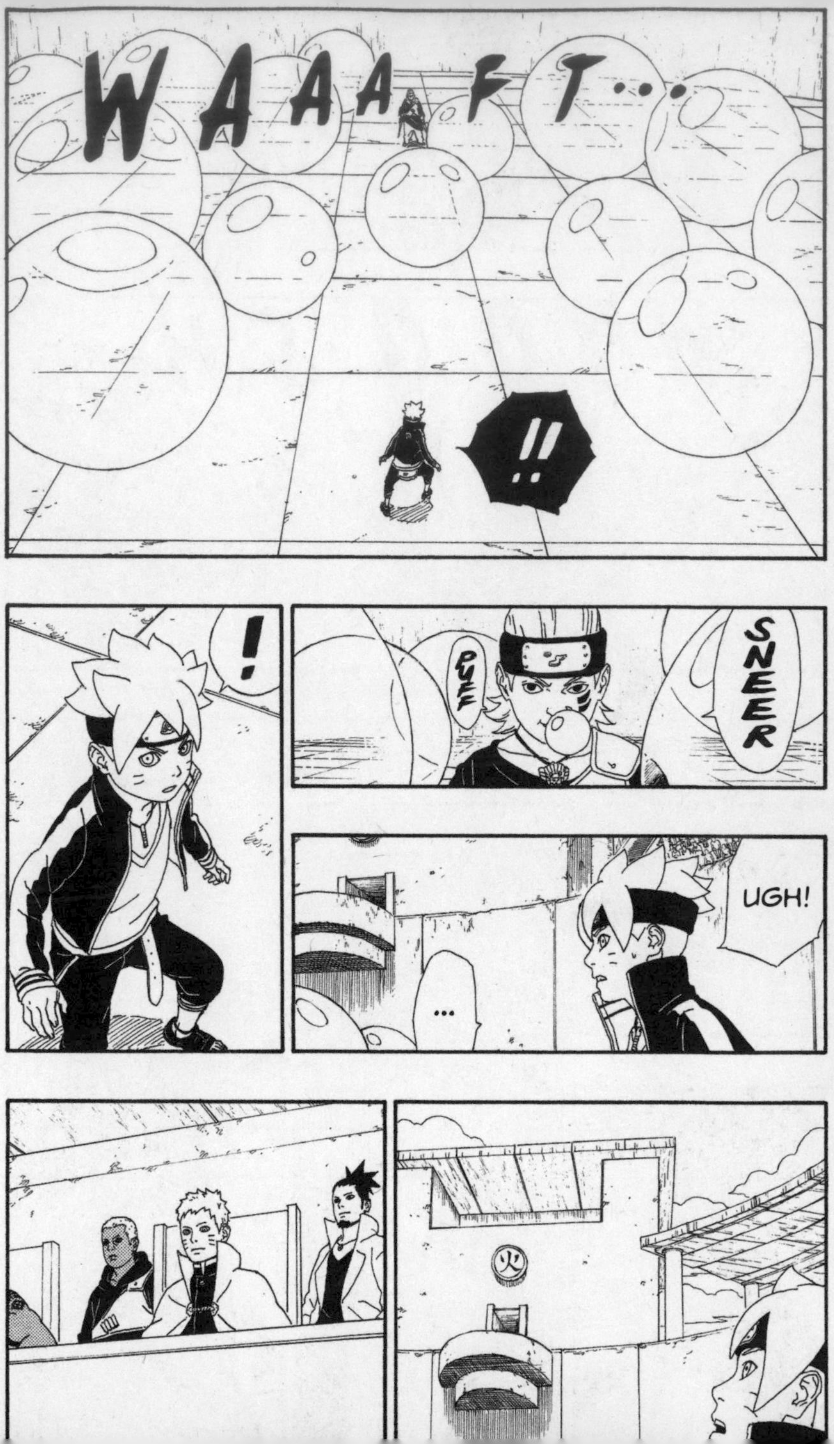
WAAAFT...
!!
SNEER
PUFF
UGH!
...
!

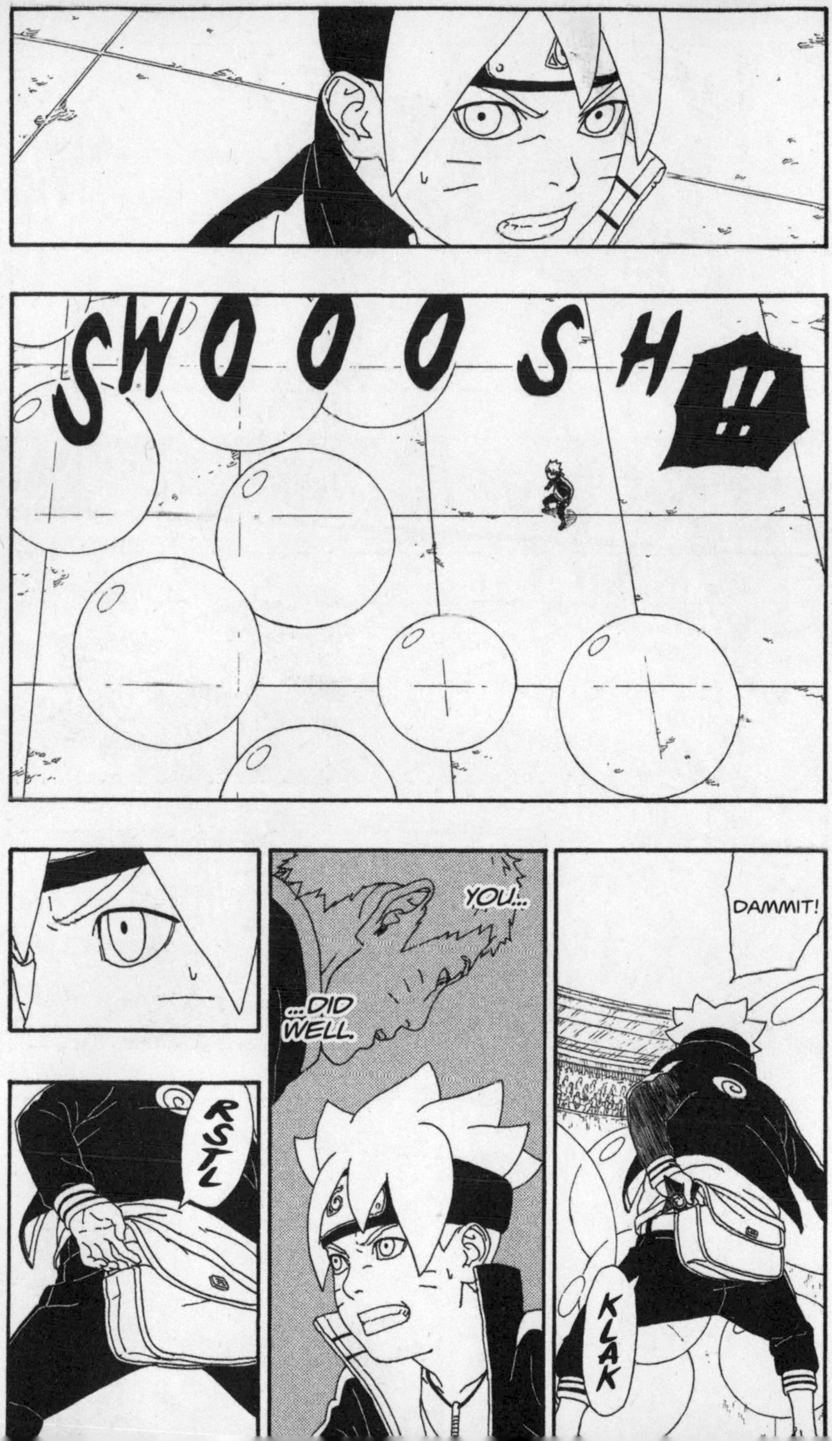
SWOOOSH!!
DAMMIT!
KLAK
YOU...
...DID WELL.
RSTL

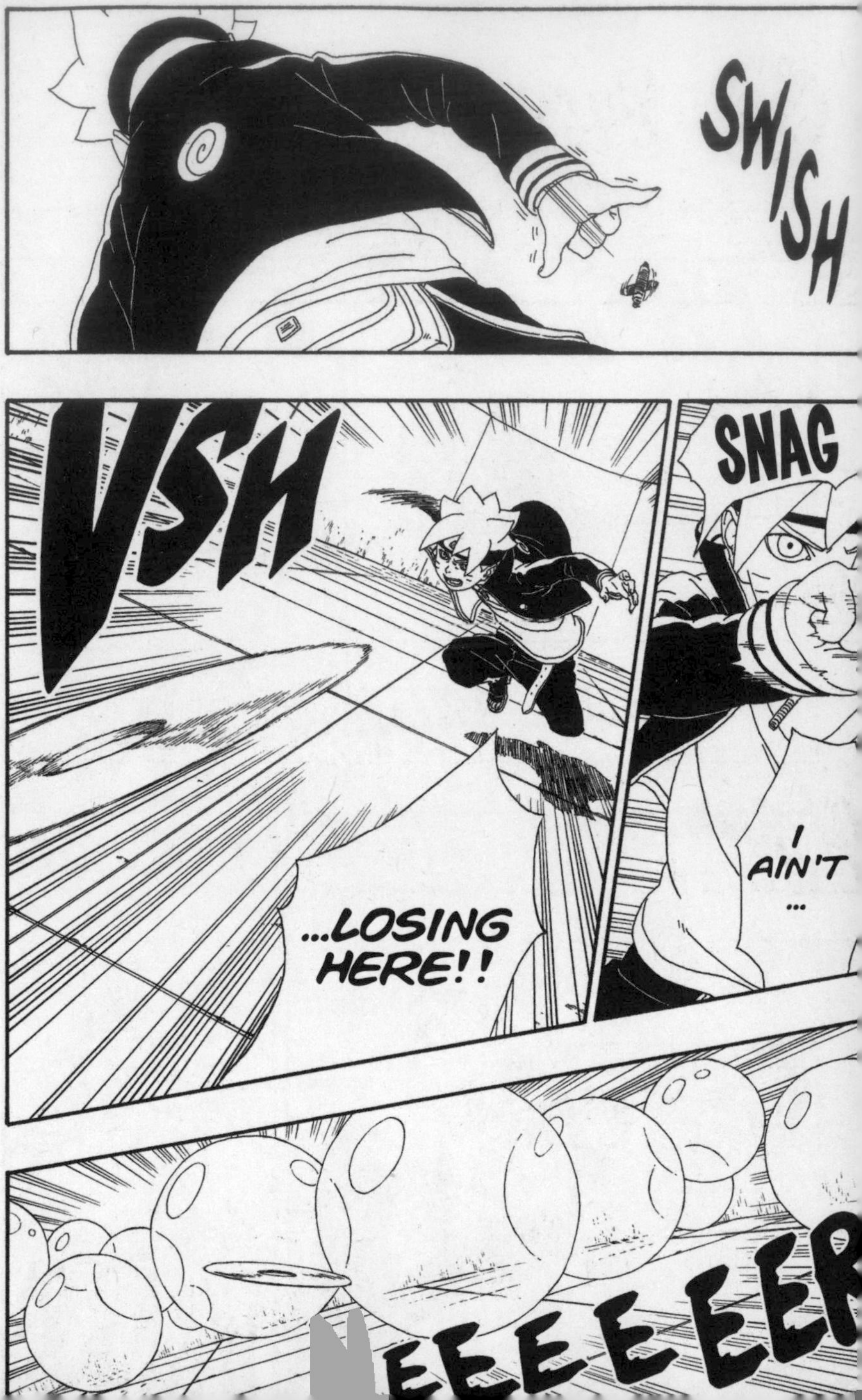
SWISH
SNAG
I AIN'T ...
VSH
...LOSING HERE!!
EEEEEER

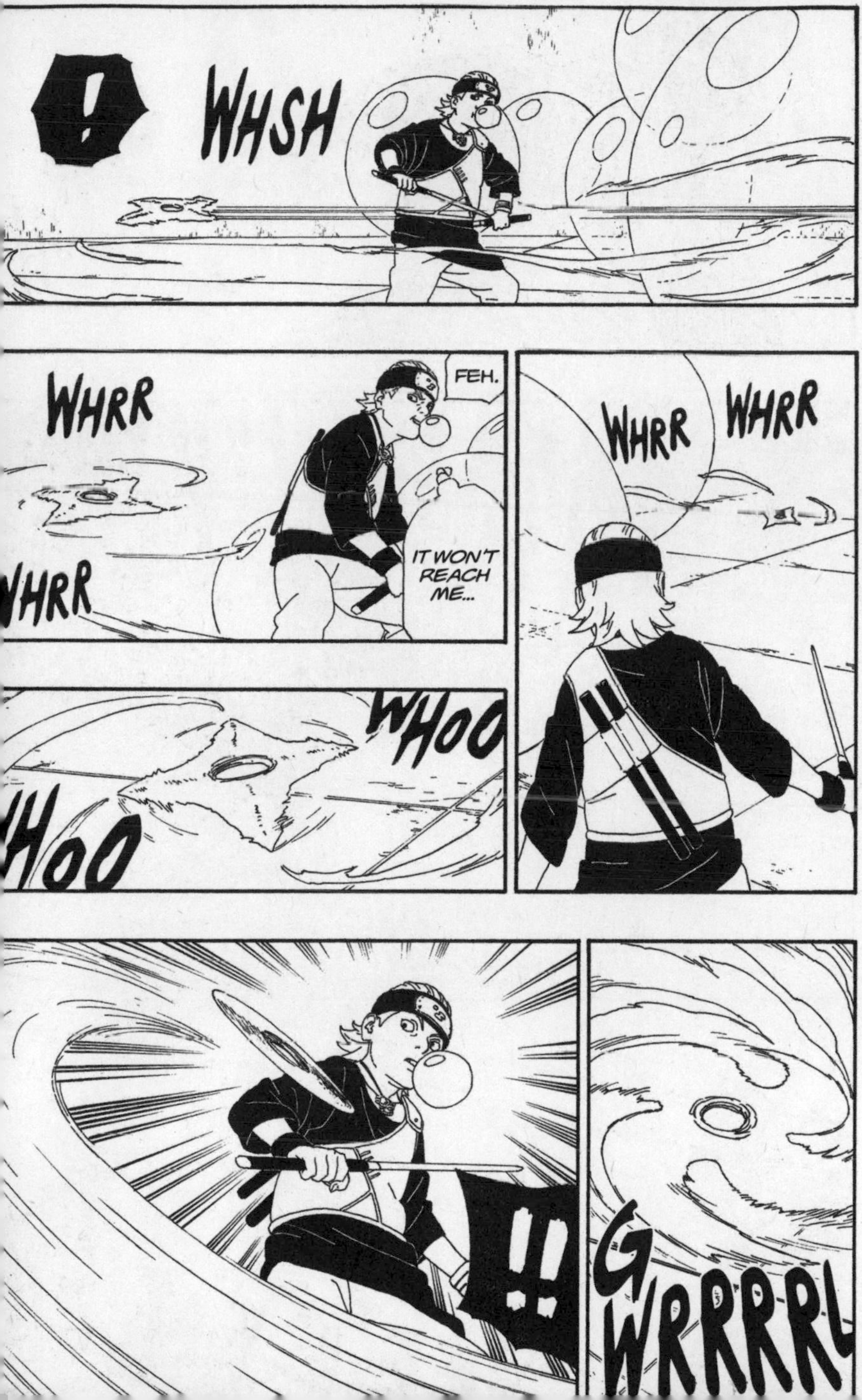
WHSH
!
WHRR WHRR
FEH.
WHRR
IT WON'T REACH ME...
WHRR
WHOO
WHOO
G WRRRRL
!!

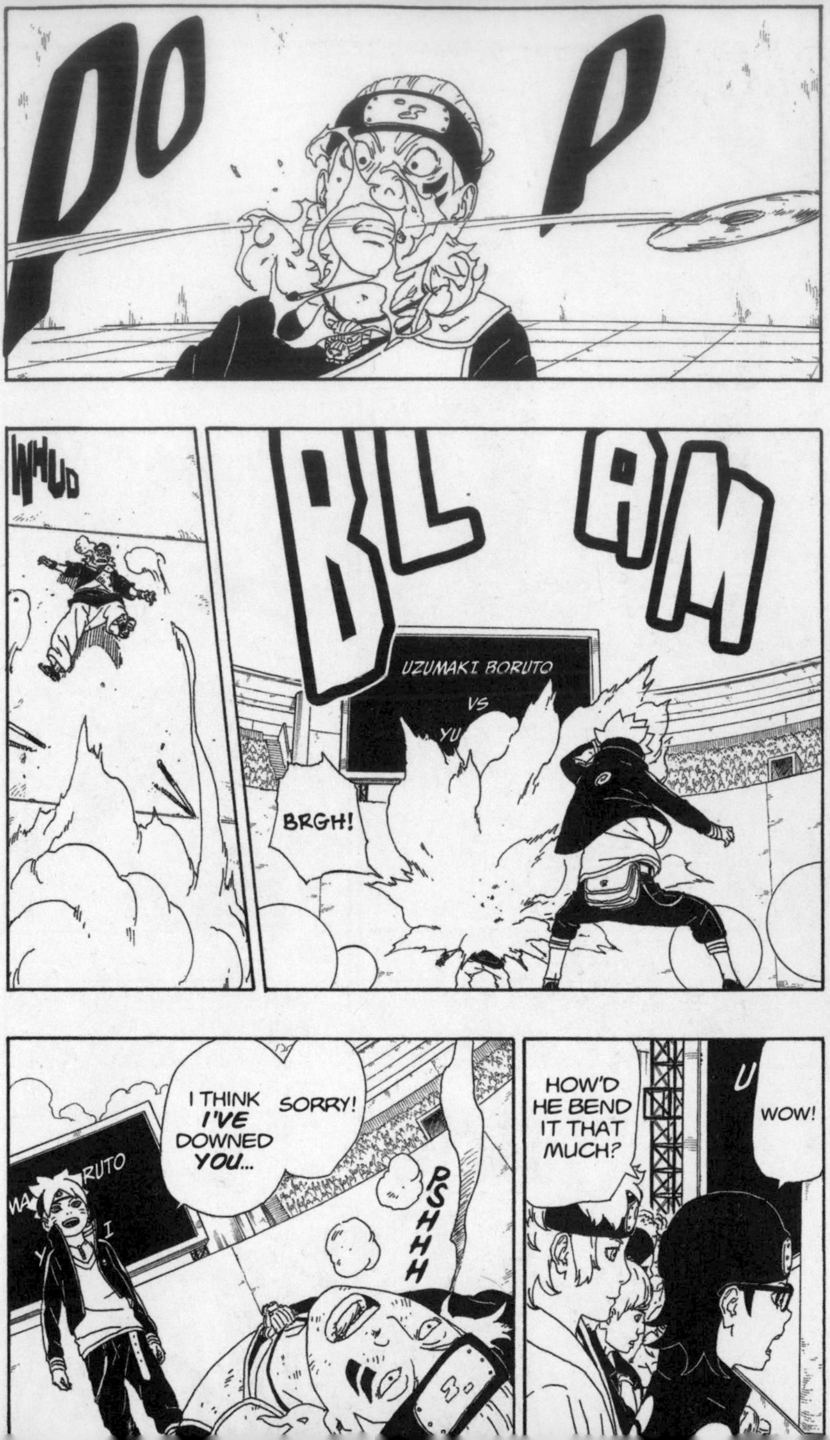
DO P
BL AM
UZUMAKI BORUTO
VS
YU
BRGH!
WHUD
WOW!
U
HOW'D HE BEND IT THAT MUCH?
SORRY!
I THINK *I'VE* DOWNED *YOU*...
PSHHH
RUTO

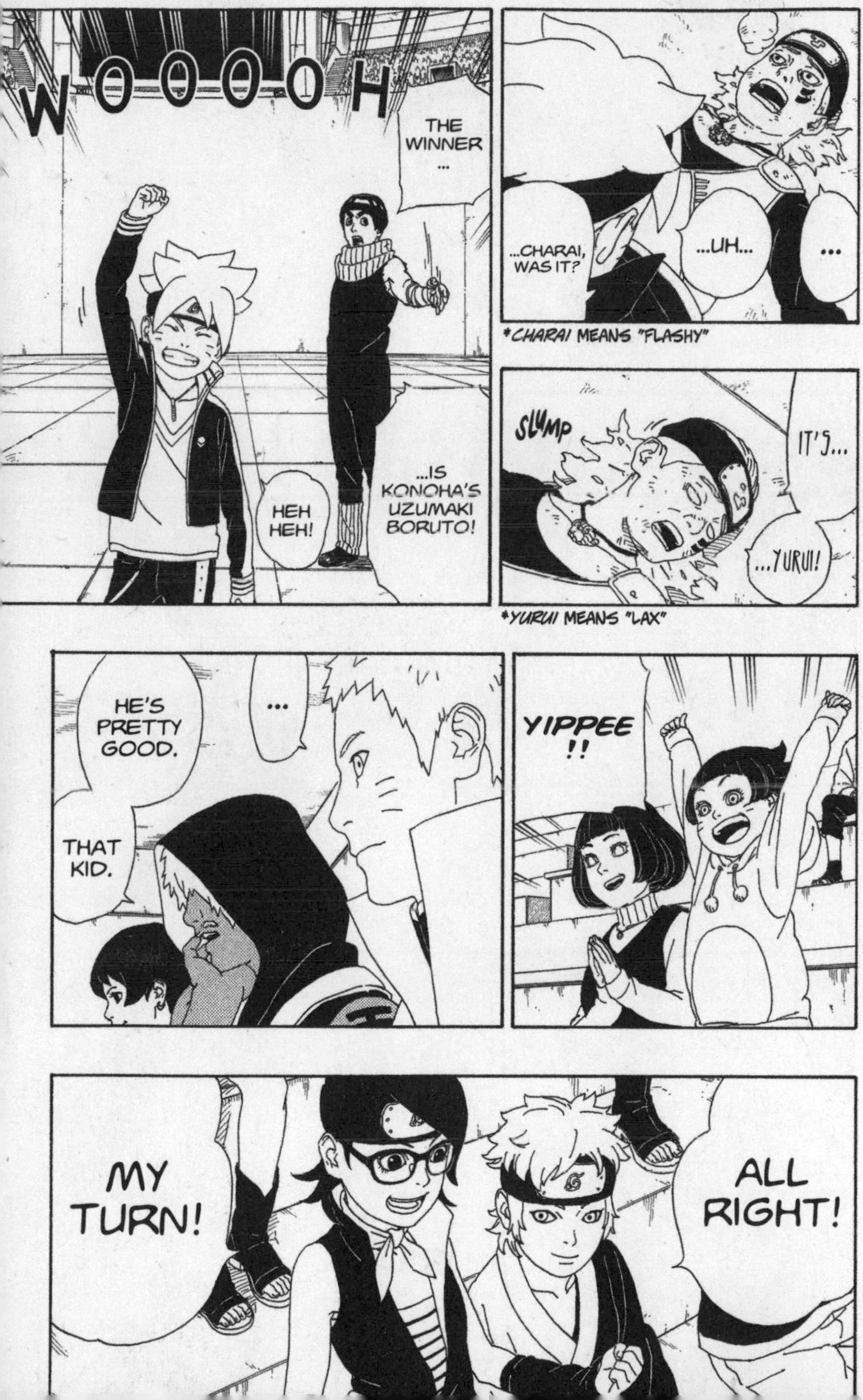
...
...UH...
...CHARAI, WAS IT?
*CHARAI MEANS "FLASHY"
SLUMP
IT'S...
...YURUI!
*YURUI MEANS "LAX"
WOOOOOH
THE WINNER ...
...IS KONOHA'S UZUMAKI BORUTO!
HEH HEH!
YIPPEE !!
...
HE'S PRETTY GOOD.
THAT KID.
ALL RIGHT!
MY TURN!

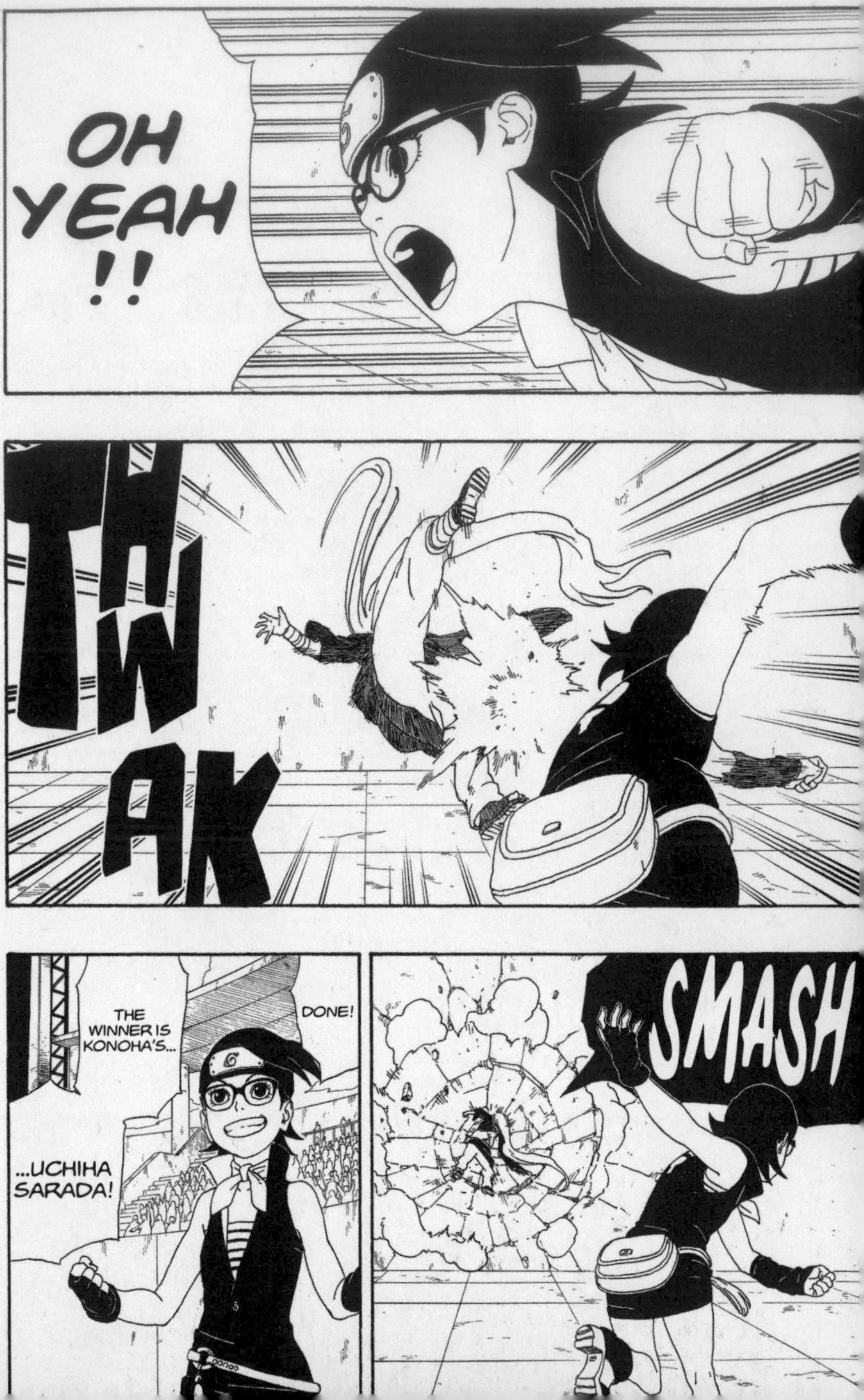
OH YEAH !!
THWAK
SMASH
DONE!
THE WINNER IS KONOHA'S...
...UCHIHA SARADA!

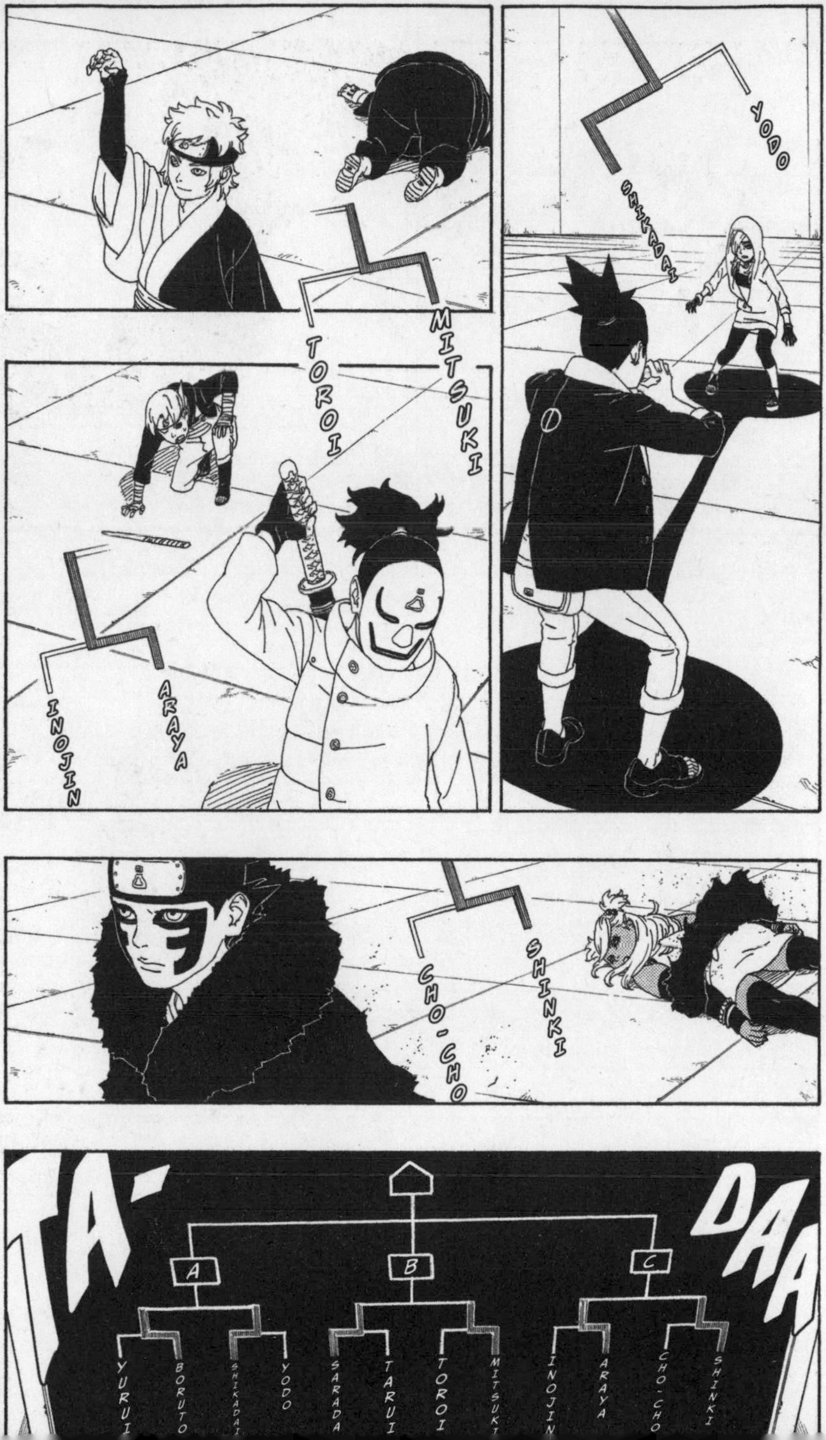
YODO
SHIKADAI
MITSUKI
TOROI
ARAYA
INOJIN
SHINKI
CHO-CHO
TA-
DAA
A
B
C
YURUI
BORUTO
SHIKADAI
YODO
SARADA
TARUI
TOROI
MITSUKI
INOJIN
ARAYA
CHO-CHO
SHINKI

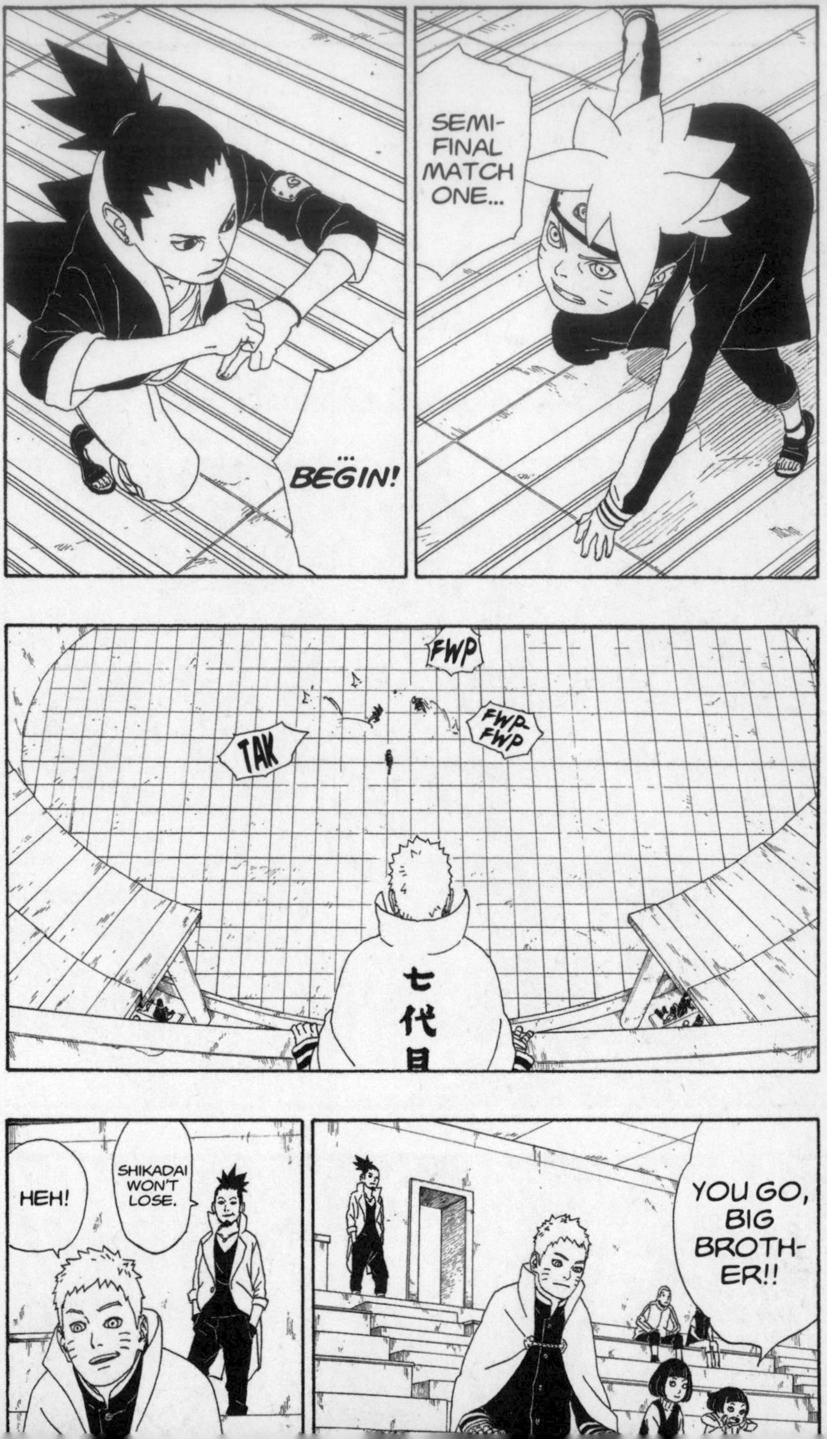
SEMI-FINAL MATCH ONE...
...BEGIN!
FWP
FWP FWP
TAK
七代目
YOU GO, BIG BROTHER!!
SHIKADAI WON'T LOSE.
HEH!

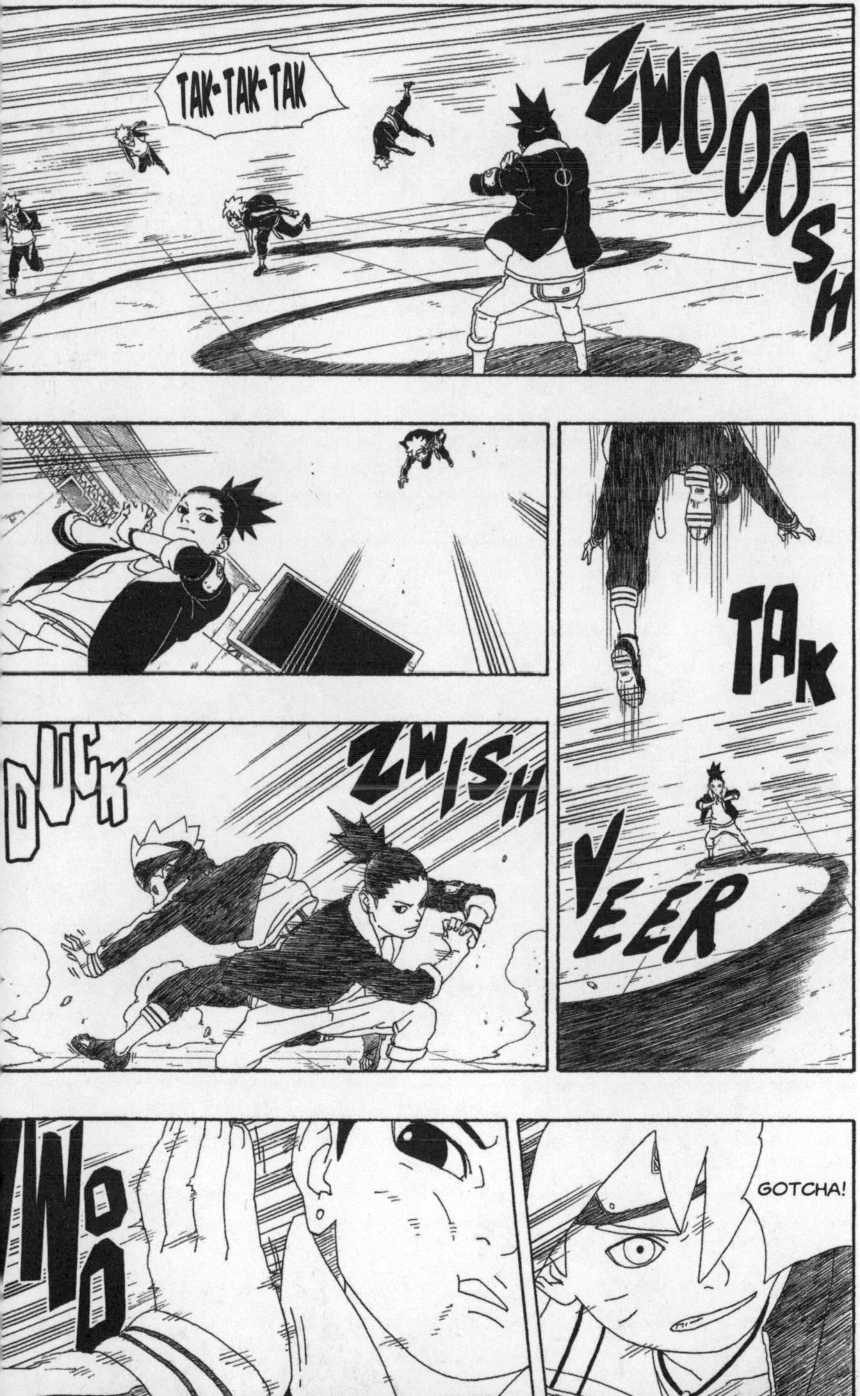
ZWOOOSH
TAK-TAK-TAK
TAK
VEER
ZWISH
DUCK
GOTCHA!
WOOO

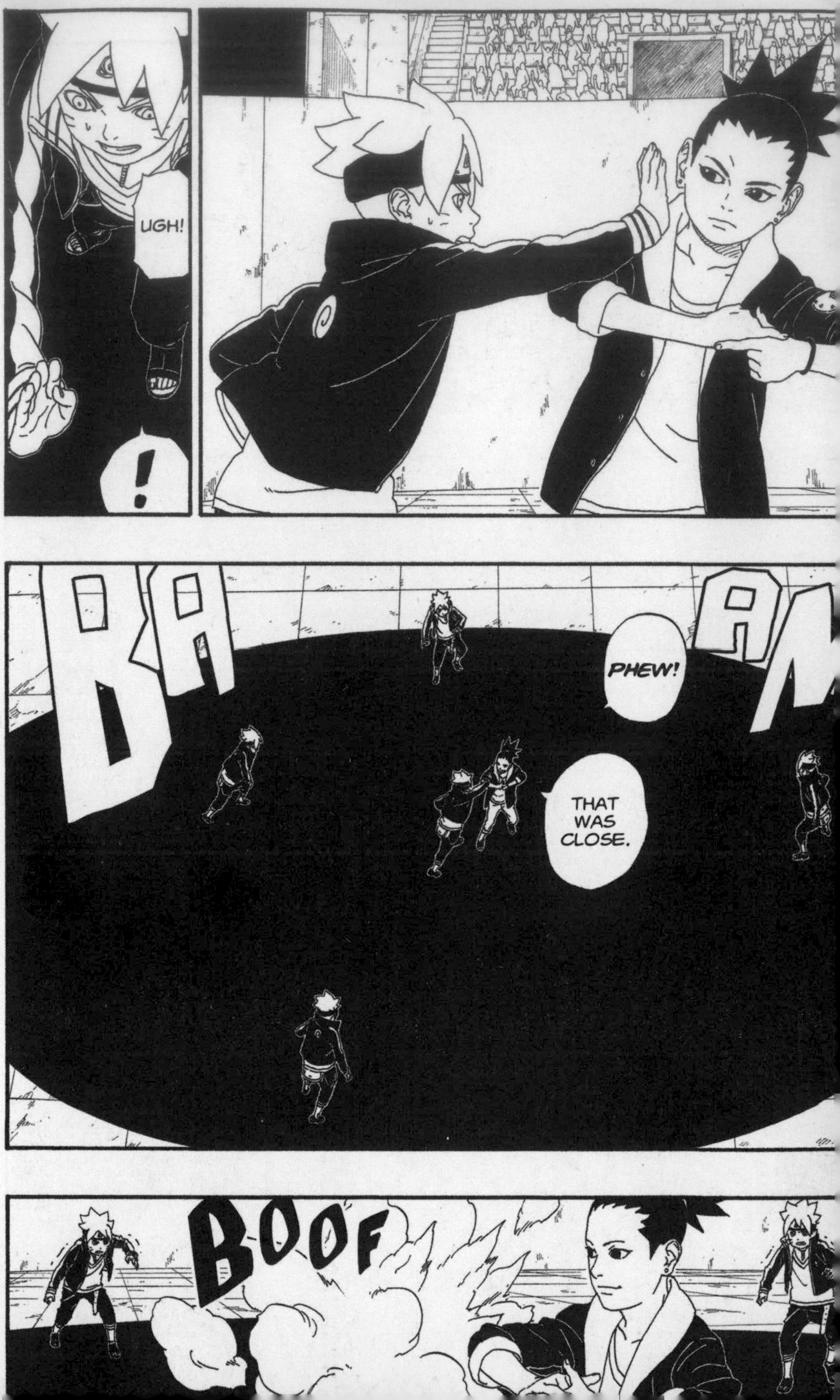
UGH!
!
BAAM
PHEW!
THAT WAS CLOSE.
BOOF

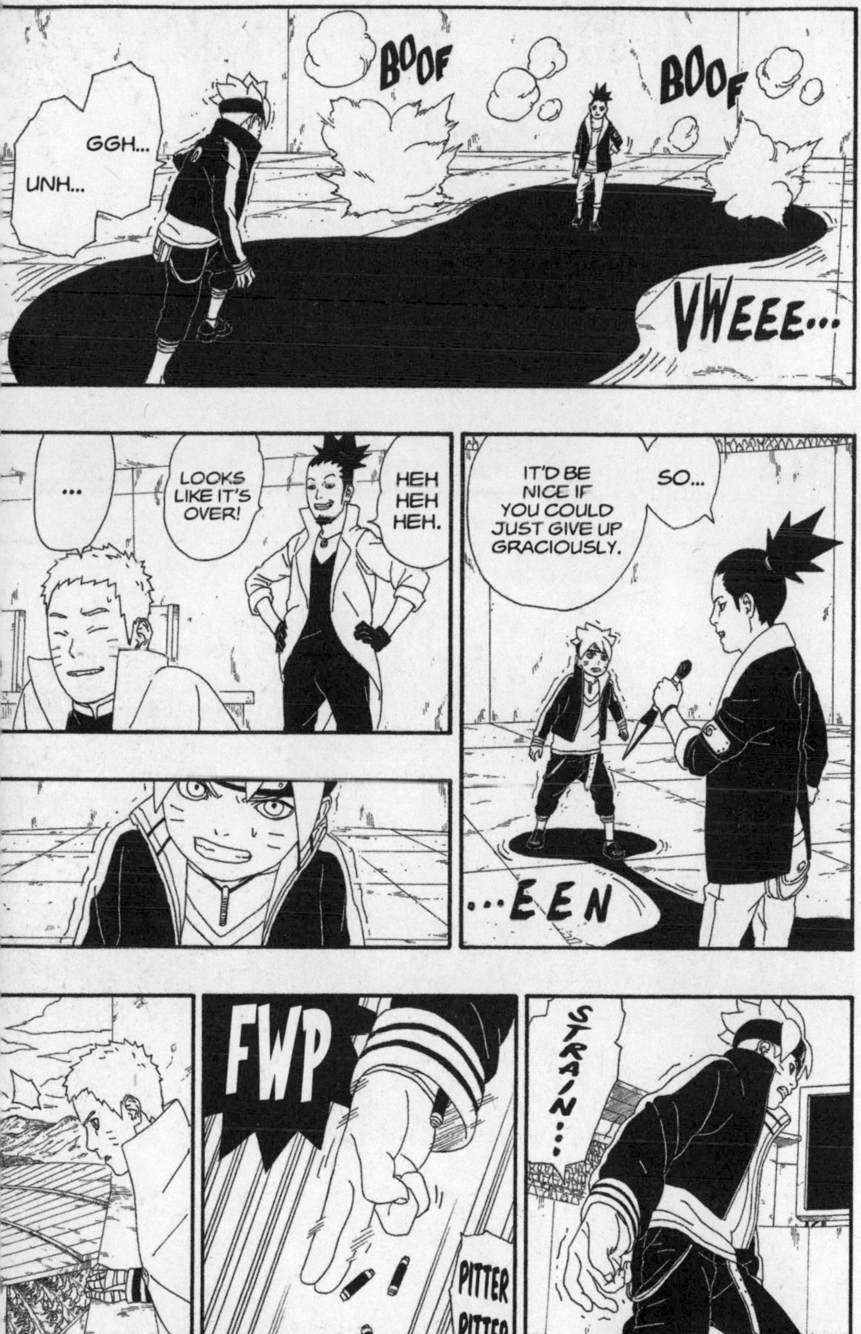
BOOF
BOOF
GGH...
UNH...
VWEEE...
SO...
IT'D BE NICE IF YOU COULD JUST GIVE UP GRACIOUSLY.
...EEN
HEH HEH HEH.
LOOKS LIKE IT'S OVER!
...
STRAIN...
FWP
PITTER PITTER

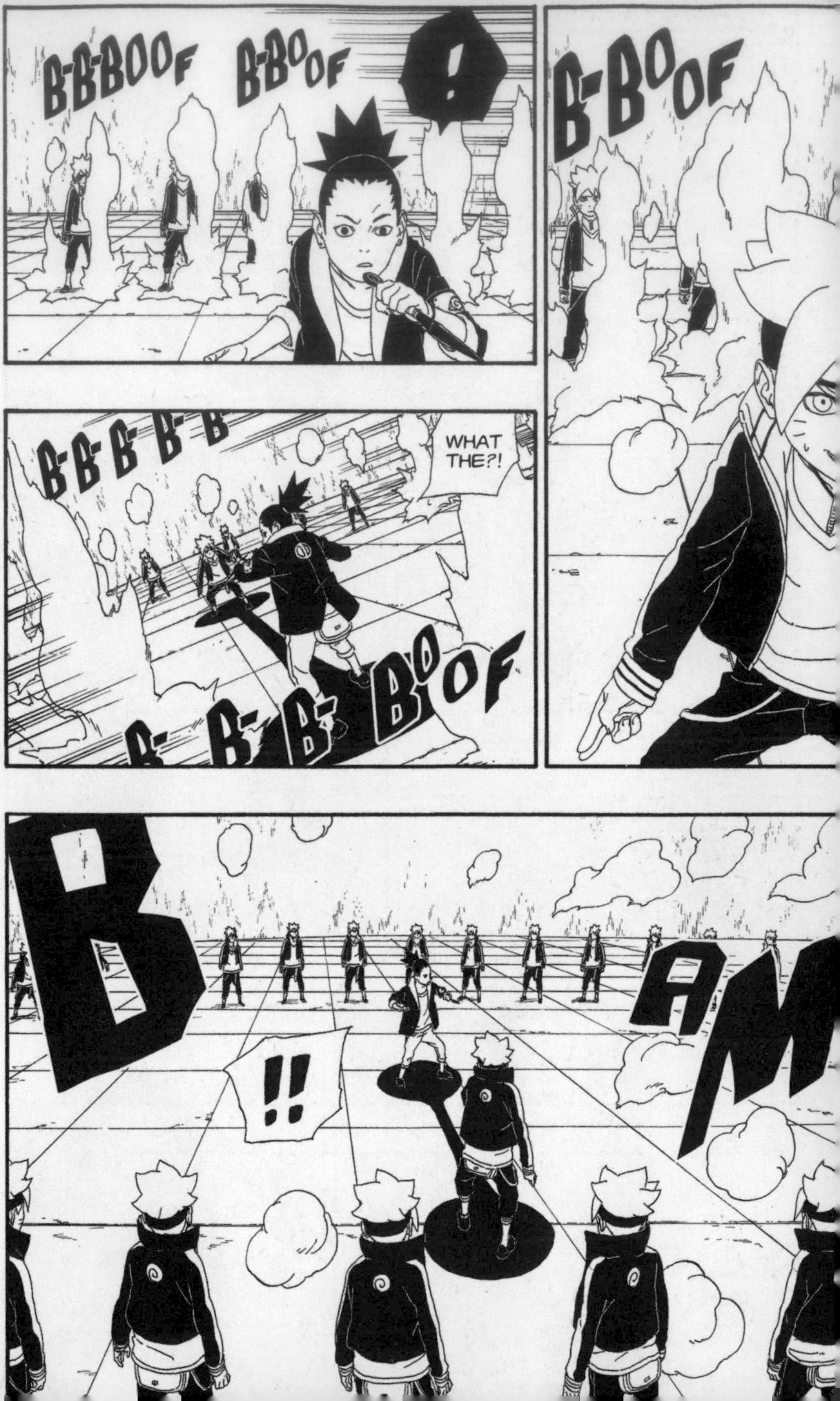

B-BOOF
B-B-BOOF
B-BOOF
!
WHAT THE?!
B-B-B-B-B
B-B-B-BOOF
!!
BAM

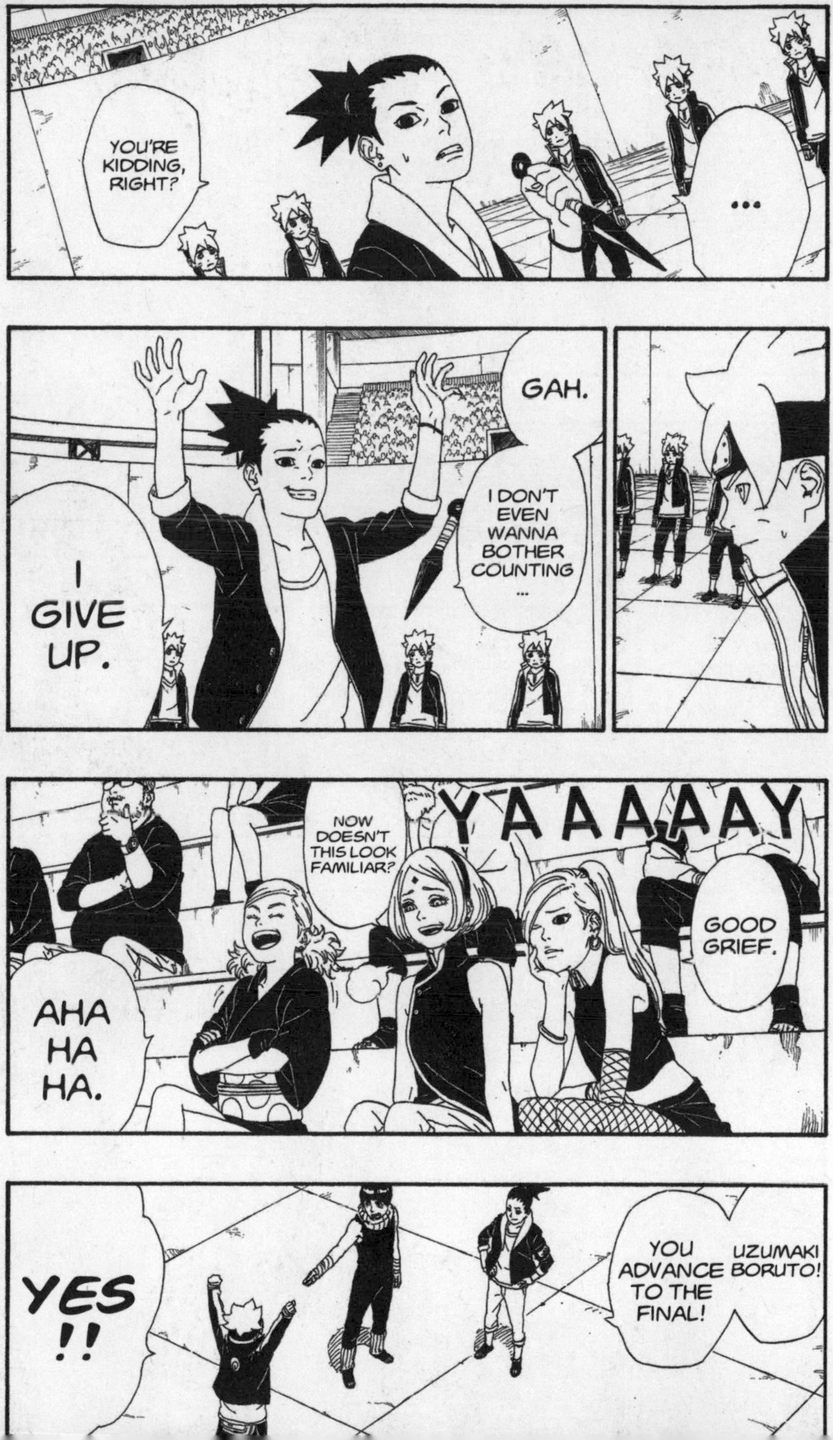
...
YOU'RE KIDDING, RIGHT?
GAH.
I DON'T EVEN WANNA BOTHER COUNTING...
I GIVE UP.
YAAAAAY
GOOD GRIEF.
NOW DOESN'T THIS LOOK FAMILIAR?
AHA HA HA.
UZUMAKI BORUTO!
YOU ADVANCE TO THE FINAL!
YES!!

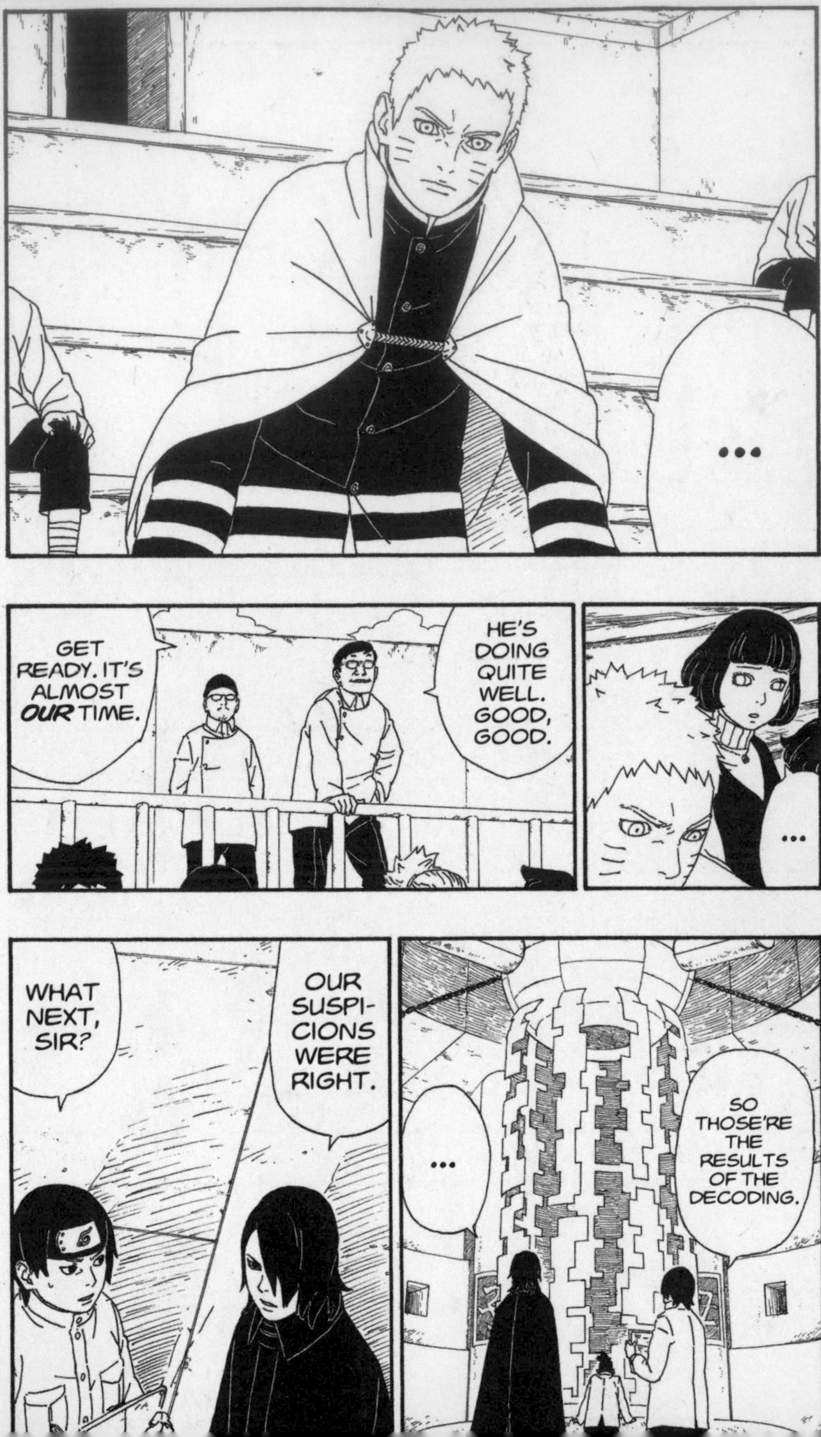
...
...
HE'S DOING QUITE WELL. GOOD, GOOD.
GET READY. IT'S ALMOST OUR TIME.
SO THOSE'RE THE RESULTS OF THE DECODING.
...
OUR SUSPICIONS WERE RIGHT.
WHAT NEXT, SIR?

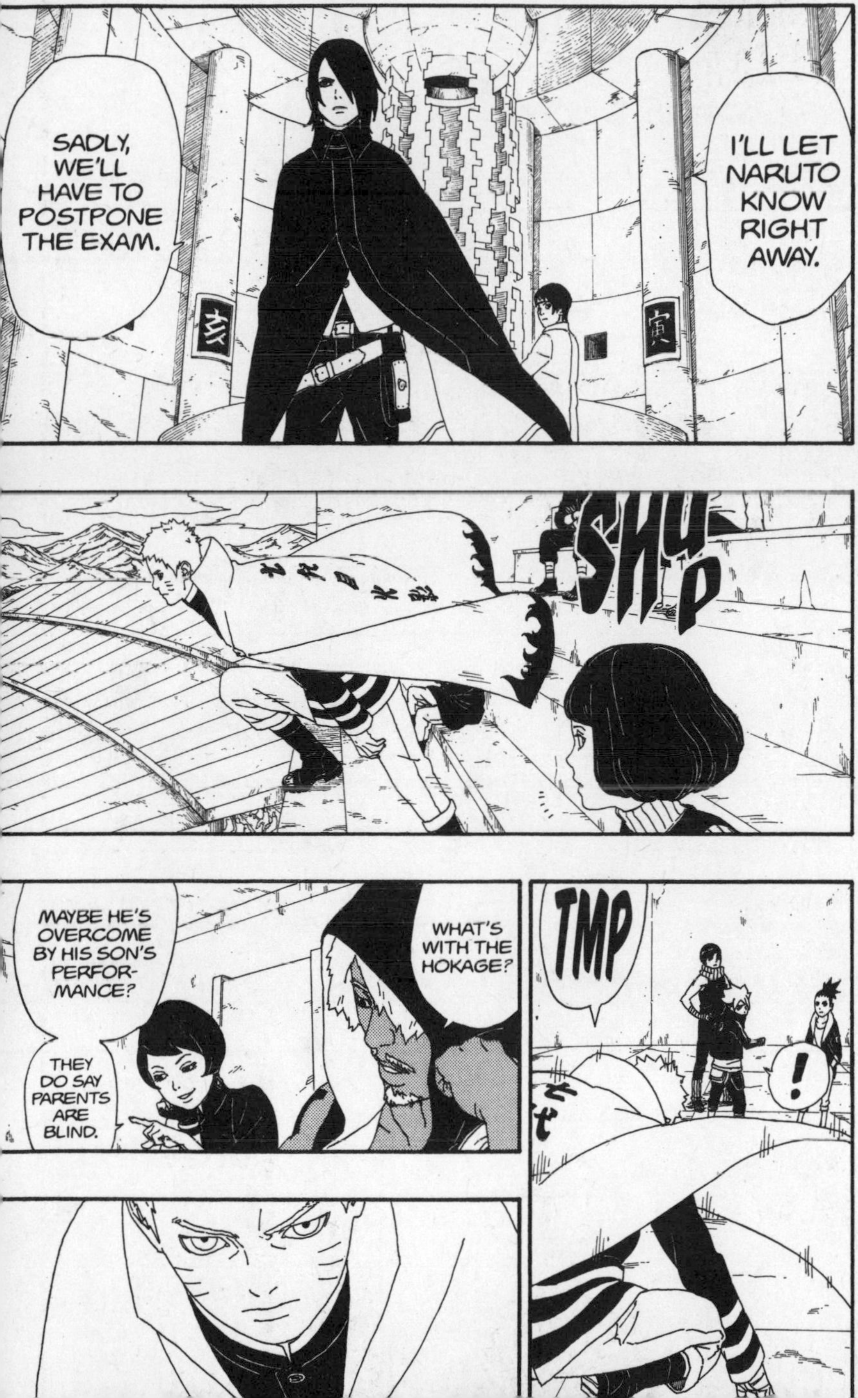
I'LL LET NARUTO KNOW RIGHT AWAY.
SADLY, WE'LL HAVE TO POSTPONE THE EXAM.
SHUP
TMP
!
WHAT'S WITH THE HOKAGE?
MAYBE HE'S OVERCOME BY HIS SON'S PERFOR-MANCE?
THEY DO SAY PARENTS ARE BLIND.

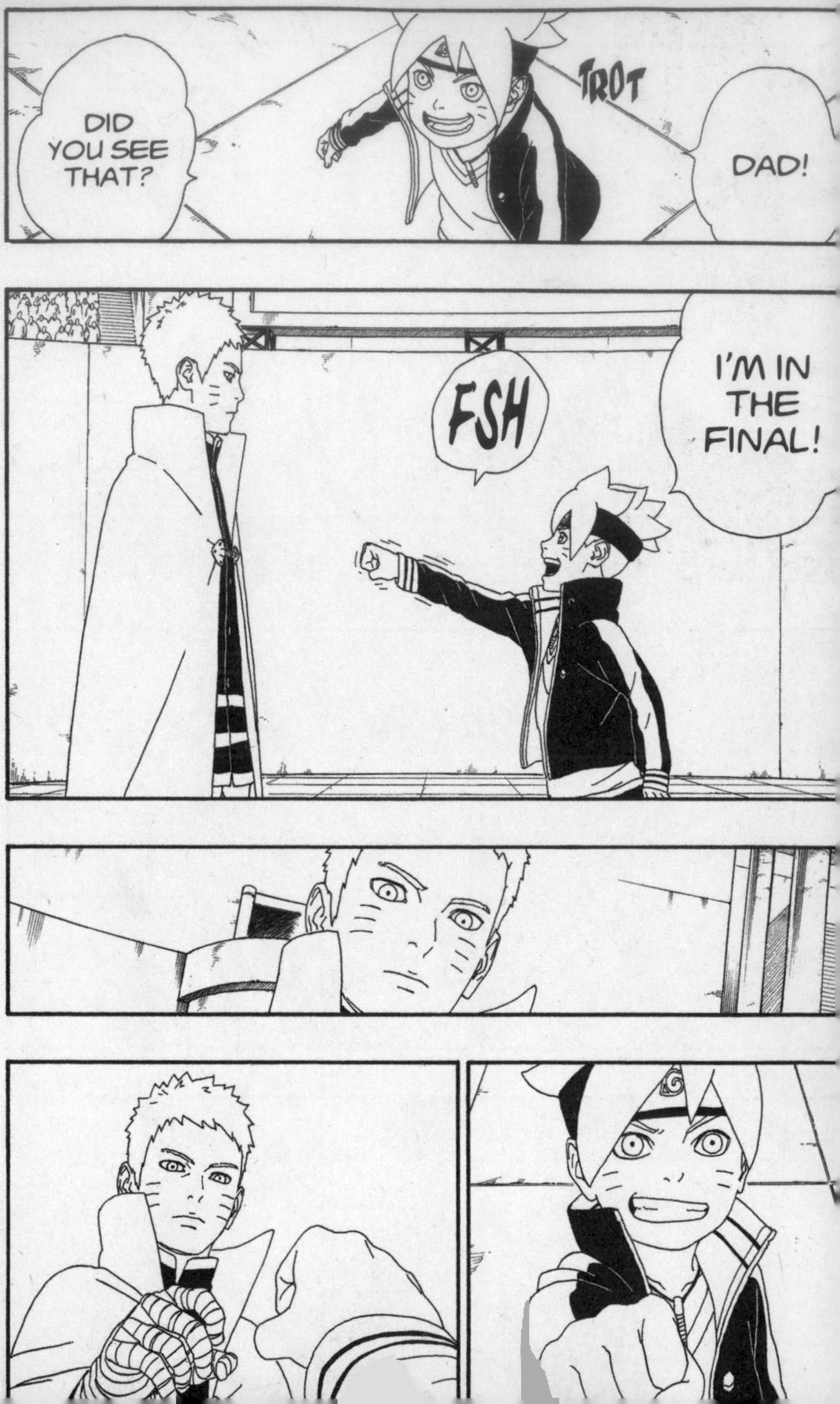
DAD!
TROT
DID YOU SEE THAT?
I'M IN THE FINAL!
FSH

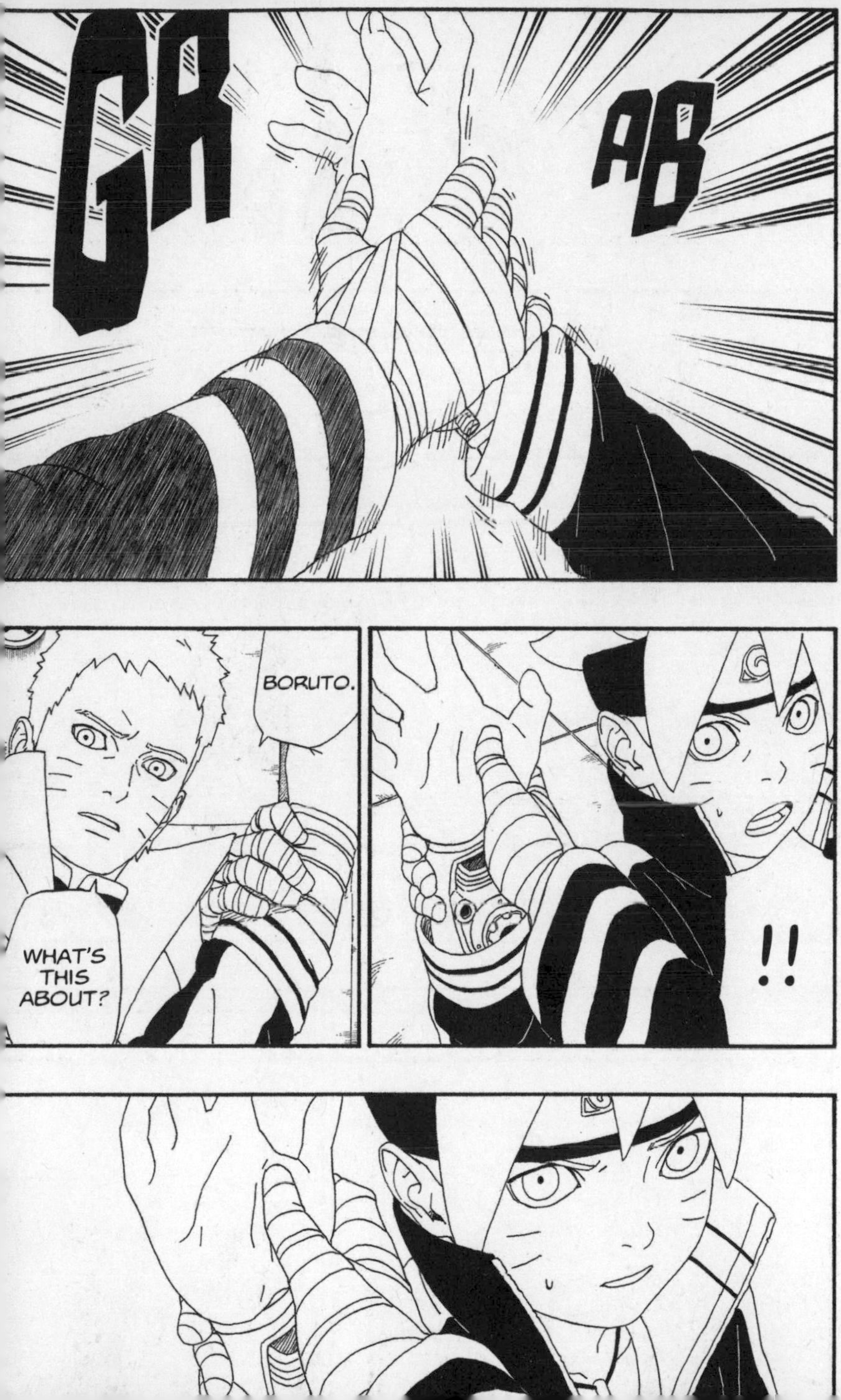
GRAB
!!
BORUTO.
WHAT'S THIS ABOUT?

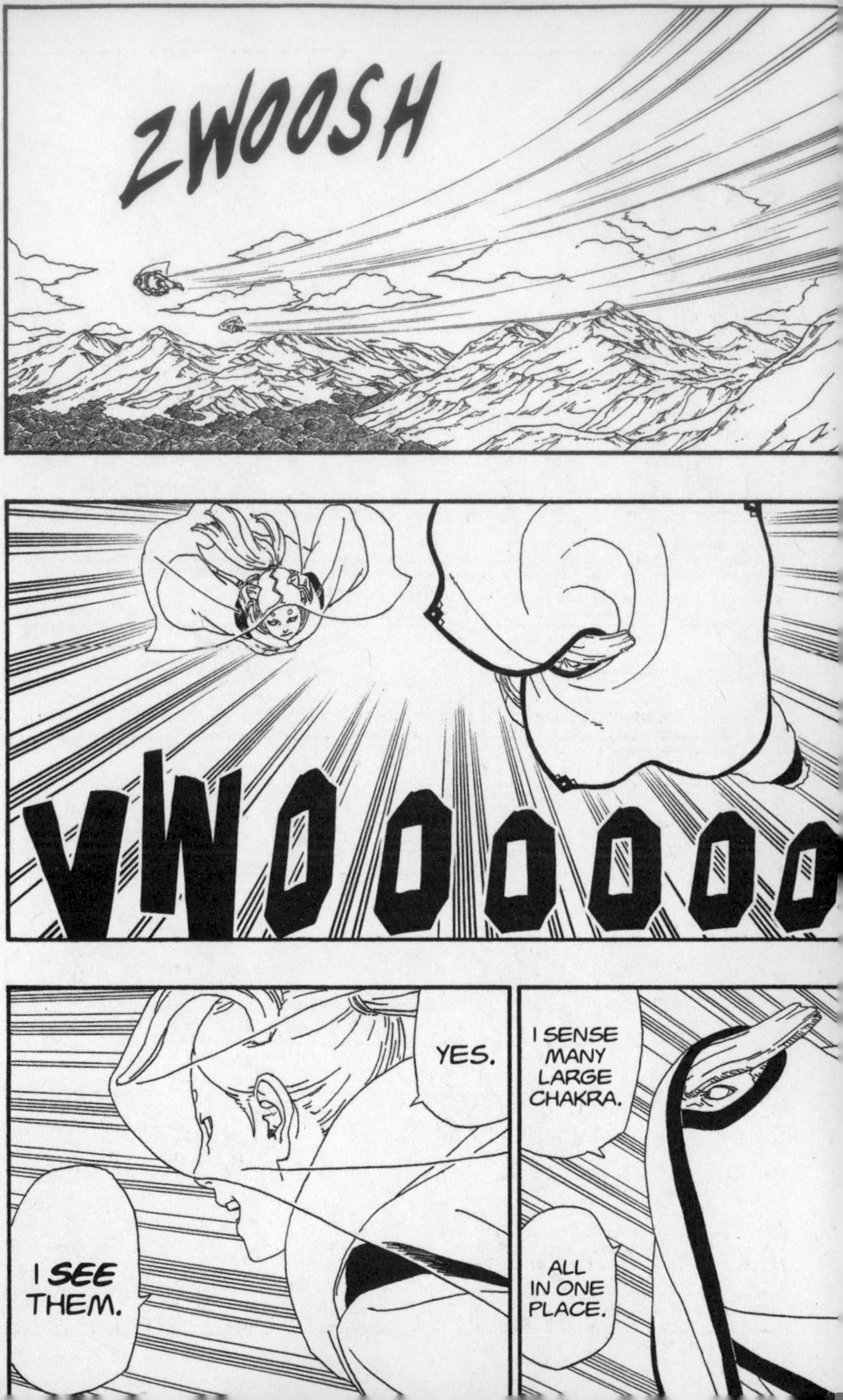
ZWOOSH
VWOOOOOO
I SENSE MANY LARGE CHAKRA.
ALL IN ONE PLACE.
YES.
I SEE THEM.

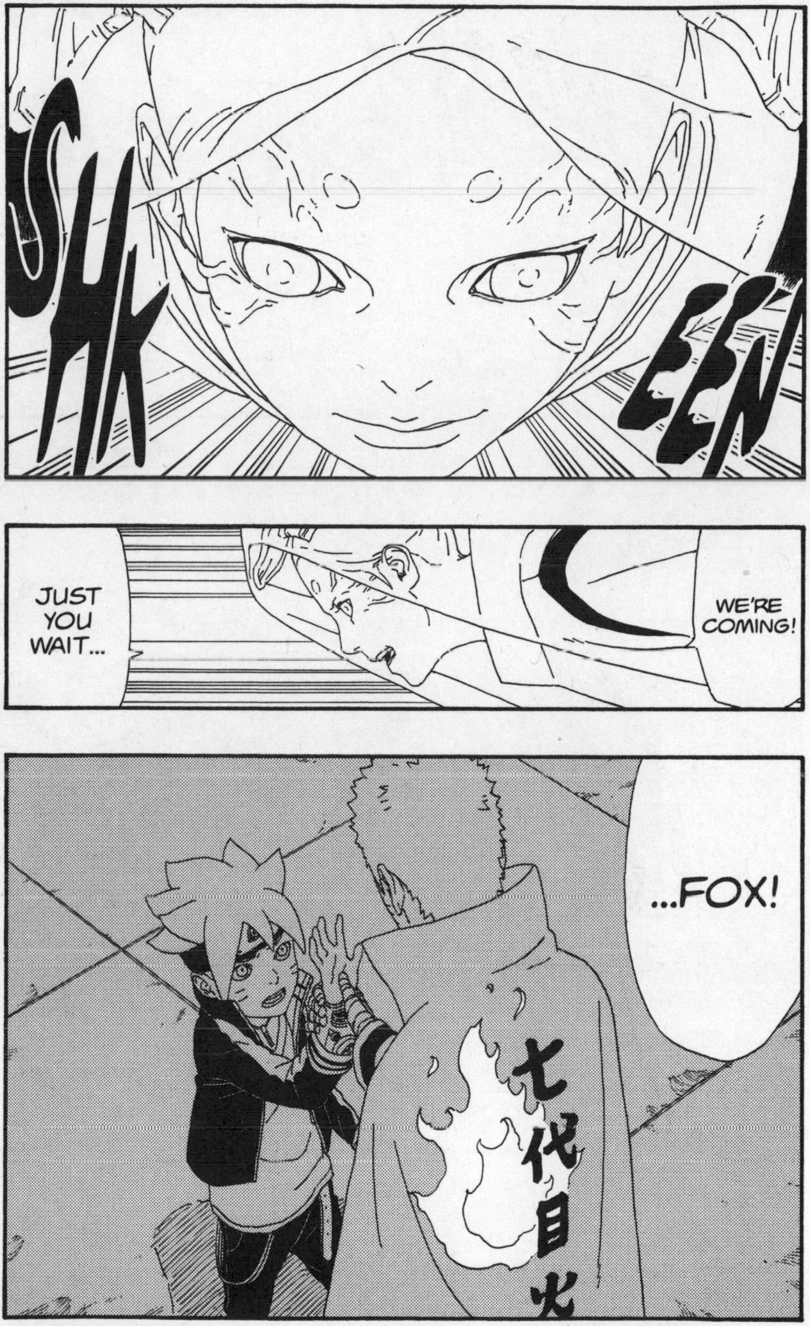
SHK
EEN
WE'RE COMING!
JUST YOU WAIT...
...FOX!
七代目火

NINJA ENCYCLOPEDIA • ENTRY 4

NARA SHIKADAI

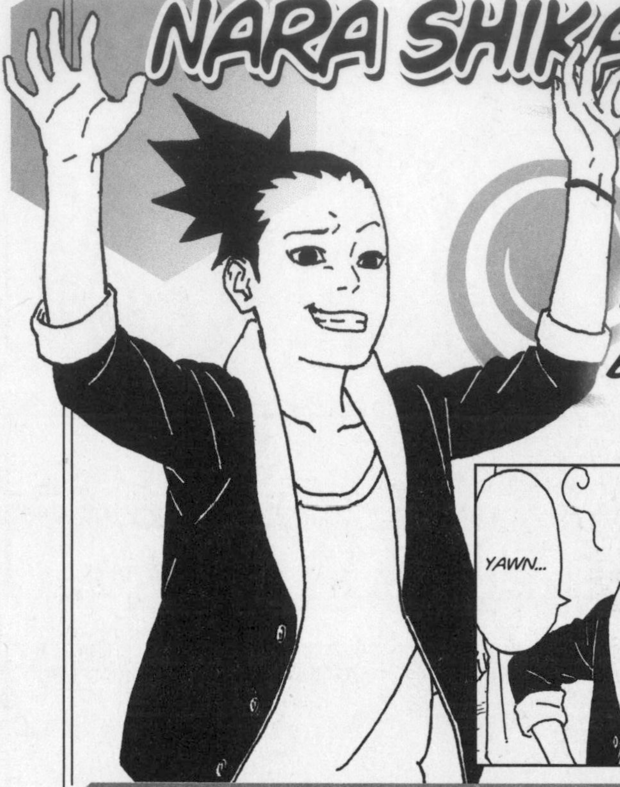

"Both training and pranks are a bother."

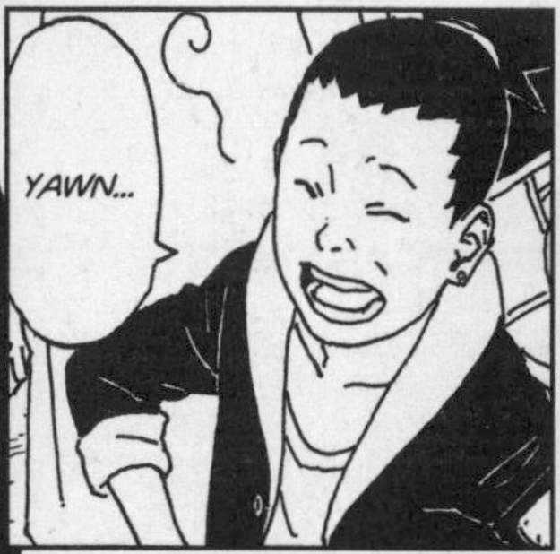
YAWN...

Attributes

Strength	90	Dexterity	112
Intelligence	180	Chakra	120
Perception	145	Negotiation	130

Skills

Observation ☆☆☆☆ Ninjutsu ☆☆☆ Intel crafting ☆☆☆☆ etc.

Ninja Arts

Shadow Possession, Shadow Paralysis, Fuuton:Kamaitachi Wind Scythe, etc.

*Average attribute value is 60 for ordinary people and 90 for genin.
Skill values range from 1 to 5☆ with 5☆ signifying super top-notch.

Number 5: Momoshiki and Kinshiki!!

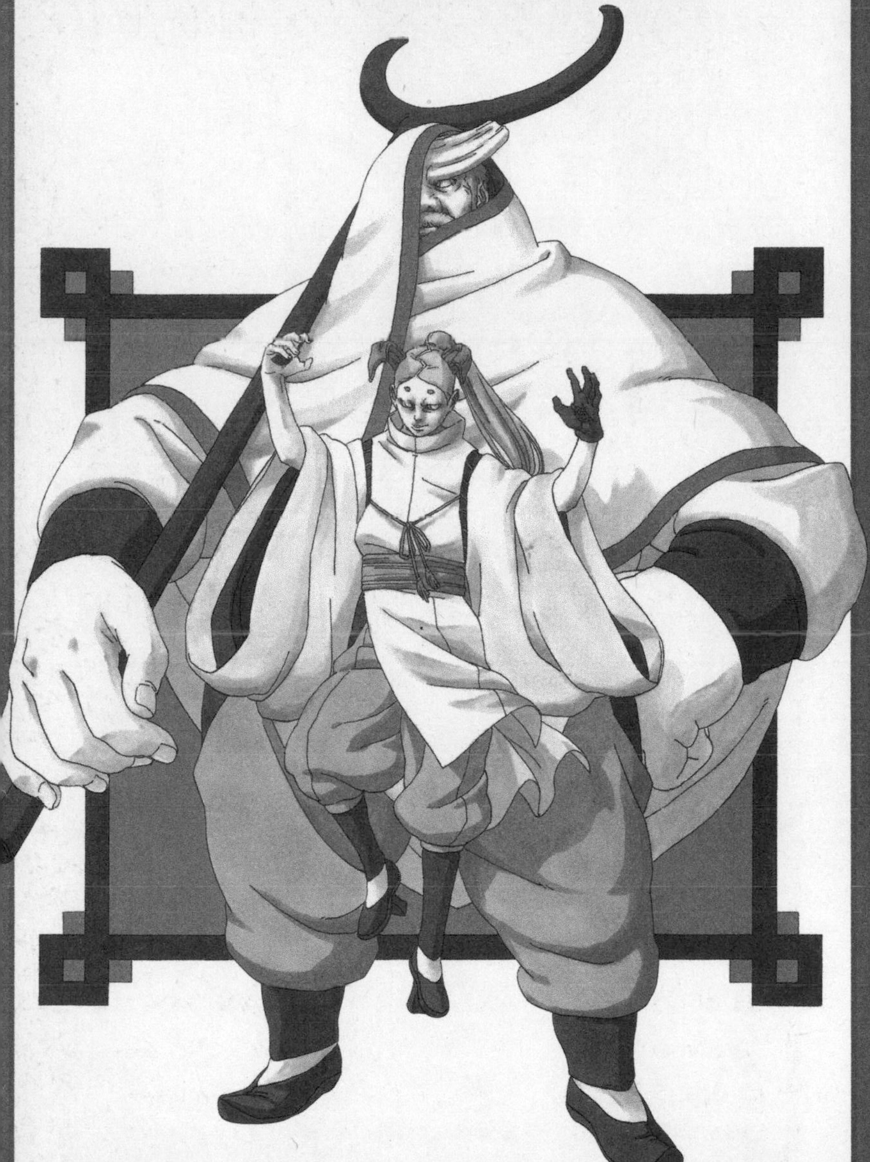

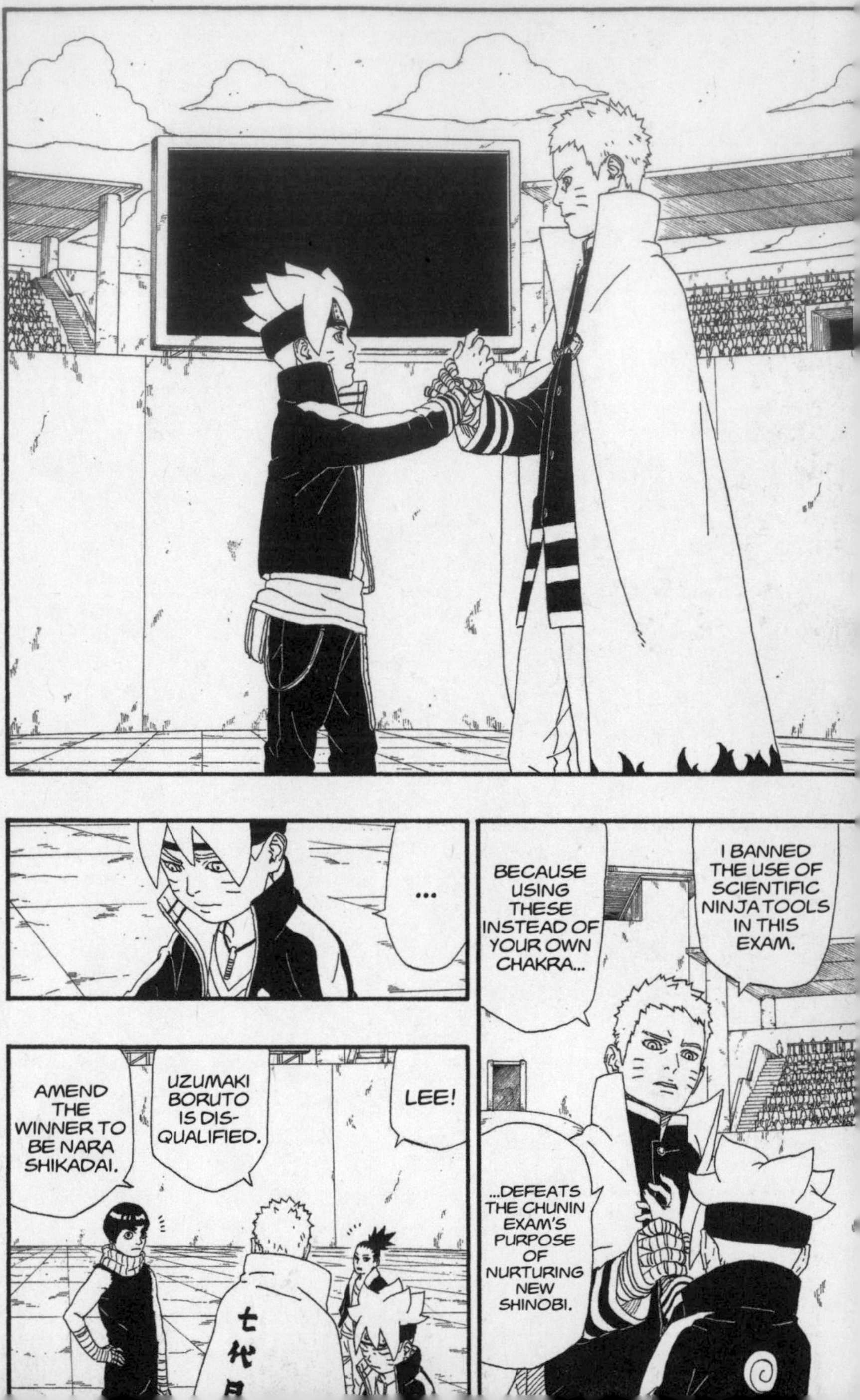
I BANNED THE USE OF SCIENTIFIC NINJA TOOLS IN THIS EXAM.
BECAUSE USING THESE INSTEAD OF YOUR OWN CHAKRA...
...DEFEATS THE CHUNIN EXAM'S PURPOSE OF NURTURING NEW SHINOBI.
...
LEE!
UZUMAKI BORUTO IS DIS-QUALIFIED.
AMEND THE WINNER TO BE NARA SHIKADAI.

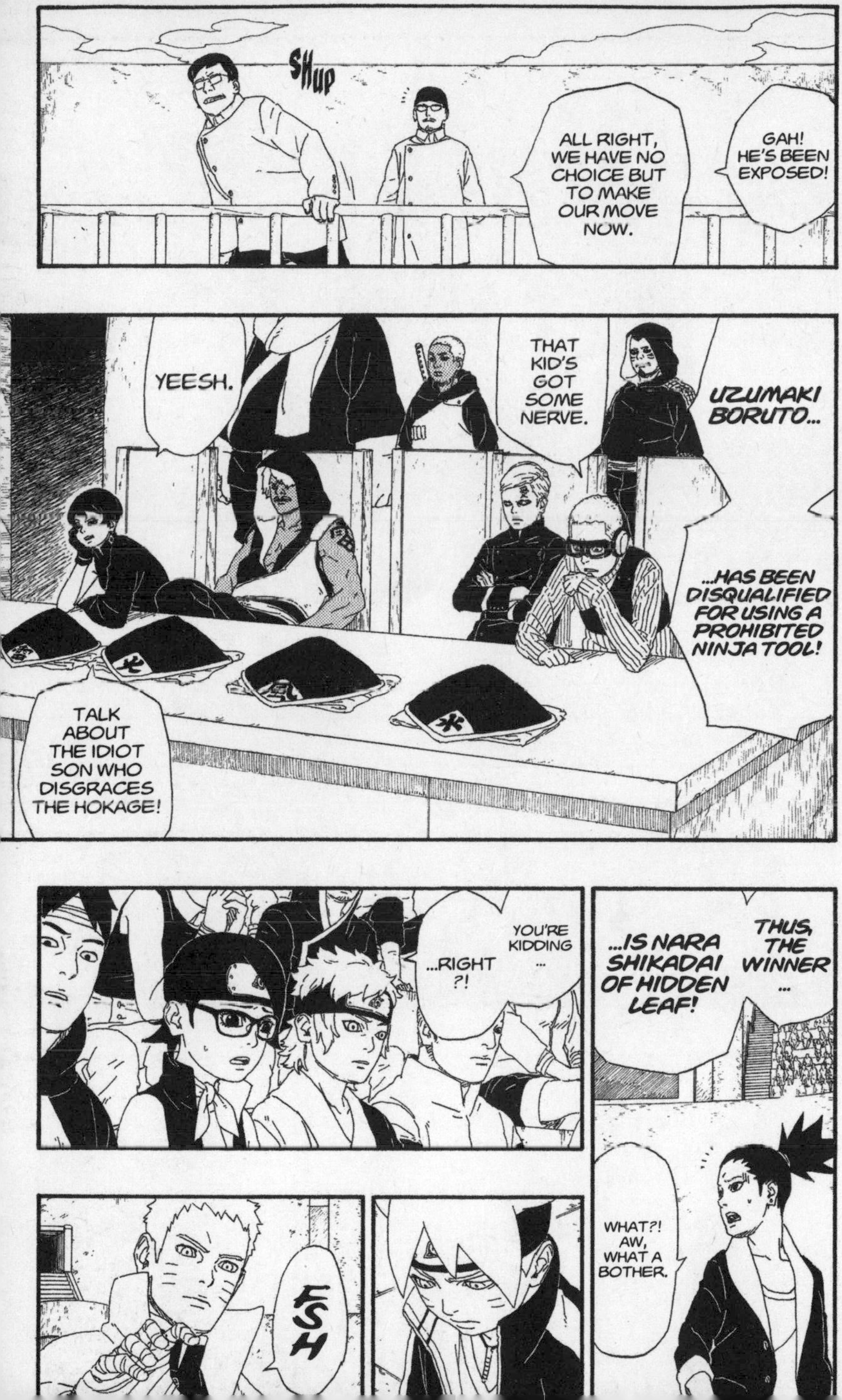
GAH! HE'S BEEN EXPOSED!
ALL RIGHT, WE HAVE NO CHOICE BUT TO MAKE OUR MOVE NOW.
SHUP
UZUMAKI BORUTO...
...HAS BEEN DISQUALIFIED FOR USING A PROHIBITED NINJA TOOL!
THAT KID'S GOT SOME NERVE.
YEESH.
TALK ABOUT THE IDIOT SON WHO DISGRACES THE HOKAGE!
THUS, THE WINNER...
...IS NARA SHIKADAI OF HIDDEN LEAF!
WHAT?! AW, WHAT A BOTHER.
YOU'RE KIDDING...
...RIGHT?!
FSH

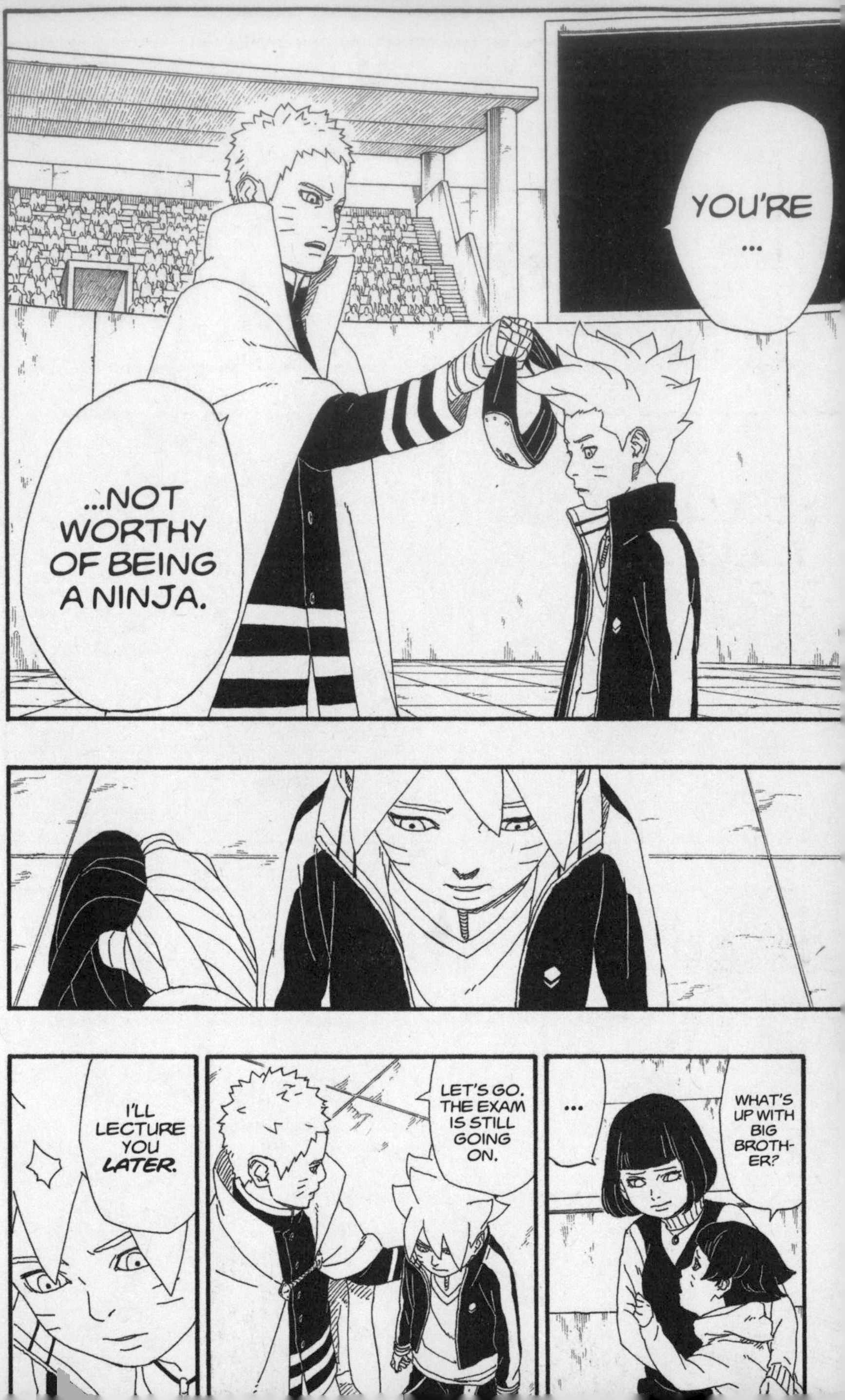
YOU'RE ...
...NOT WORTHY OF BEING A NINJA.
WHAT'S UP WITH BIG BROTH-ER?
...
LET'S GO. THE EXAM IS STILL GOING ON.
I'LL LECTURE YOU *LATER*.

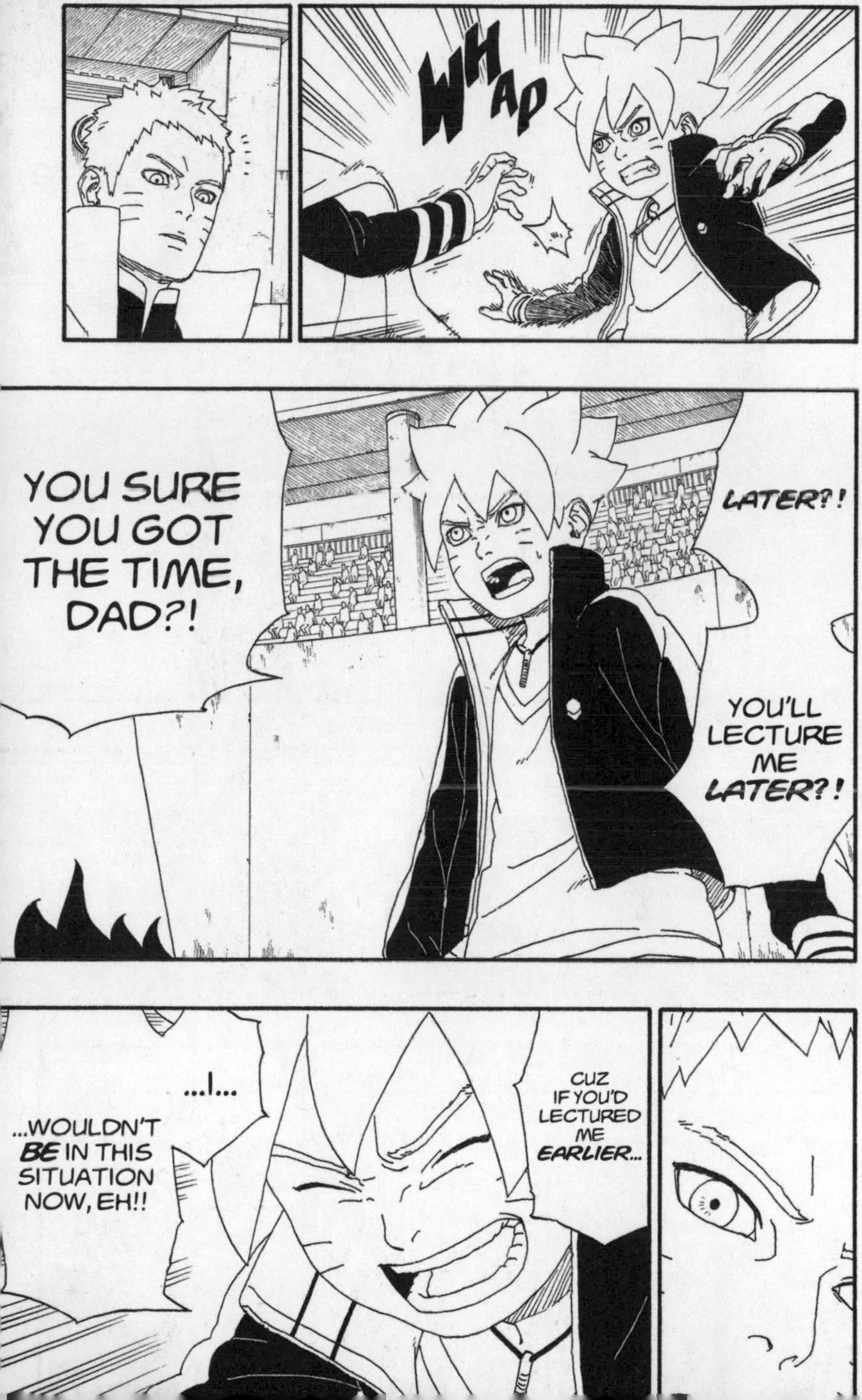
WHAP
LATER?!
YOU'LL LECTURE ME LATER?!
YOU SURE YOU GOT THE TIME, DAD?!
CUZ IF YOU'D LECTURED ME EARLIER...
...I...
...WOULDN'T BE IN THIS SITUATION NOW, EH!!

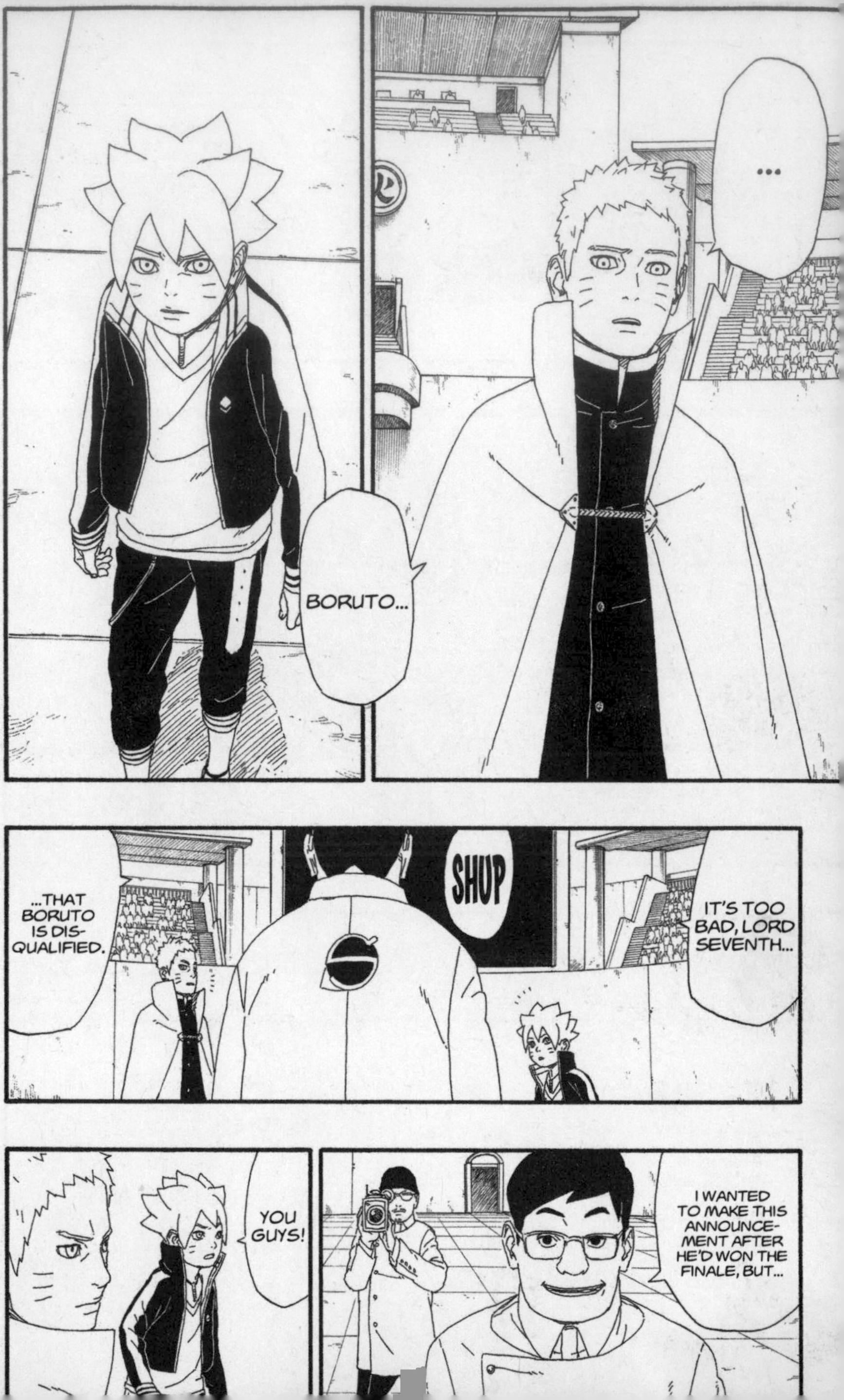
...
BORUTO...
IT'S TOO BAD, LORD SEVENTH...
SHUP
...THAT BORUTO IS DIS-QUALIFIED.
I WANTED TO MAKE THIS ANNOUNCE-MENT AFTER HE'D WON THE FINALE, BUT...
YOU GUYS!

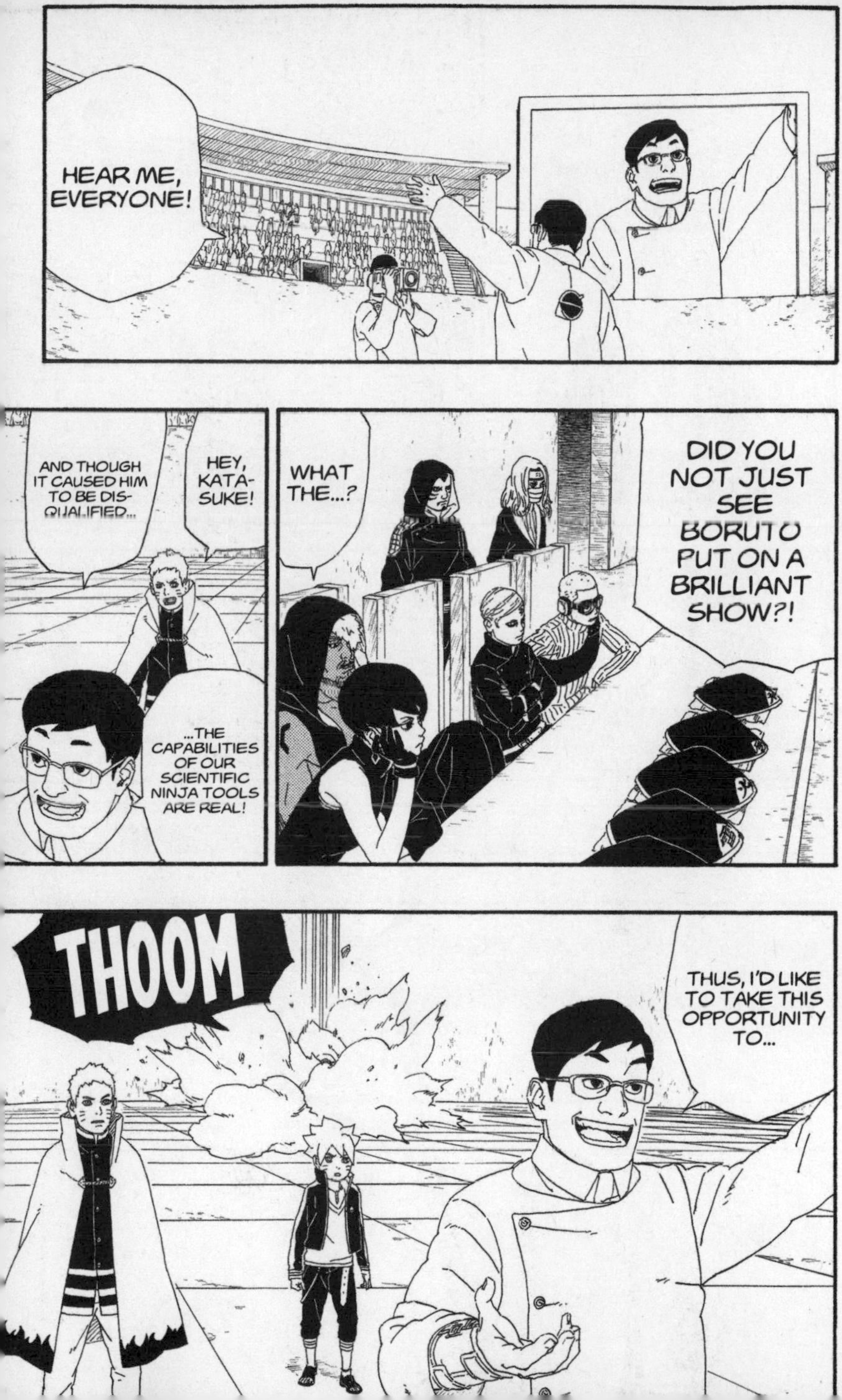
HEAR ME, EVERYONE!
DID YOU NOT JUST SEE BORUTO PUT ON A BRILLIANT SHOW?!
WHAT THE...?
HEY, KATA-SUKE!
AND THOUGH IT CAUSED HIM TO BE DIS-QUALIFIED...
...THE CAPABILITIES OF OUR SCIENTIFIC NINJA TOOLS ARE REAL!
THUS, I'D LIKE TO TAKE THIS OPPORTUNITY TO...
THOOM

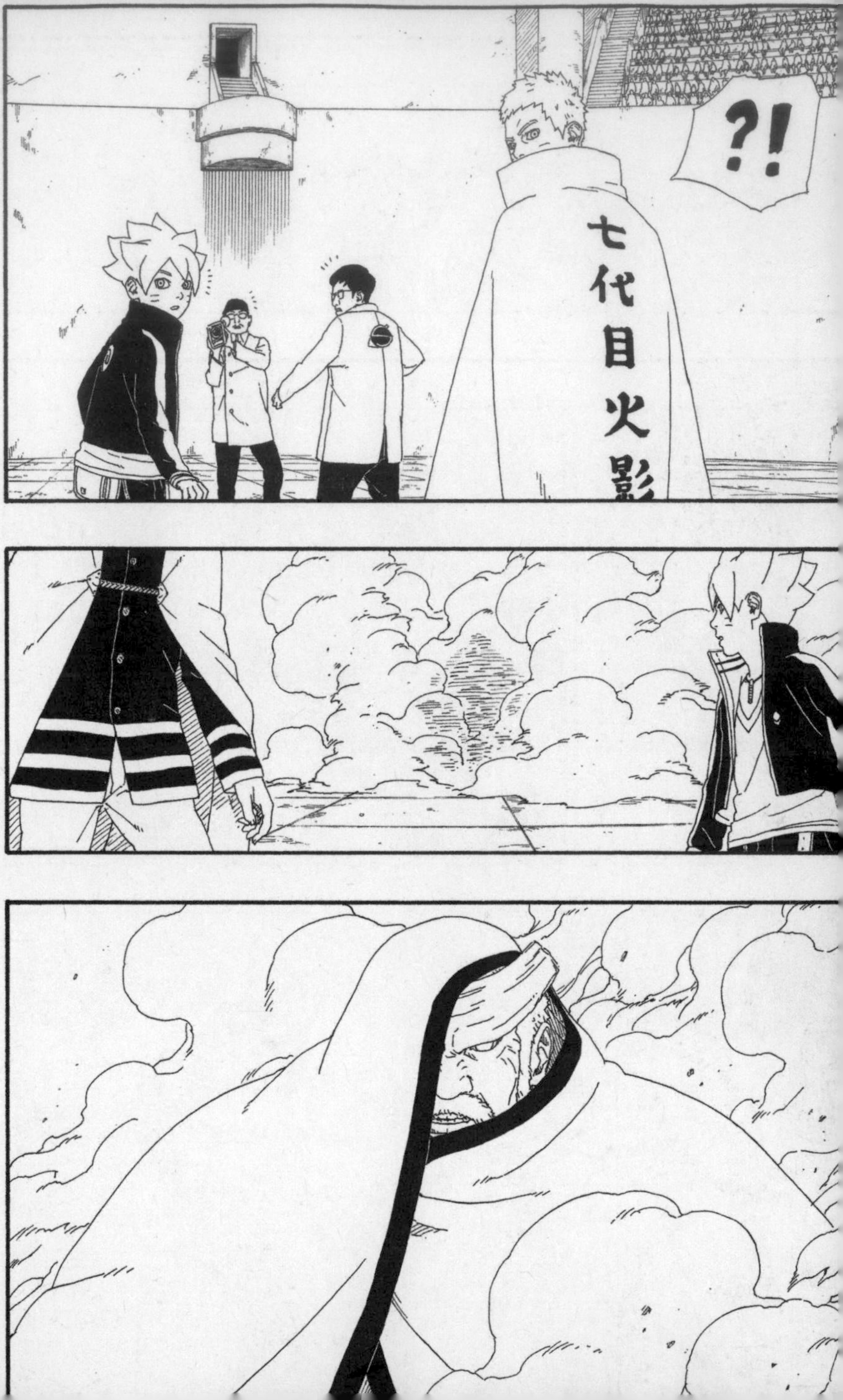
?!
七代目火影

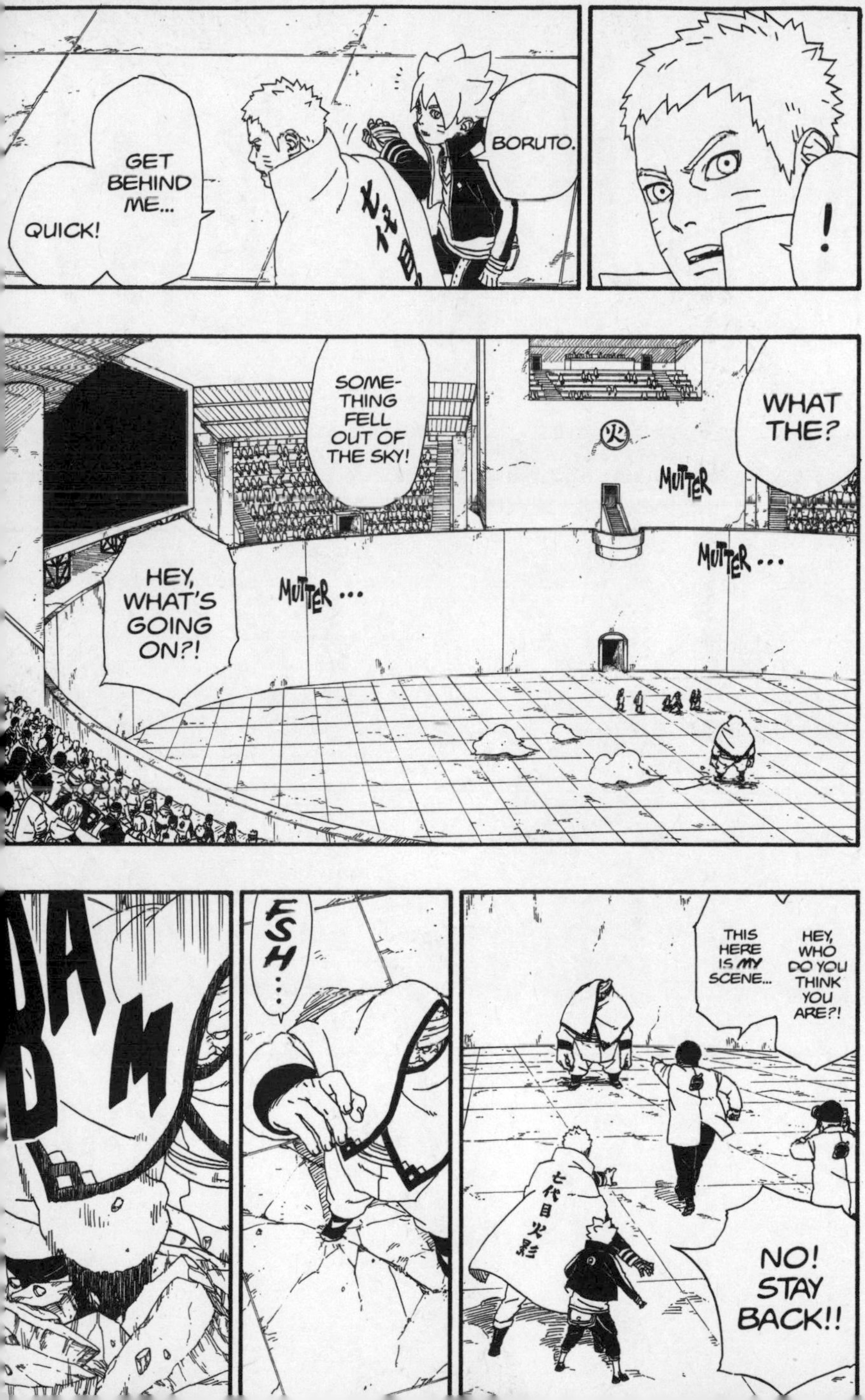
!
BORUTO.
GET BEHIND ME... QUICK!
WHAT THE?
MUTTER
MUTTER ...
SOME-THING FELL OUT OF THE SKY!
MUTTER ...
HEY, WHAT'S GOING ON?!
HEY, WHO DO YOU THINK YOU ARE?!
THIS HERE IS *MY* SCENE...
七代目火影
NO! STAY BACK!!
FSH...

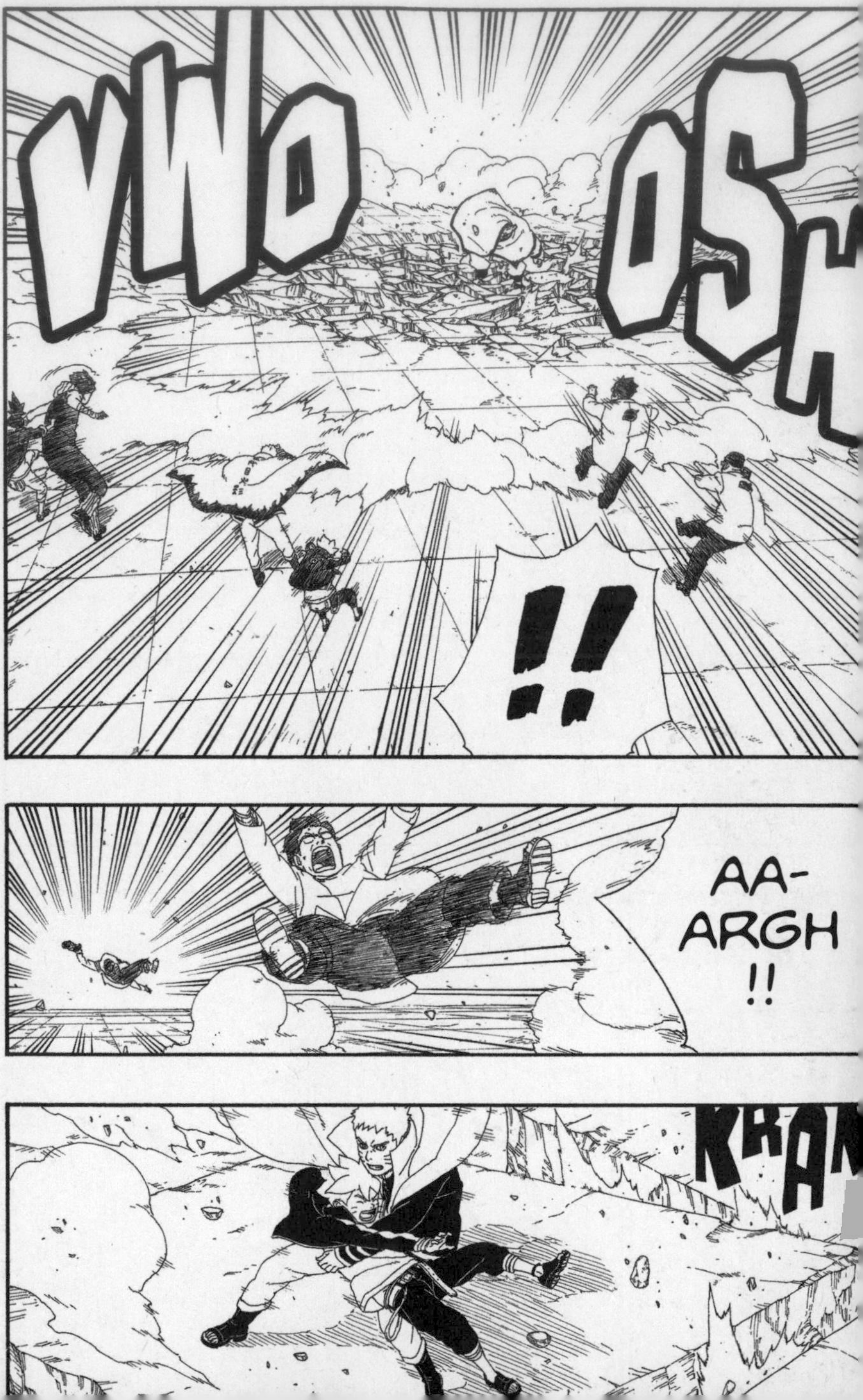
VWOOSH
!!
AA-
ARGH
!!
KRAN

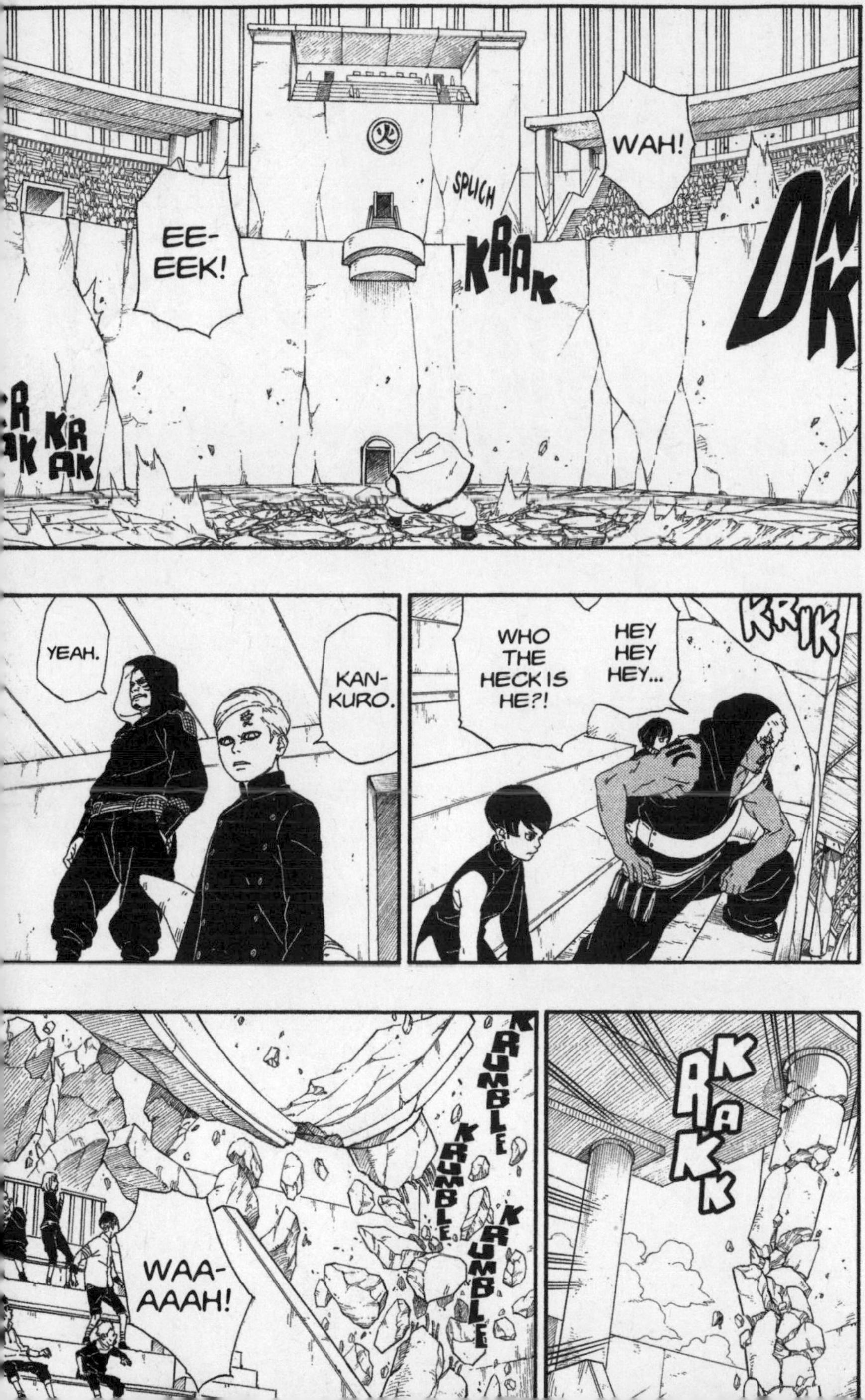

DONK
WAH!
SPLICH
KRAK
EE-EEK!
KRAK
KRAK
KRIK
HEY HEY HEY...
WHO THE HECK IS HE?!
KAN-KURO.
YEAH.
KRAKK
KRUMBLE
KRUMBLE
KRUMBLE
WAA-AAAH!

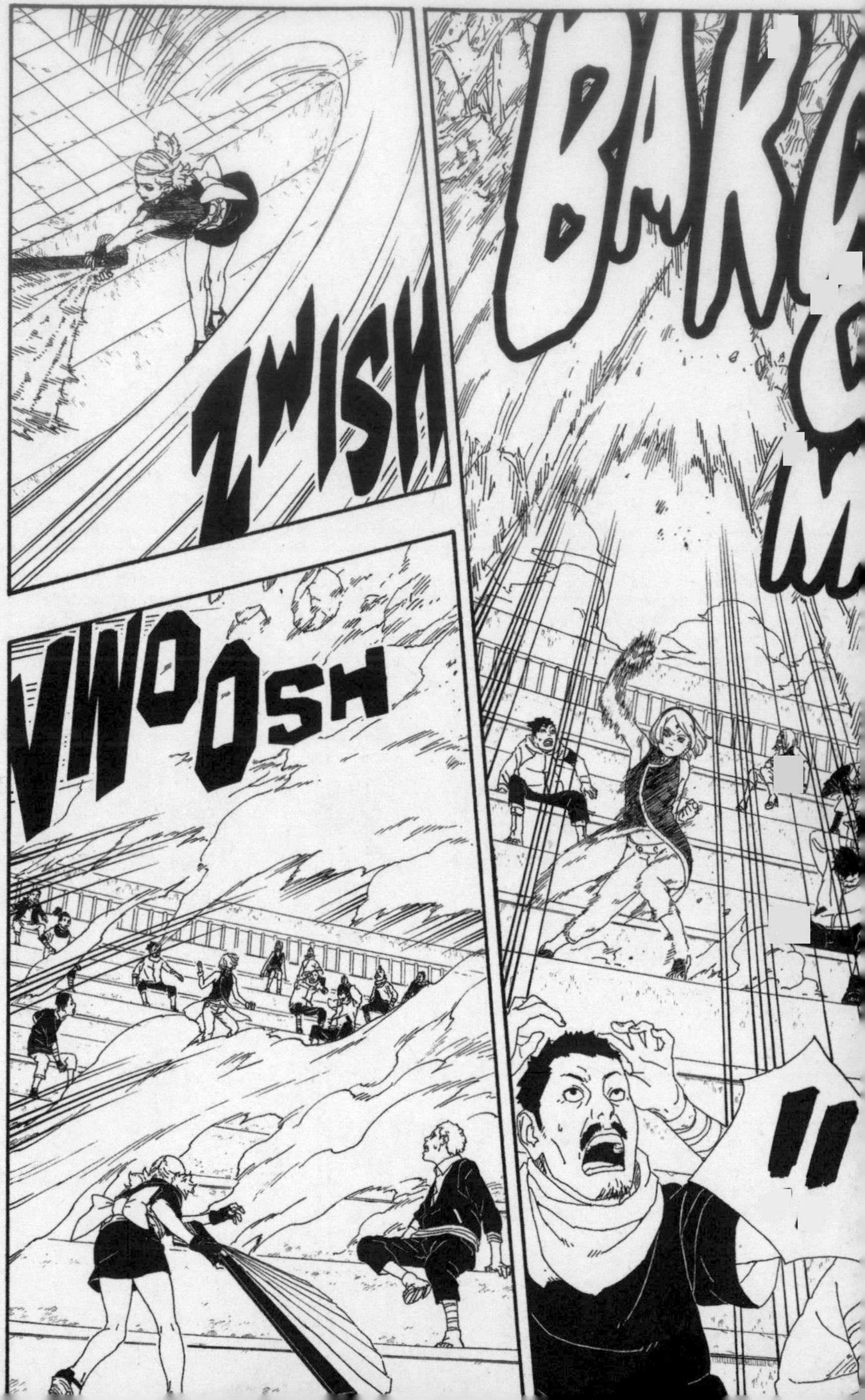
ZWISH
VWOOSH

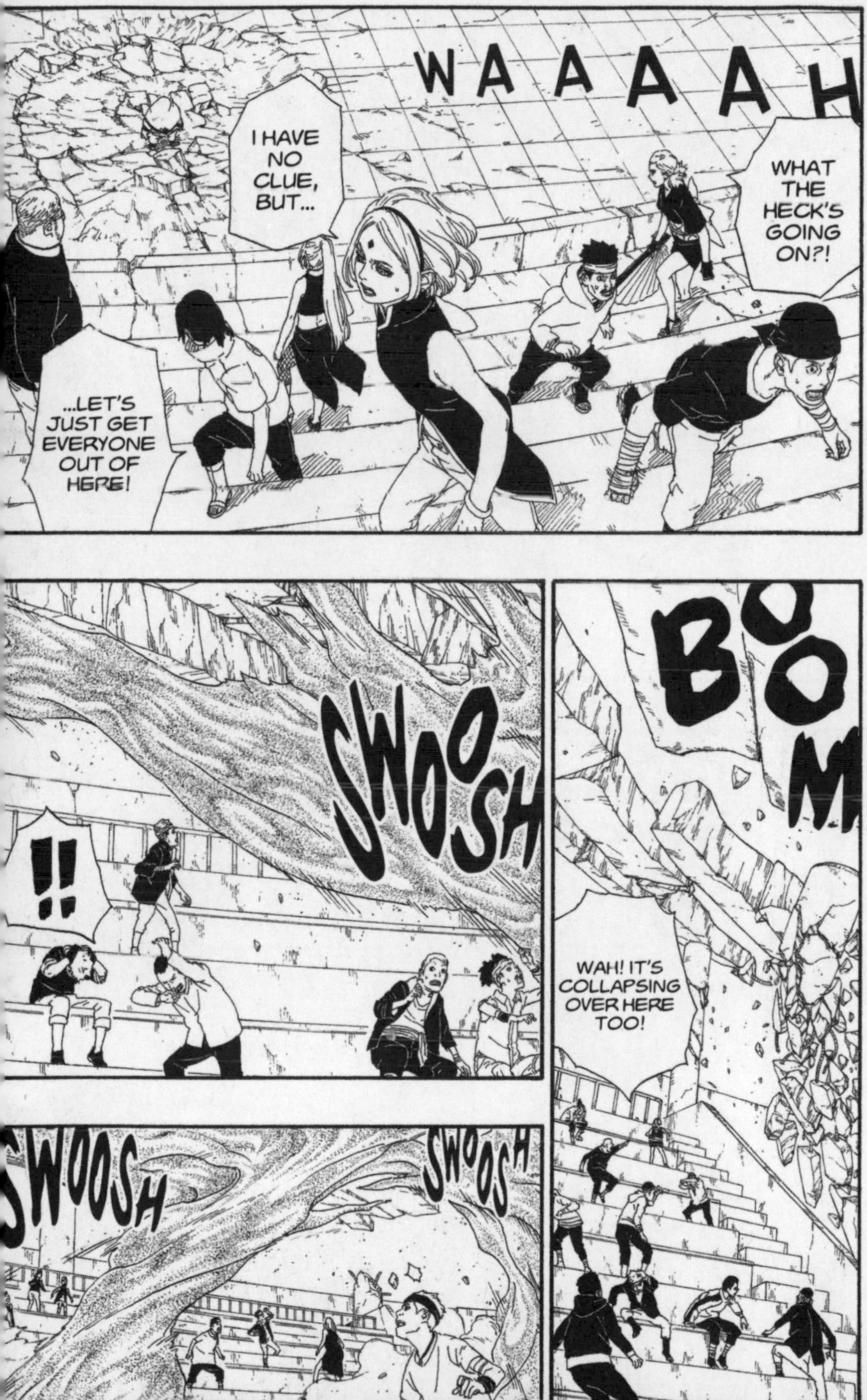
WAAAAH
WHAT THE HECK'S GOING ON?!
I HAVE NO CLUE, BUT...
...LET'S JUST GET EVERYONE OUT OF HERE!
BOOM
WAH! IT'S COLLAPSING OVER HERE TOO!
SWOOSH
!!
SWOOSH
SWOOSH

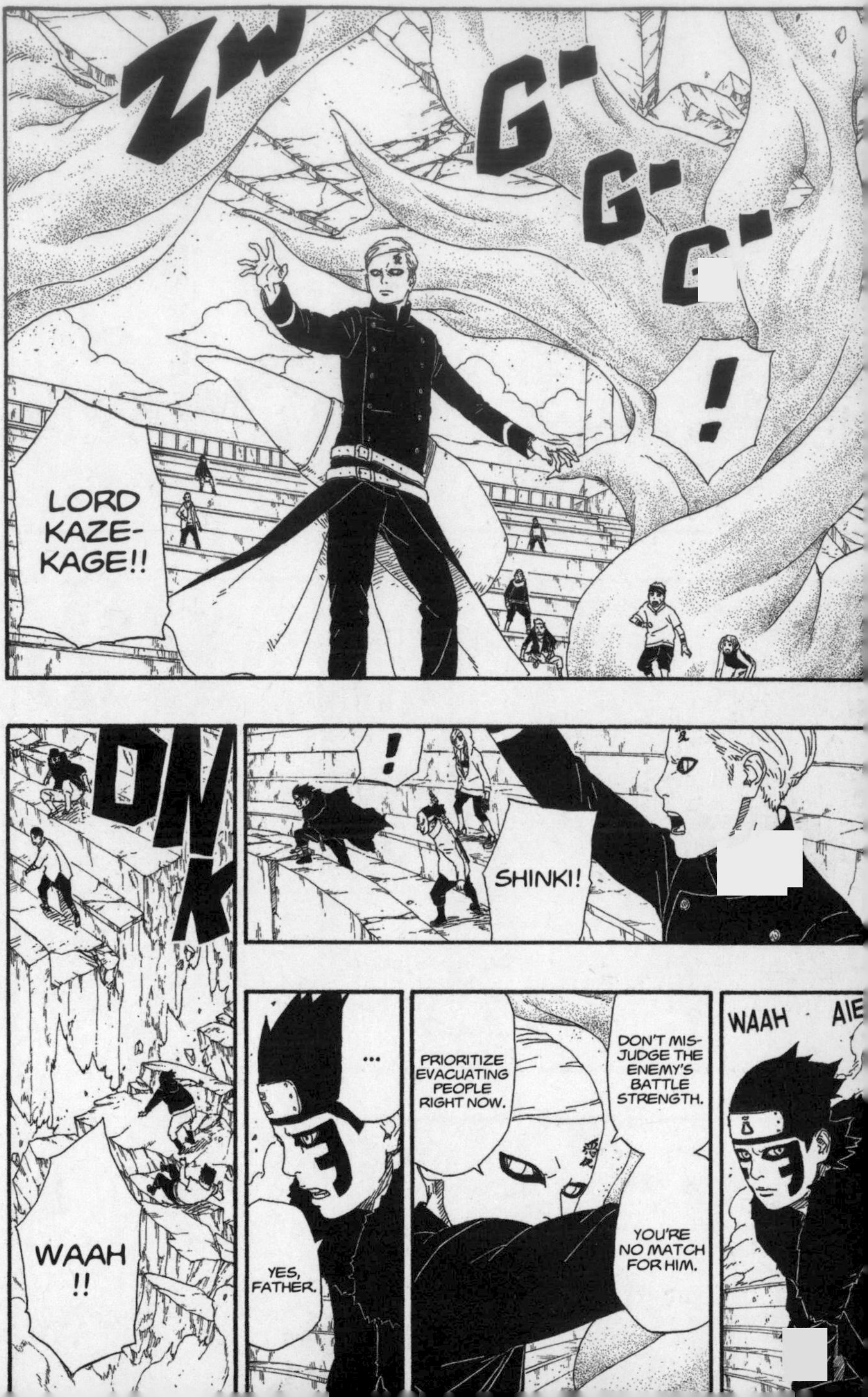
ZW G- G- G-
!
LORD KAZE-KAGE!!
!
SHINKI!
WAAH
AIE
DON'T MIS-JUDGE THE ENEMY'S BATTLE STRENGTH.
YOU'RE NO MATCH FOR HIM.
PRIORITIZE EVACUATING PEOPLE RIGHT NOW.
...
YES, FATHER.
DOWK
WAAH!!

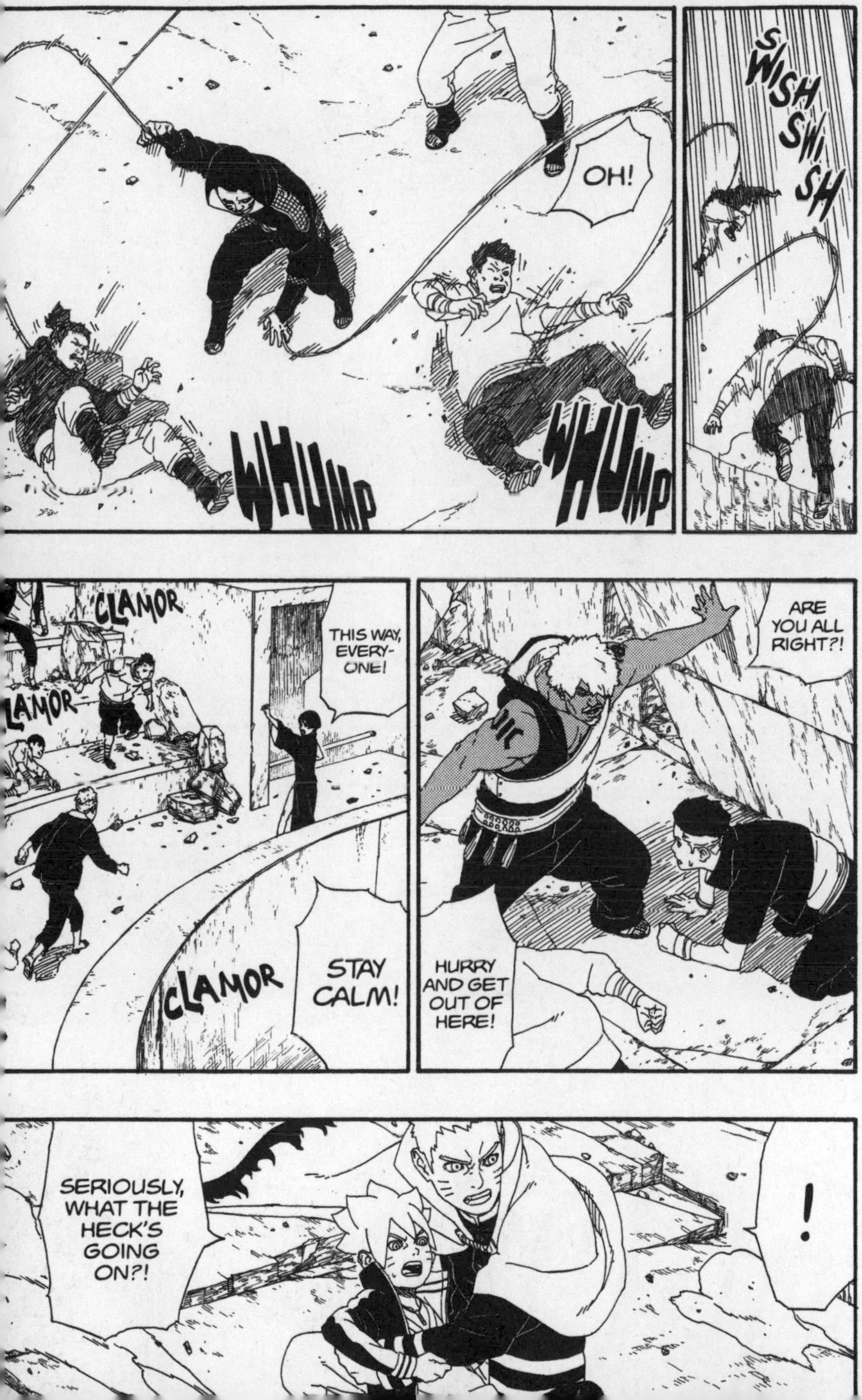
SWISH SWISH SWISH
OH!
WHUMP
WHUMP
ARE YOU ALL RIGHT?!
HURRY AND GET OUT OF HERE!
THIS WAY, EVERY-ONE!
CLAMOR
CLAMOR
STAY CALM!
CLAMOR
!
SERIOUSLY, WHAT THE HECK'S GOING ON?!

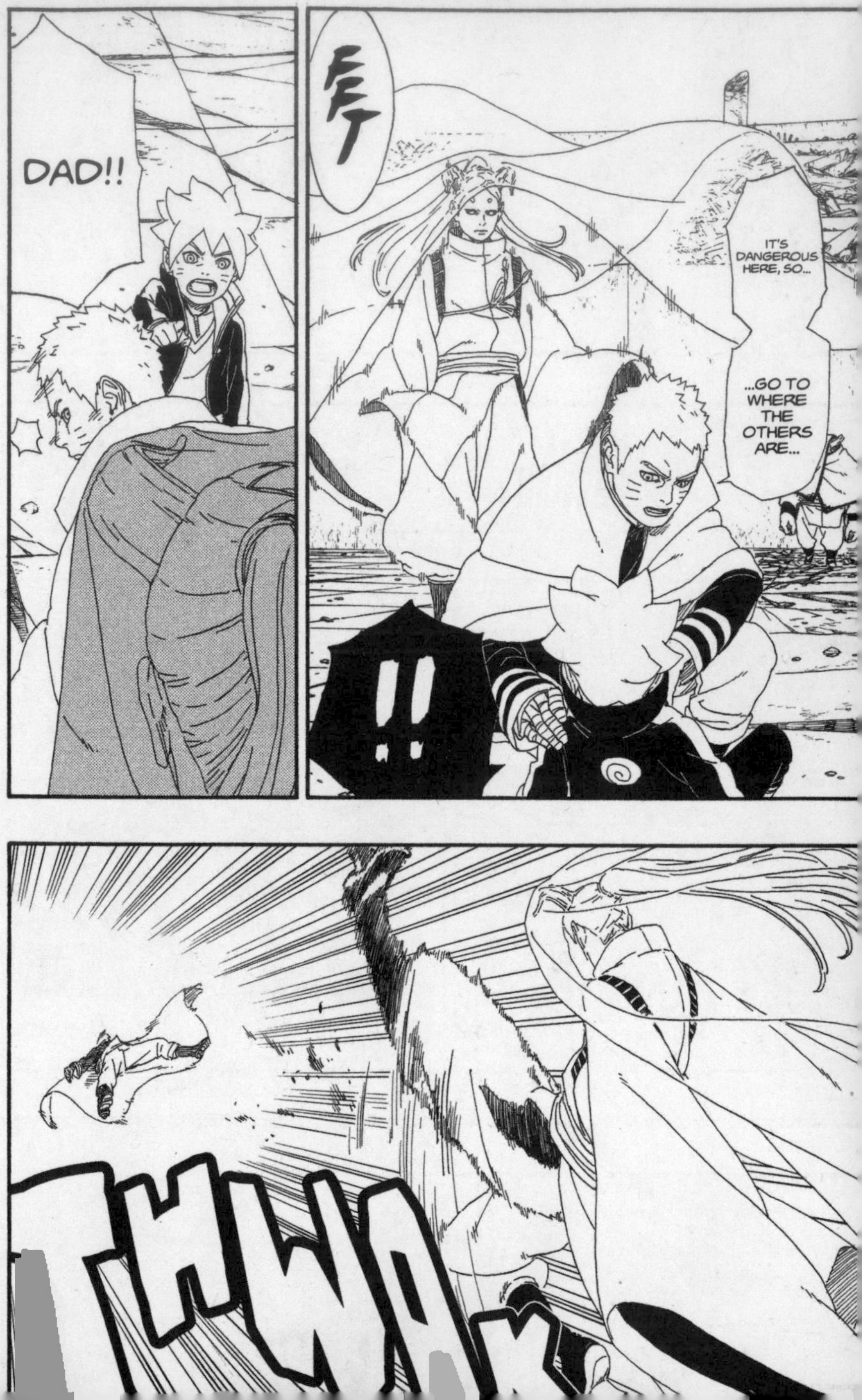
IT'S DANGEROUS HERE, SO...
...GO TO WHERE THE OTHERS ARE...
FFT
!!
DAD!!
THWA

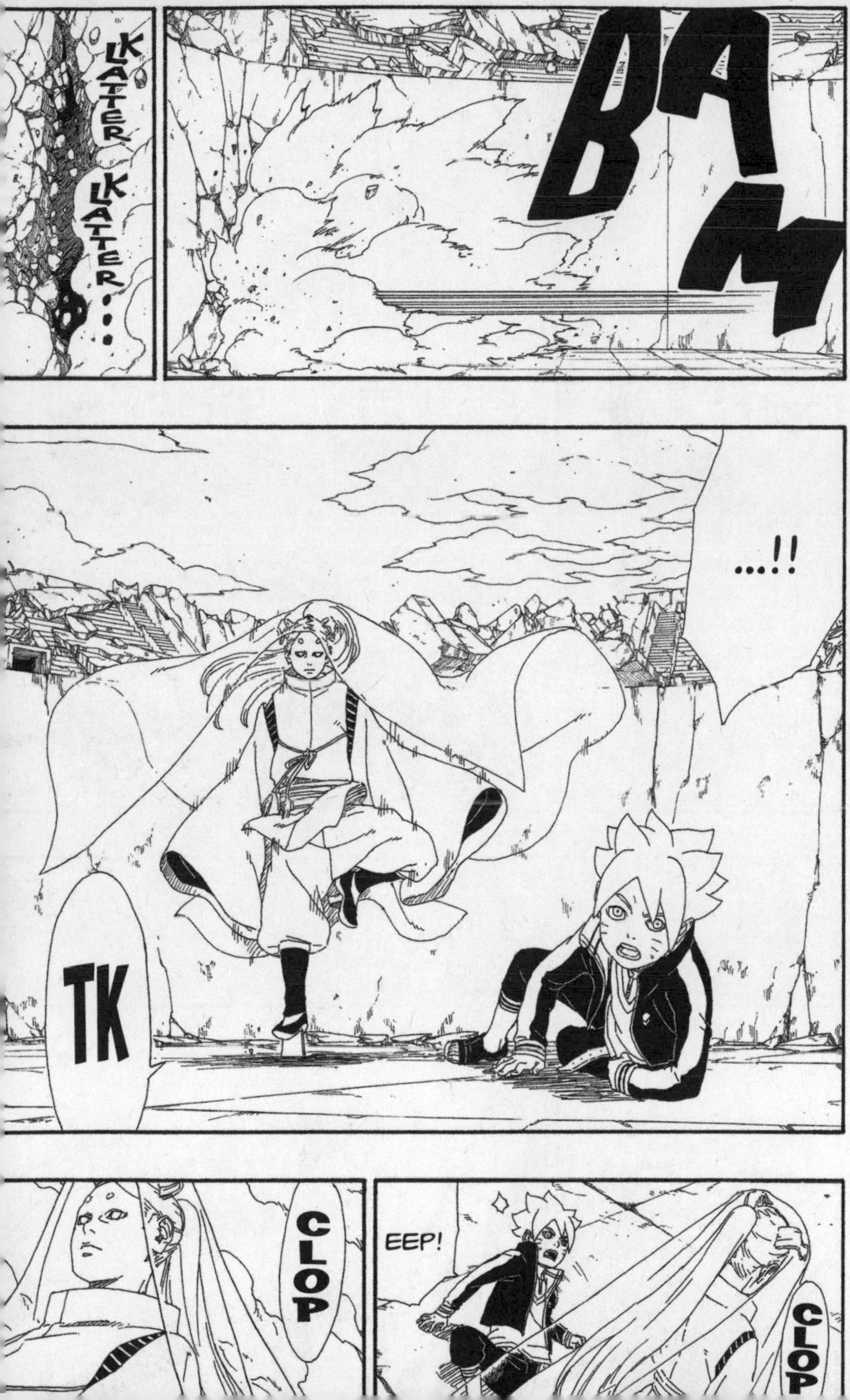
BAM
KLATTER KLATTER...
...!!
TK
EEP!
CLOP
CLOP

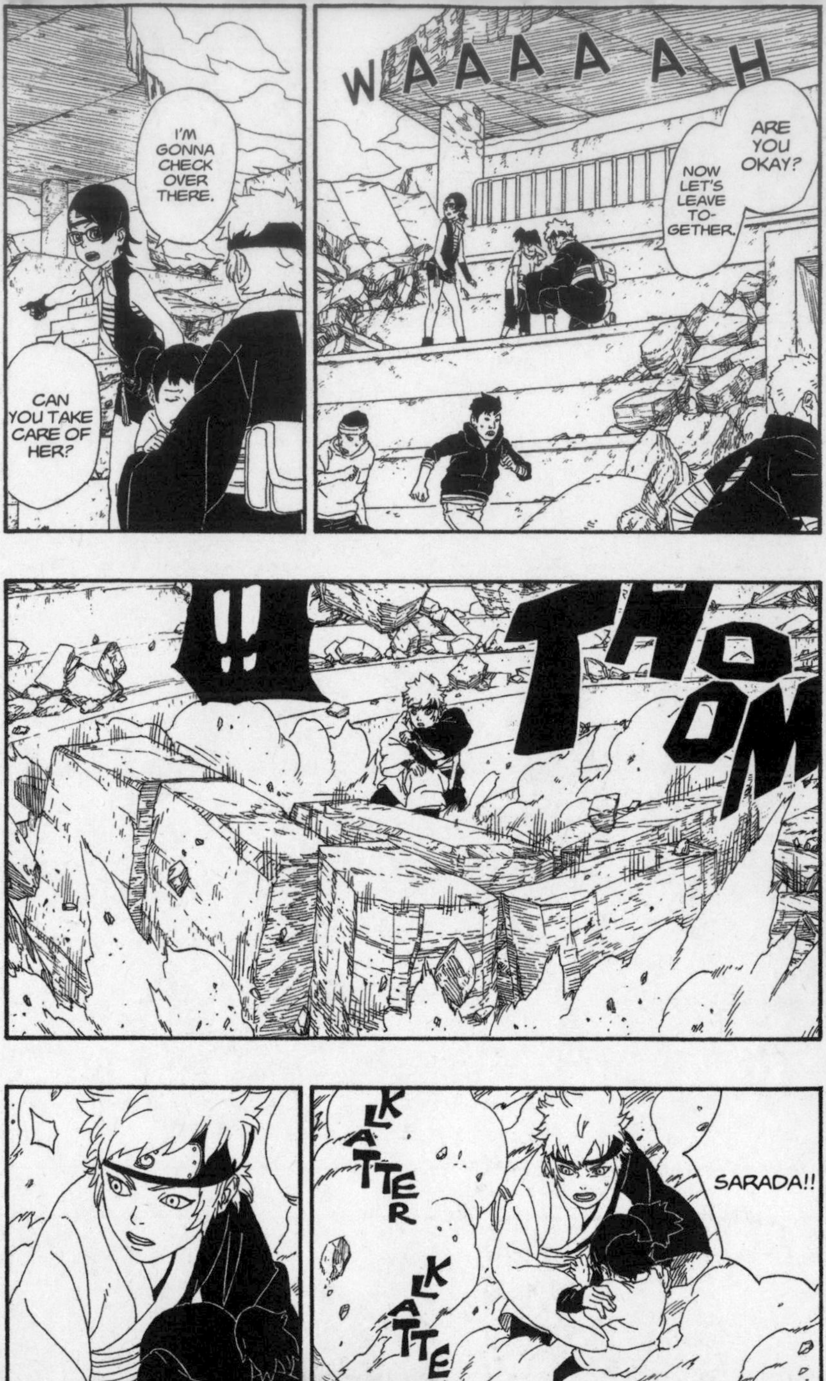
WAAAAAH
ARE YOU OKAY?
NOW LET'S LEAVE TO-GETHER.
I'M GONNA CHECK OVER THERE.
CAN YOU TAKE CARE OF HER?
THOOM
!!
SARADA!!
KLATTER
KLATTER

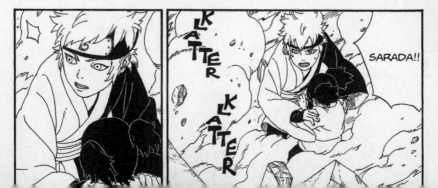

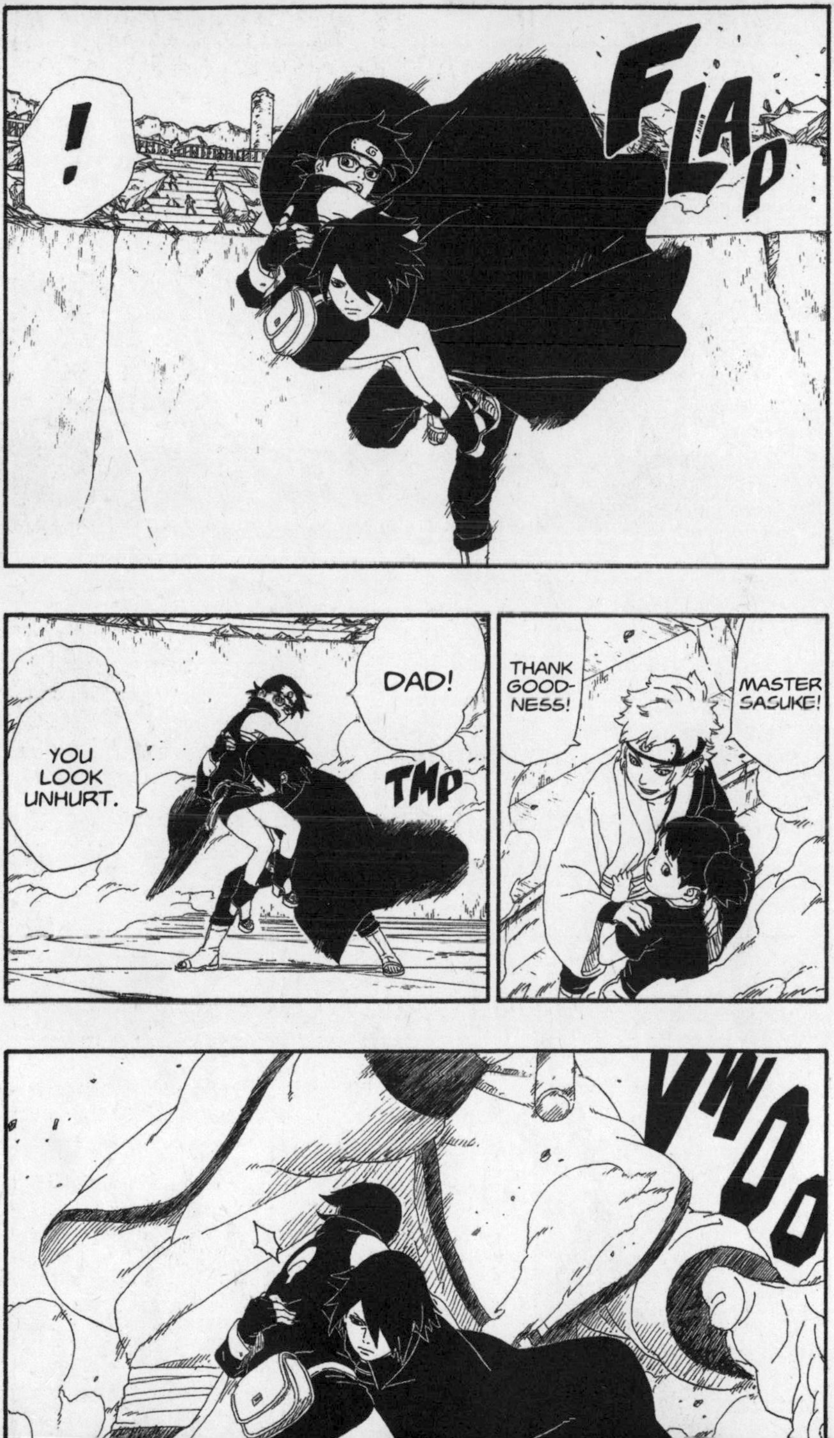
FLAP
!
MASTER SASUKE!
THANK GOODNESS!
DAD!
TMP
YOU LOOK UNHURT.
VWOO

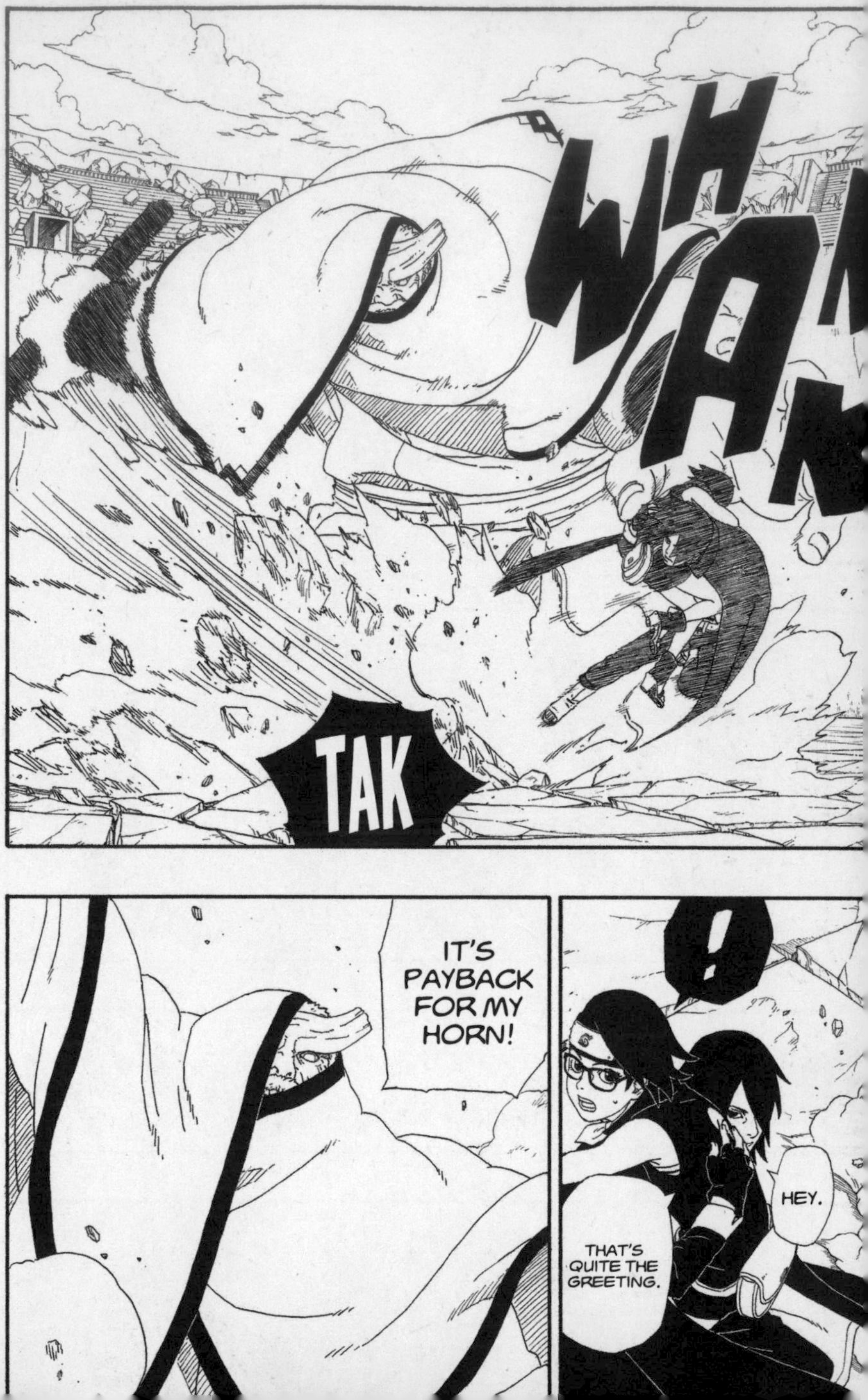
TAK
HEY.
THAT'S QUITE THE GREETING.
IT'S PAYBACK FOR MY HORN!

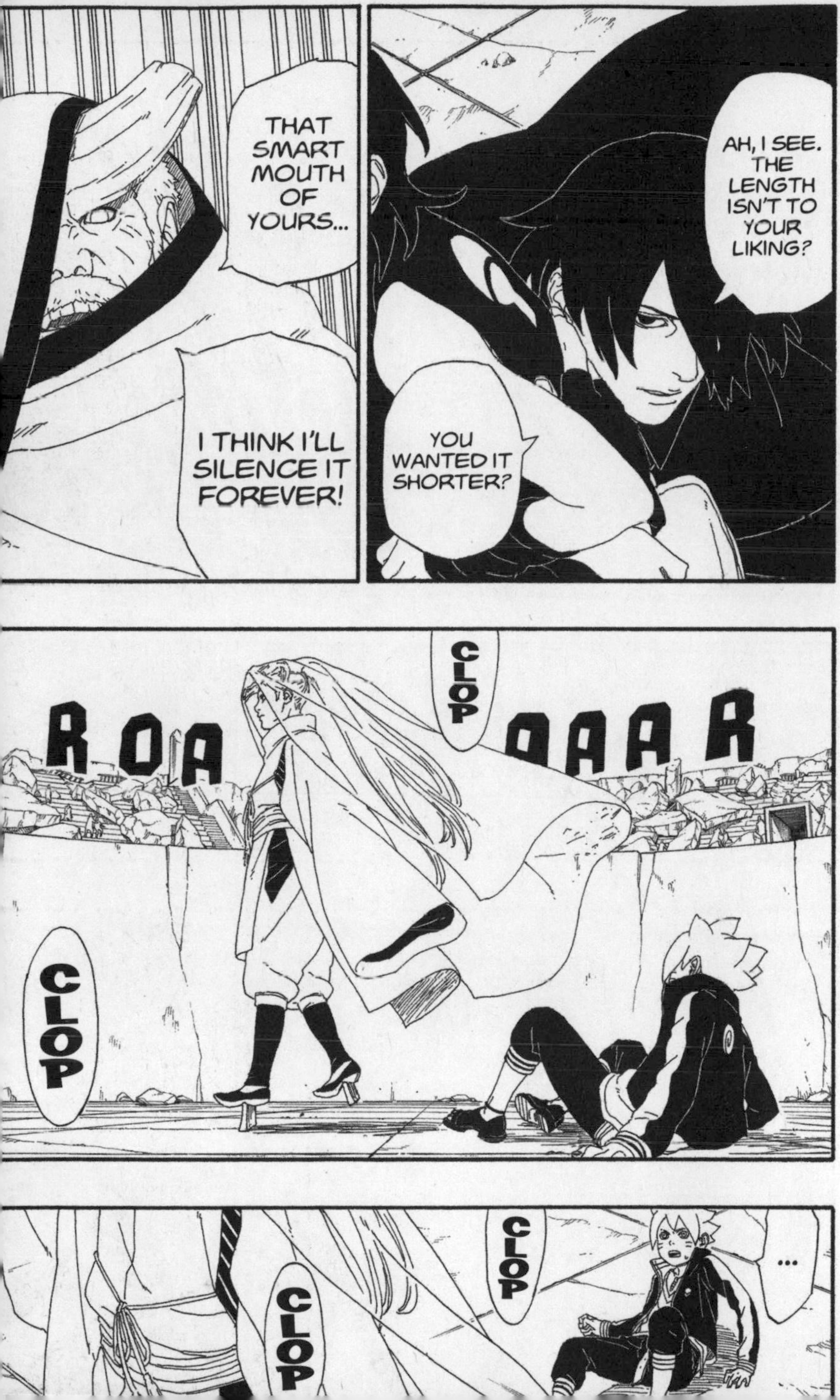
AH, I SEE. THE LENGTH ISN'T TO YOUR LIKING?
YOU WANTED IT SHORTER?
THAT SMART MOUTH OF YOURS...
I THINK I'LL SILENCE IT FOREVER!
ROA OAAR
CLOP
CLOP
...
CLOP
CLOP

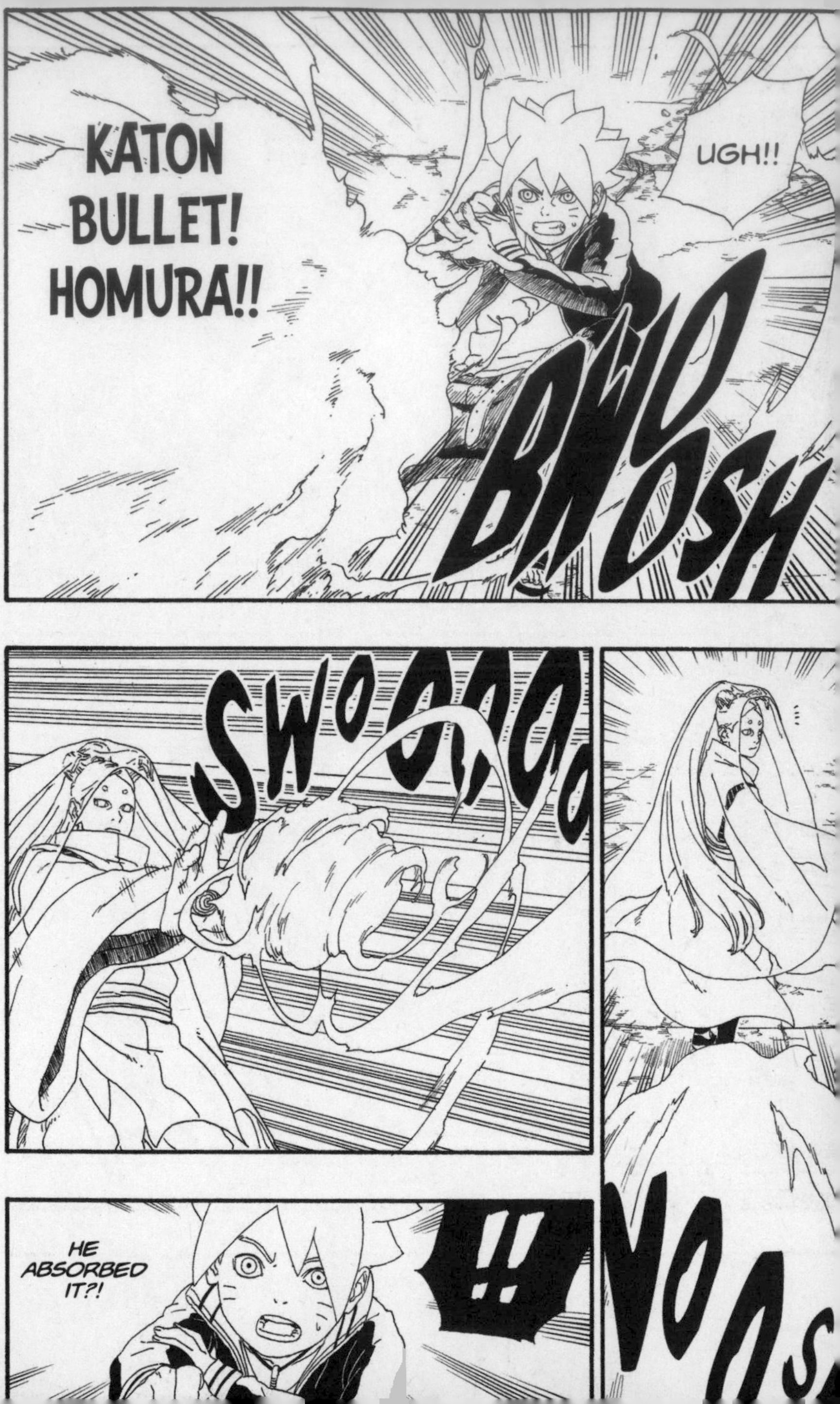
UGH!!
KATON BULLET! HOMURA!!
BWOOSH
...
SWOOOOO
!!
HE ABSORBED IT?!

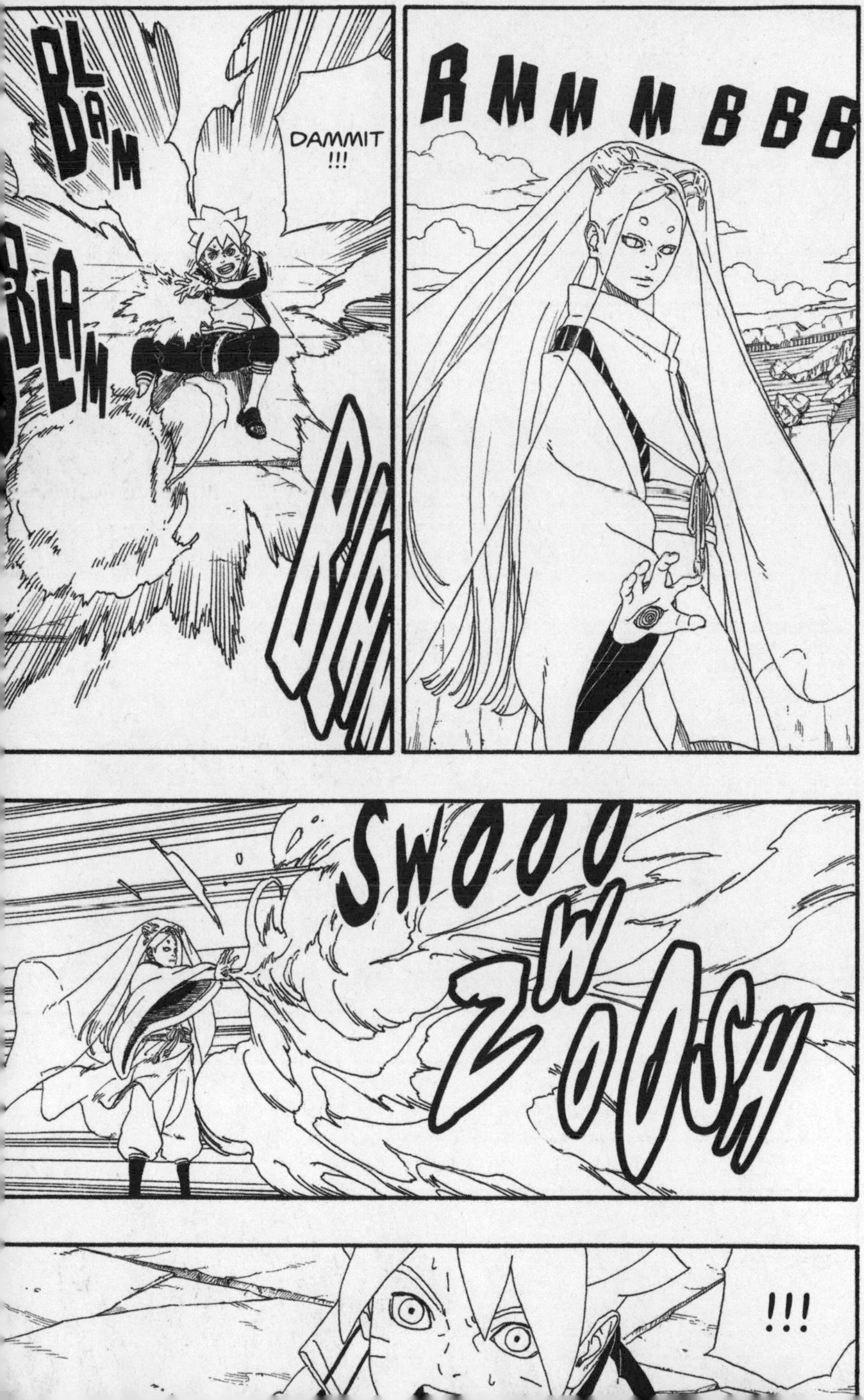
RMMMBBB
BLAM
BLAM
DAMMIT!!!
SWOOO
ZWOOSH
!!!

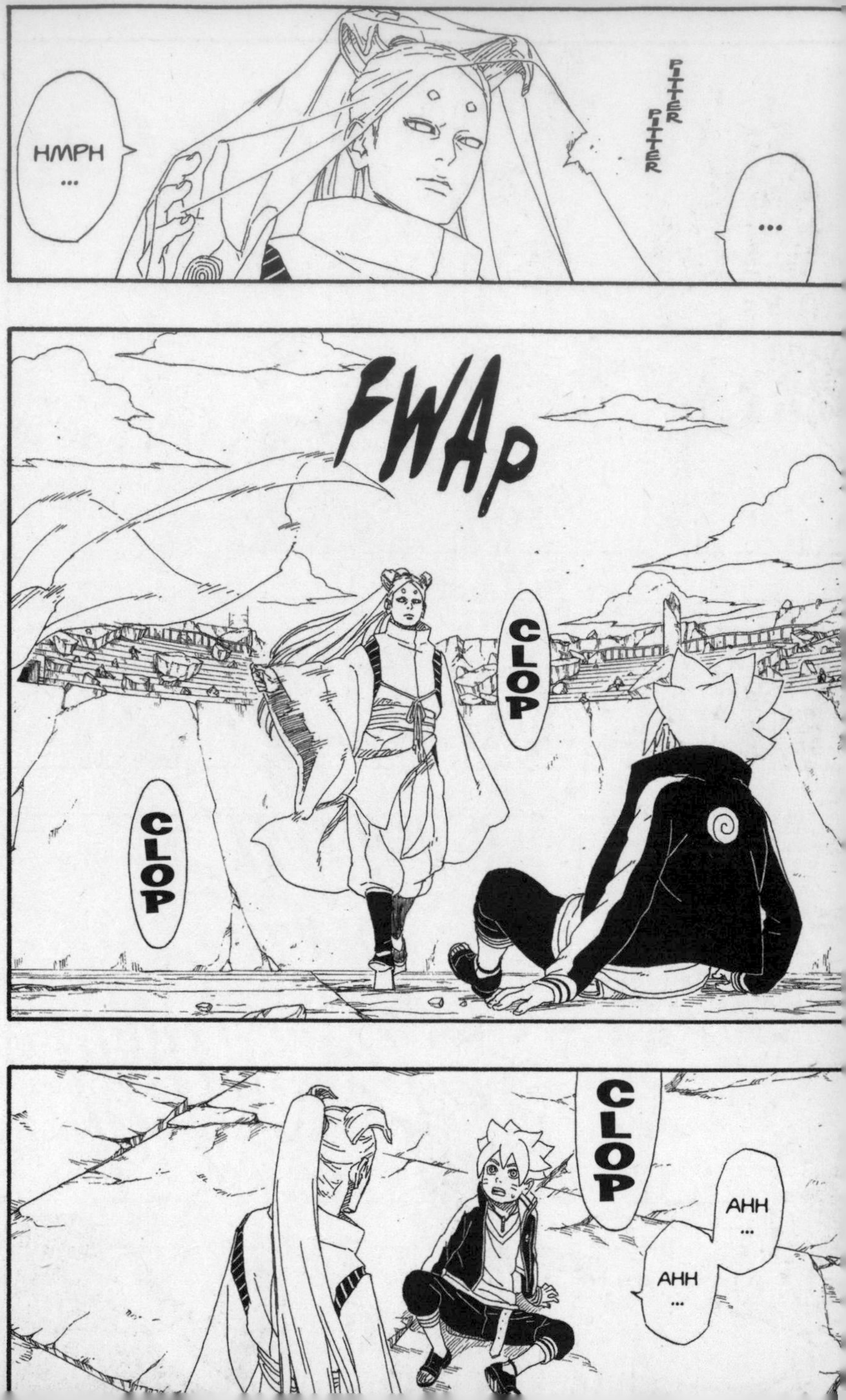
...
PITTER PITTER
HMPH ...
FWAP
CLOP
CLOP
CLOP
AHH ...
AHH ...

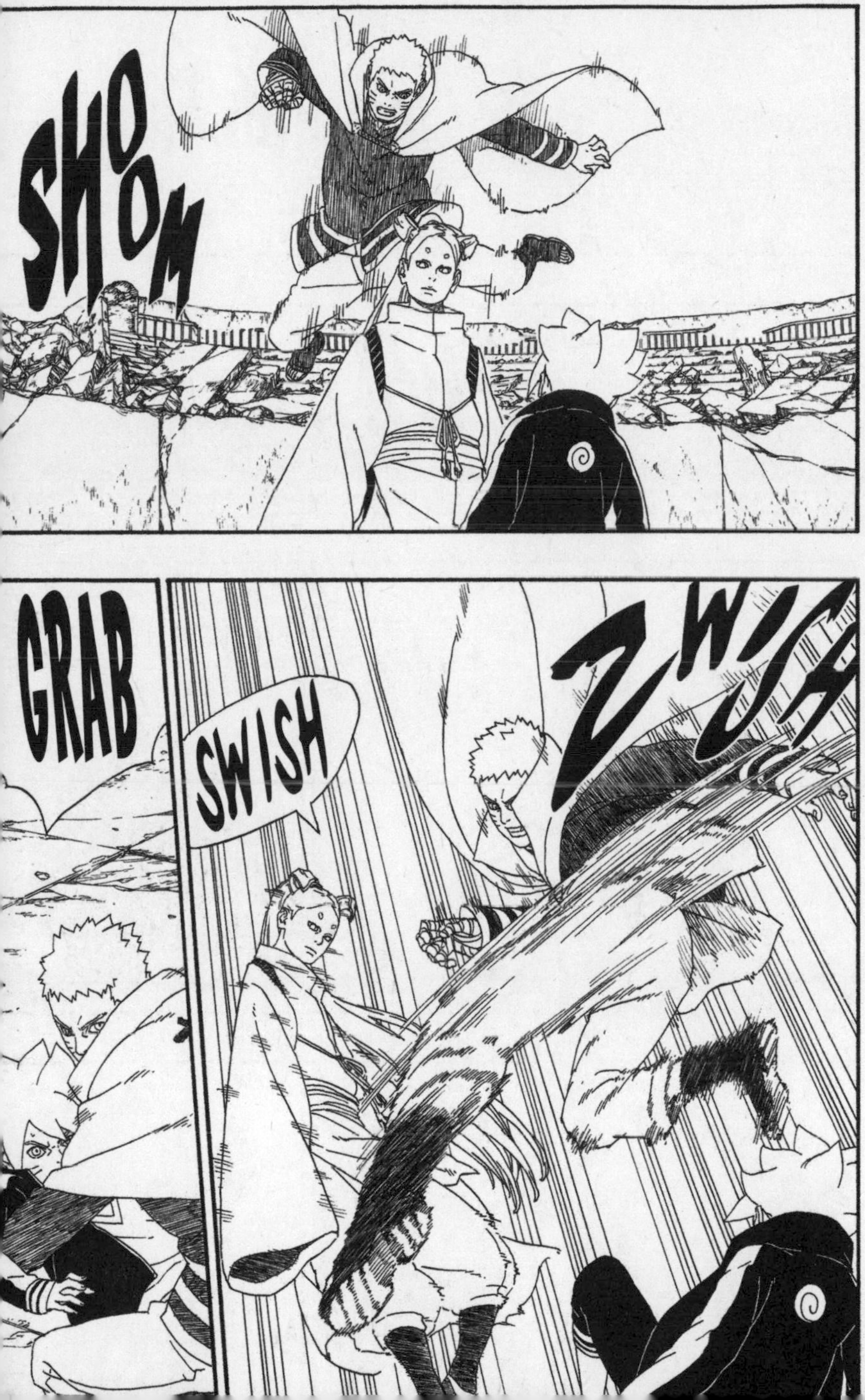
SHOOM
ZWISH
SWISH
GRAB

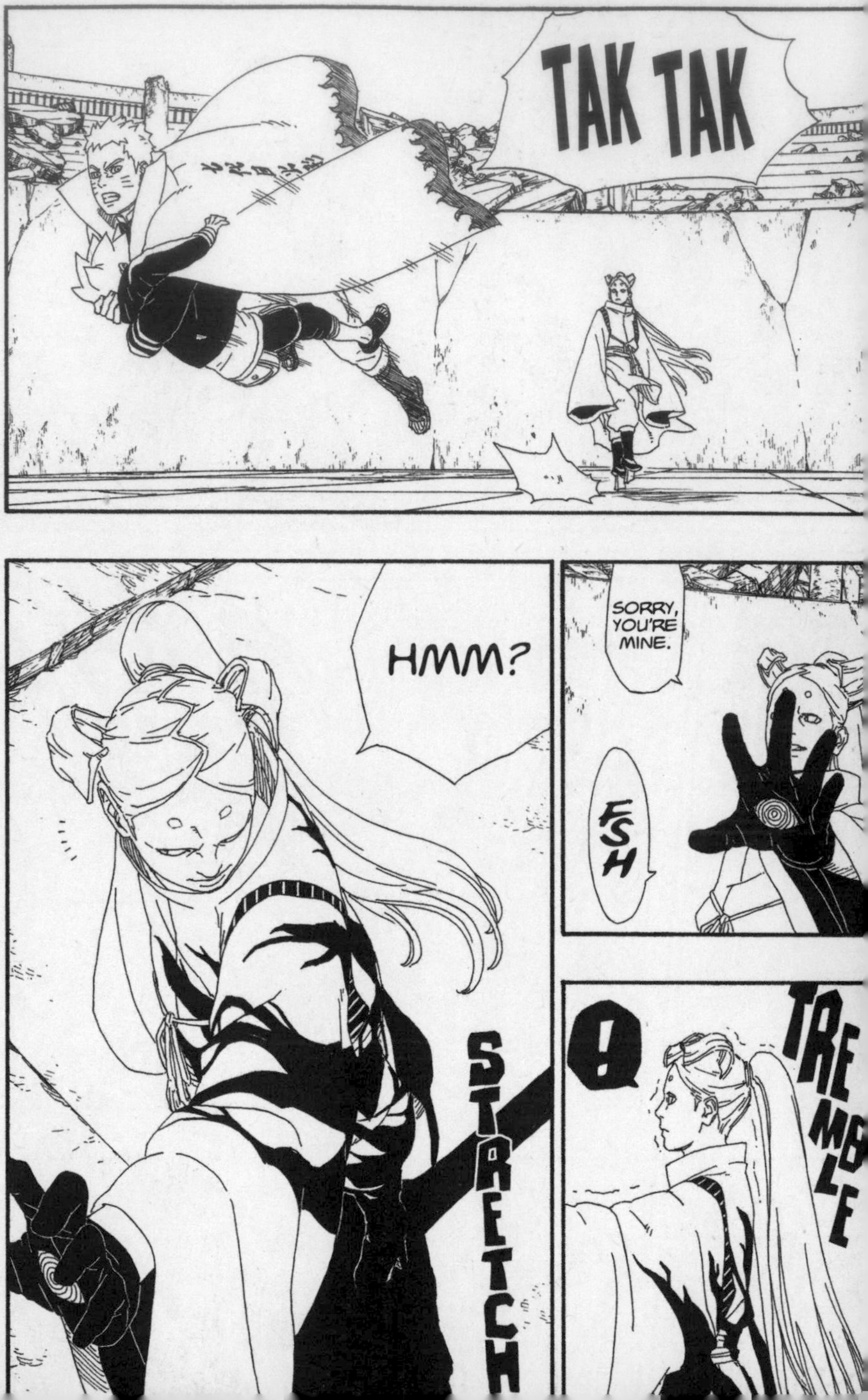
TAK TAK
SORRY, YOU'RE MINE.
FSH
!
TREMBLE
HMM?
STRETCH

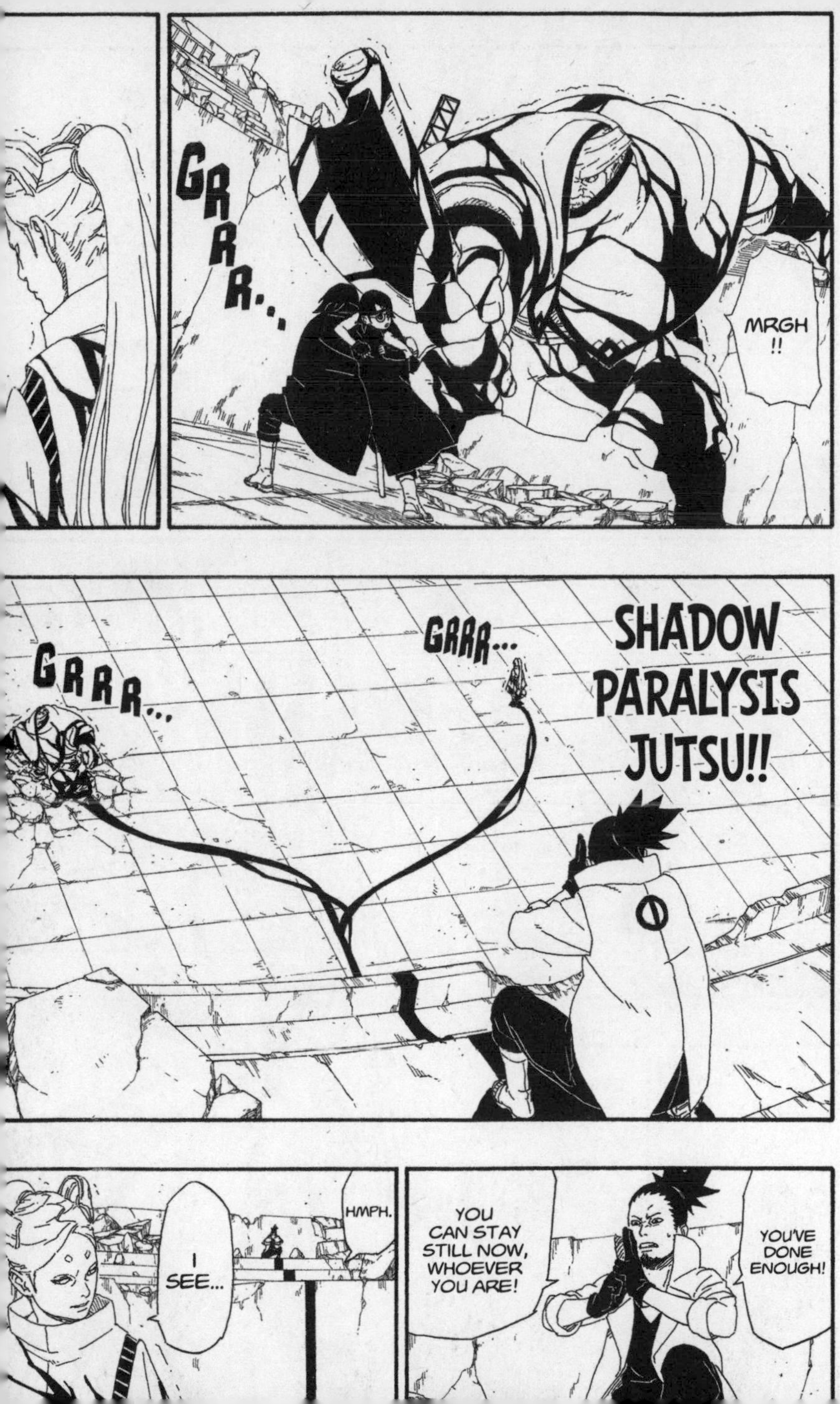
GRRR...
MRGH!!
SHADOW PARALYSIS JUTSU!!
GRRR...
GRRRR...
YOU'VE DONE ENOUGH!
YOU CAN STAY STILL NOW, WHOEVER YOU ARE!
HMPH.
I SEE...

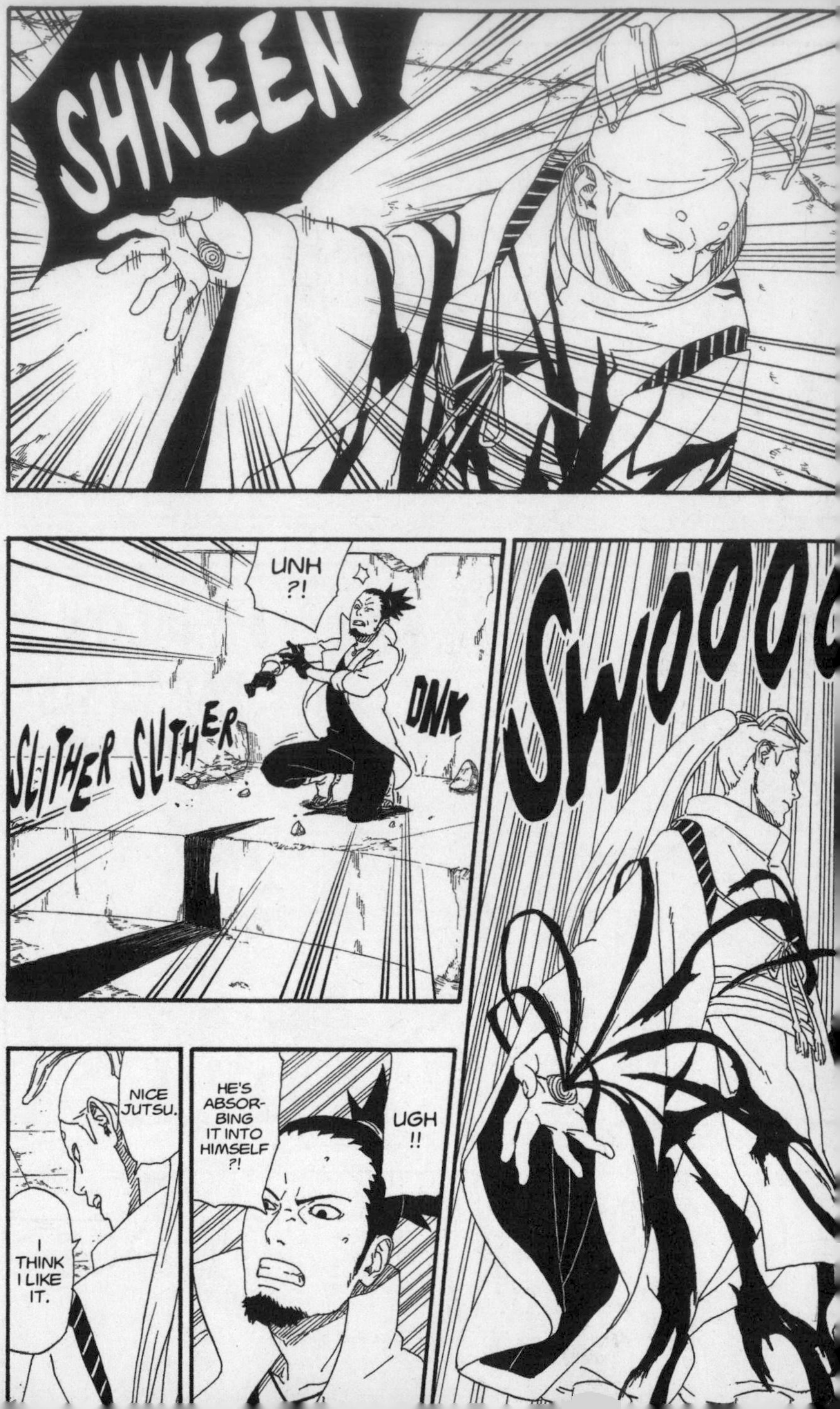
SHKEEN
SWOOO
UNH ?!
DNK
SLITHER SLITHER
UGH !!
HE'S ABSORBING IT INTO HIMSELF ?!
NICE JUTSU.
I THINK I LIKE IT.

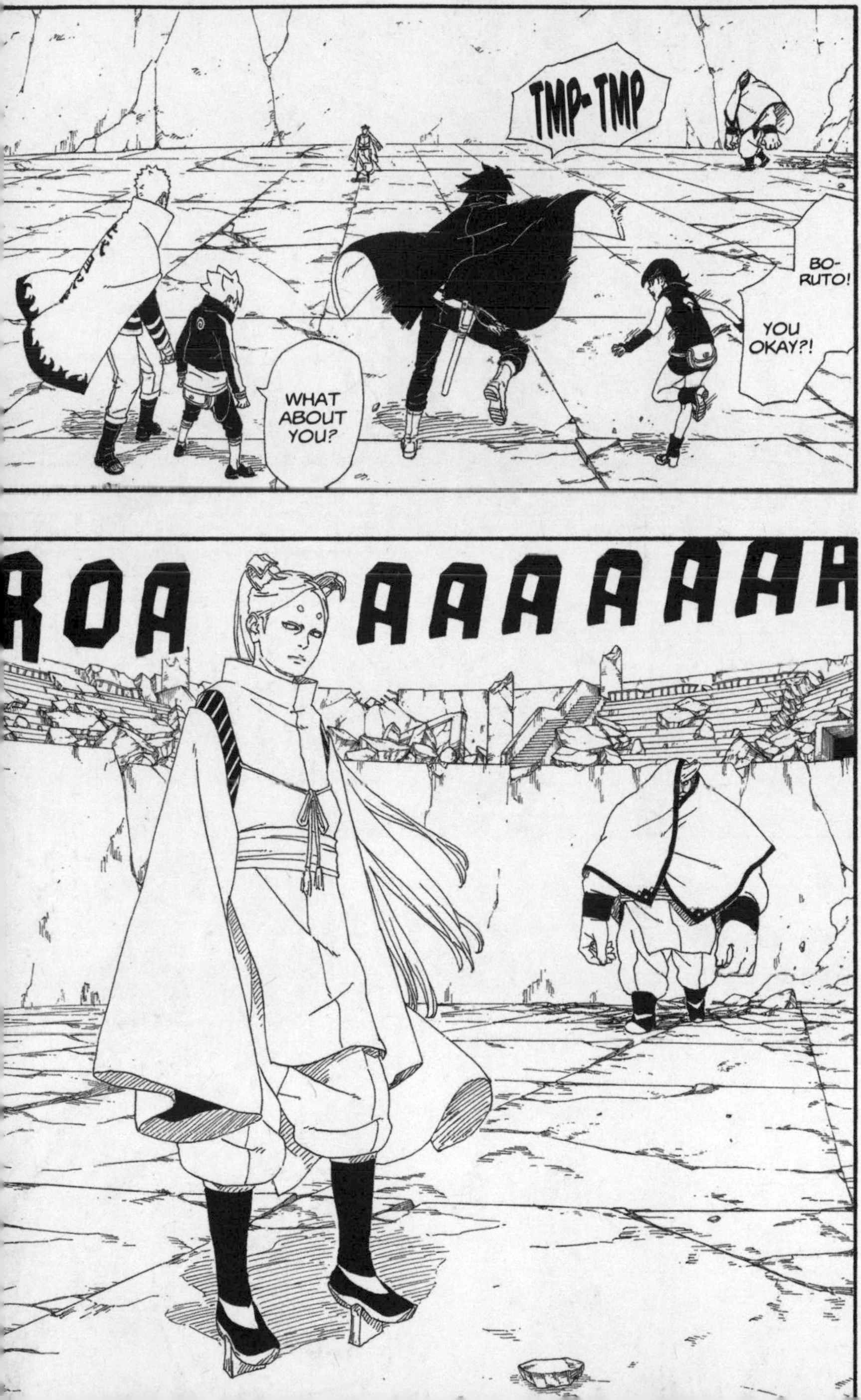
TMP-TMP
BO-RUTO!
YOU OKAY?!
WHAT ABOUT YOU?
ROA AAAAAAAR

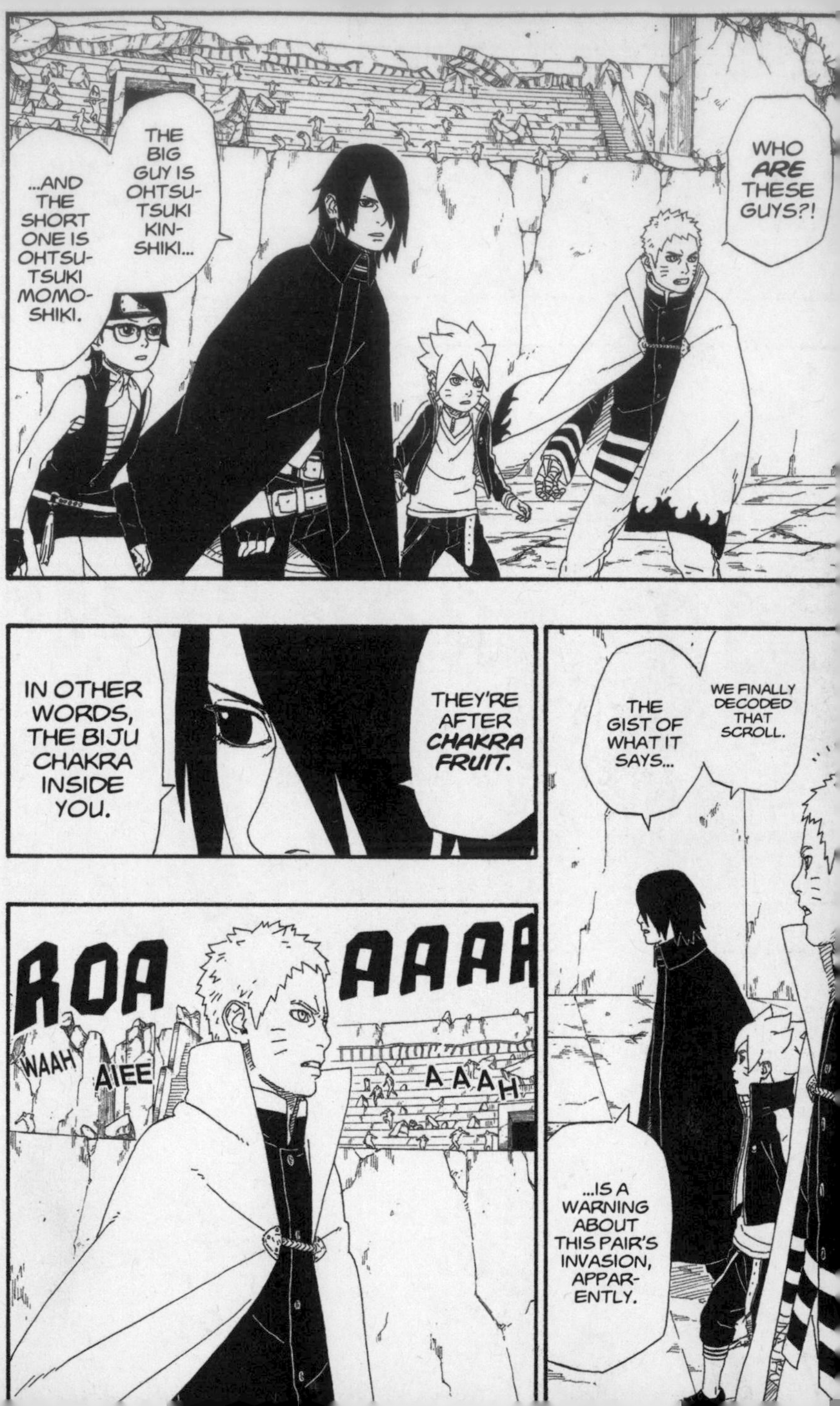
WHO ARE THESE GUYS?!
THE BIG GUY IS OHTSU-TSUKI KIN-SHIKI...
...AND THE SHORT ONE IS OHTSU-TSUKI MOMO-SHIKI.
WE FINALLY DECODED THAT SCROLL.
THE GIST OF WHAT IT SAYS...
...IS A WARNING ABOUT THIS PAIR'S INVASION, APPAR-ENTLY.
THEY'RE AFTER CHAKRA FRUIT.
IN OTHER WORDS, THE BIJU CHAKRA INSIDE YOU.
ROA AAAA
AAAH
AIEE
WAAH

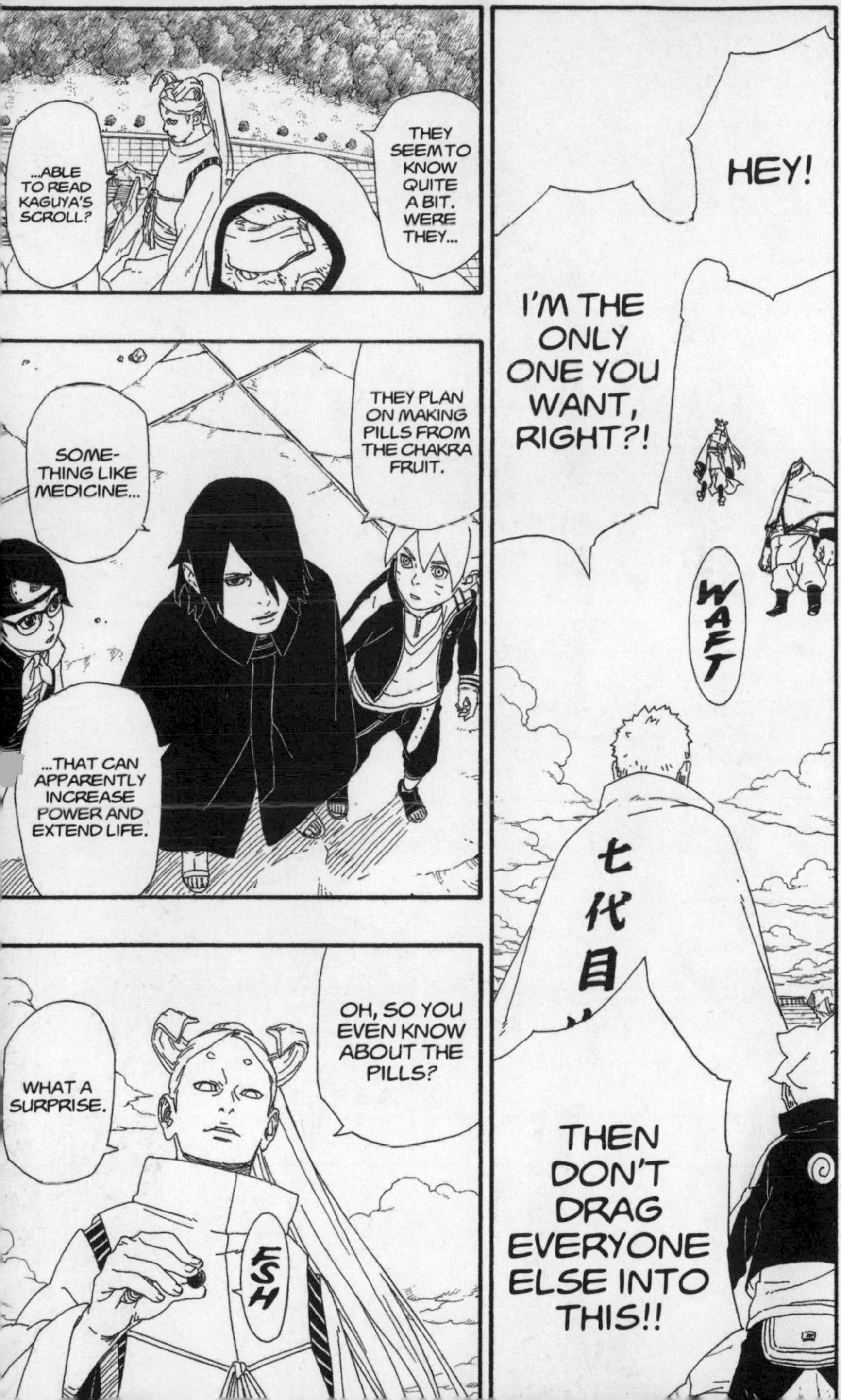
HEY!
I'M THE ONLY ONE YOU WANT, RIGHT?!
WAFT
七代目
THEN DON'T DRAG EVERYONE ELSE INTO THIS!!
THEY SEEM TO KNOW QUITE A BIT. WERE THEY...
...ABLE TO READ KAGUYA'S SCROLL?
THEY PLAN ON MAKING PILLS FROM THE CHAKRA FRUIT.
SOME-THING LIKE MEDICINE...
...THAT CAN APPARENTLY INCREASE POWER AND EXTEND LIFE.
OH, SO YOU EVEN KNOW ABOUT THE PILLS?
FSH
WHAT A SURPRISE.

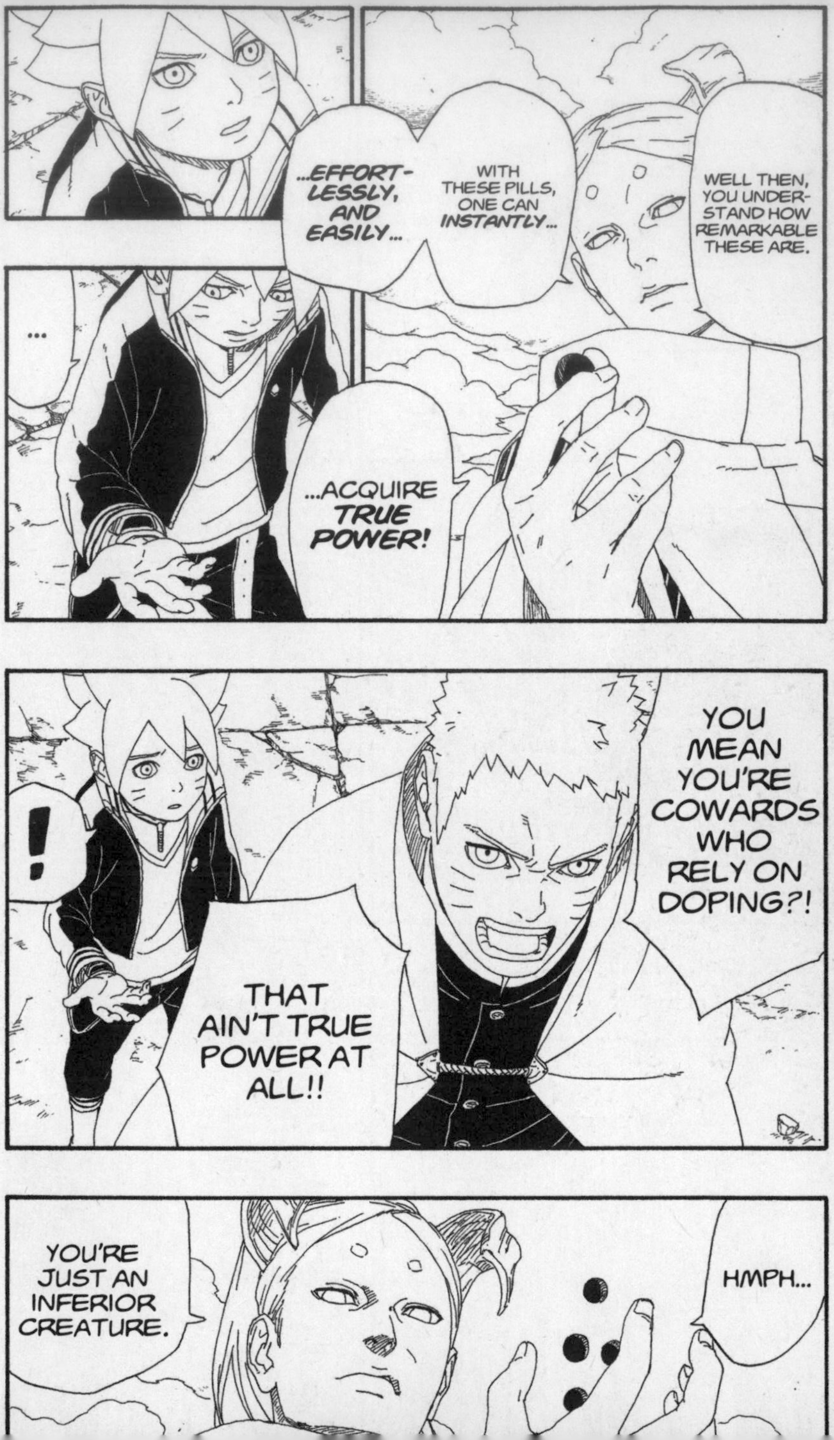
WELL THEN, YOU UNDERSTAND HOW REMARKABLE THESE ARE.
WITH THESE PILLS, ONE CAN INSTANTLY...
...EFFORTLESSLY, AND EASILY...
...ACQUIRE TRUE POWER!
...
YOU MEAN YOU'RE COWARDS WHO RELY ON DOPING?!
THAT AIN'T TRUE POWER AT ALL!!
!
HMPH...
YOU'RE JUST AN INFERIOR CREATURE.

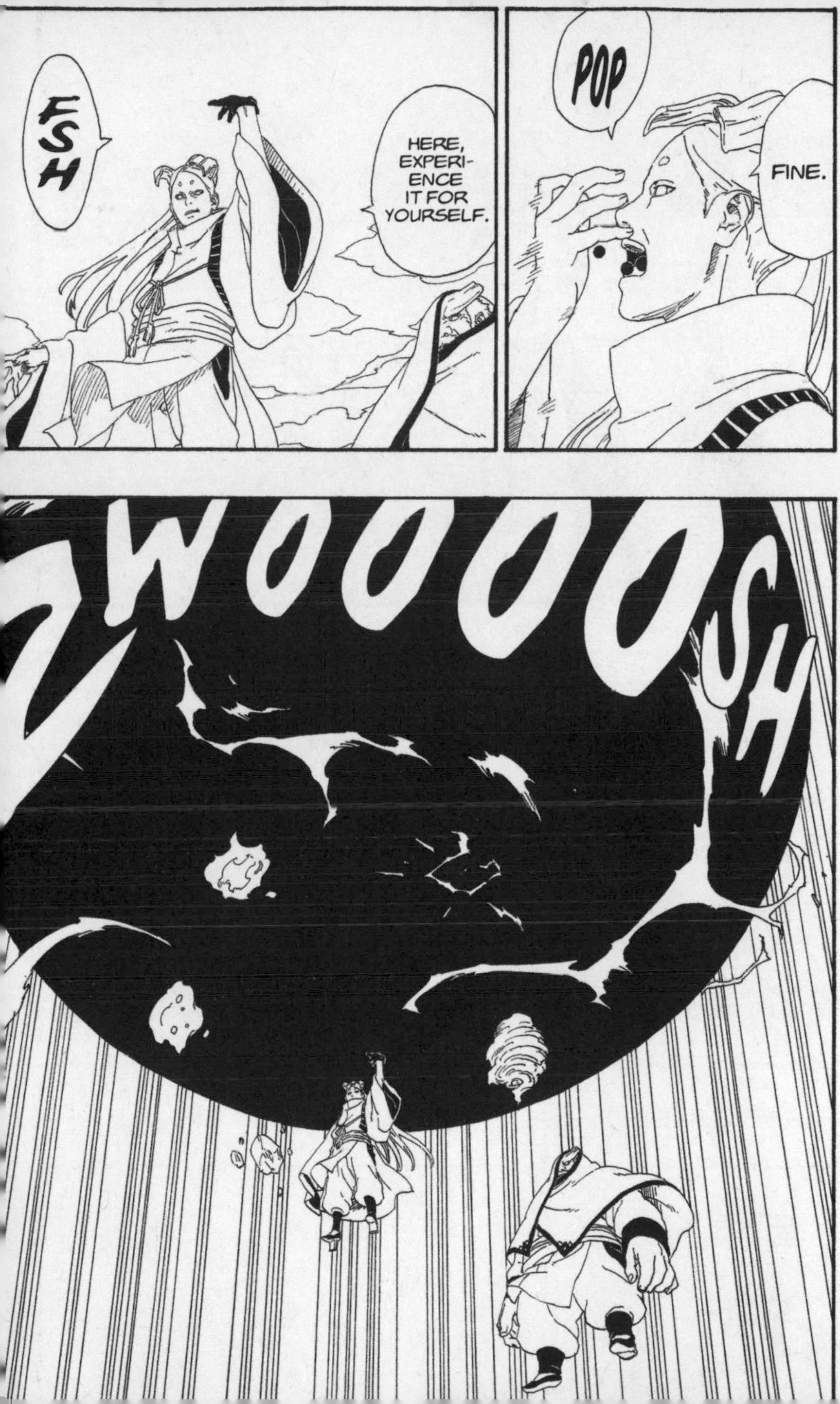
FINE.
POP
HERE, EXPERIENCE IT FOR YOURSELF.
FSH
WOOOOSH

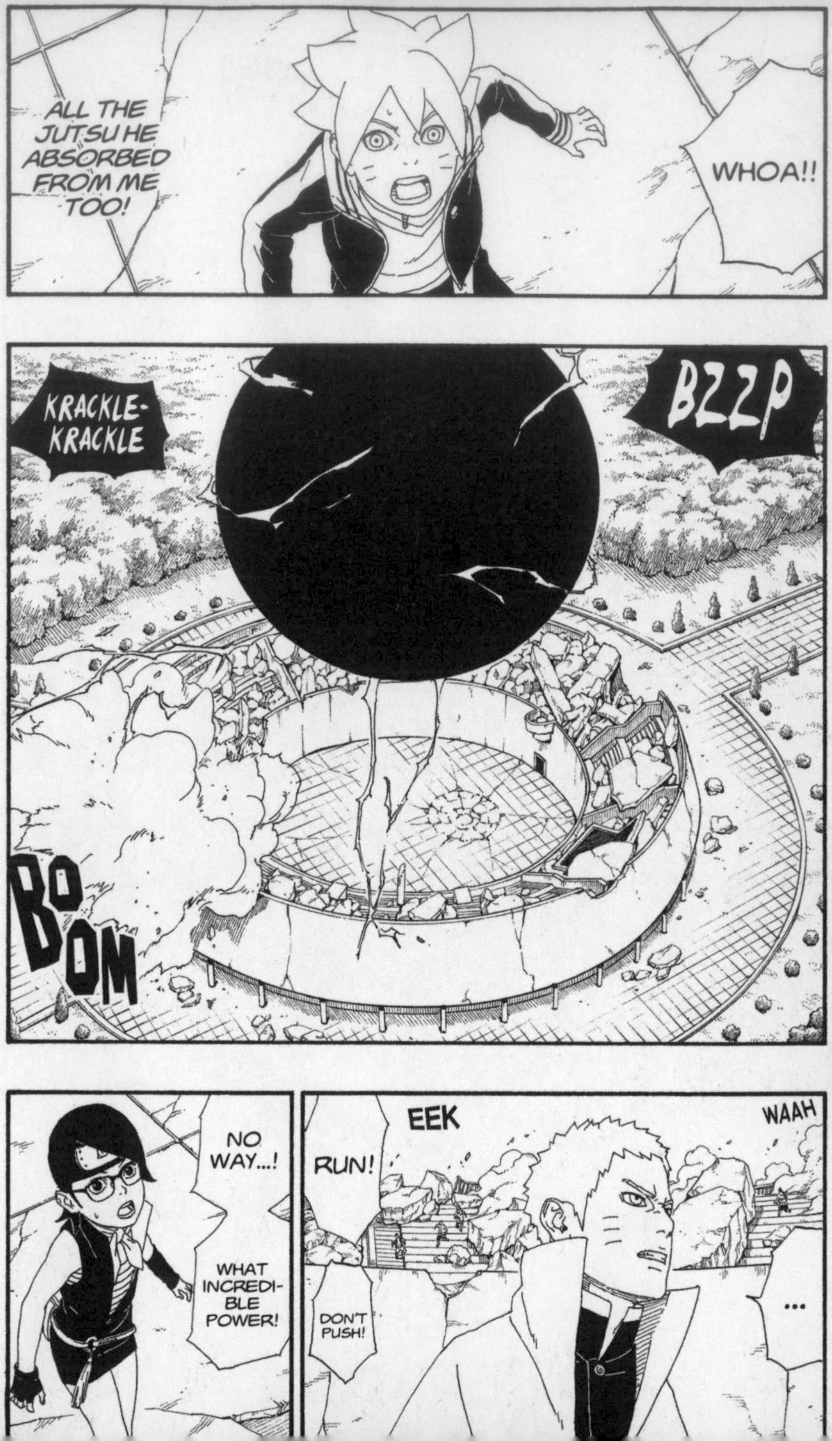
WHOA!!
ALL THE JUTSU HE ABSORBED FROM ME TOO!
BZZP
KRACKLE-KRACKLE
BOOM
WAAH
EEK
RUN!
...
DON'T PUSH!
NO WAY...!
WHAT INCREDIBLE POWER!

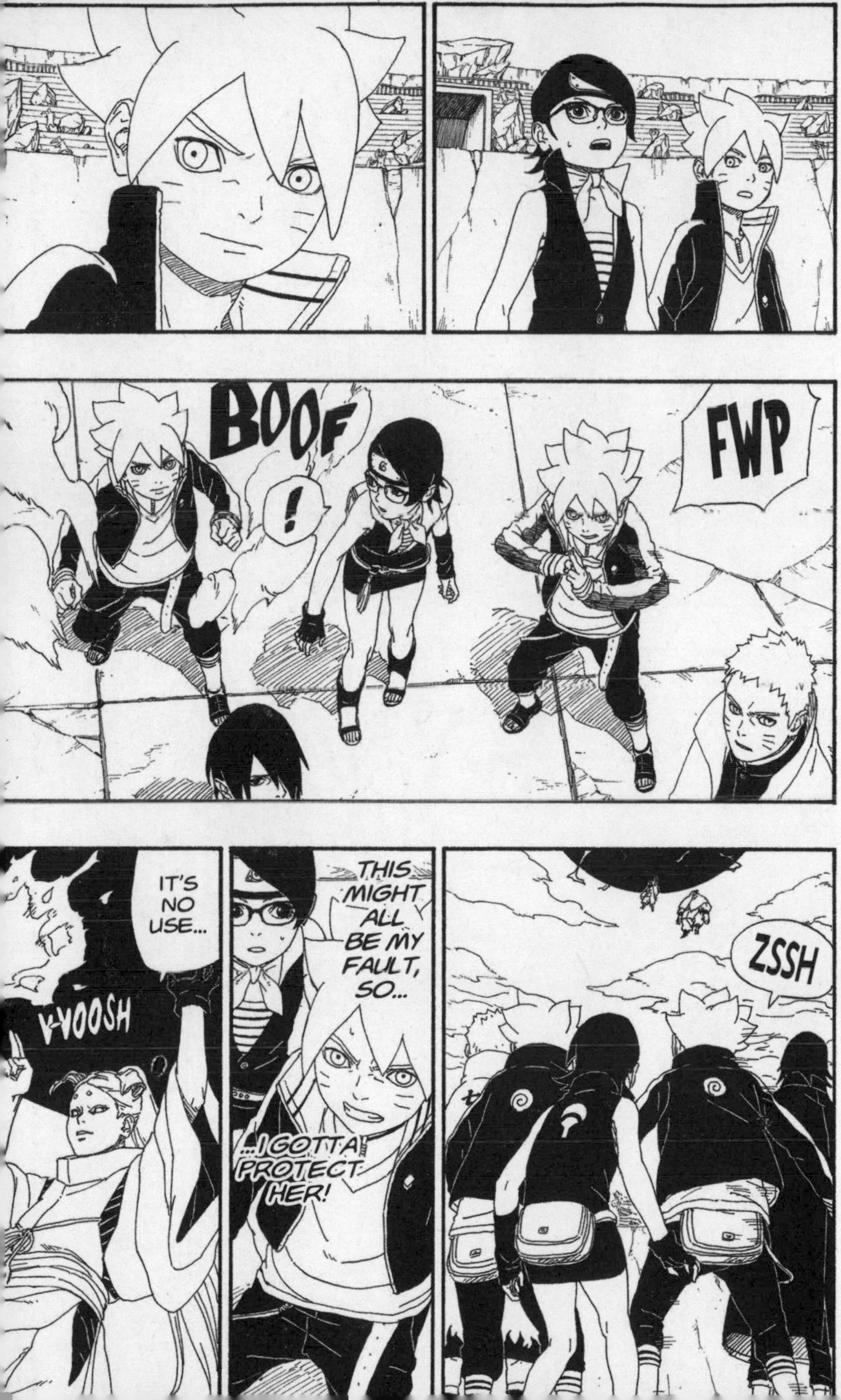
FWP
BOOF
!
ZSSH
THIS MIGHT ALL BE MY FAULT, SO...
...I GOTTA PROTECT HER!
IT'S NO USE...
V-VOOSH

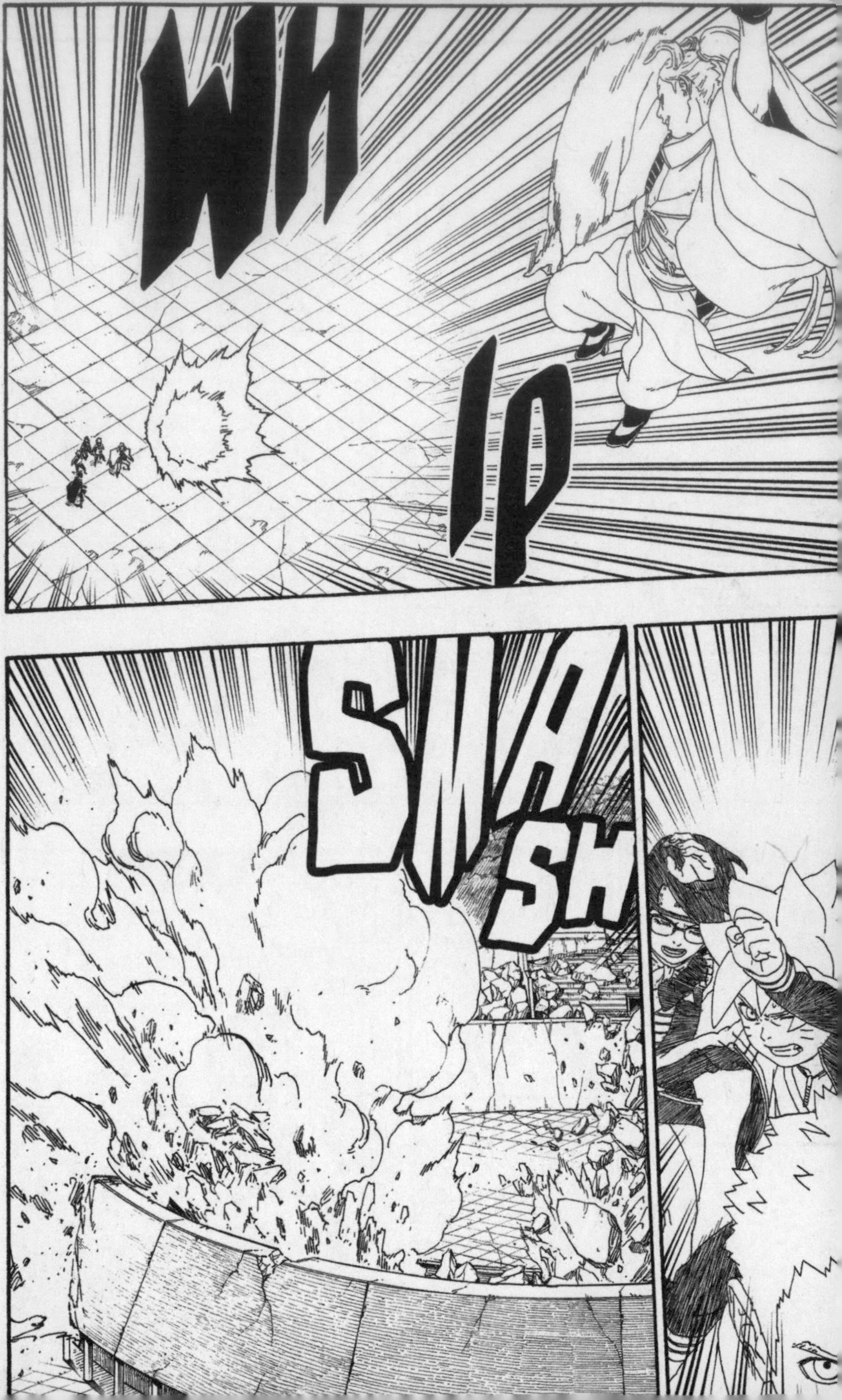
WHIP
SMASH

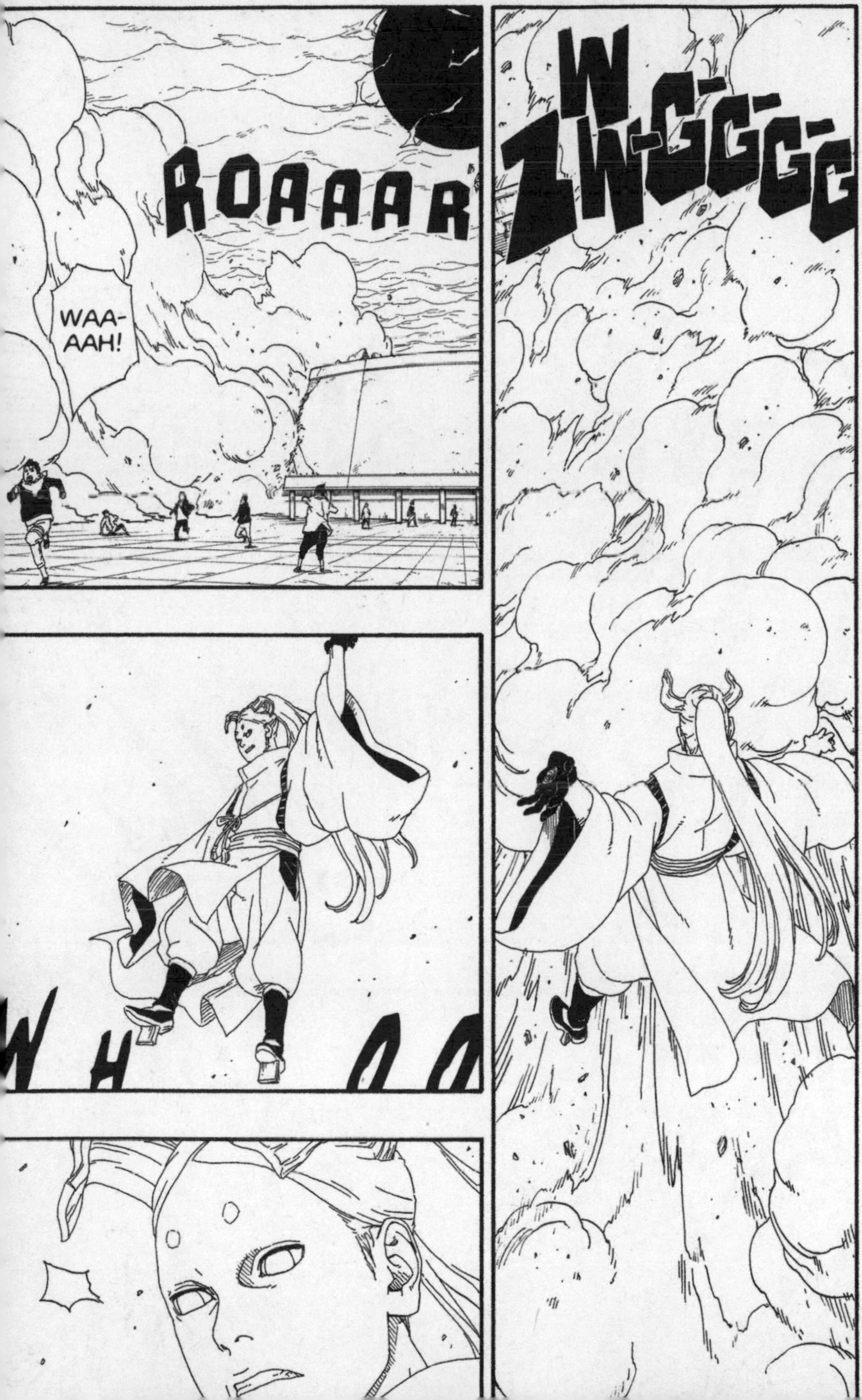
ZWN-G-G-G-G
ROAAAR
WAA-AAH!
WHOO

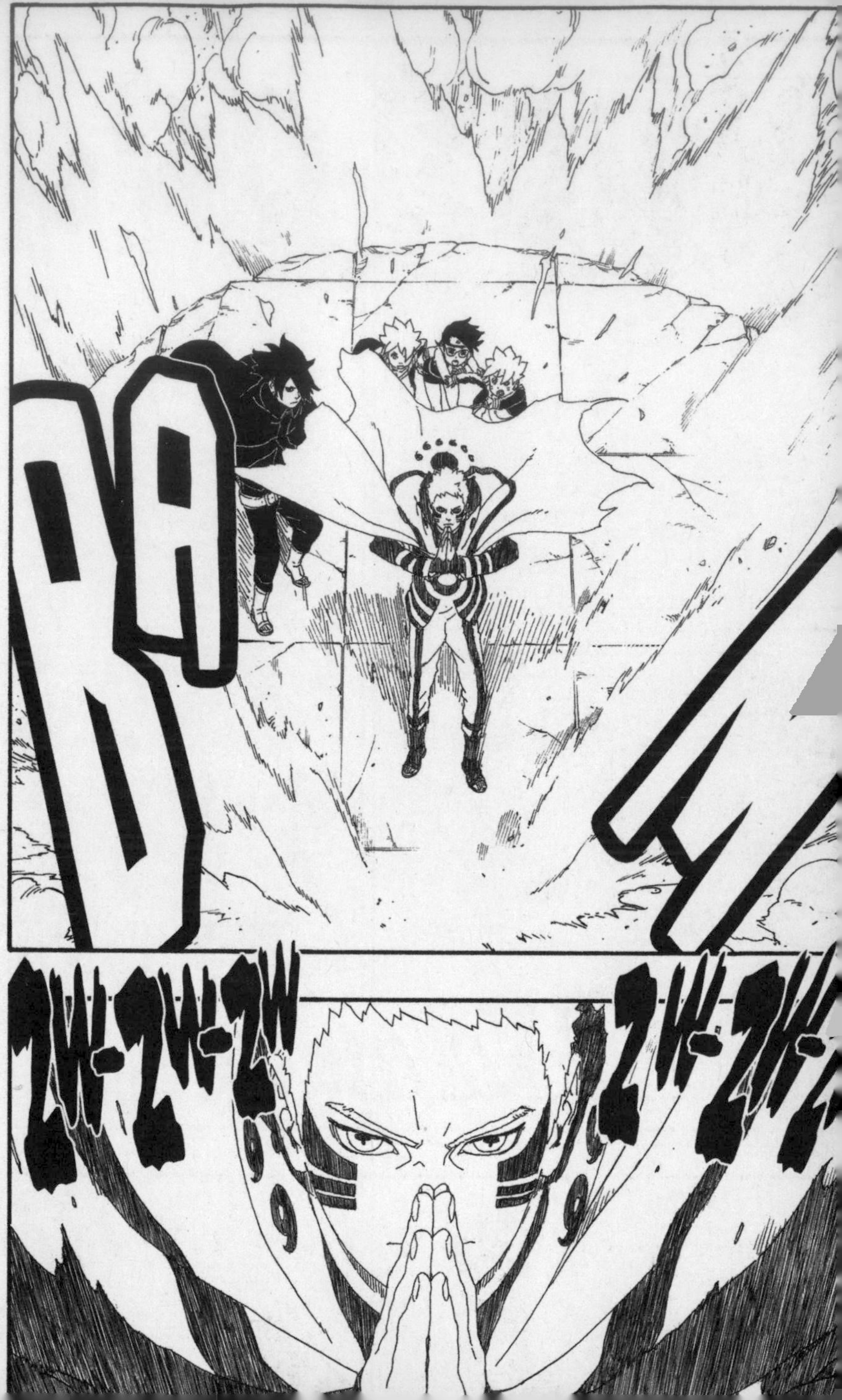
BA
ZW-ZW-ZW
ZW-ZW-

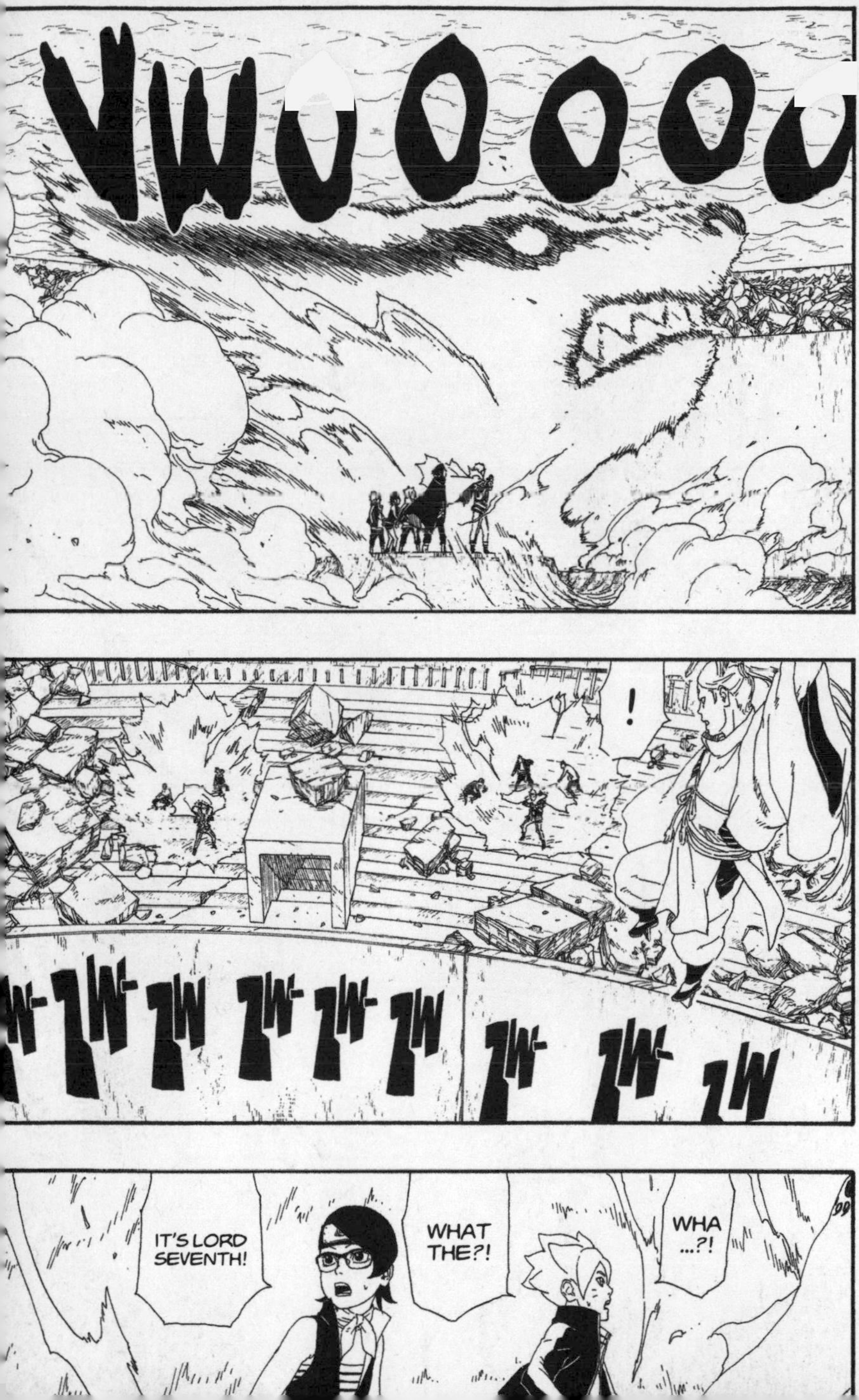
VWOOOOO
!
ZW- ZW- ZW ZW- ZW- ZW ZW- ZW- ZW
WHA ...?!
WHAT THE?!
IT'S LORD SEVENTH!

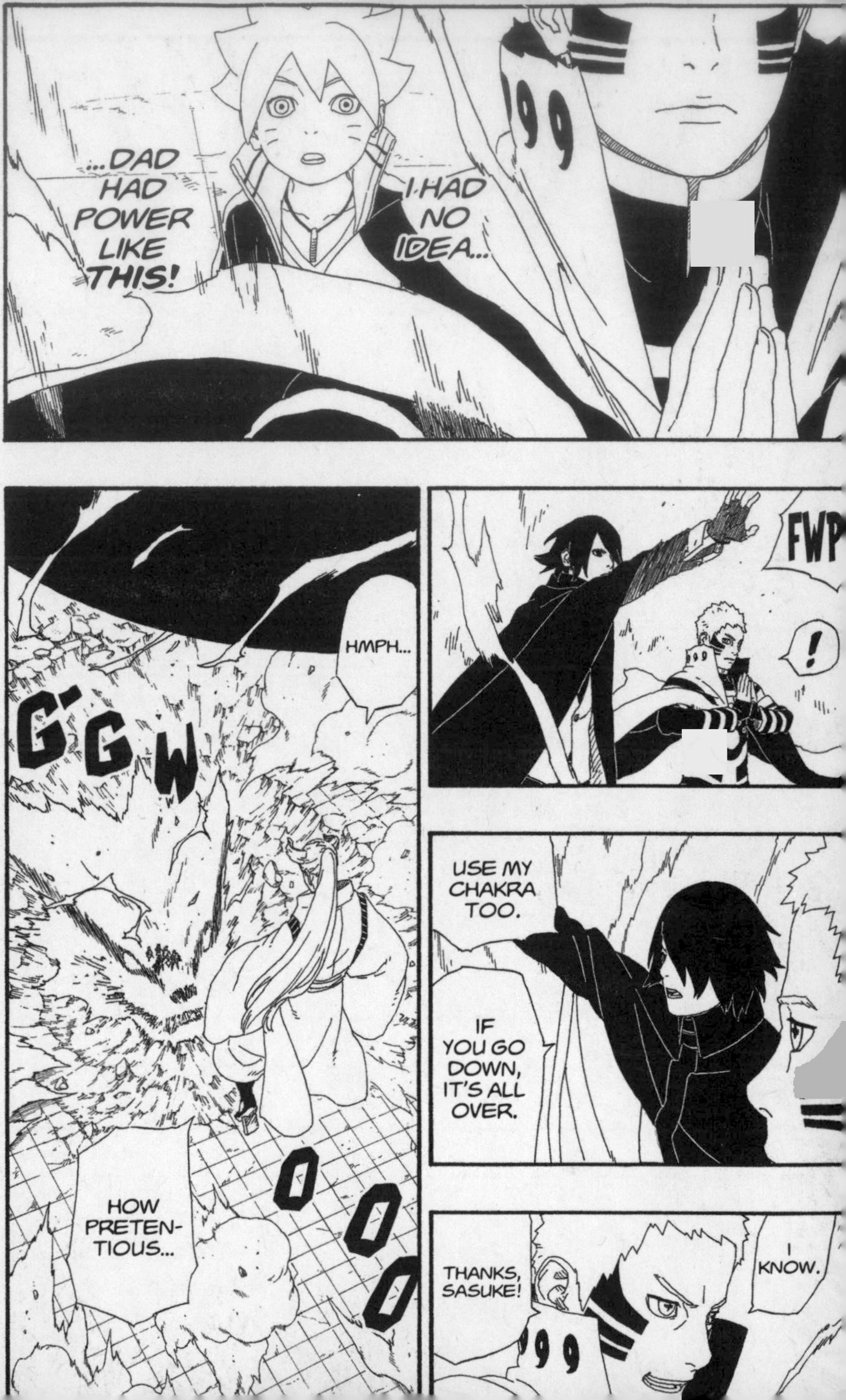
I HAD NO IDEA...
...DAD HAD POWER LIKE THIS!
FWP
!
USE MY CHAKRA TOO.
IF YOU GO DOWN, IT'S ALL OVER.
I KNOW.
THANKS, SASUKE!
HMPH...
GGW
HOW PRETEN-TIOUS...
OOO

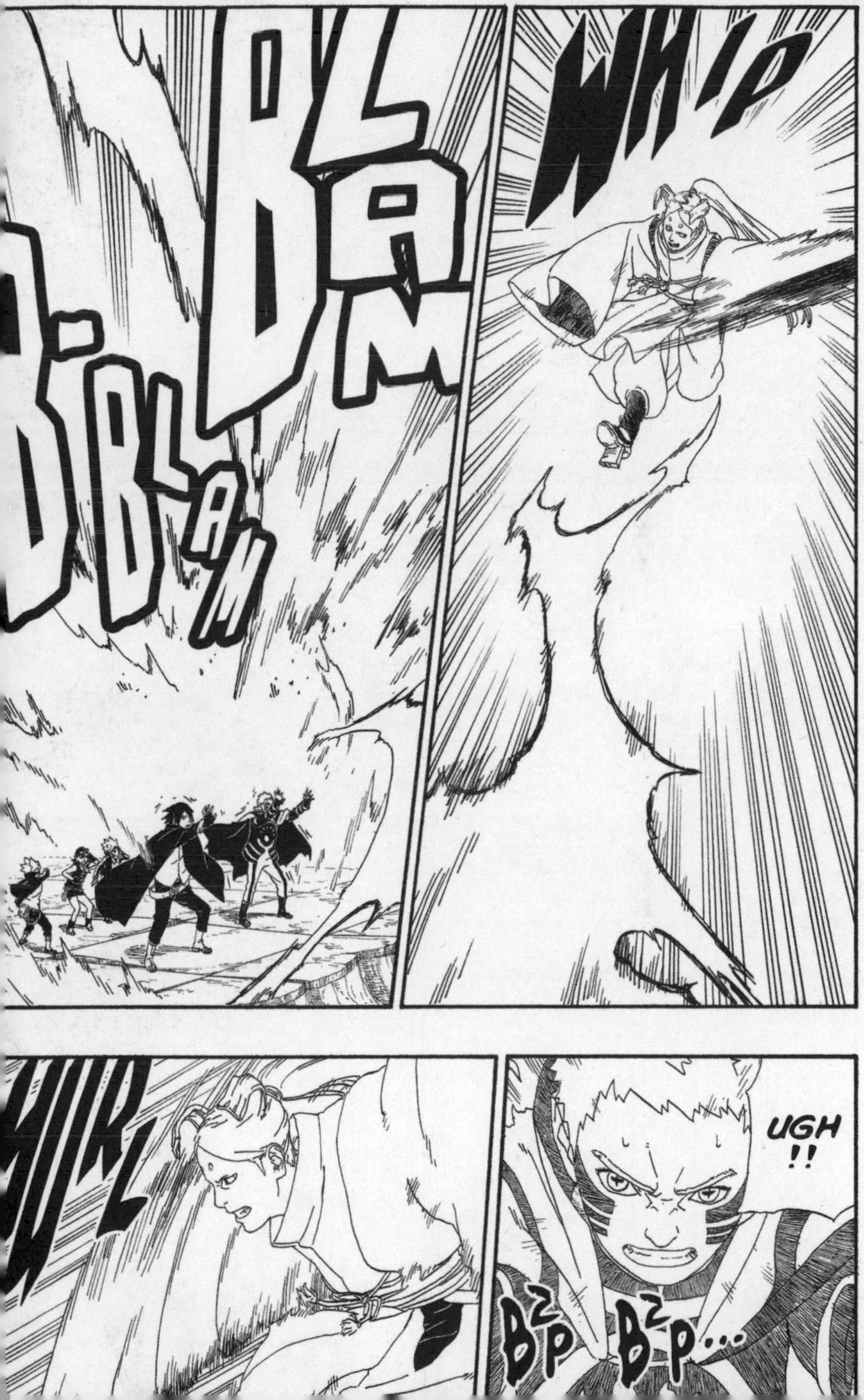
WHIP
BLAM
BLAM
UGH!!
BZZP BZZP...
WHIRL

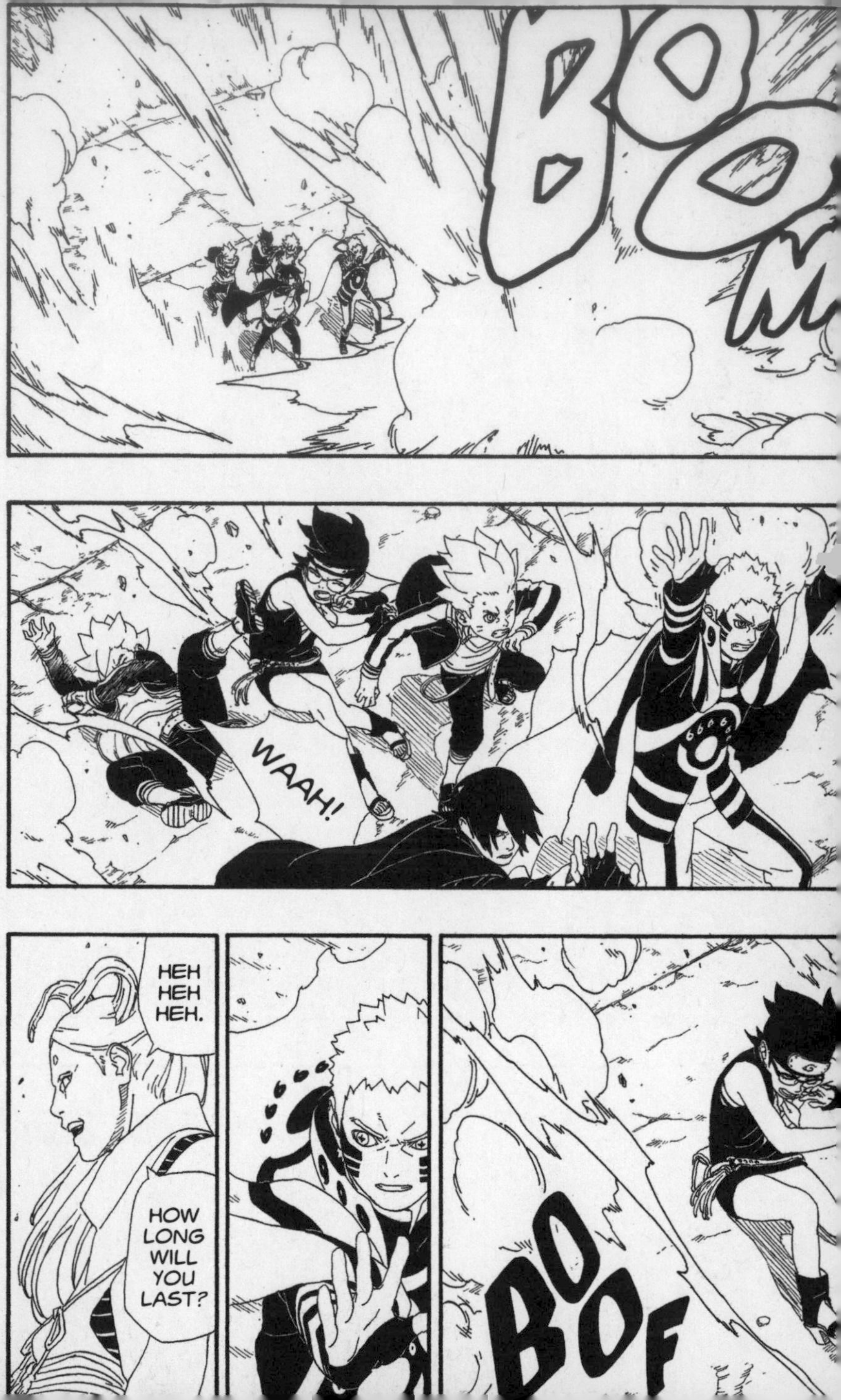
BOOM
WAAH!
BOOF
HEH HEH HEH.
HOW LONG WILL YOU LAST?

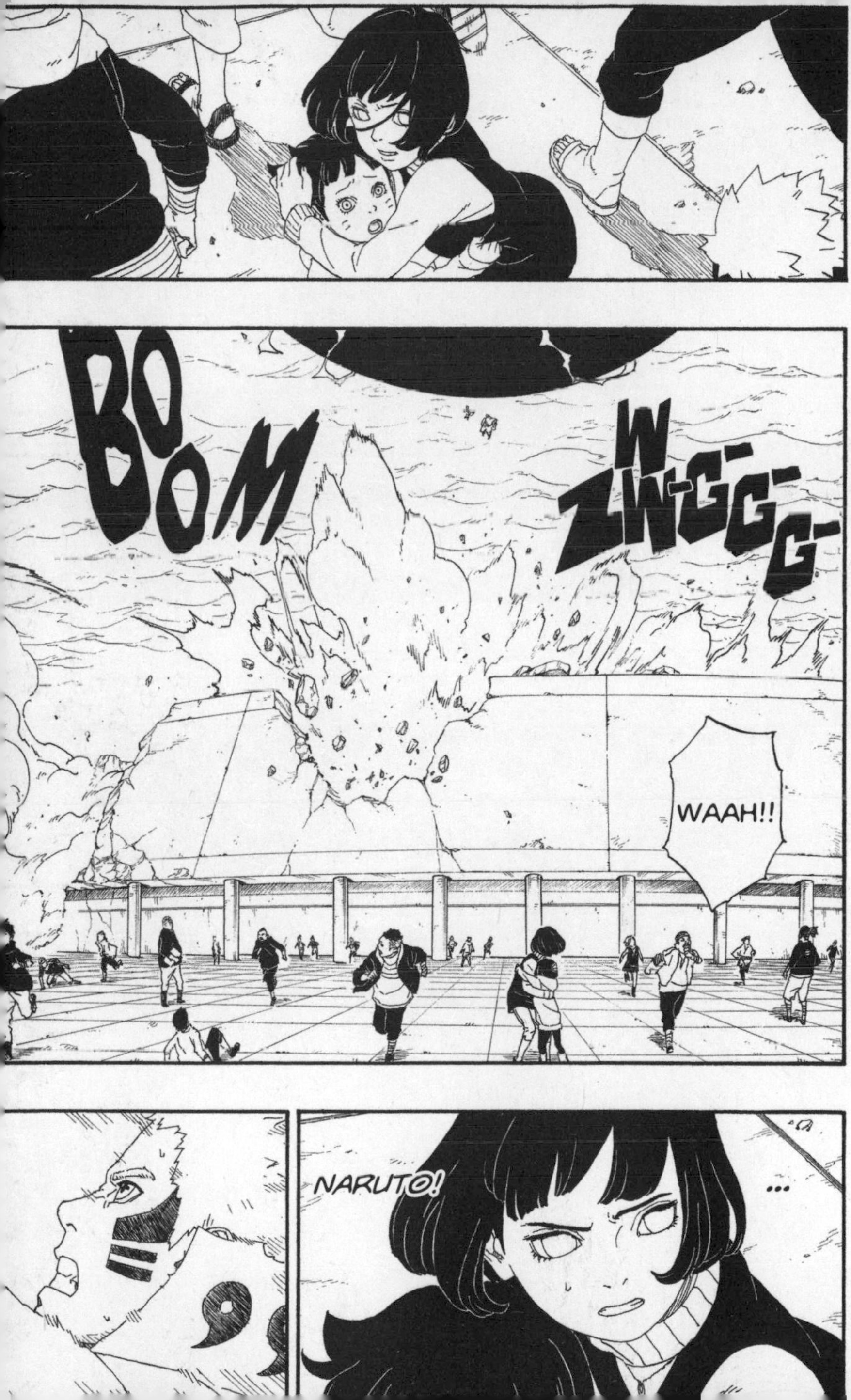
WZING-G-G-G-
BOOM
WAAH!!
...
NARUTO!

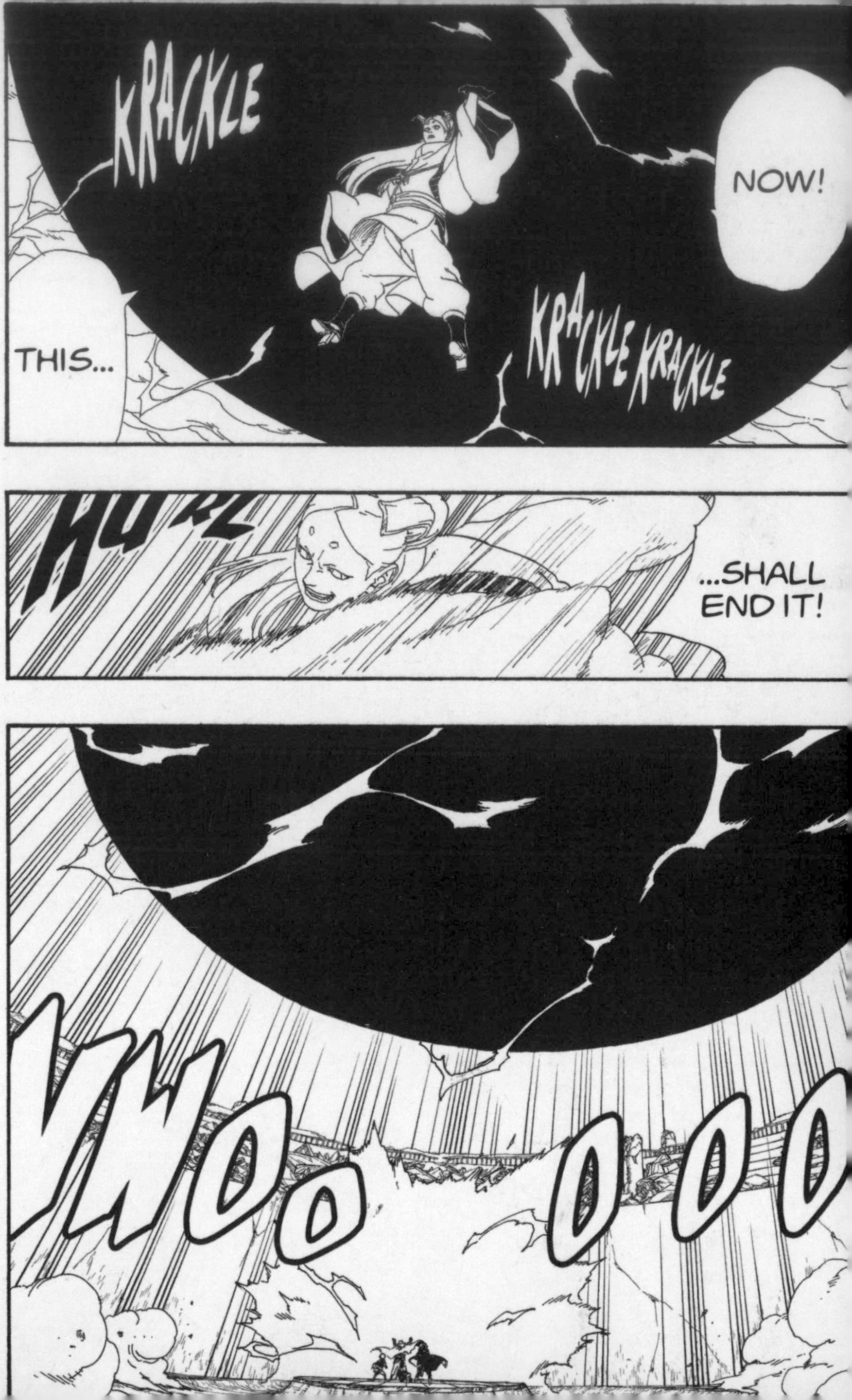
NOW!
KRACKLE
KRACKLE KRACKLE
THIS...
...SHALL END IT!

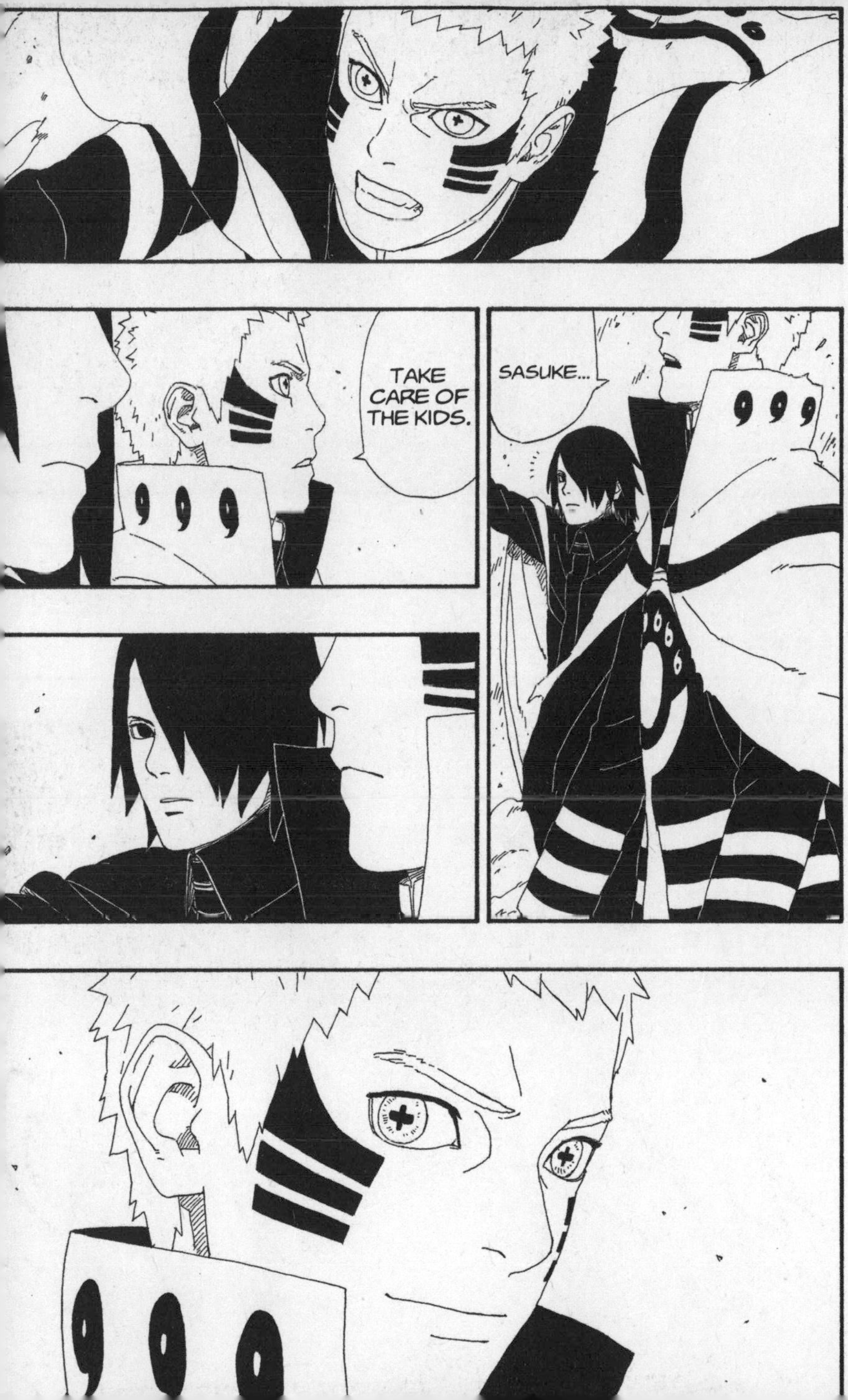
SASUKE...
TAKE CARE OF THE KIDS.

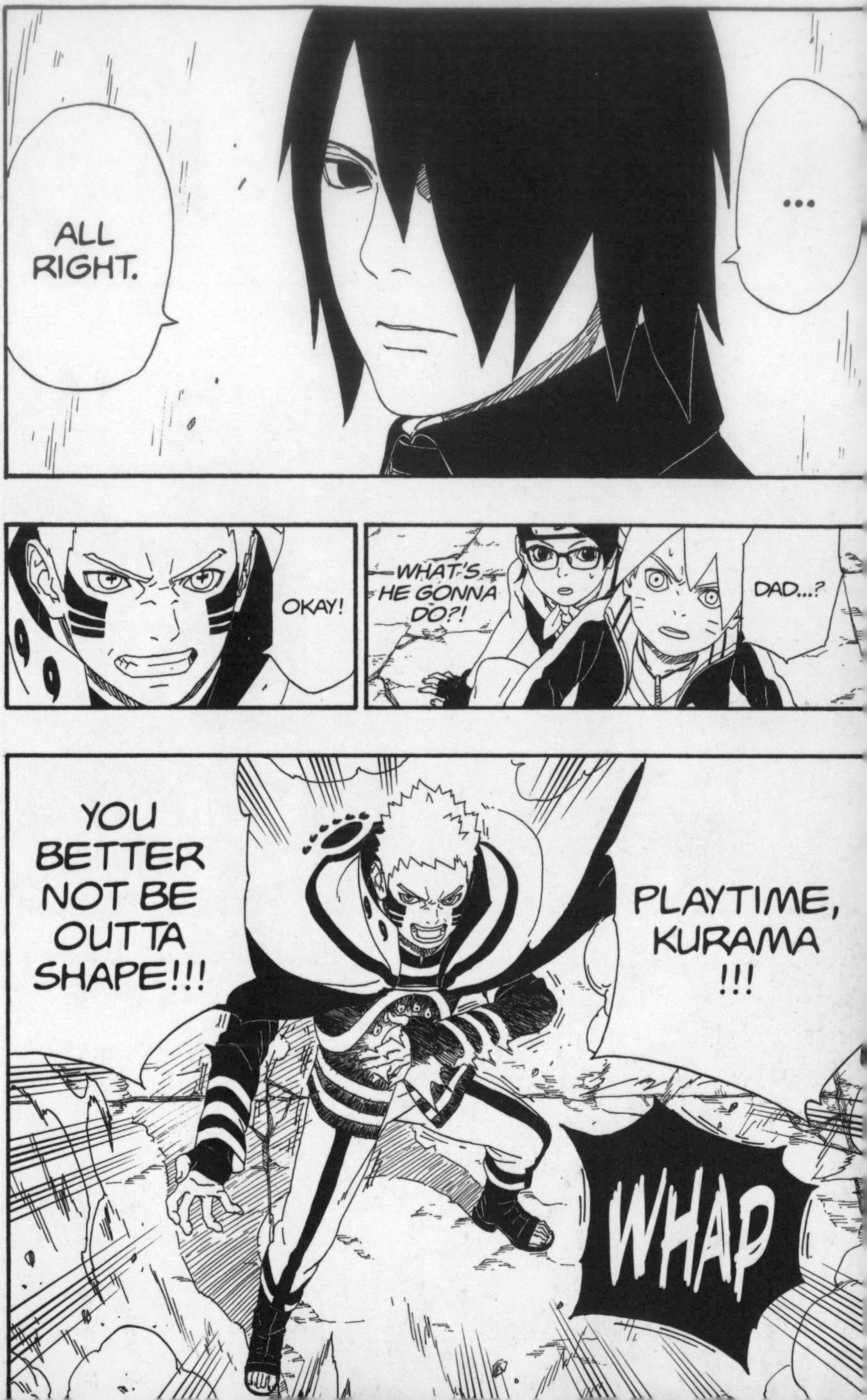
...
ALL RIGHT.
DAD...?
WHAT'S HE GONNA DO?!
OKAY!
PLAYTIME, KURAMA !!!
YOU BETTER NOT BE OUTTA SHAPE!!!
WHAP

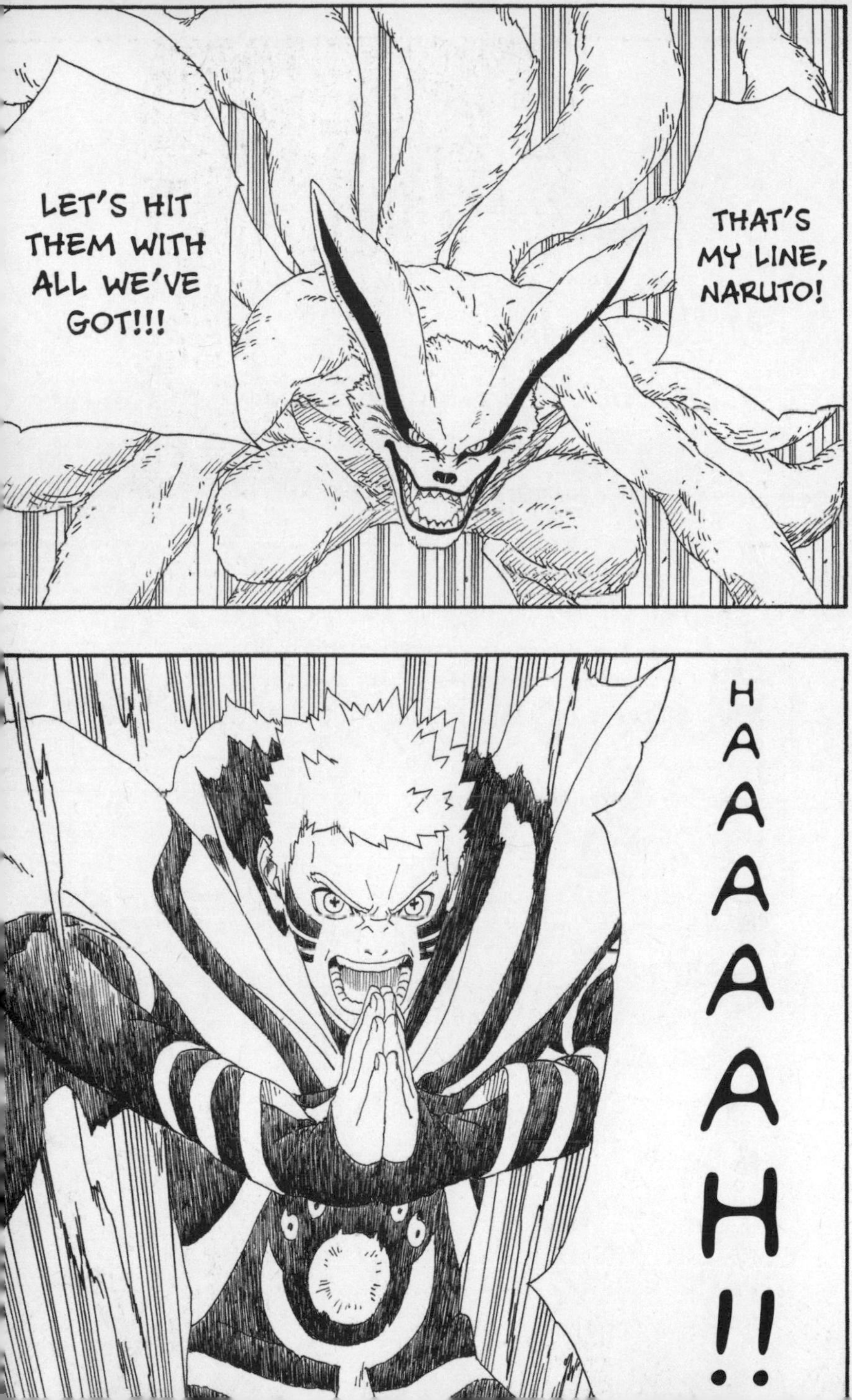
THAT'S MY LINE, NARUTO!
LET'S HIT THEM WITH ALL WE'VE GOT!!!
HAAAAAAH!!

NINJA ENCYCLOPEDIA • ENTRY 5

YAMANAKA INOJIN

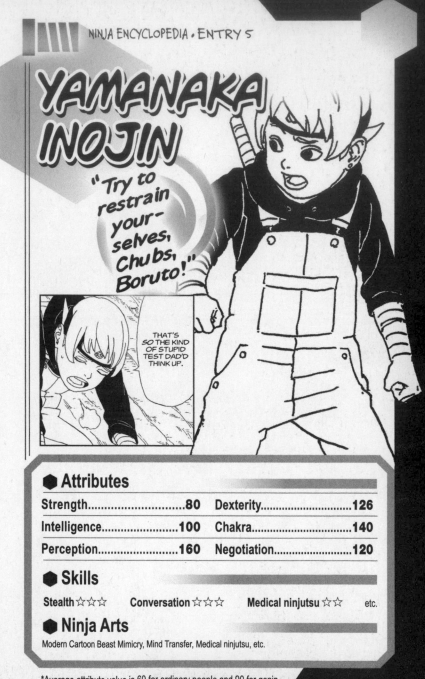

"Try to restrain your-selves, Chubs, Boruto!"

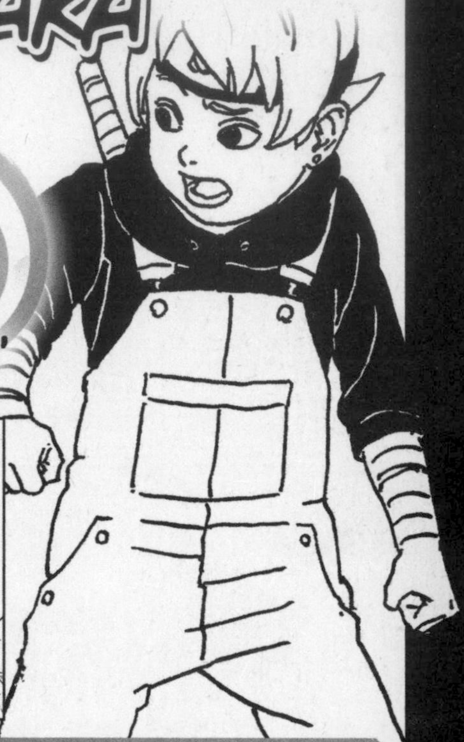

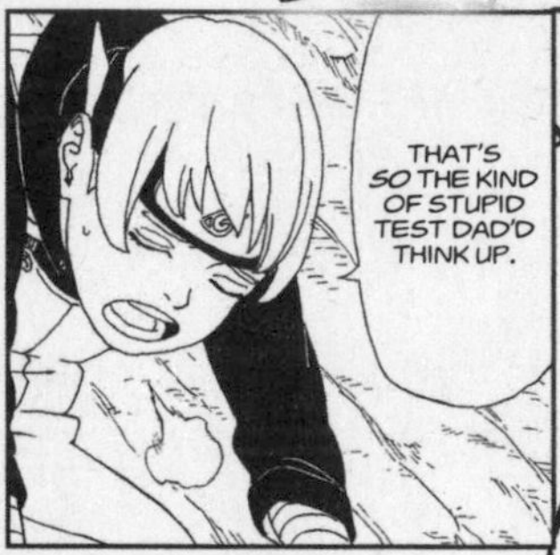
THAT'S SO THE KIND OF STUPID TEST DAD'D THINK UP.

Attributes

Strength	80	Dexterity	126
Intelligence	100	Chakra	140
Perception	160	Negotiation	120

Skills

Stealth ☆☆☆ Conversation ☆☆☆ Medical ninjutsu ☆☆ etc.

Ninja Arts

Modern Cartoon Beast Mimicry, Mind Transfer, Medical ninjutsu, etc.

*Average attribute value is 60 for ordinary people and 90 for genin.
Skill values range from 1 to 5☆ with 5☆ signifying super top-notch.

Number 6: Buffoon

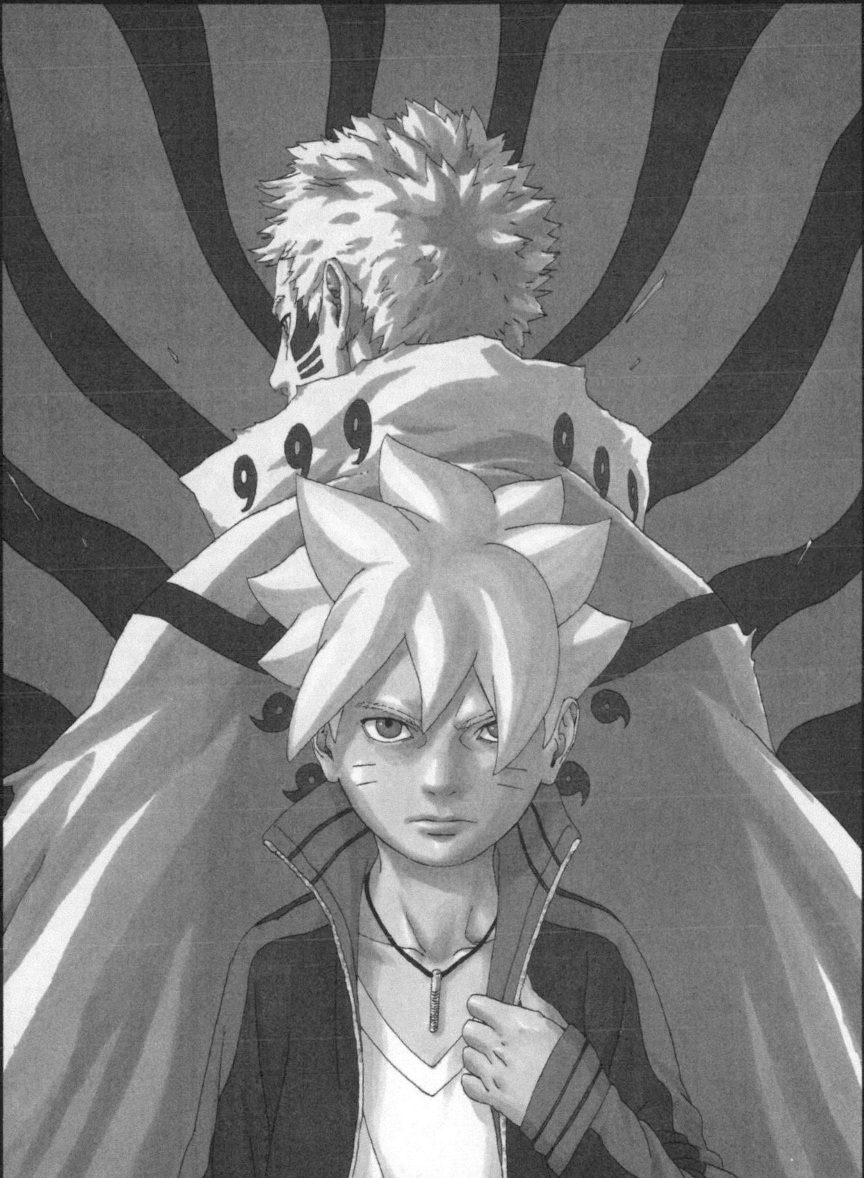

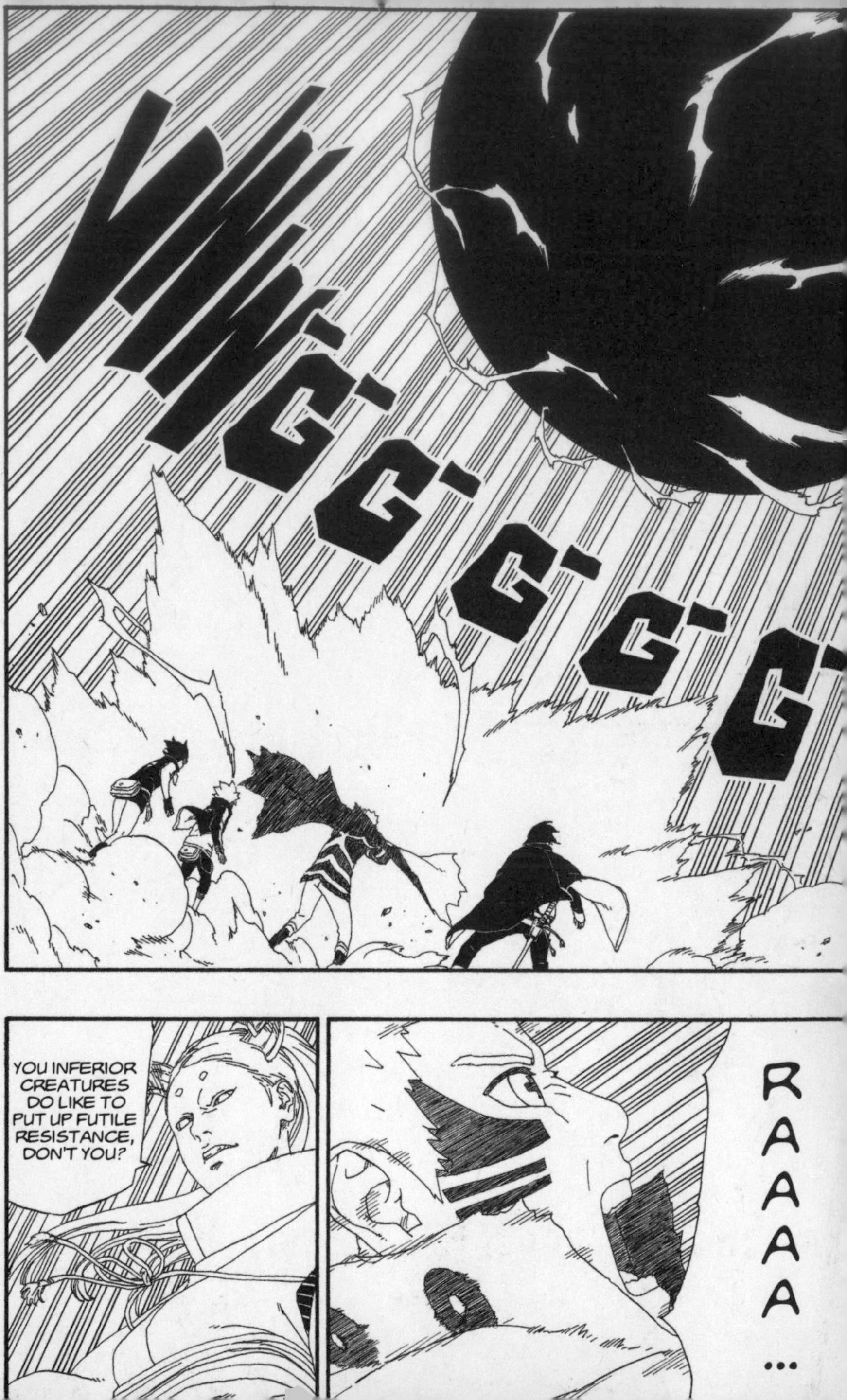
VWGGGG
RAAAA...
YOU INFERIOR CREATURES DO LIKE TO PUT UP FUTILE RESISTANCE, DON'T YOU?

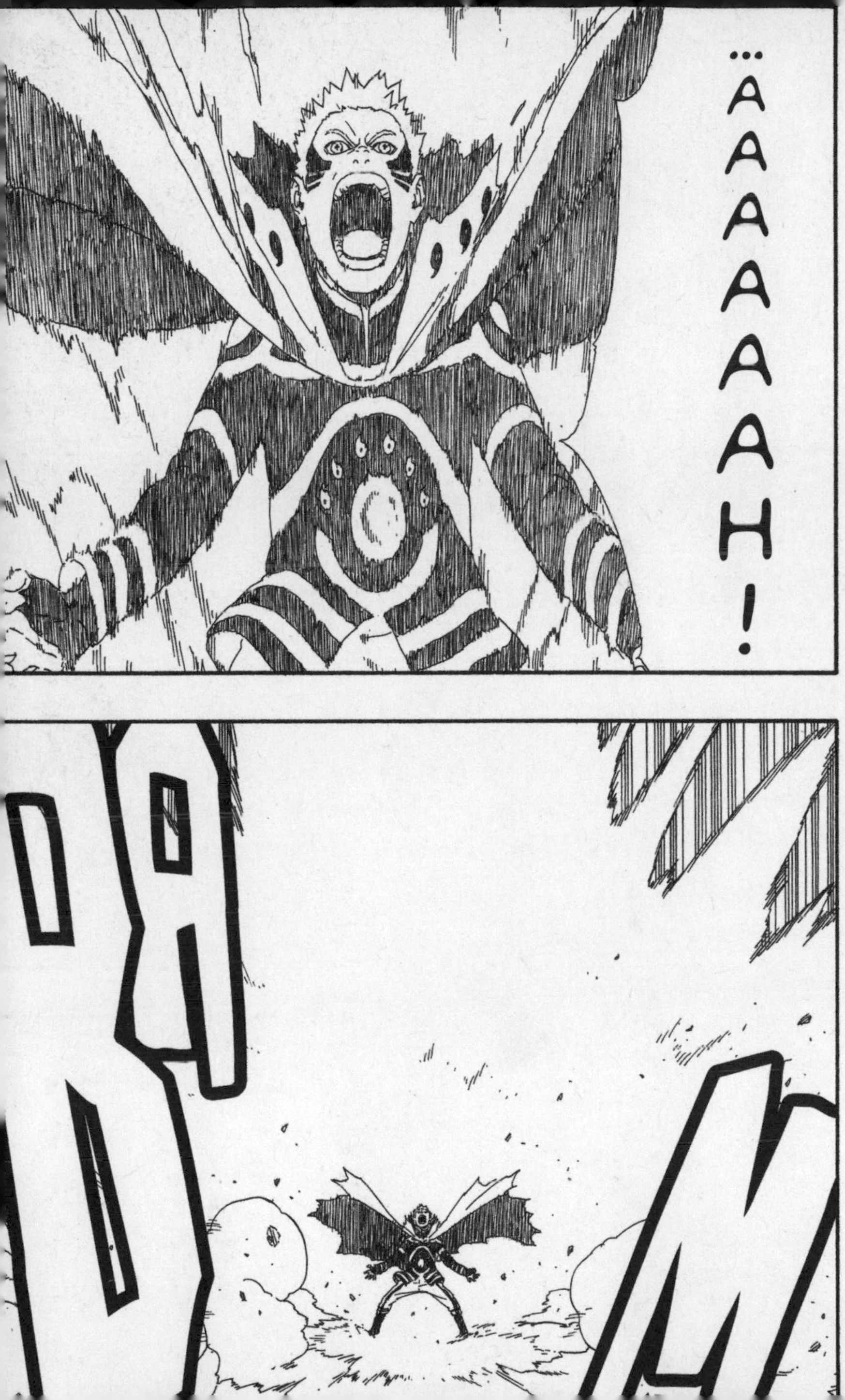
...AAAAAAH!

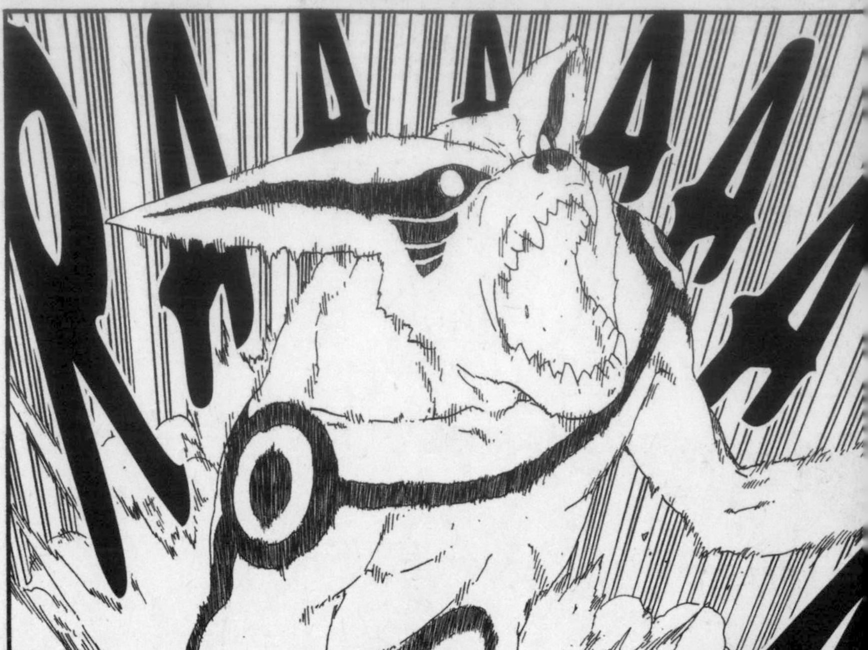
RAAAAAAA
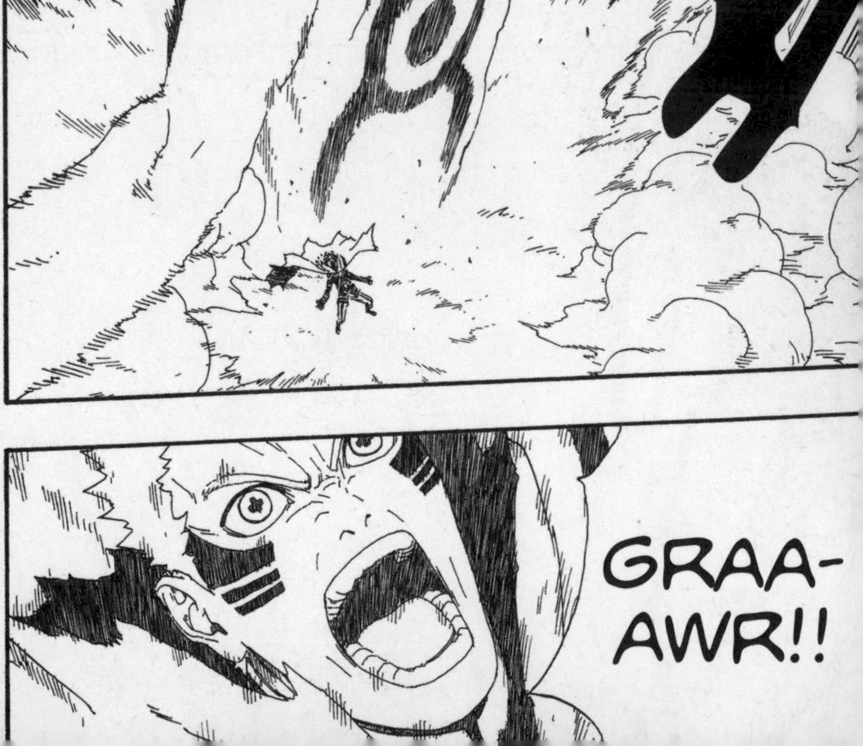
GRAA-
AWR!!

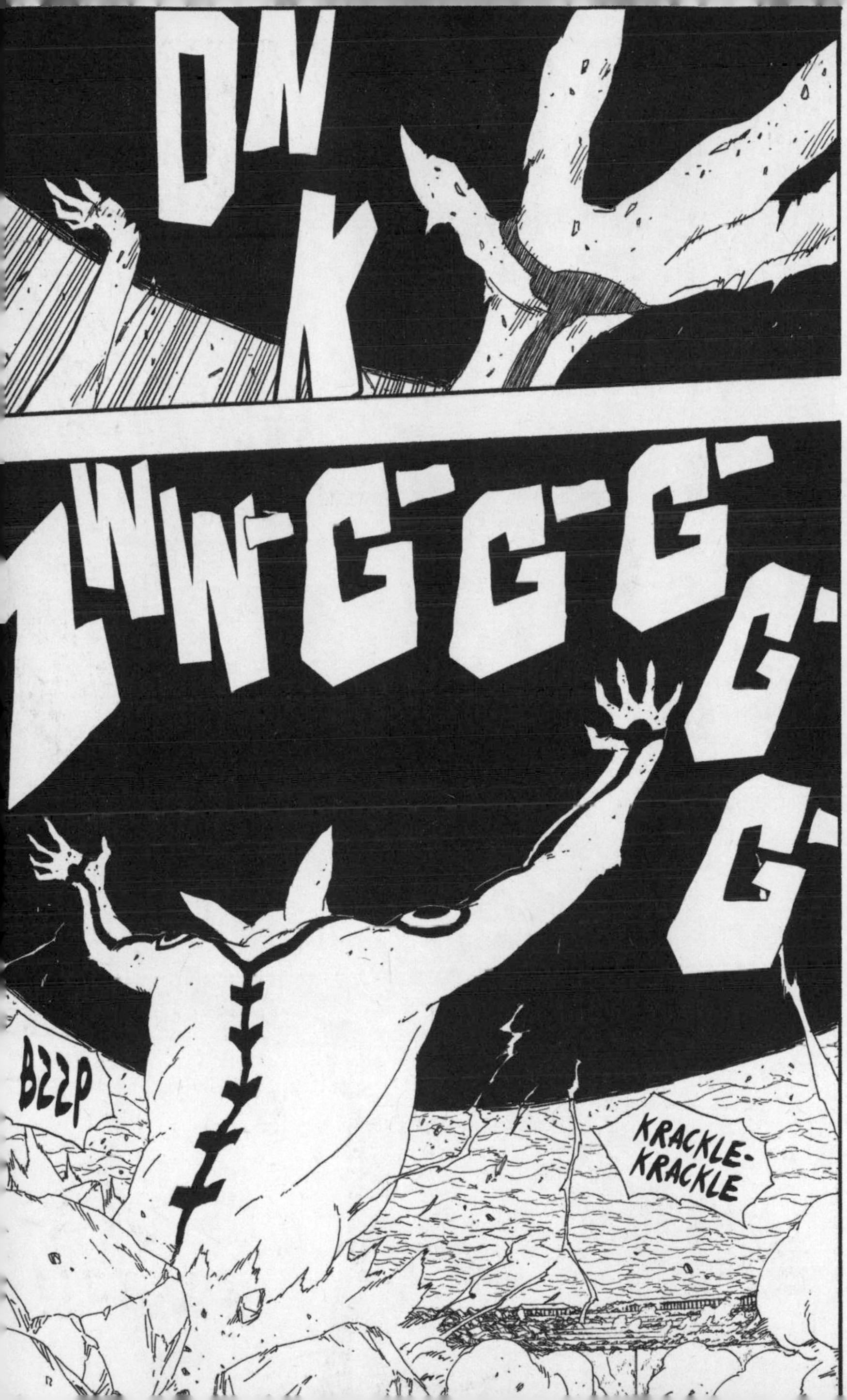
DNK
ZWN-G-G-G-G-G
KRACKLE-KRACKLE
BZZP

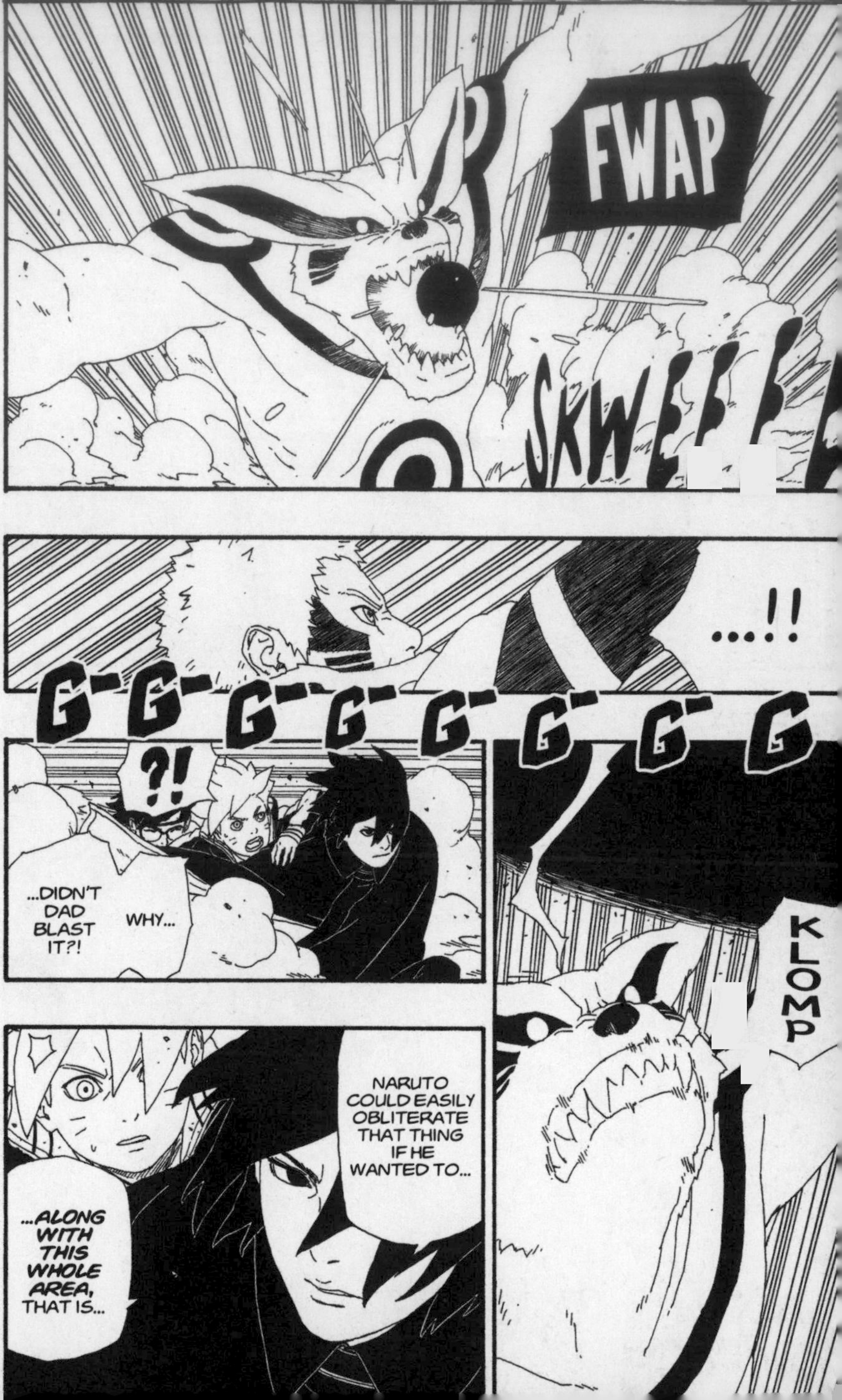
FWAP
SKWEEE
...!!
G-G-G-G-G-G-G-G
KLOMP
?!
WHY...
...DIDN'T DAD BLAST IT?!
NARUTO COULD EASILY OBLITERATE THAT THING IF HE WANTED TO...
...ALONG WITH THIS WHOLE AREA, THAT IS...

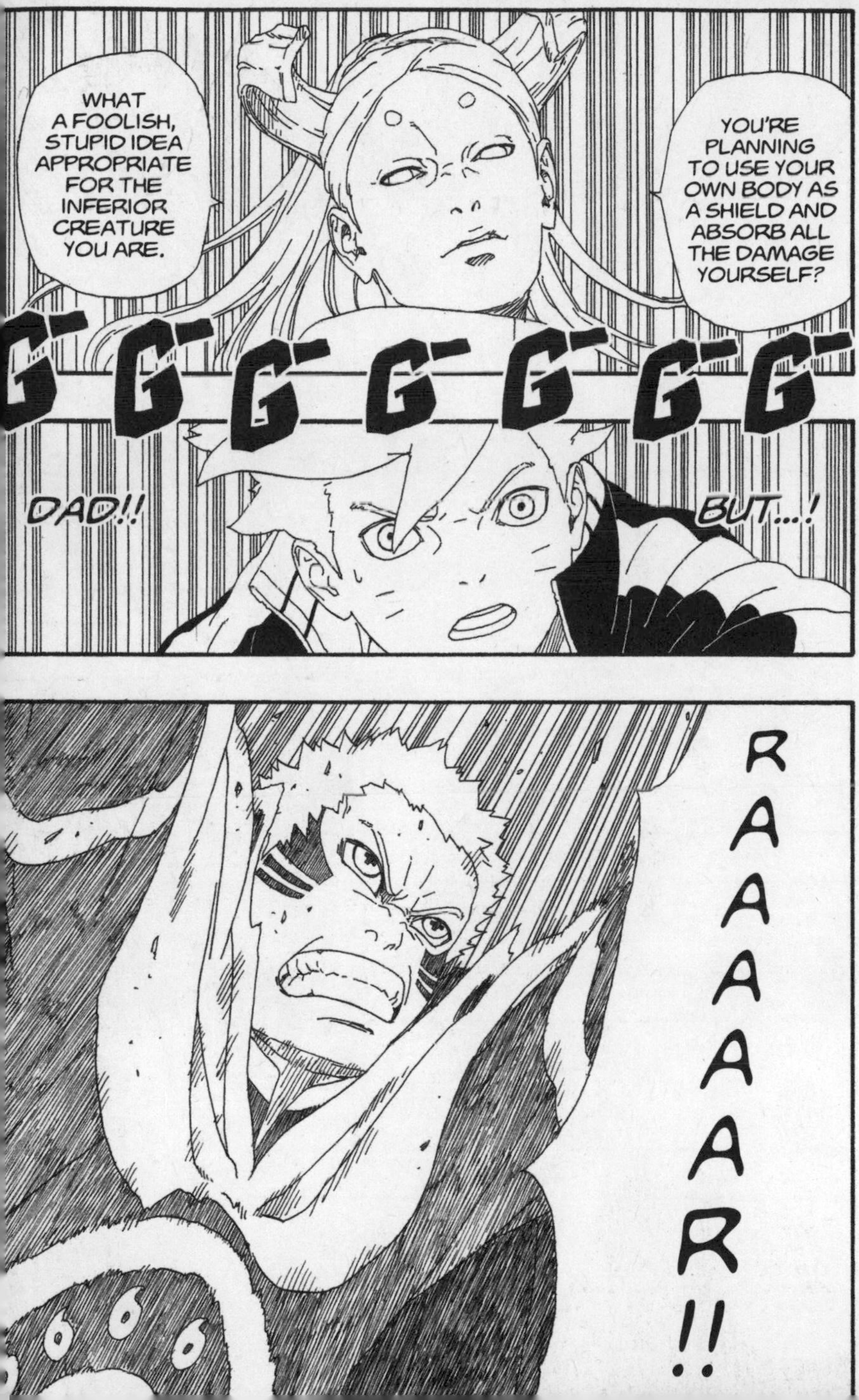
YOU'RE PLANNING TO USE YOUR OWN BODY AS A SHIELD AND ABSORB ALL THE DAMAGE YOURSELF?
WHAT A FOOLISH, STUPID IDEA APPROPRIATE FOR THE INFERIOR CREATURE YOU ARE.
GGGGGGG
BUT...!
DAD!!
RAAAAAR!!

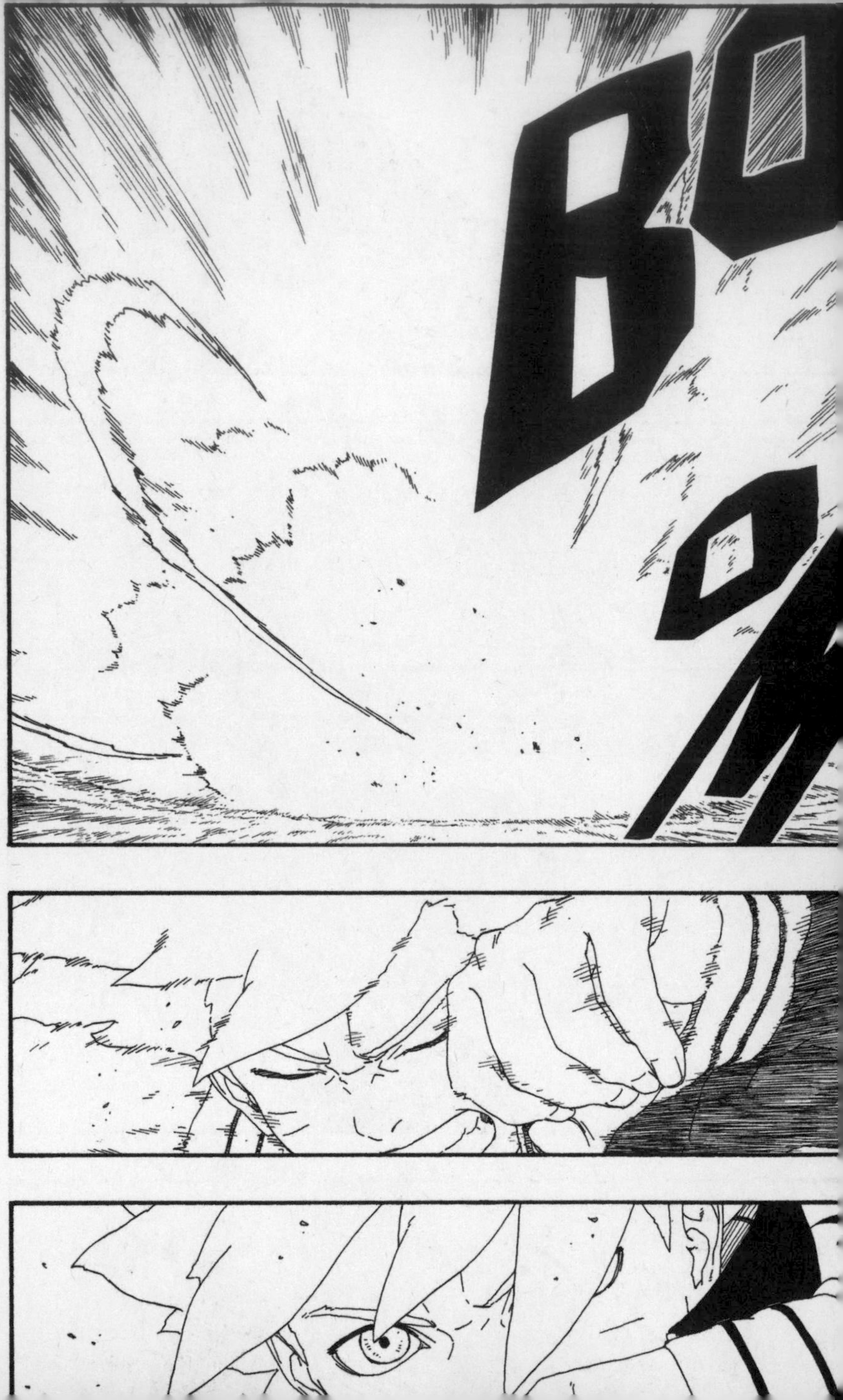
BOOM

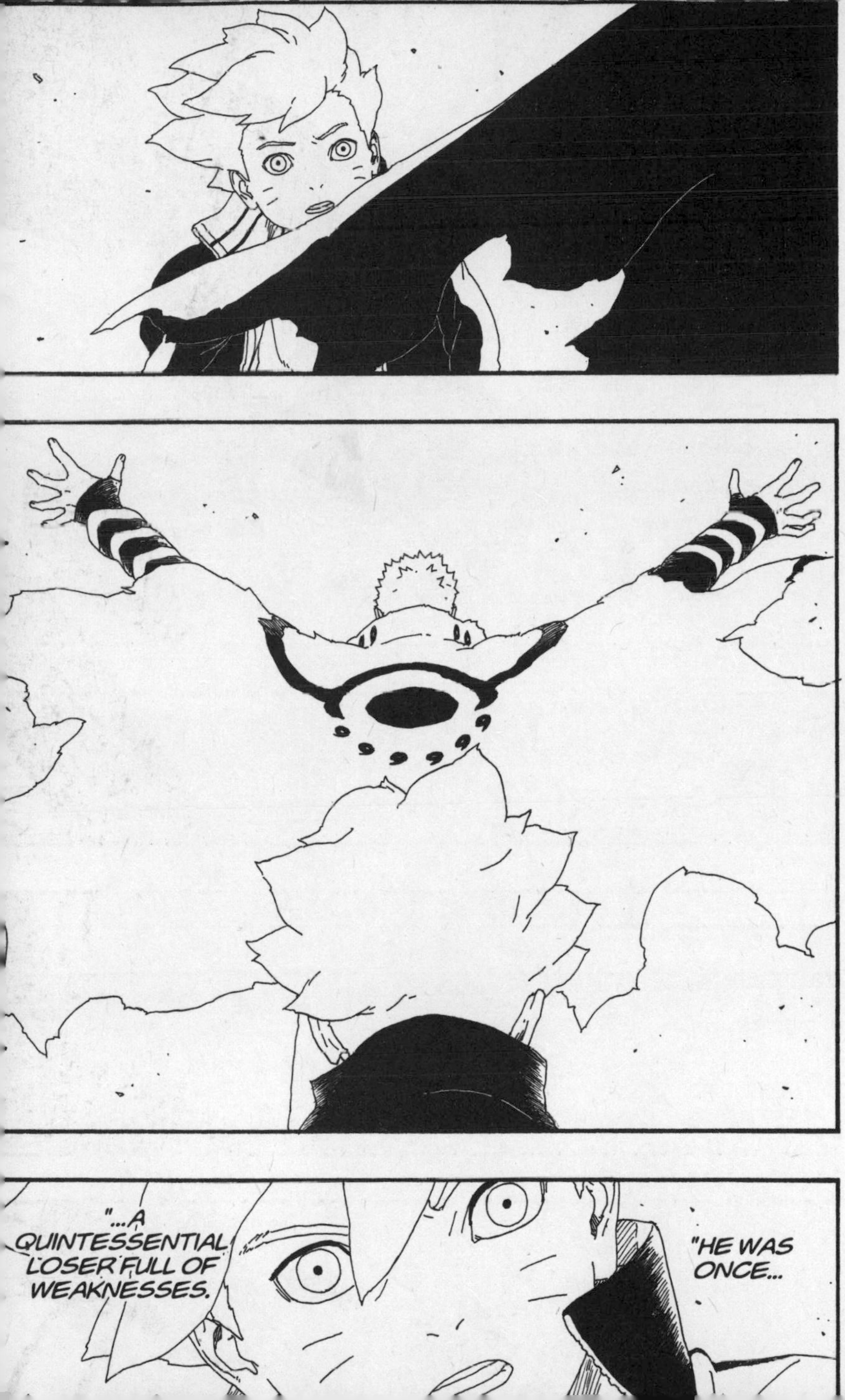
"HE WAS ONCE...
"...A QUINTESSENTIAL LOSER FULL OF WEAKNESSES.

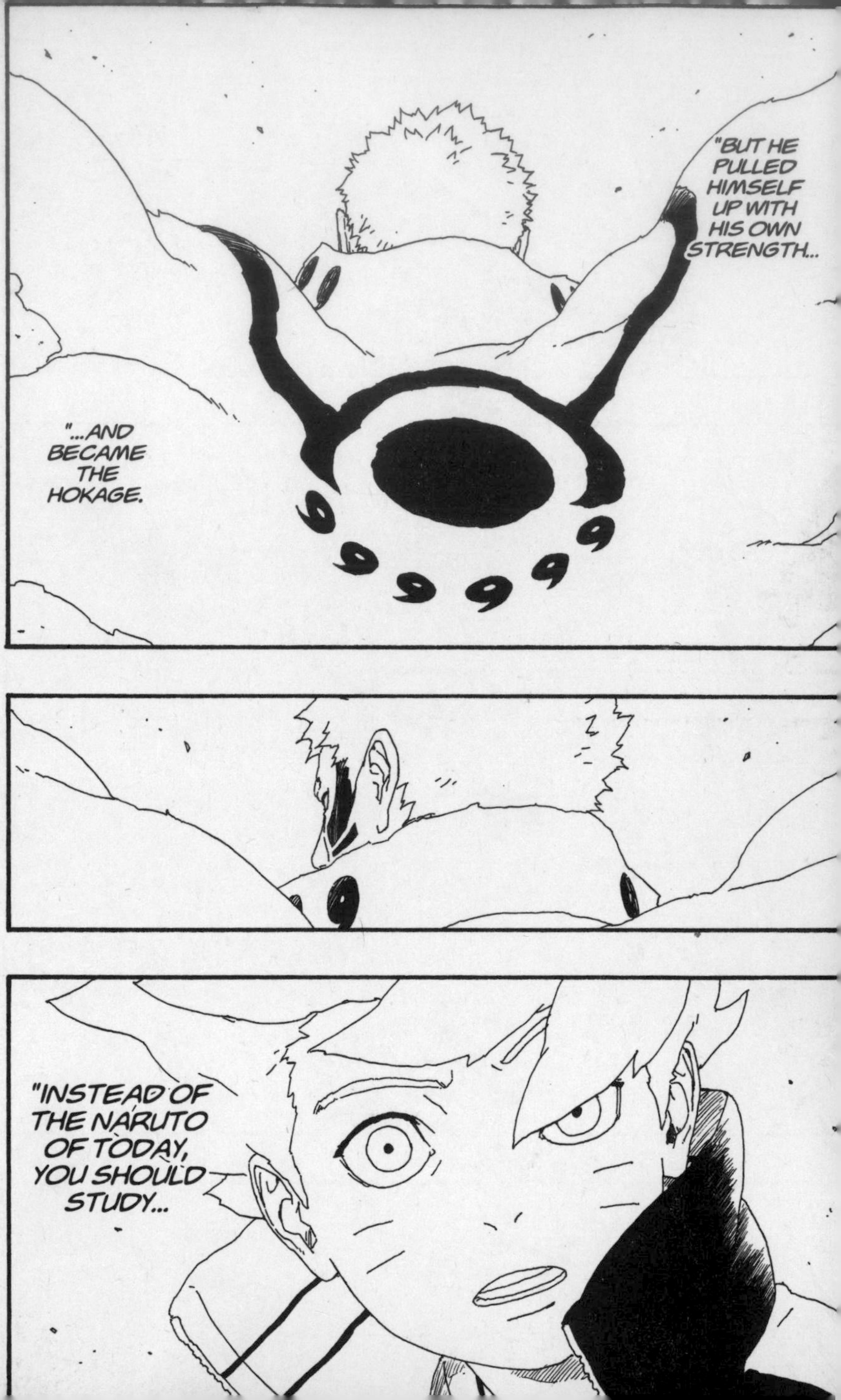
"BUT HE PULLED HIMSELF UP WITH HIS OWN STRENGTH...
"...AND BECAME THE HOKAGE.
"INSTEAD OF THE NARUTO OF TODAY, YOU SHOULD STUDY...

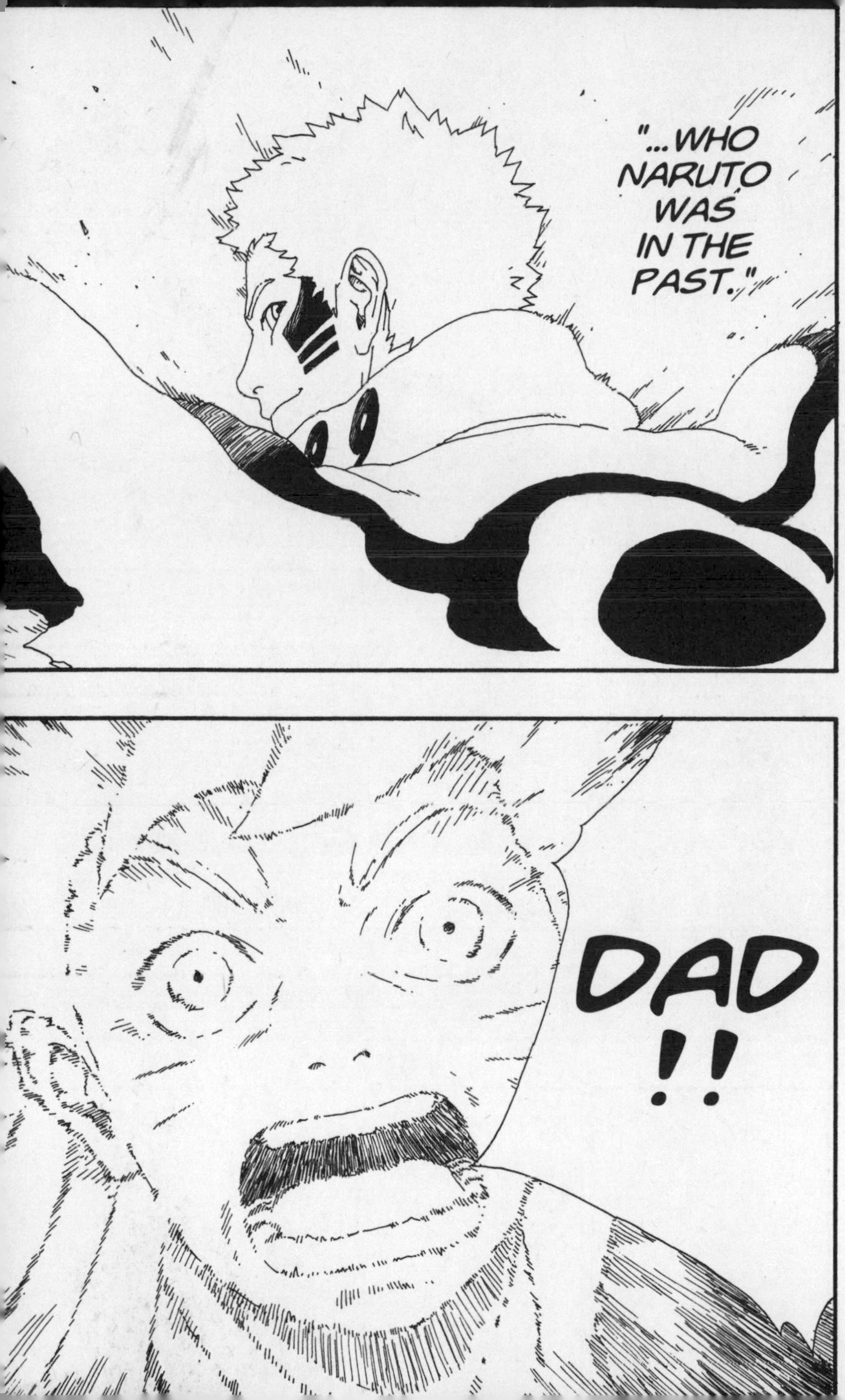
"...WHO NARUTO WAS IN THE PAST."
DAD!!

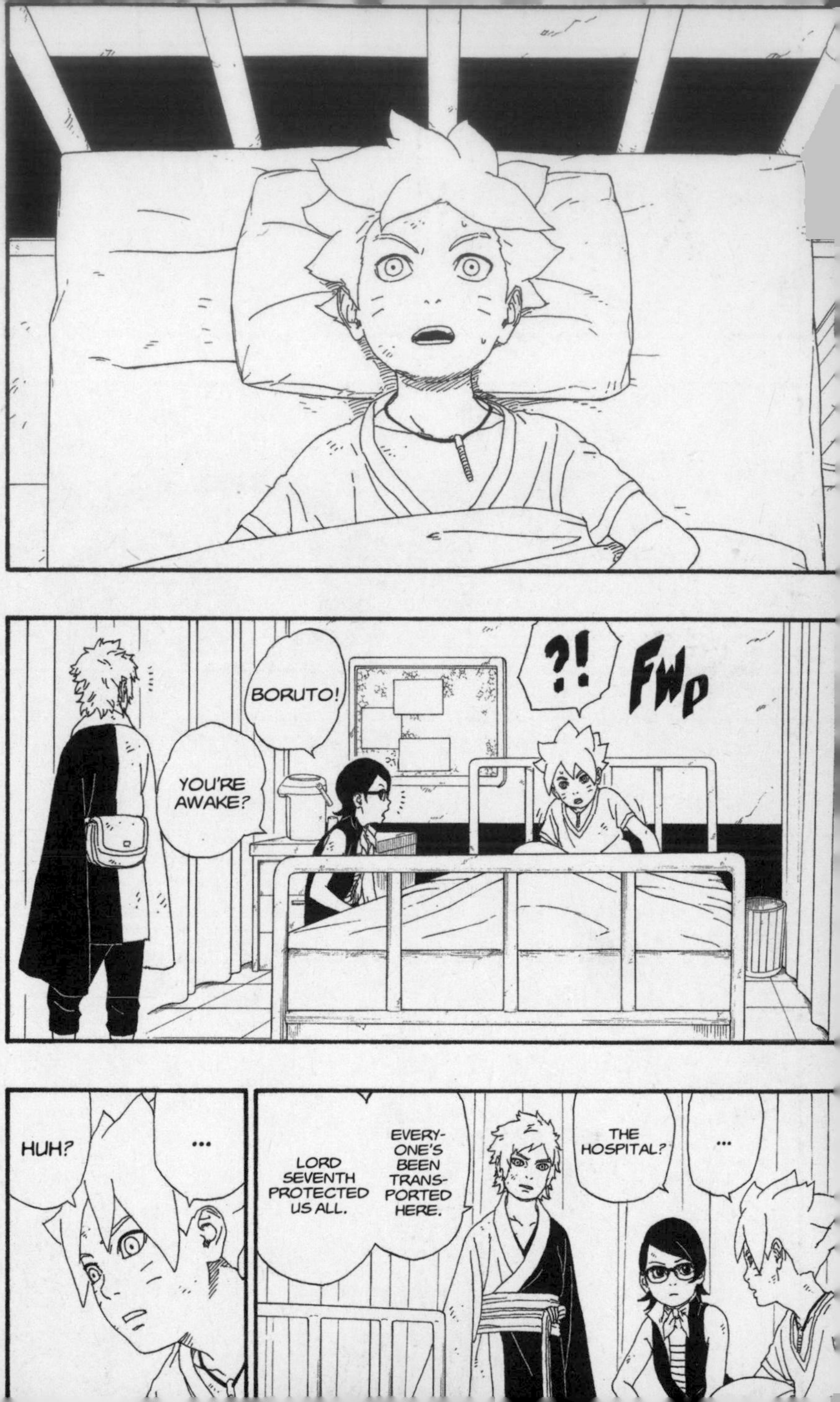
FWP
?!
BORUTO!
YOU'RE AWAKE?
...
THE HOSPITAL?
EVERY-ONE'S BEEN TRANS-PORTED HERE.
LORD SEVENTH PROTECTED US ALL.
...
HUH?

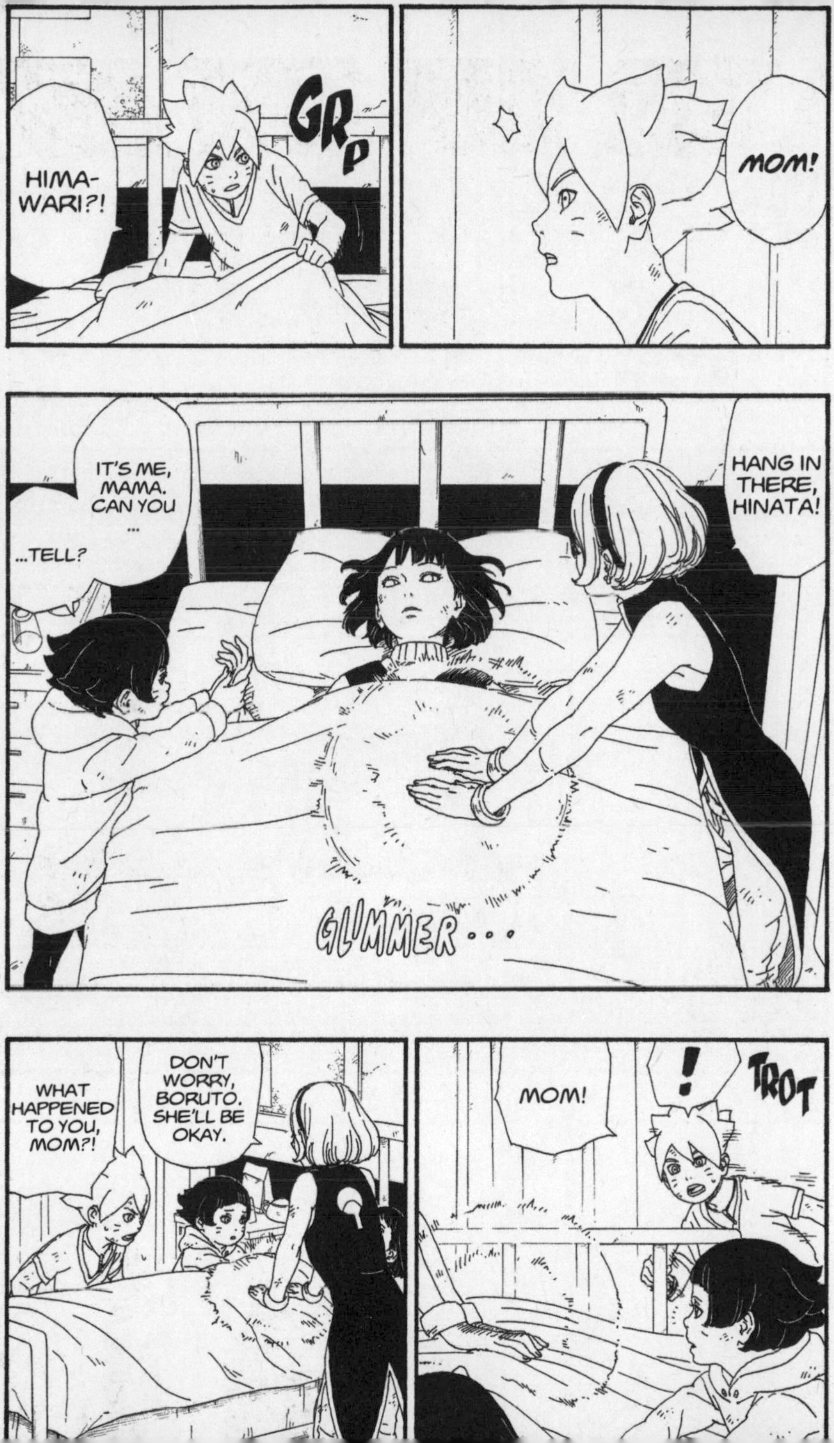
MOM!
GRP
HIMA-WARI?!
HANG IN THERE, HINATA!
IT'S ME, MAMA. CAN YOU ...
...TELL?
GLIMMER...
TROT
!
MOM!
DON'T WORRY, BORUTO. SHE'LL BE OKAY.
WHAT HAPPENED TO YOU, MOM?!

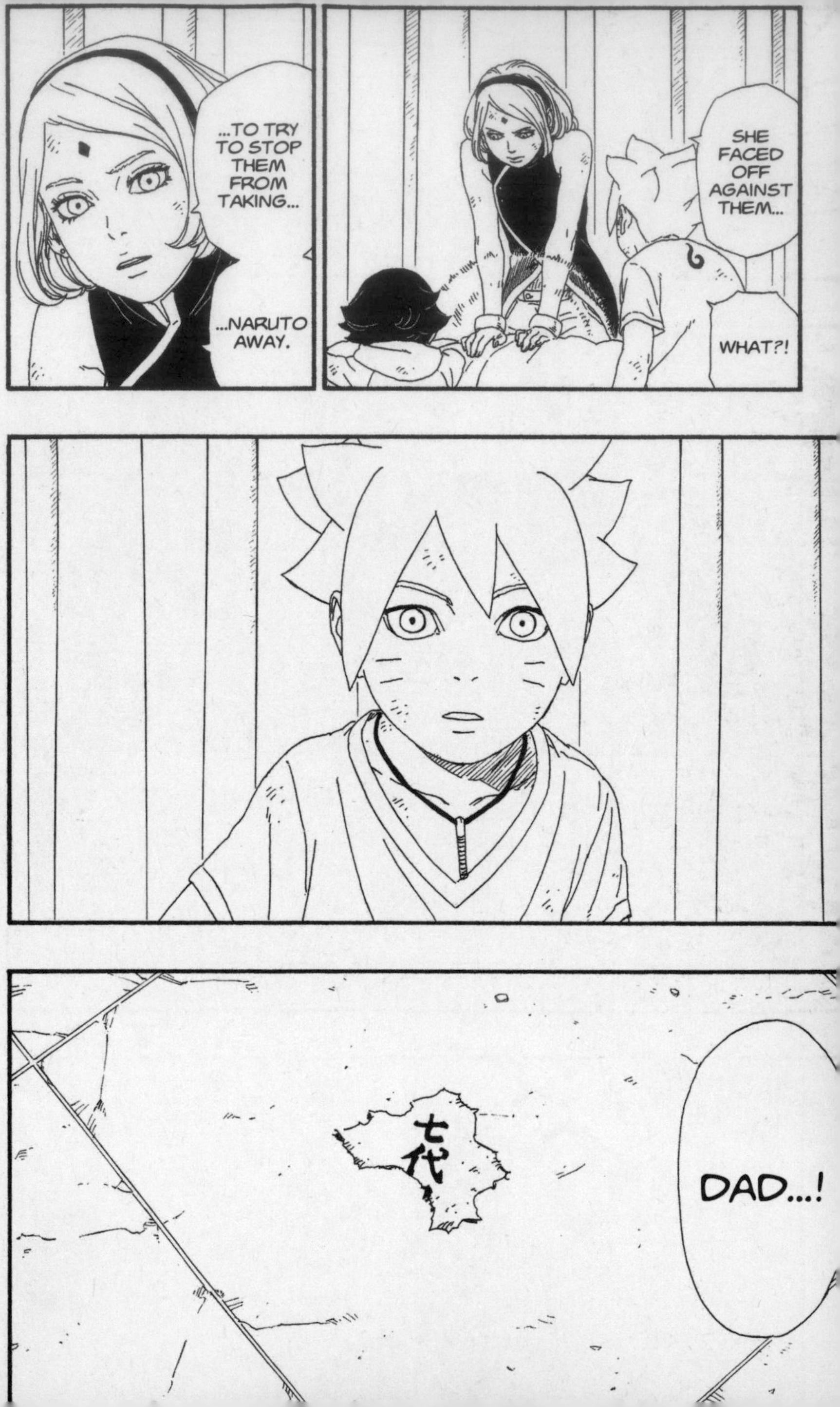
SHE FACED OFF AGAINST THEM...
WHAT?!
...TO TRY TO STOP THEM FROM TAKING...
...NARUTO AWAY.
DAD...!
七代

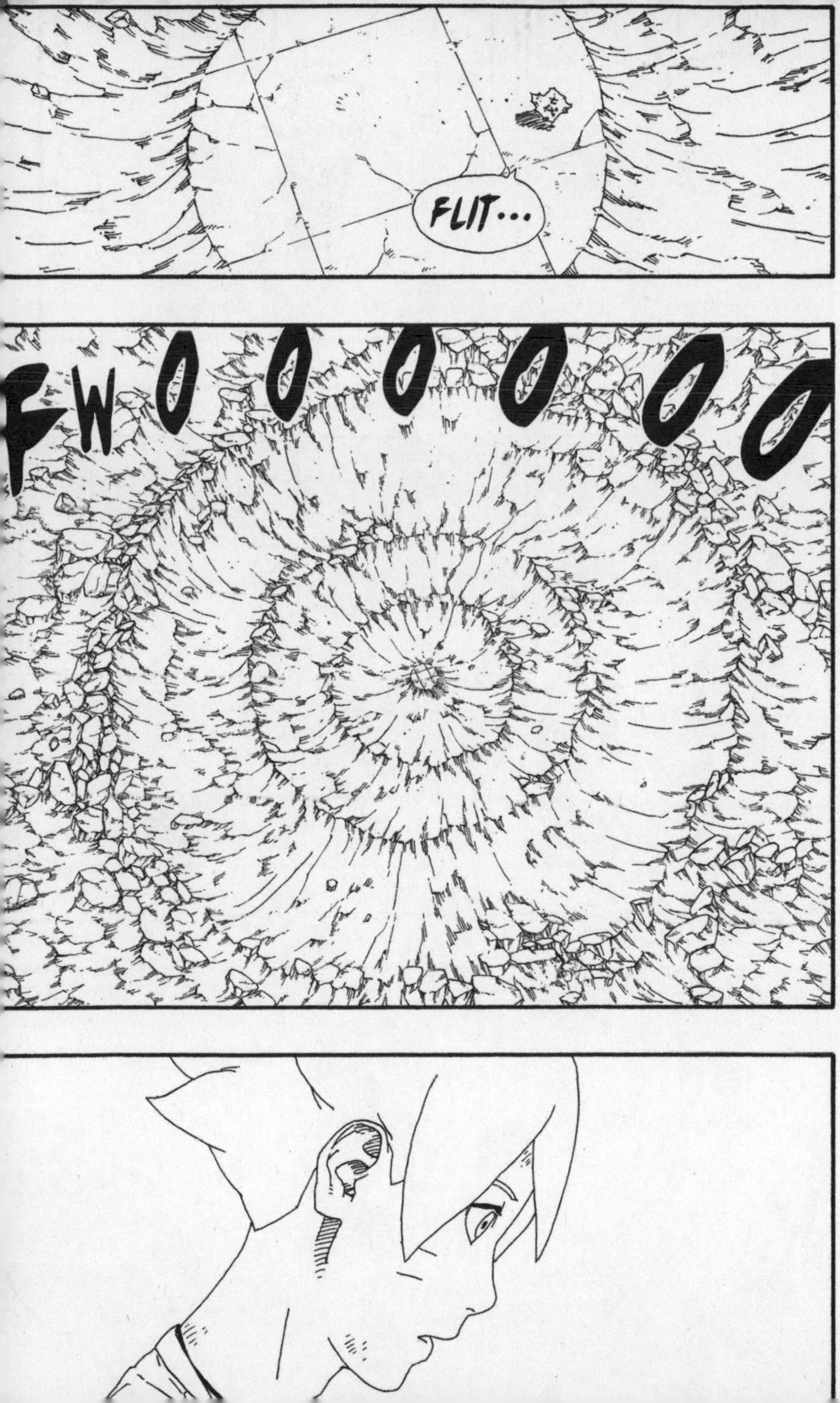
FLIT...
FWOOOOOOO

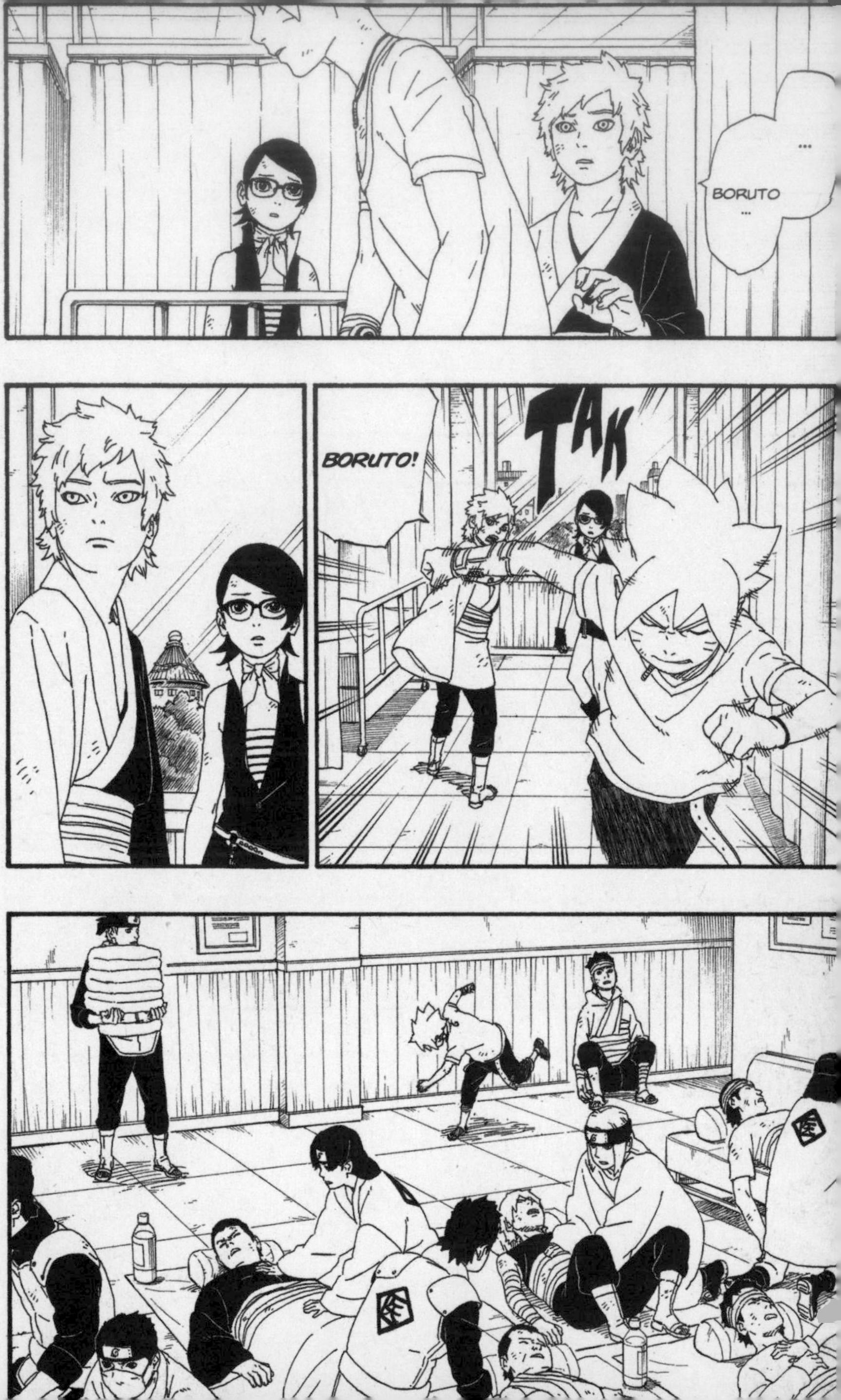
...
BORUTO
...
TAK
BORUTO!

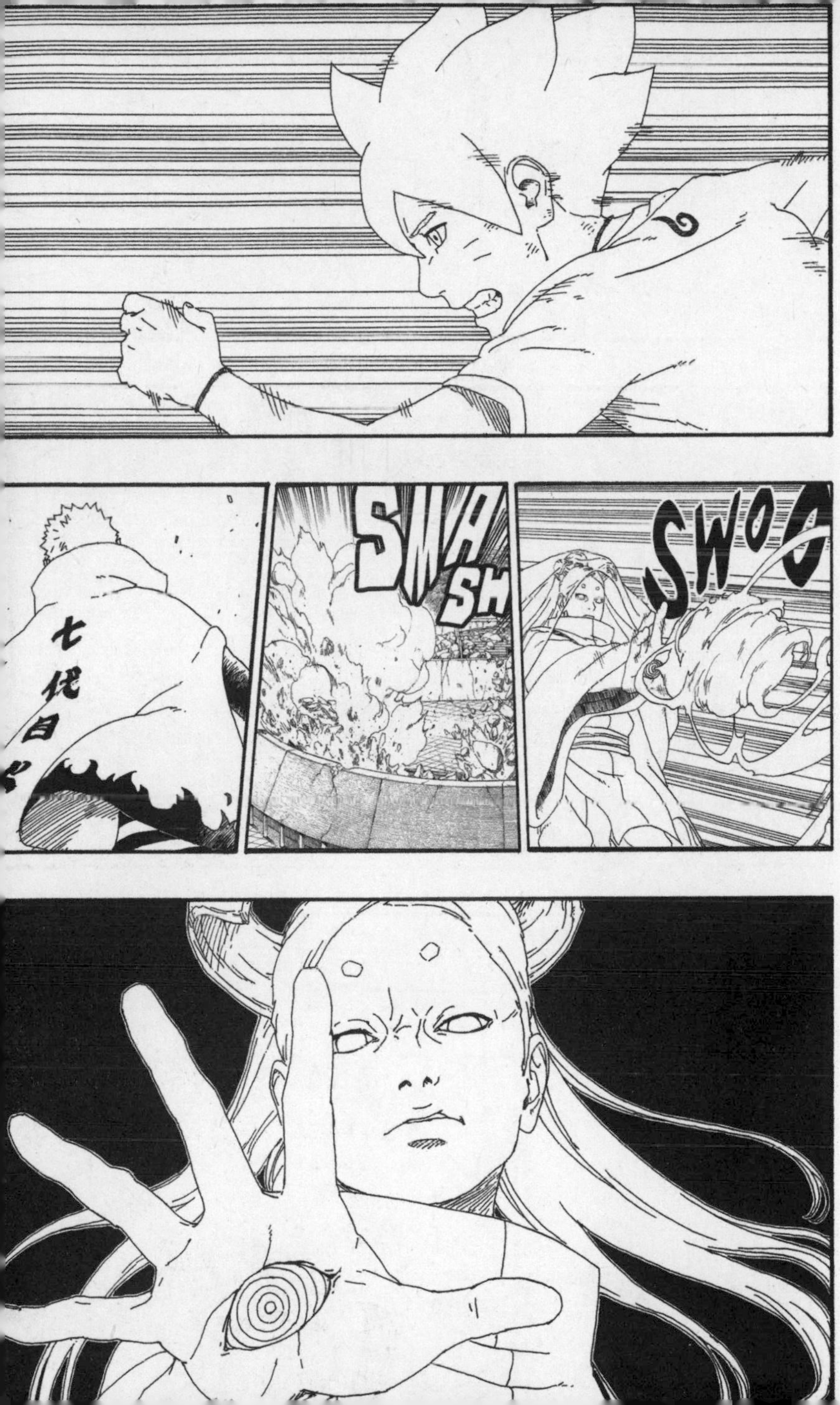
SWO
SWASH
七代目

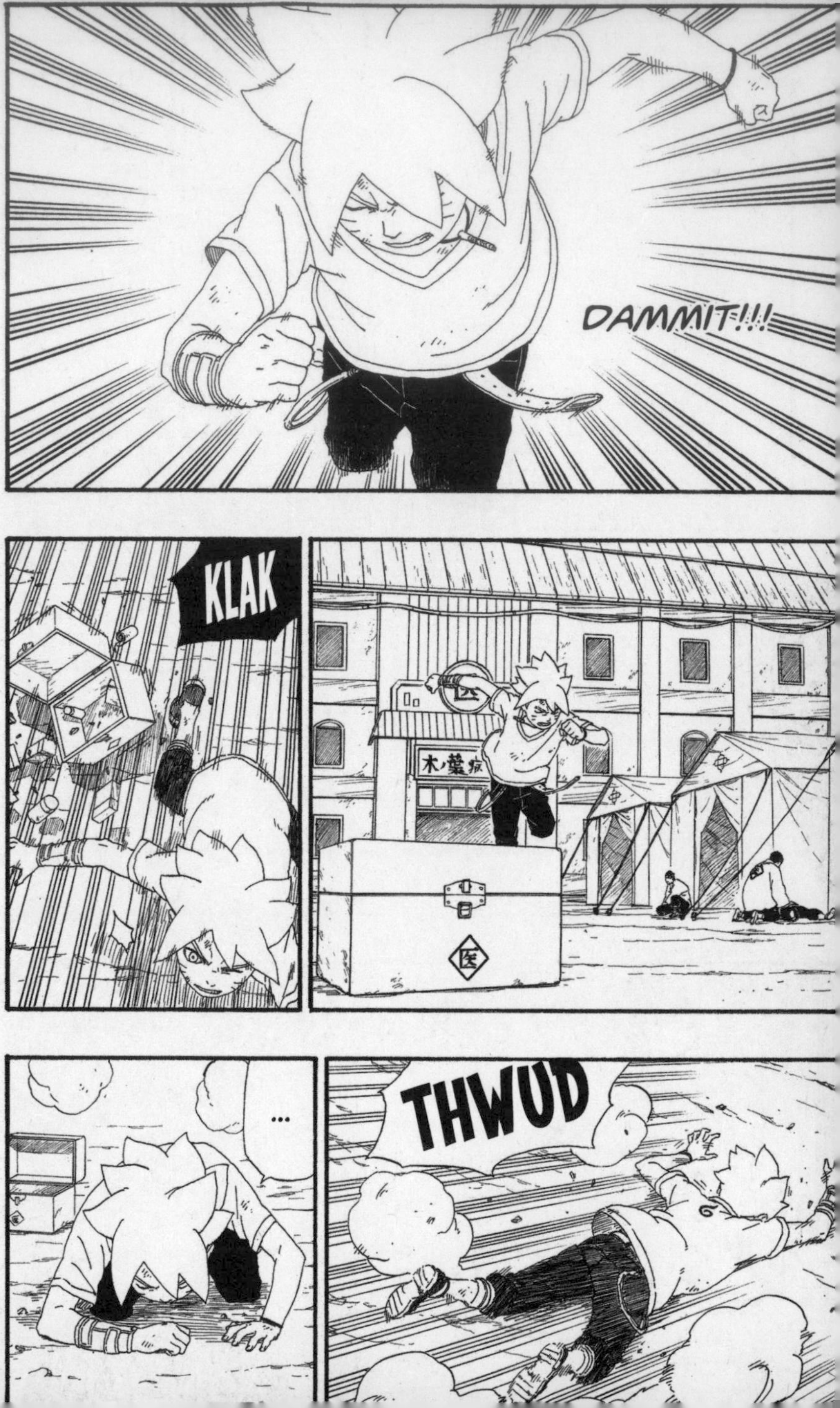
DAMMIT!!!
KLAK
THWUD
...

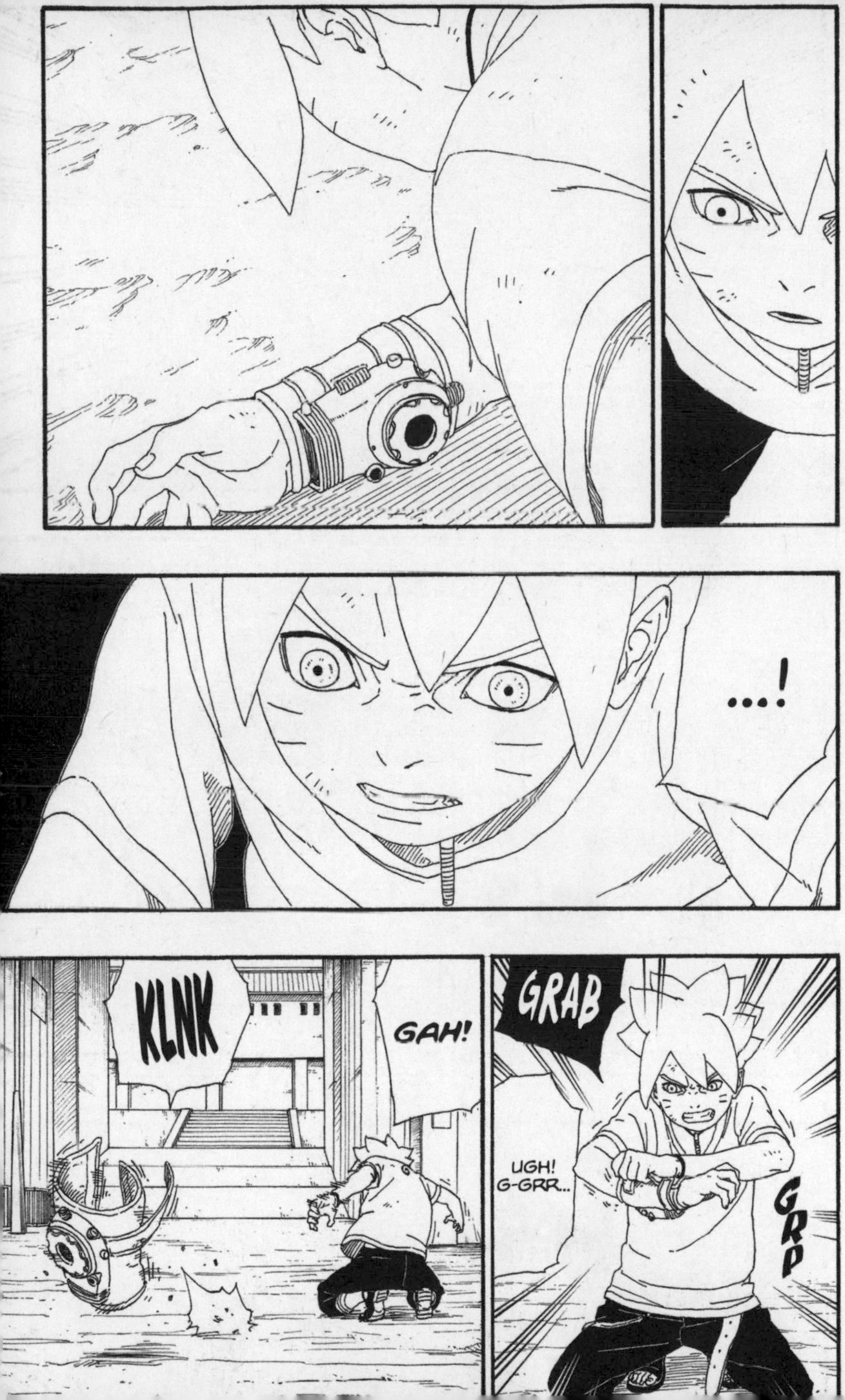
...!
GRAB
UGH! G-GRR...
GRP
GAH!
KLNK

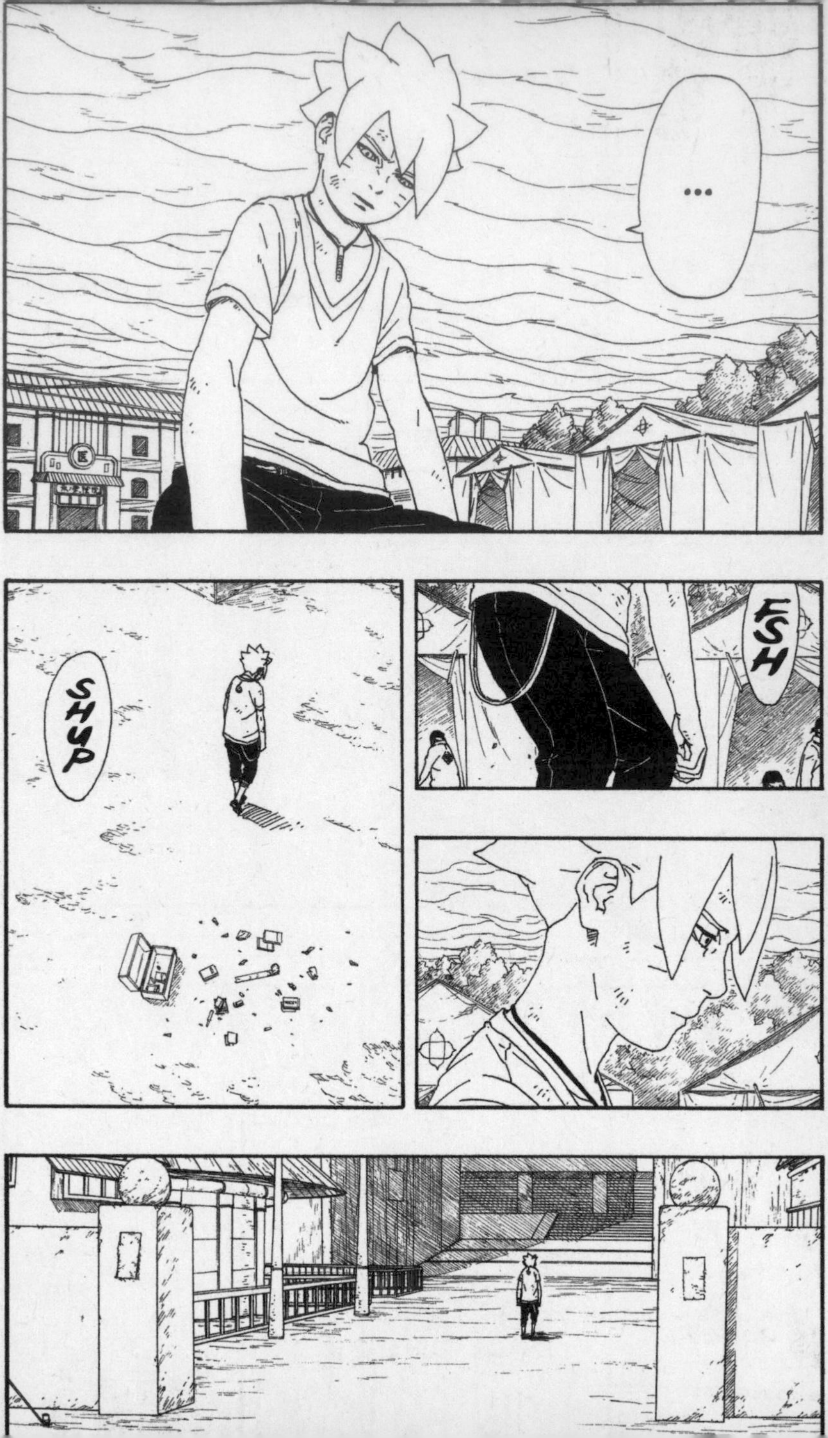
...
FSH
SHUP

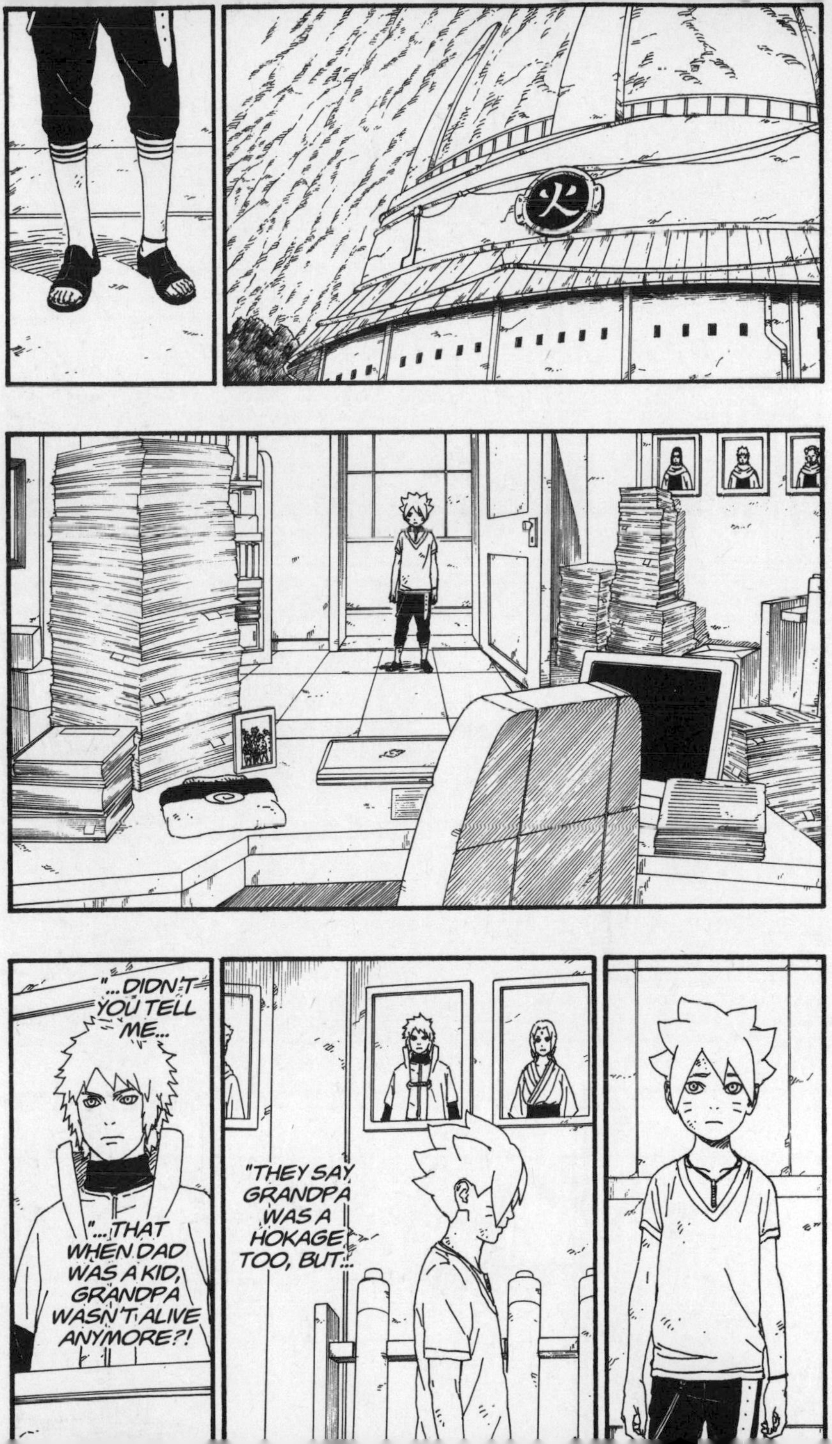
"THEY SAY GRANDPA WAS A HOKAGE TOO, BUT...
"...DIDN'T YOU TELL ME...
"...THAT WHEN DAD WAS A KID, GRANDPA WASN'T ALIVE ANYMORE?!

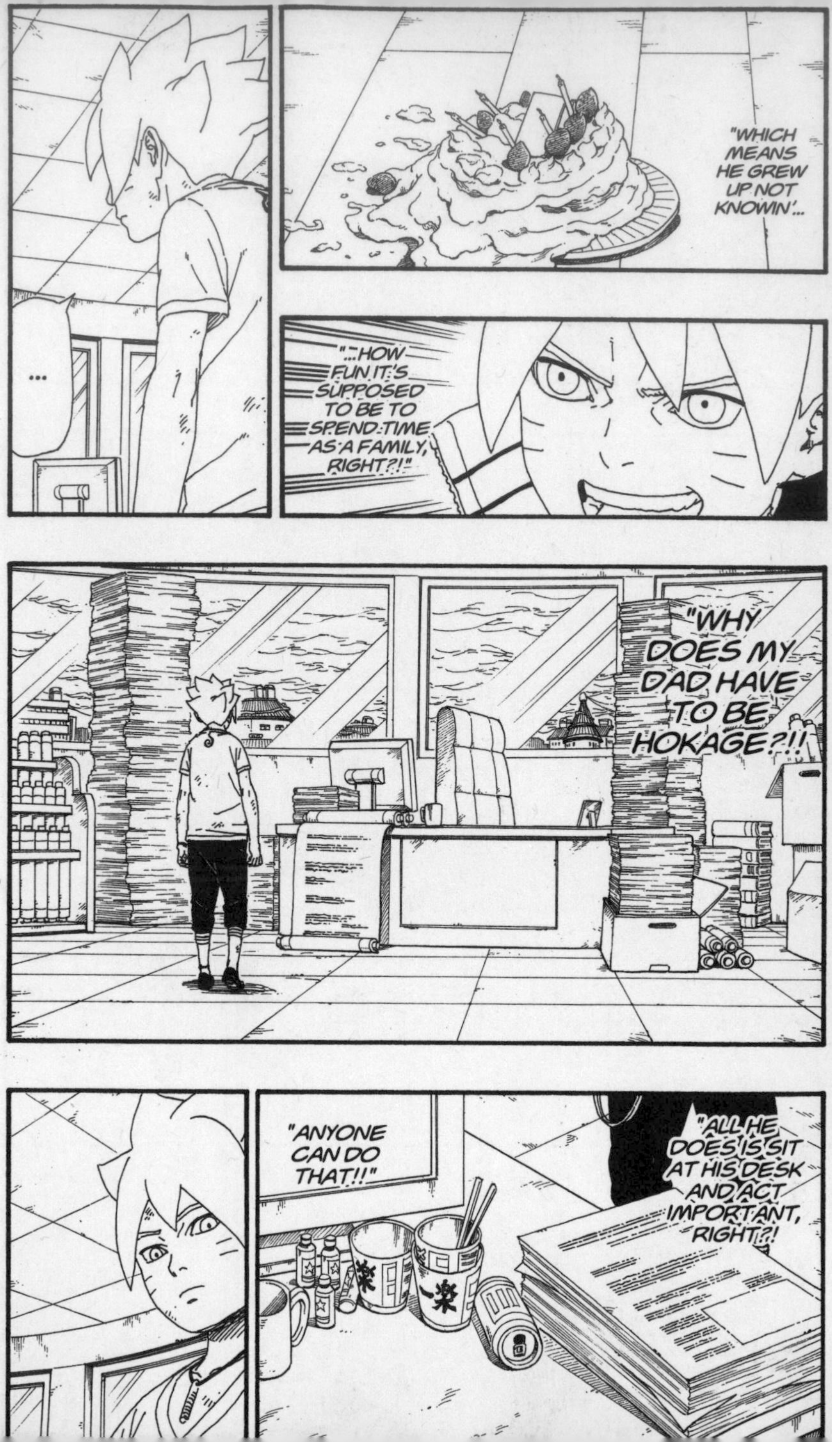
"WHICH MEANS HE GREW UP NOT KNOWIN'...
"...HOW FUN IT'S SUPPOSED TO BE TO SPEND TIME AS A FAMILY, RIGHT?!"
...
"WHY DOES MY DAD HAVE TO BE HOKAGE?!!
"ALL HE DOES IS SIT AT HIS DESK AND ACT IMPORTANT, RIGHT?!
"ANYONE CAN DO THAT!!"

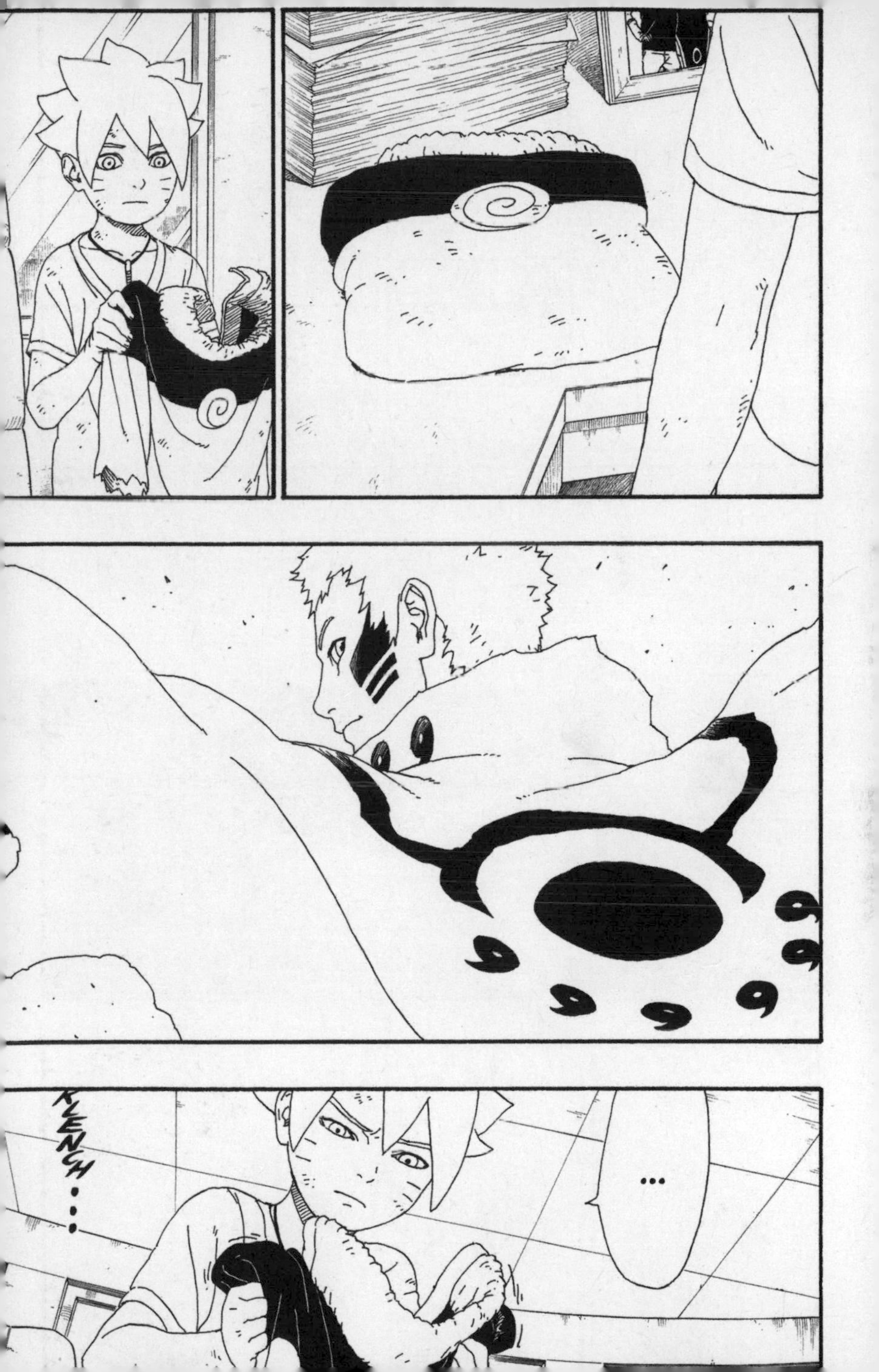
...
KLENCH...

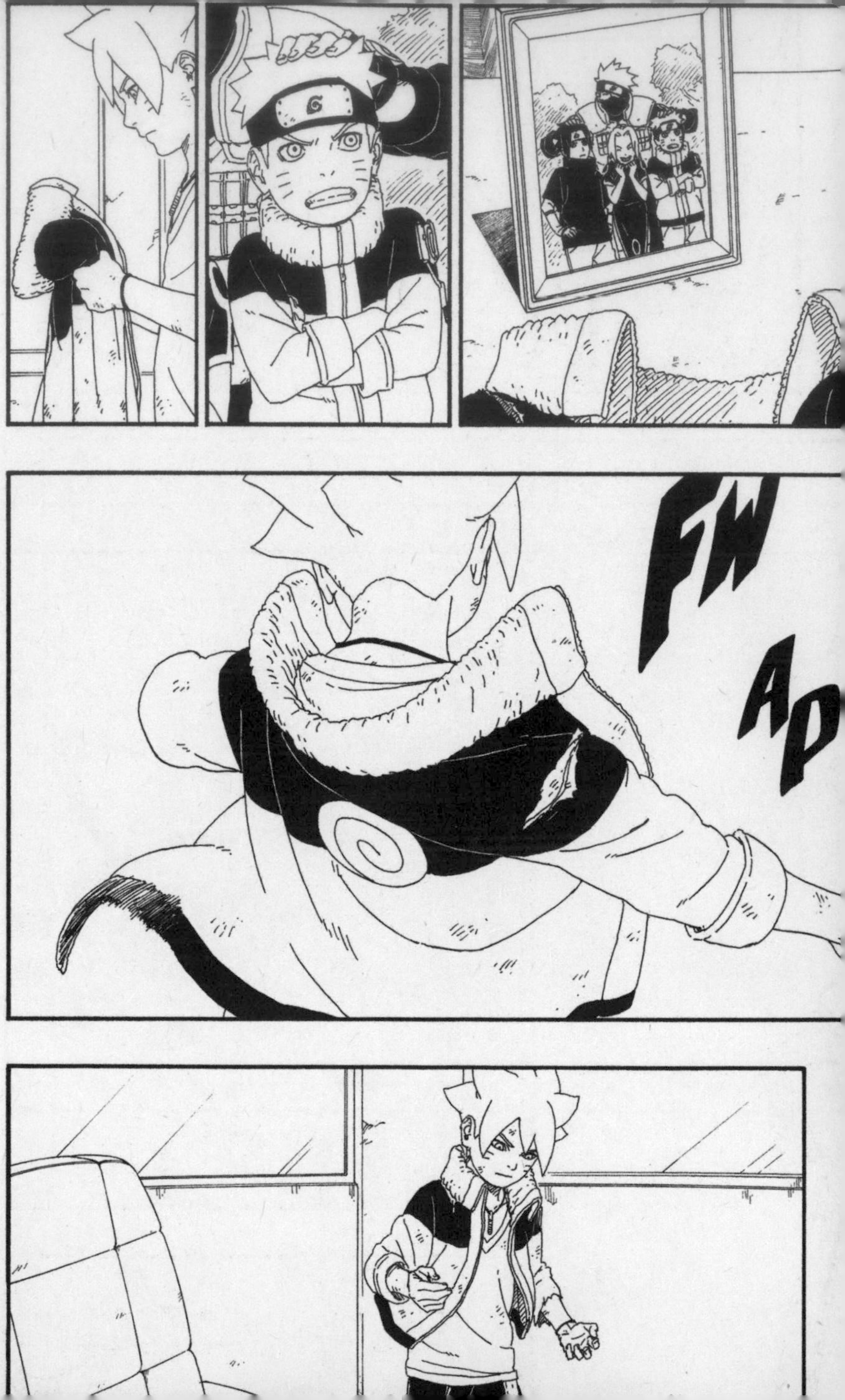
FWAP

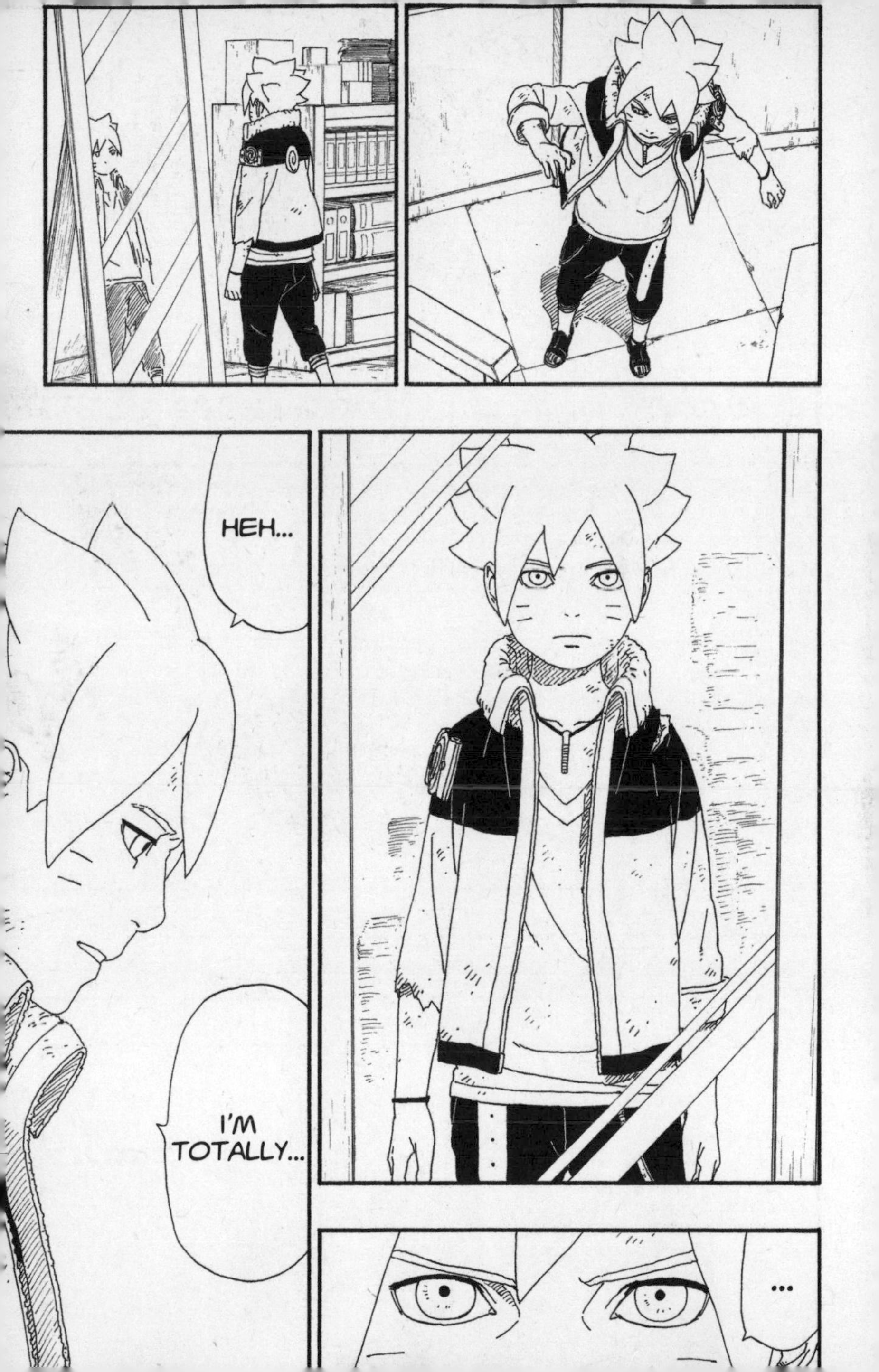
...
HEH...
I'M TOTALLY...

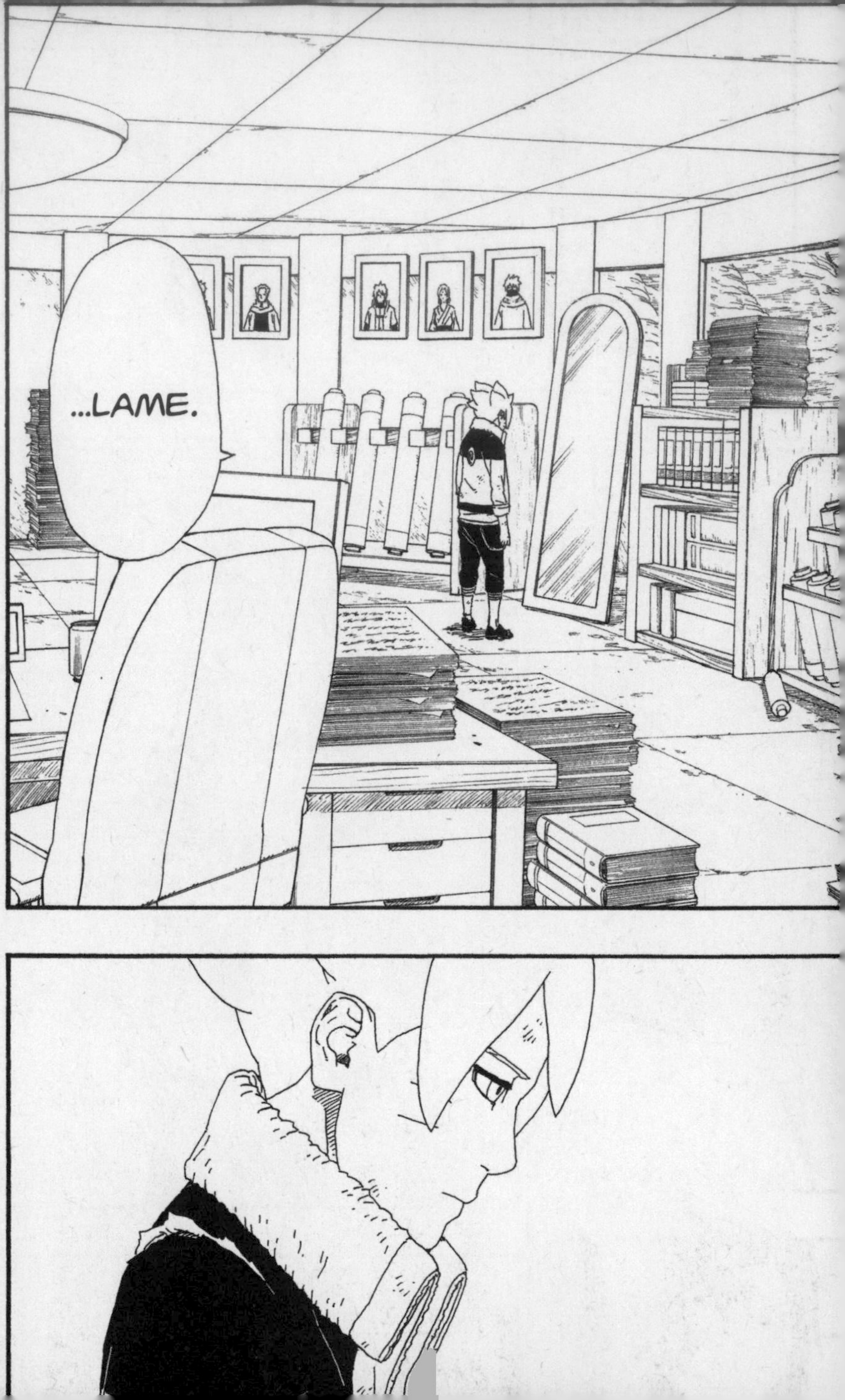
...LAME.

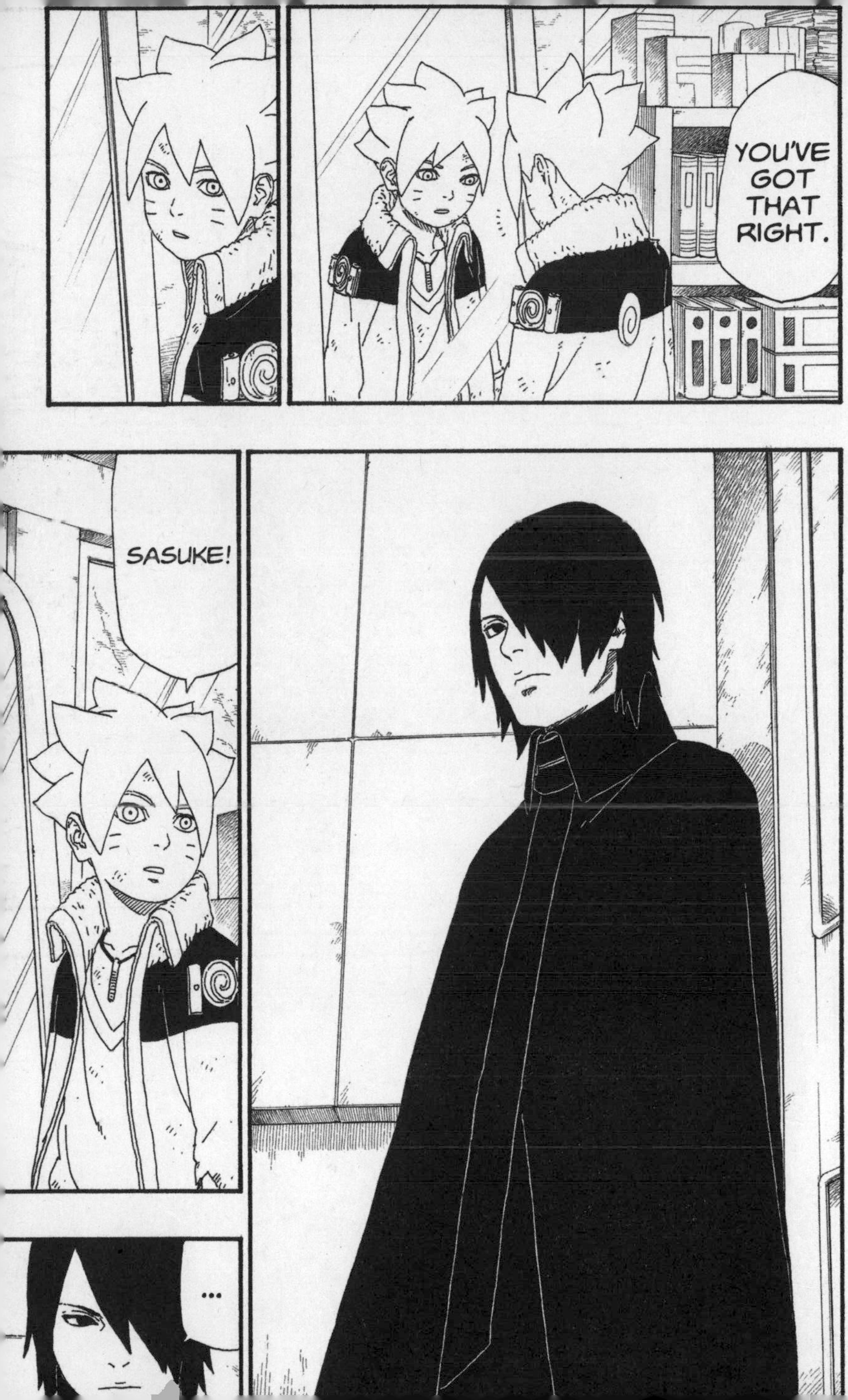
YOU'VE GOT THAT RIGHT.
SASUKE!
...

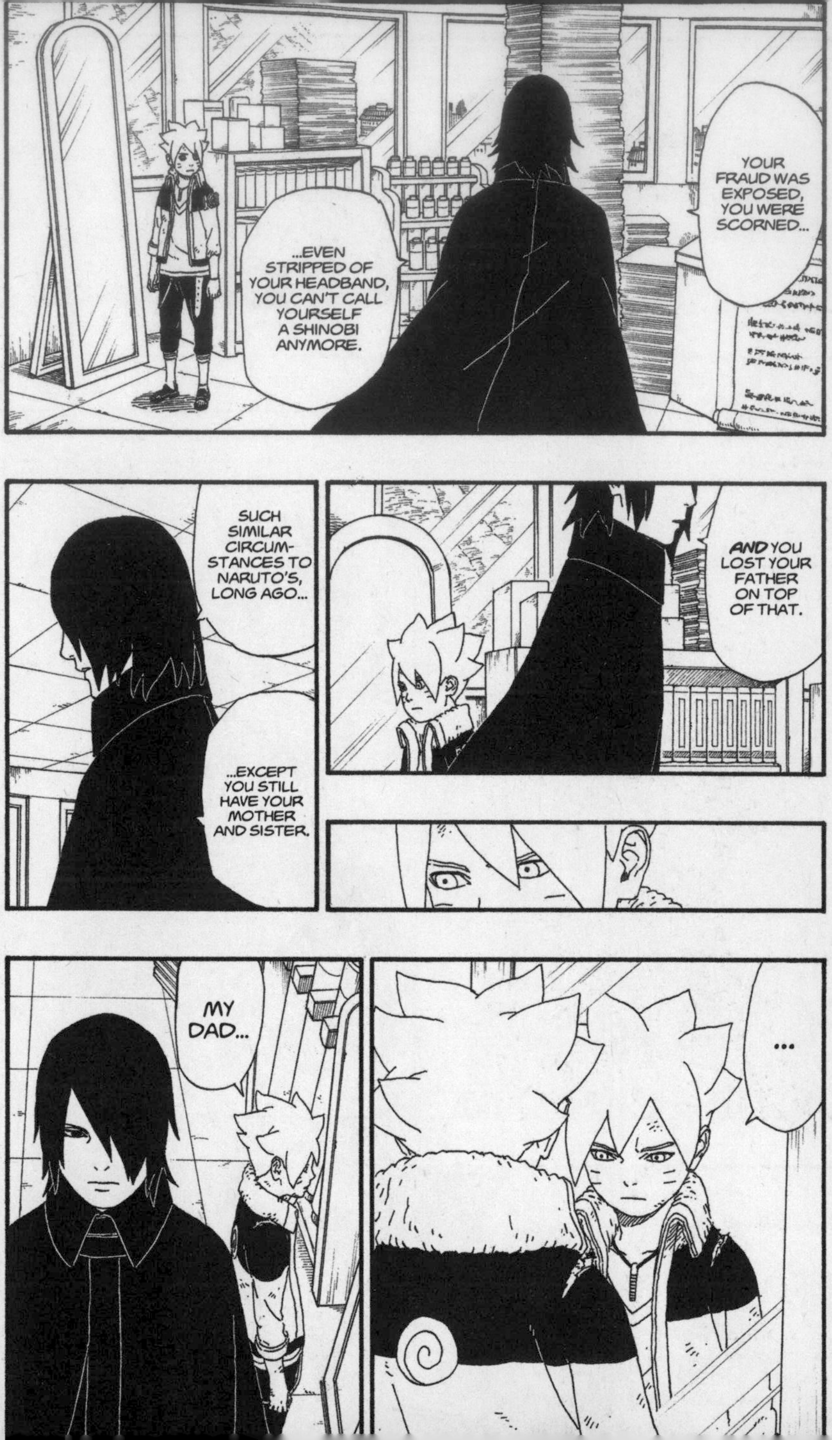
YOUR FRAUD WAS EXPOSED, YOU WERE SCORNED...
...EVEN STRIPPED OF YOUR HEADBAND, YOU CAN'T CALL YOURSELF A SHINOBI ANYMORE.
AND YOU LOST YOUR FATHER ON TOP OF THAT.
SUCH SIMILAR CIRCUM-STANCES TO NARUTO'S, LONG AGO...
...EXCEPT YOU STILL HAVE YOUR MOTHER AND SISTER.
...
MY DAD...

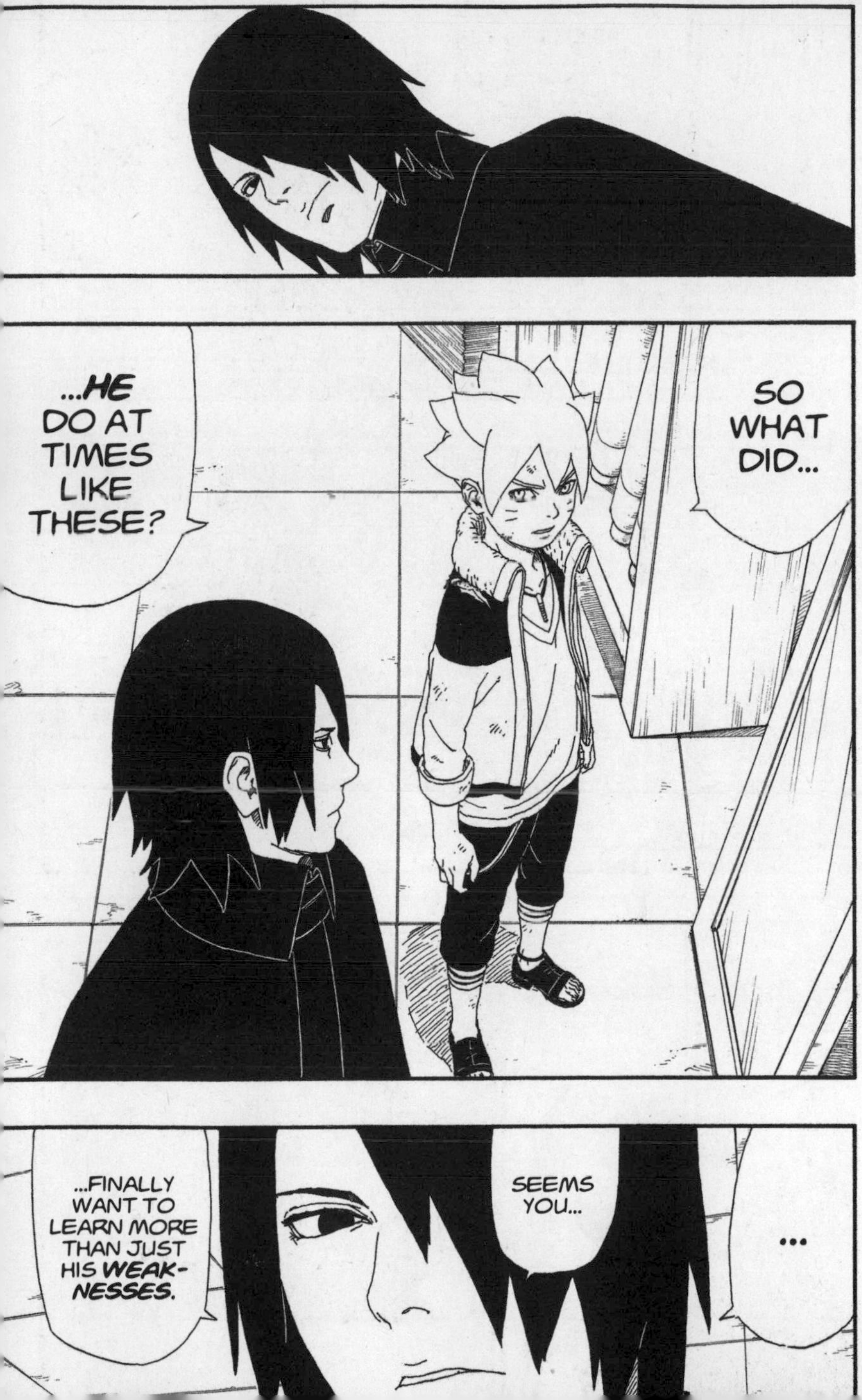
SO WHAT DID...
...HE DO AT TIMES LIKE THESE?
...
SEEMS YOU...
...FINALLY WANT TO LEARN MORE THAN JUST HIS WEAKNESSES.

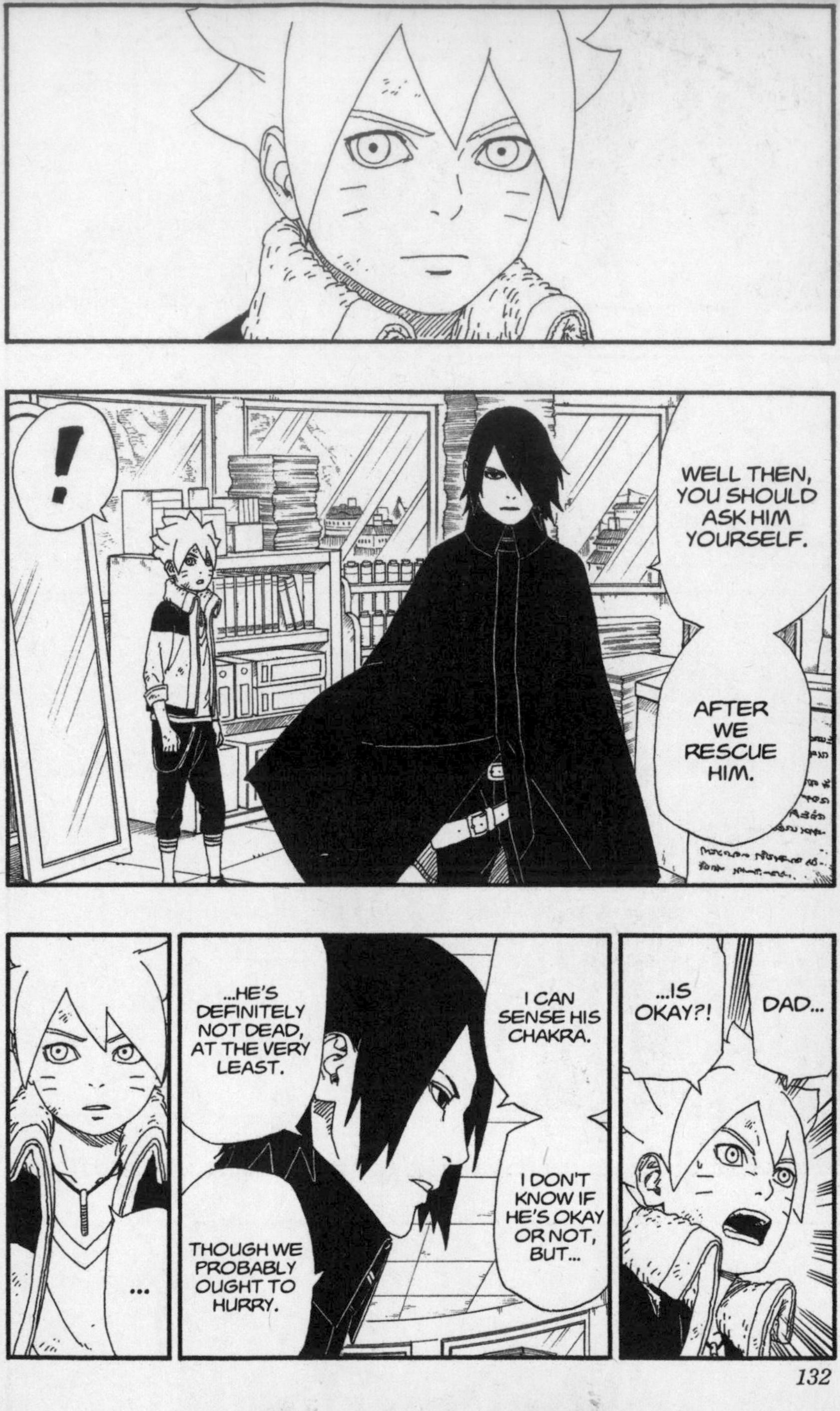
WELL THEN, YOU SHOULD ASK HIM YOURSELF.
AFTER WE RESCUE HIM.
!
DAD...
...IS OKAY?!
I CAN SENSE HIS CHAKRA.
...HE'S DEFINITELY NOT DEAD, AT THE VERY LEAST.
I DON'T KNOW IF HE'S OKAY OR NOT, BUT...
THOUGH WE PROBABLY OUGHT TO HURRY.
...

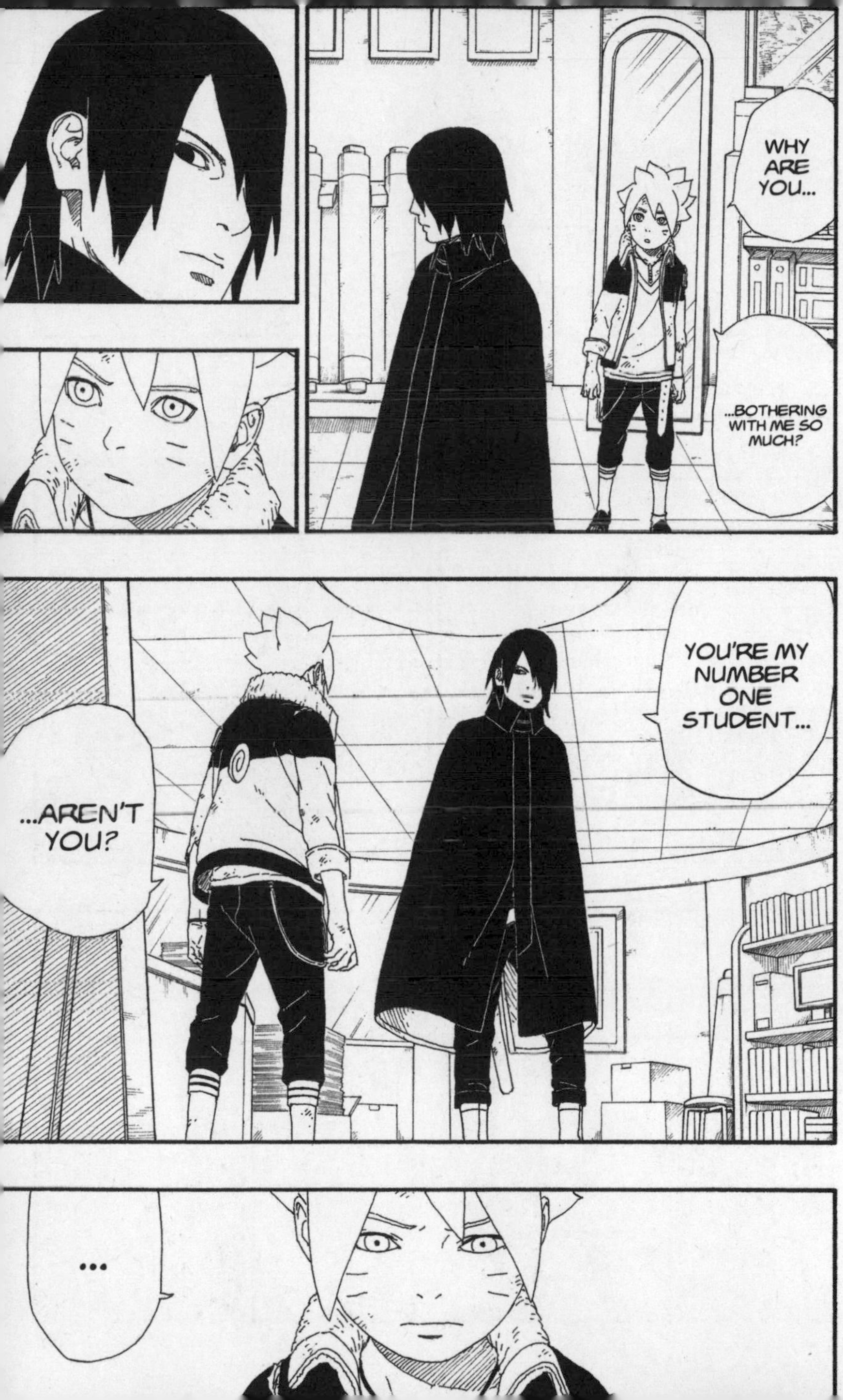
WHY ARE YOU...
...BOTHERING WITH ME SO MUCH?
YOU'RE MY NUMBER ONE STUDENT...
...AREN'T YOU?
...

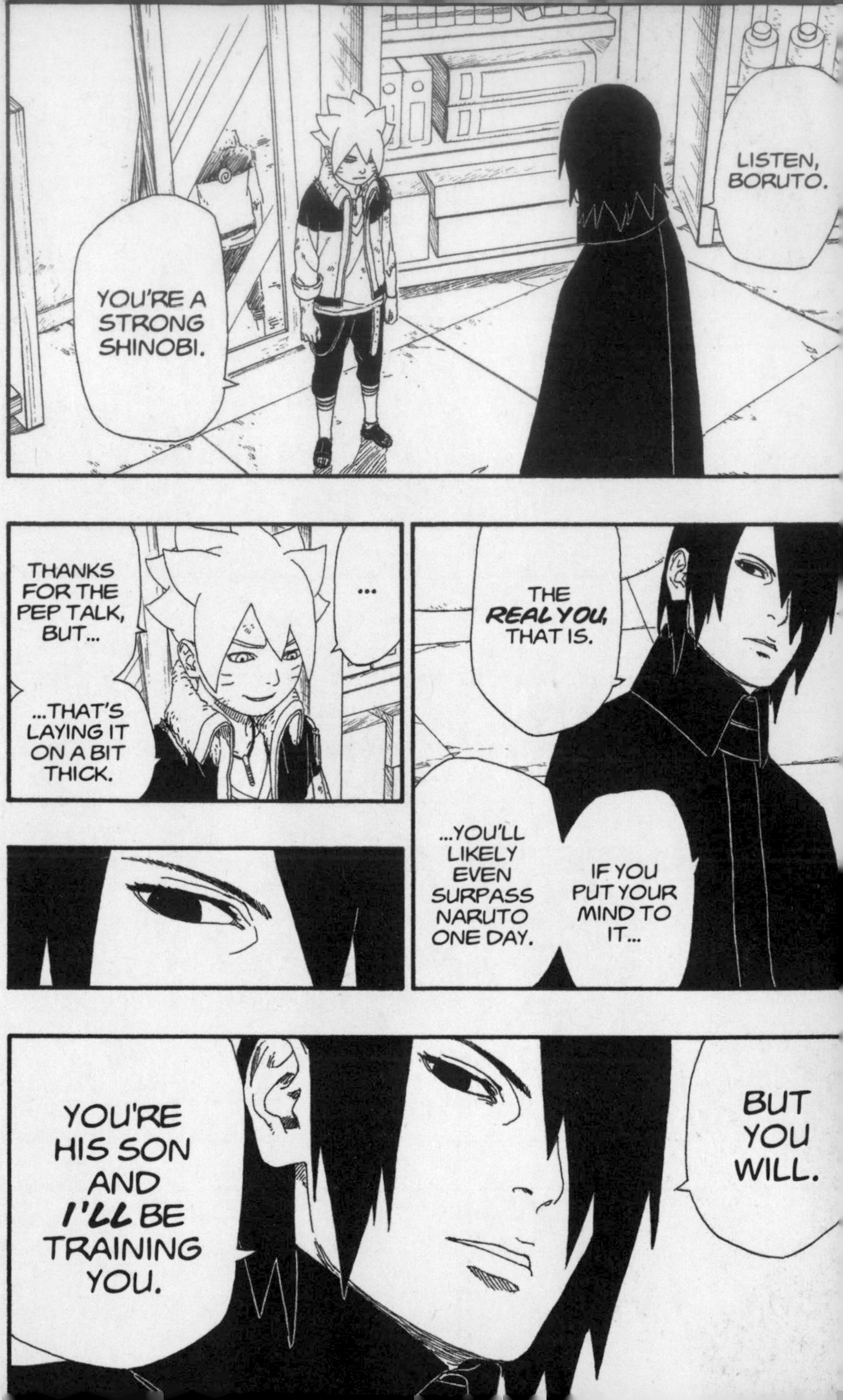
LISTEN, BORUTO.
YOU'RE A STRONG SHINOBI.
THE *REAL YOU,* THAT IS.
IF YOU PUT YOUR MIND TO IT...
...YOU'LL LIKELY EVEN SURPASS NARUTO ONE DAY.
...
THANKS FOR THE PEP TALK, BUT...
...THAT'S LAYING IT ON A BIT THICK.
BUT YOU WILL.
YOU'RE HIS SON AND *I'LL* BE TRAINING YOU.

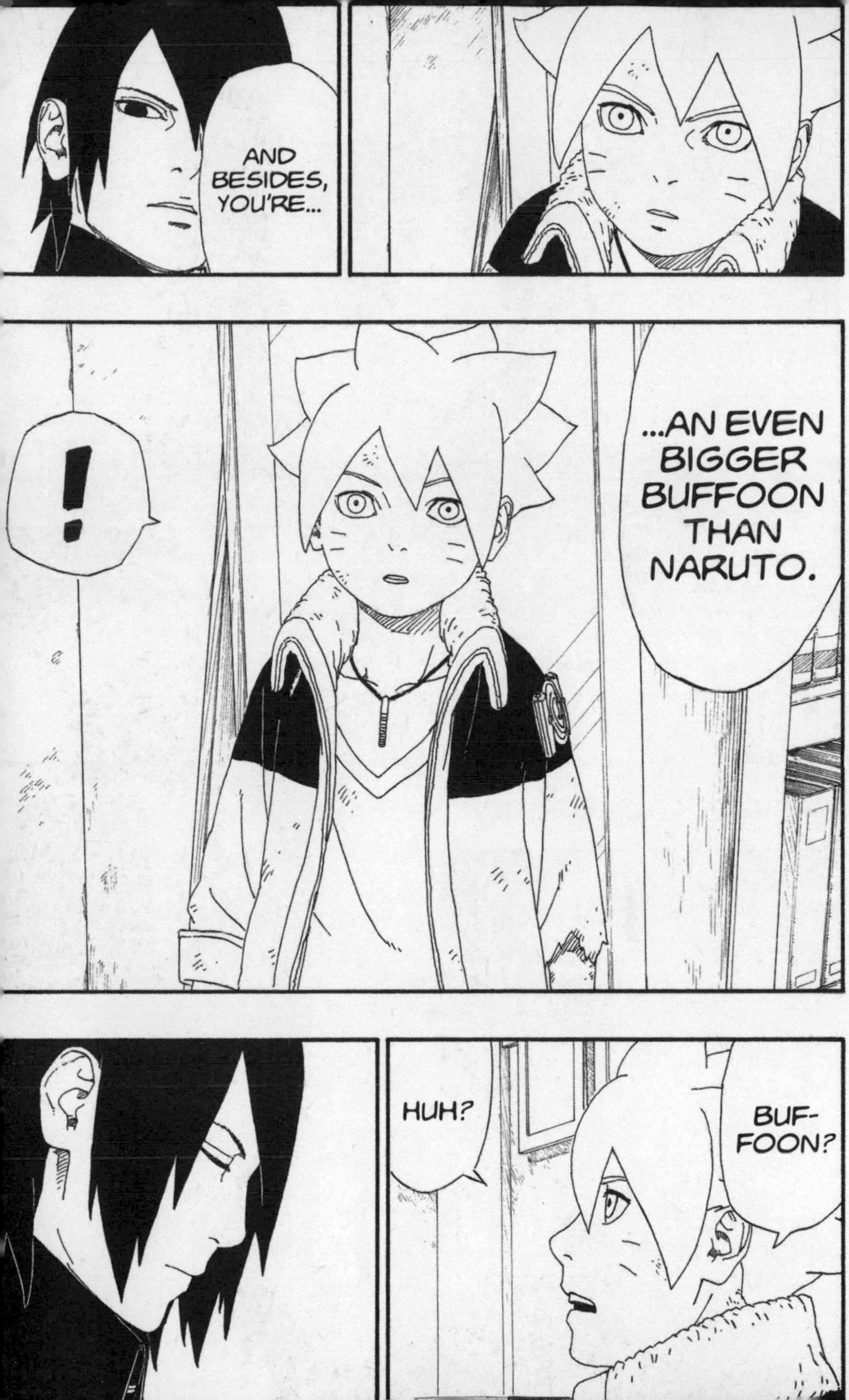
AND BESIDES, YOU'RE...
...AN EVEN BIGGER BUFFOON THAN NARUTO.
!
BUF-FOON?
HUH?

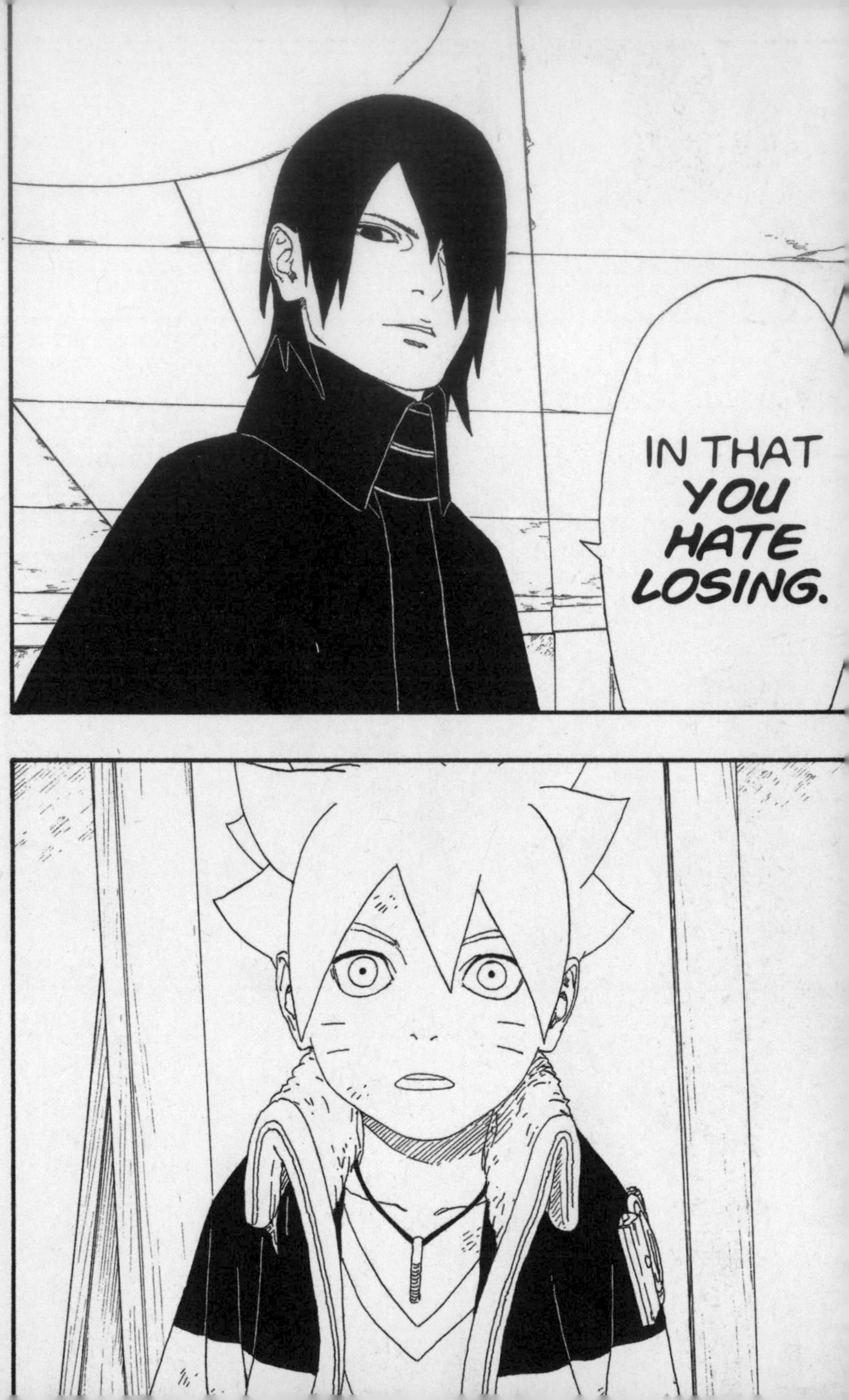
IN THAT YOU HATE LOSING.

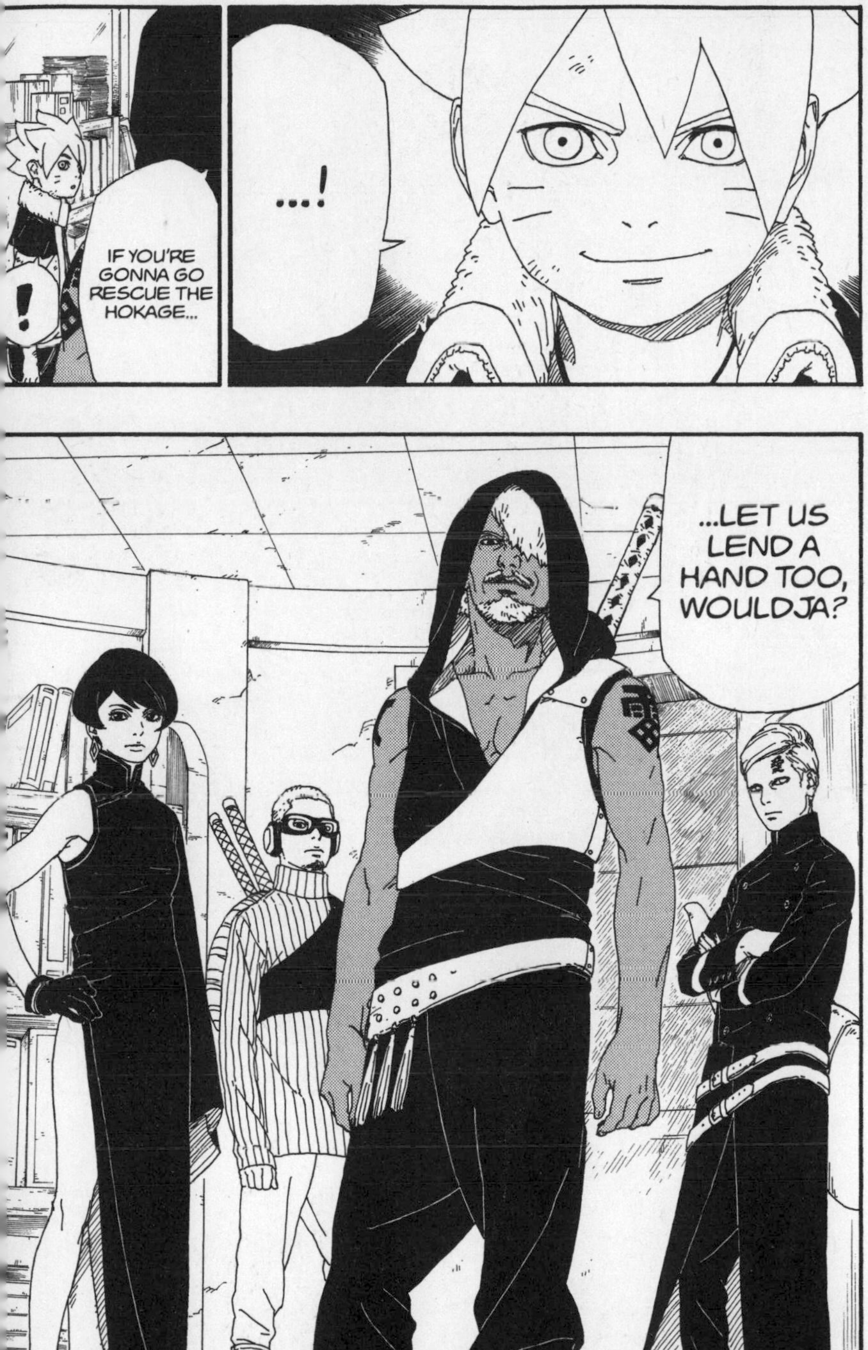
...!
IF YOU'RE GONNA GO RESCUE THE HOKAGE...
!
...LET US LEND A HAND TOO, WOULDJA?

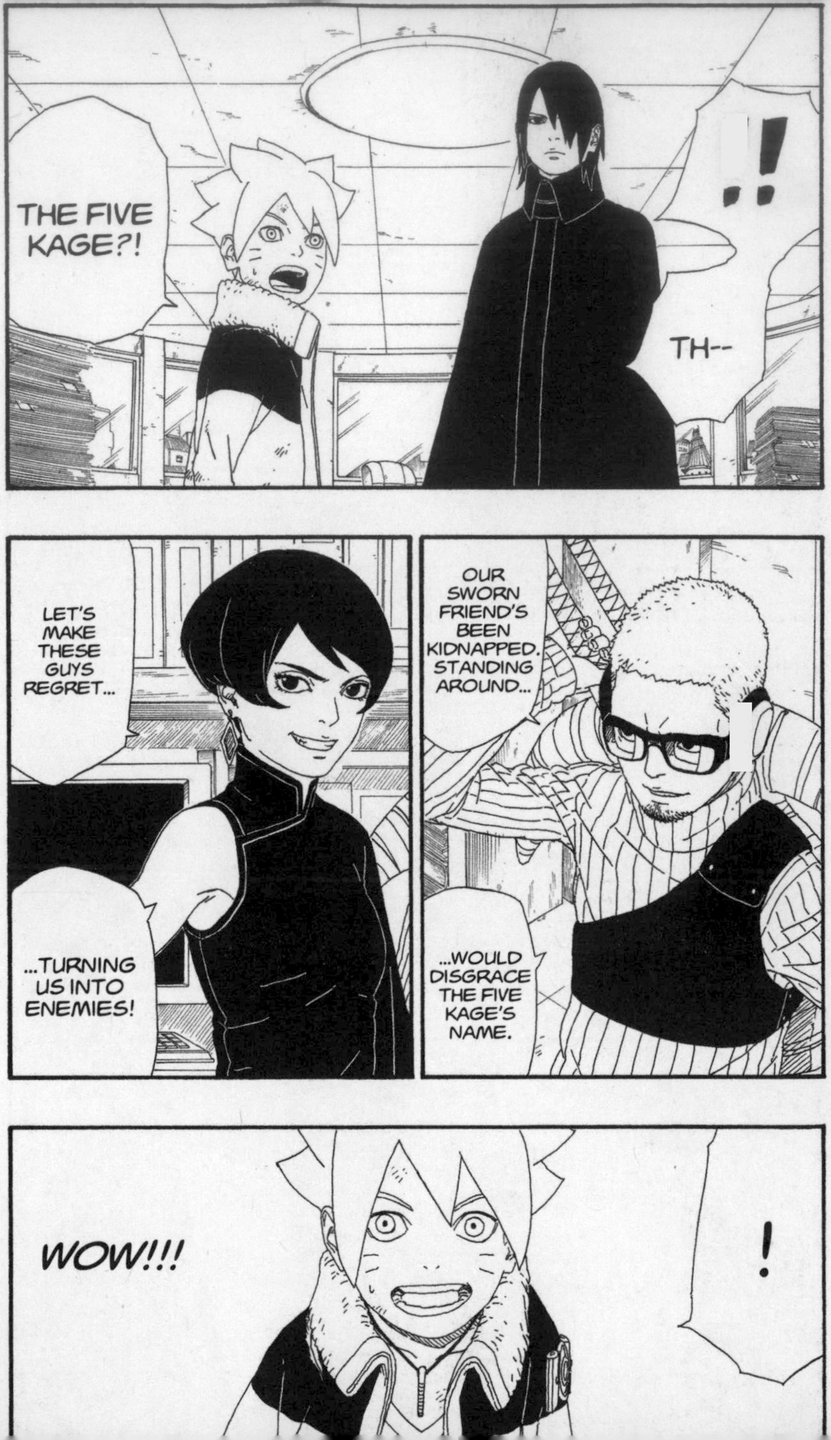
!!
TH--
THE FIVE KAGE?!
OUR SWORN FRIEND'S BEEN KIDNAPPED. STANDING AROUND...
...WOULD DISGRACE THE FIVE KAGE'S NAME.
LET'S MAKE THESE GUYS REGRET...
...TURNING US INTO ENEMIES!
!
WOW!!!

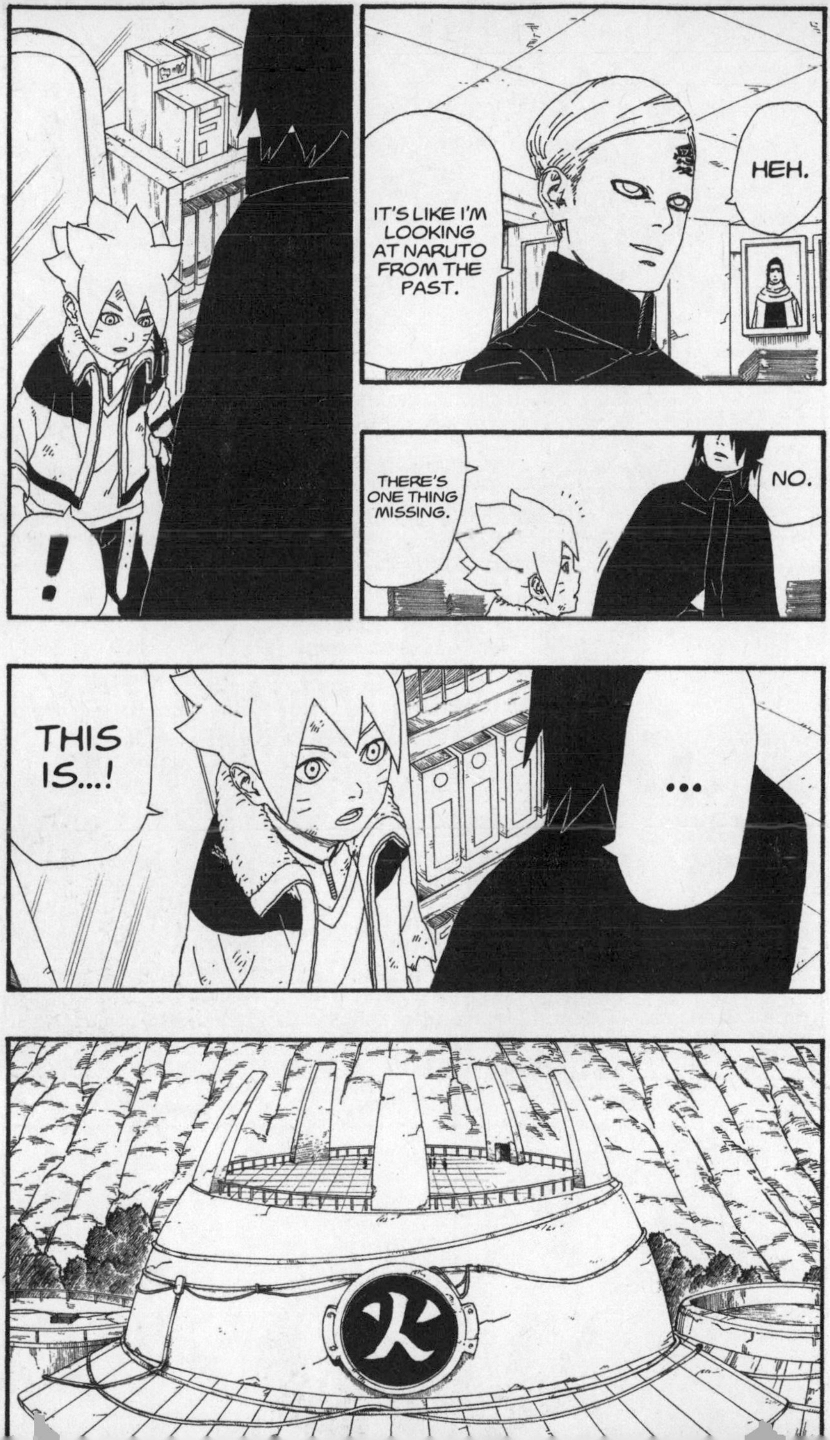
HEH.
IT'S LIKE I'M LOOKING AT NARUTO FROM THE PAST.
NO.
THERE'S ONE THING MISSING.
!
...
THIS IS...!

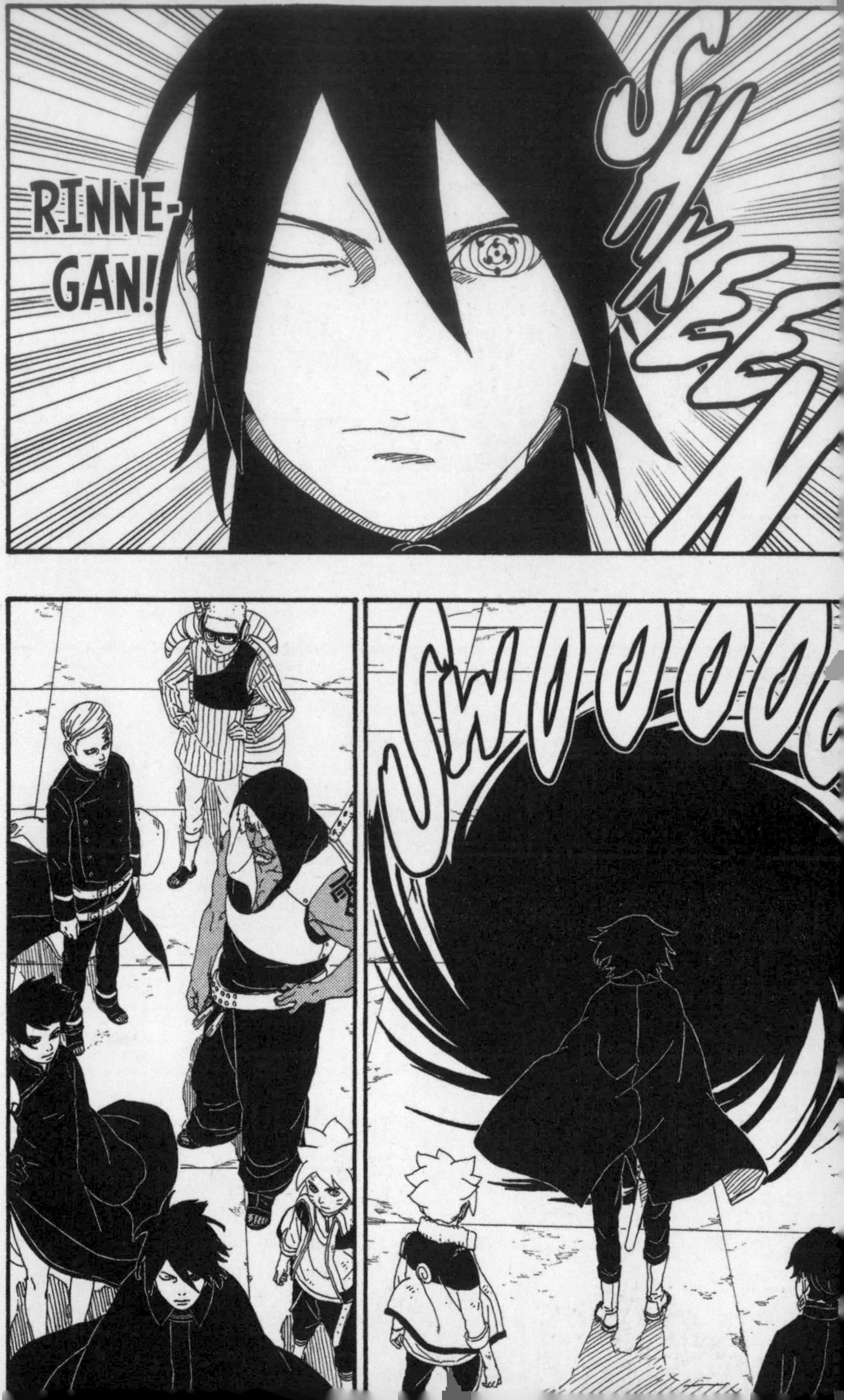
SHKEEN
RINNE-GAN!
SWOOOO

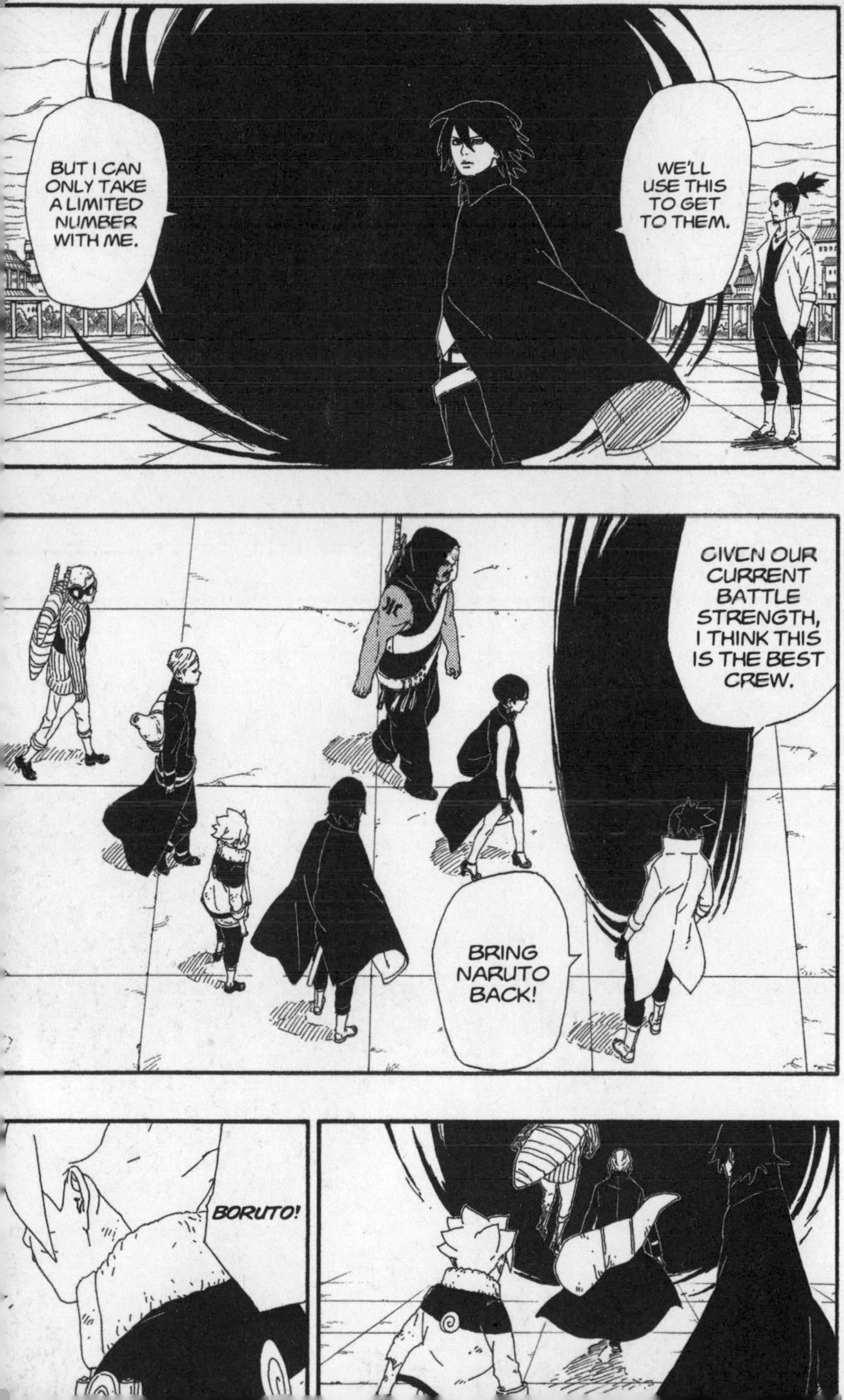
WE'LL USE THIS TO GET TO THEM.
BUT I CAN ONLY TAKE A LIMITED NUMBER WITH ME.
GIVEN OUR CURRENT BATTLE STRENGTH, I THINK THIS IS THE BEST CREW.
BRING NARUTO BACK!
BORUTO!

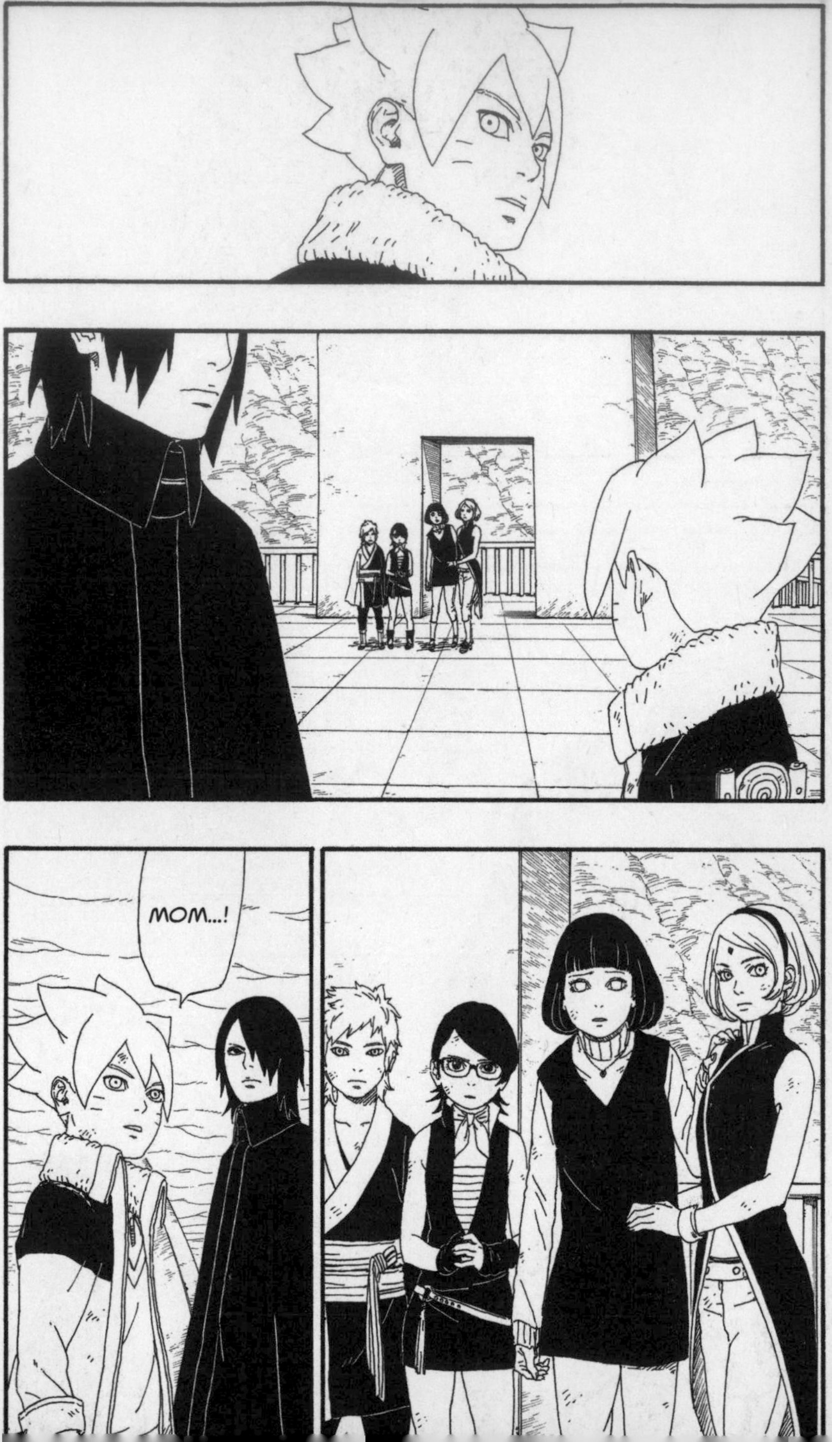
MOM...!

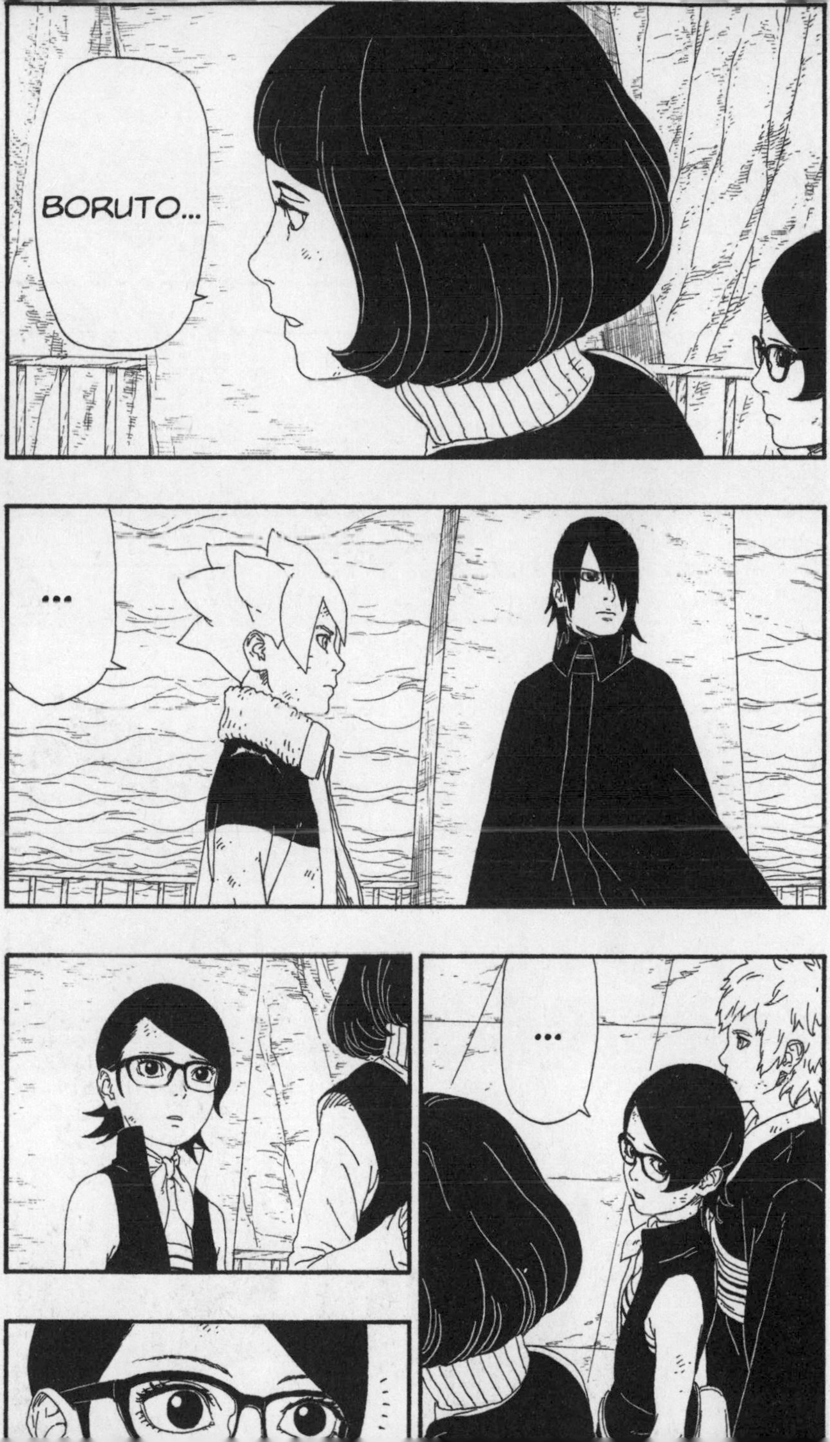
BORUTO...
...
...

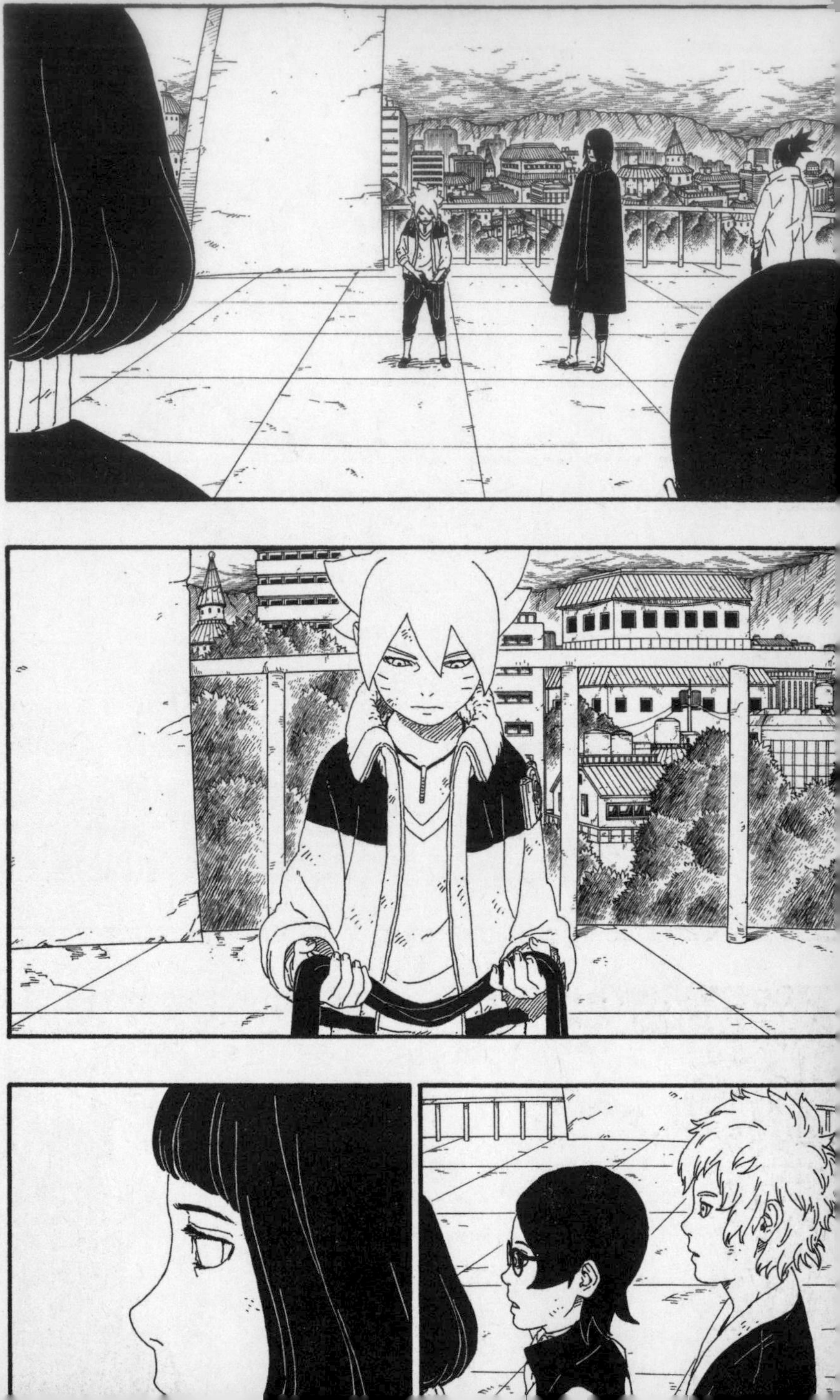

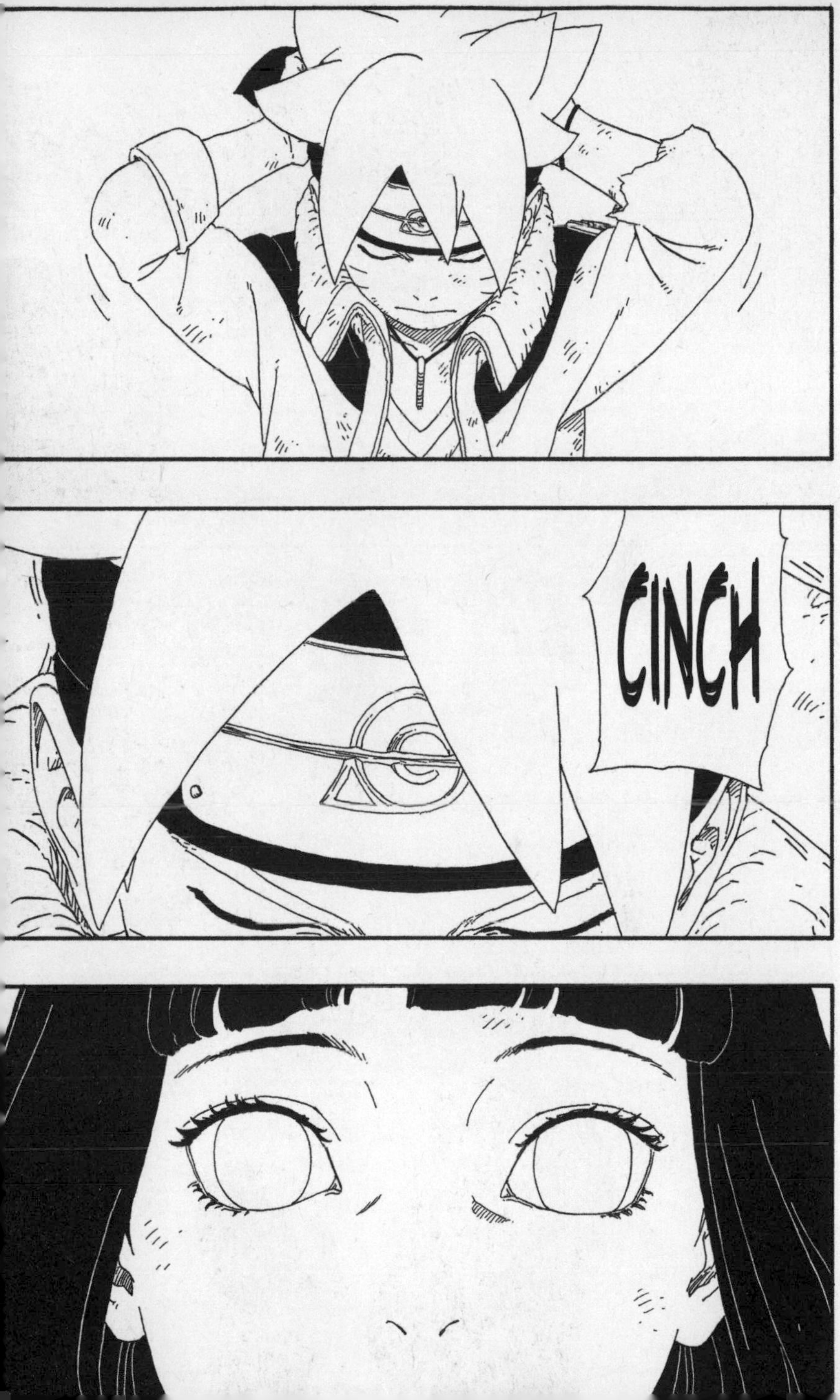
CINCH

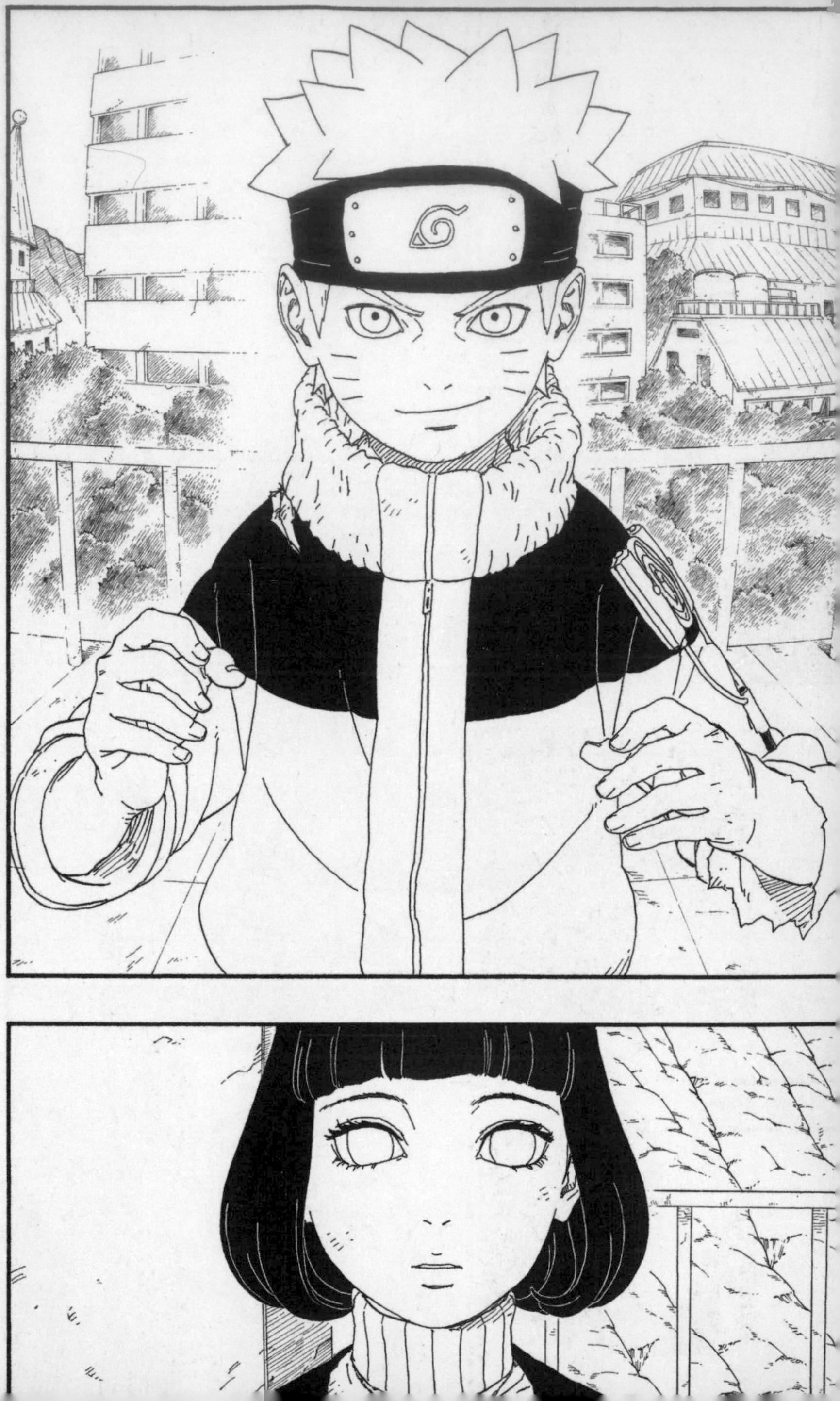

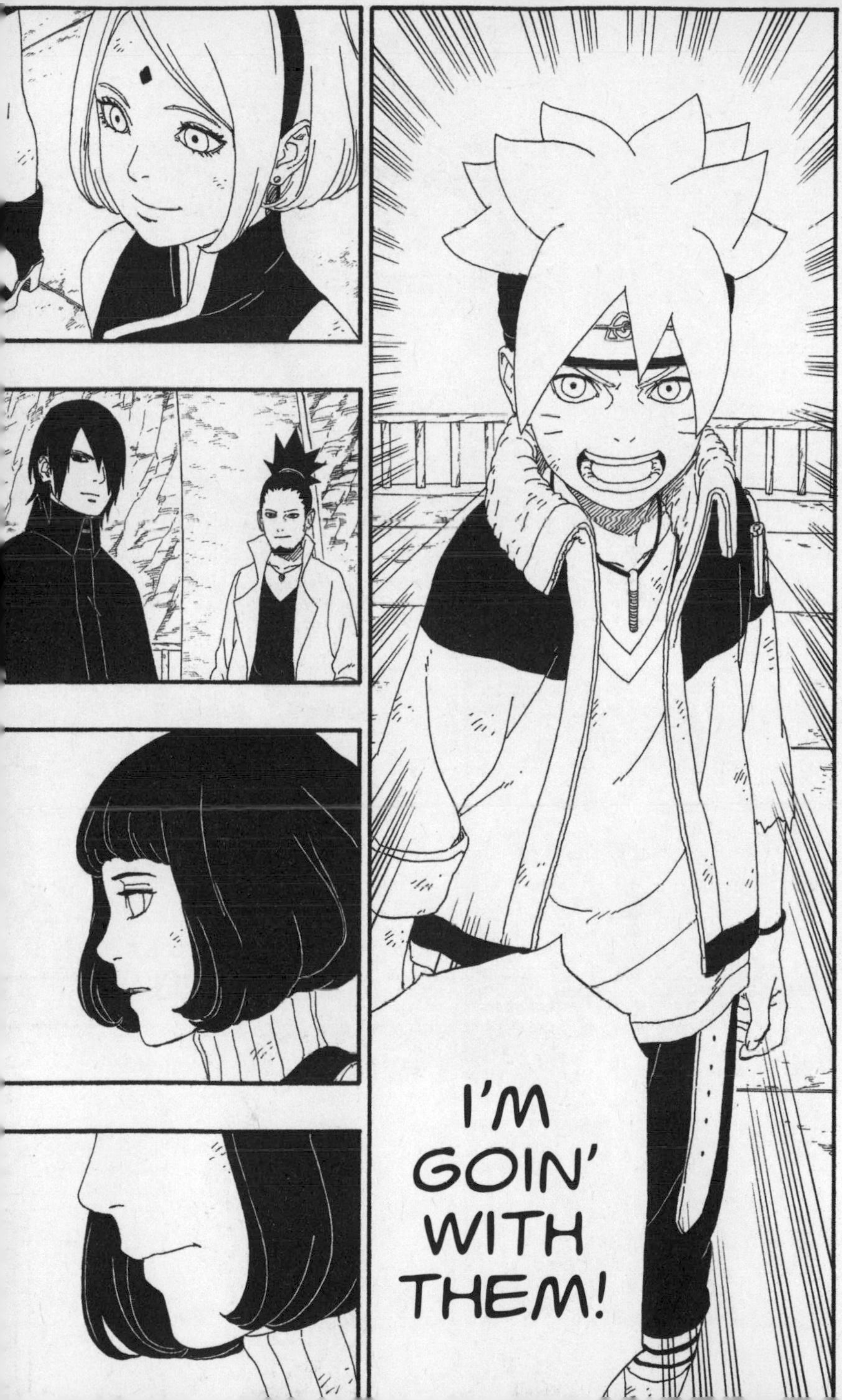
I'M GOIN' WITH THEM!

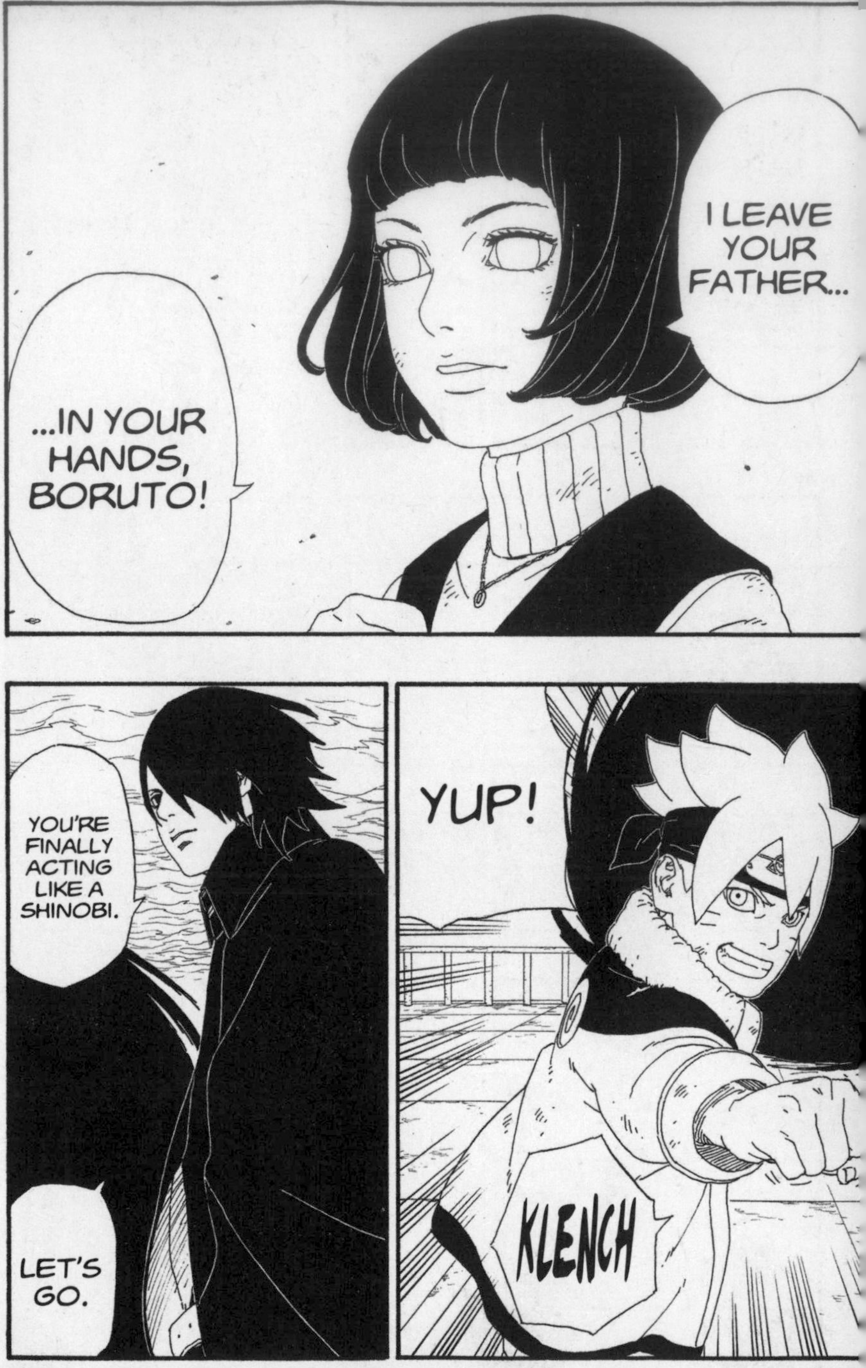
I LEAVE YOUR FATHER...
...IN YOUR HANDS, BORUTO!
YUP!
KLENCH
YOU'RE FINALLY ACTING LIKE A SHINOBI.
LET'S GO.

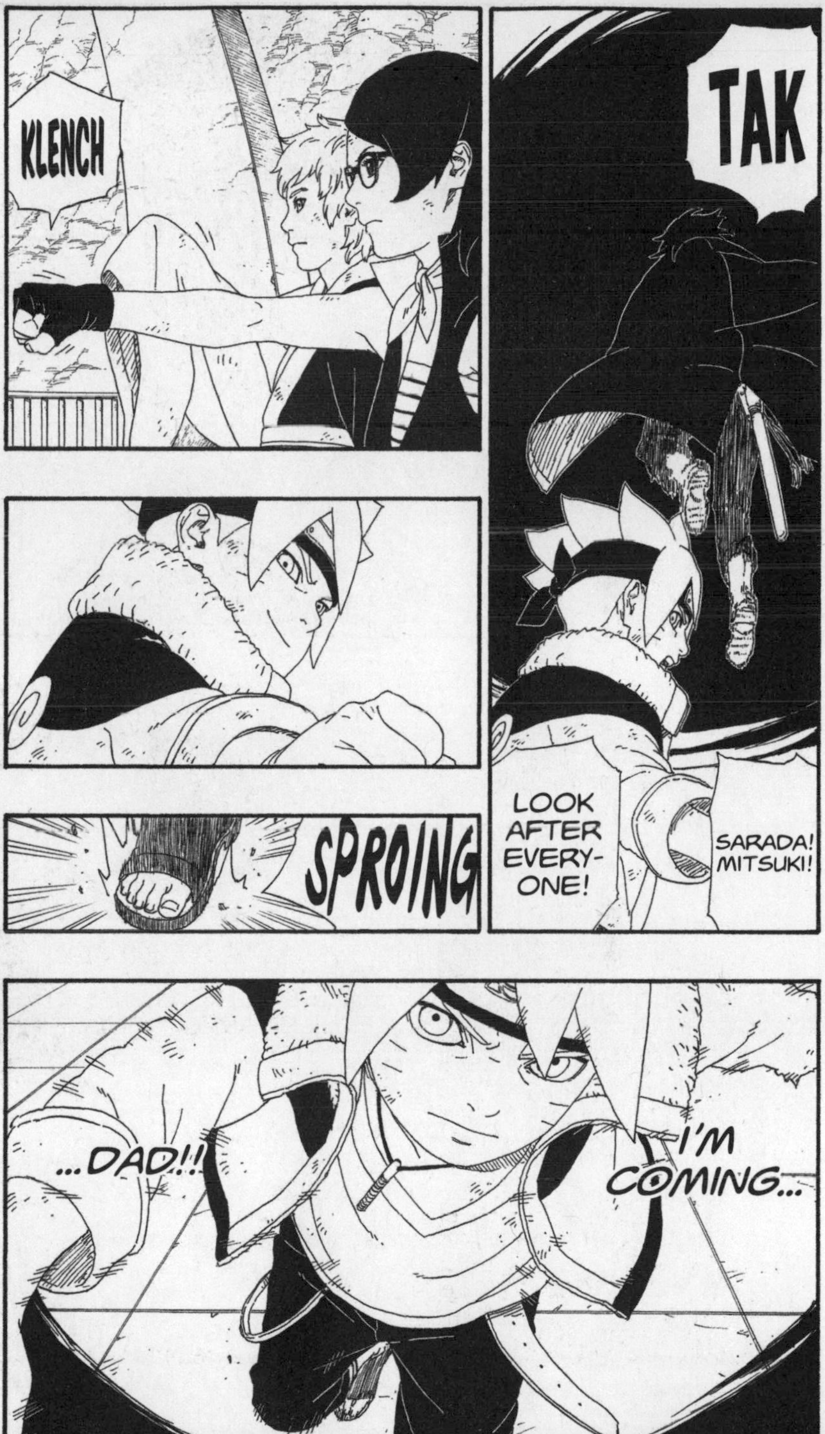
TAK
SARADA! MITSUKI!
LOOK AFTER EVERY-ONE!
KLENCH
SPROING
I'M COMING...
...DAD!!

NINJA ENCYCLOPEDIA • ENTRY 6

AKIMICHI CHO-CHO

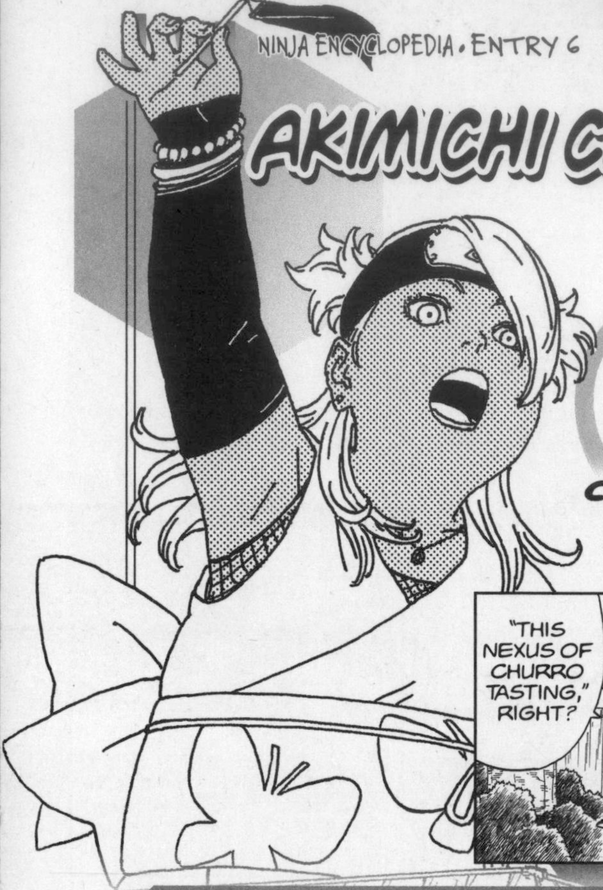

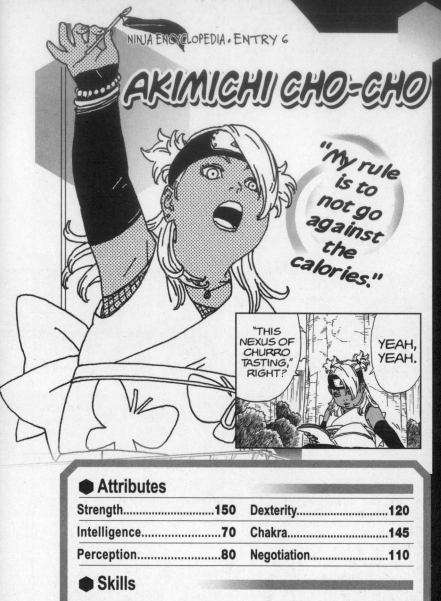

"My rule is to not go against the calories."

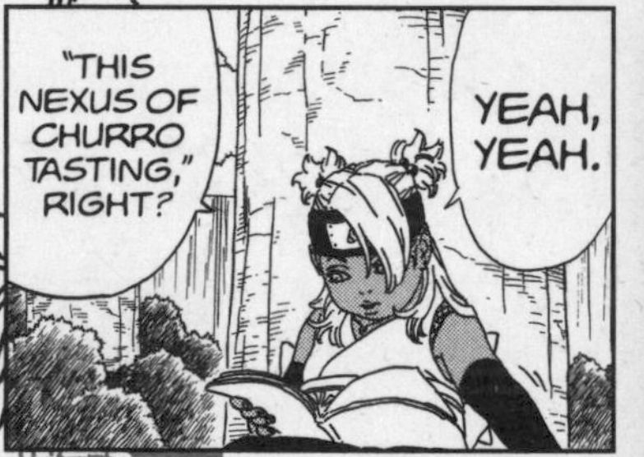
YEAH, YEAH.
"THIS NEXUS OF CHURRO TASTING," RIGHT?

● Attributes

Strength	150	Dexterity	120
Intelligence	70	Chakra	145
Perception	80	Negotiation	110

● Skills

Mental strength ☆☆☆☆ **Resistance** ☆☆☆ **Hand-to-hand combat** ☆☆☆ etc.

● Ninja Arts

Expansion, Butterfly Transformation, Human Juggernaut, Raiton Thunderclap Punch, etc.

*Average attribute value is 60 for ordinary people and 90 for genin.
Skill values range from 1 to 5☆ with 5☆ signifying super top-notch.

Number 7: Collision...!!

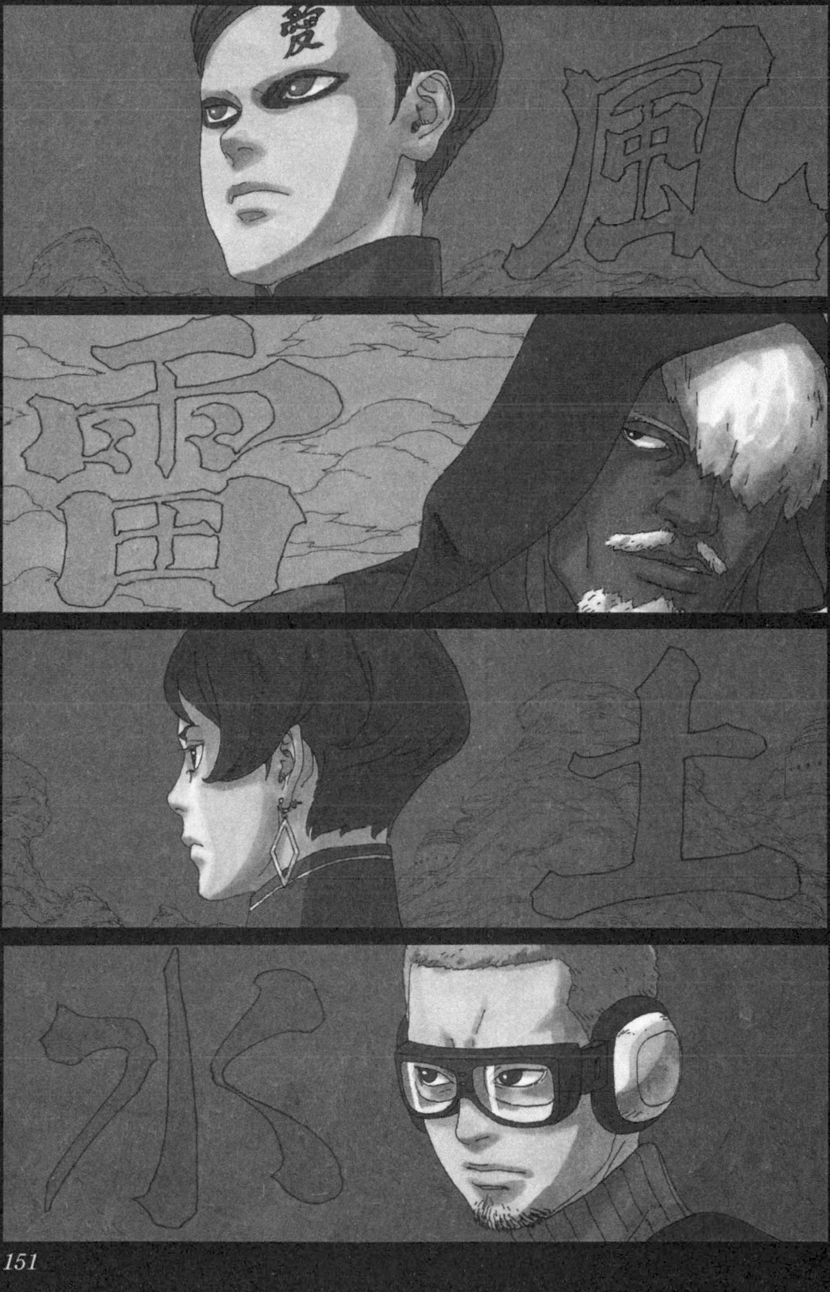
風
雷
土
水

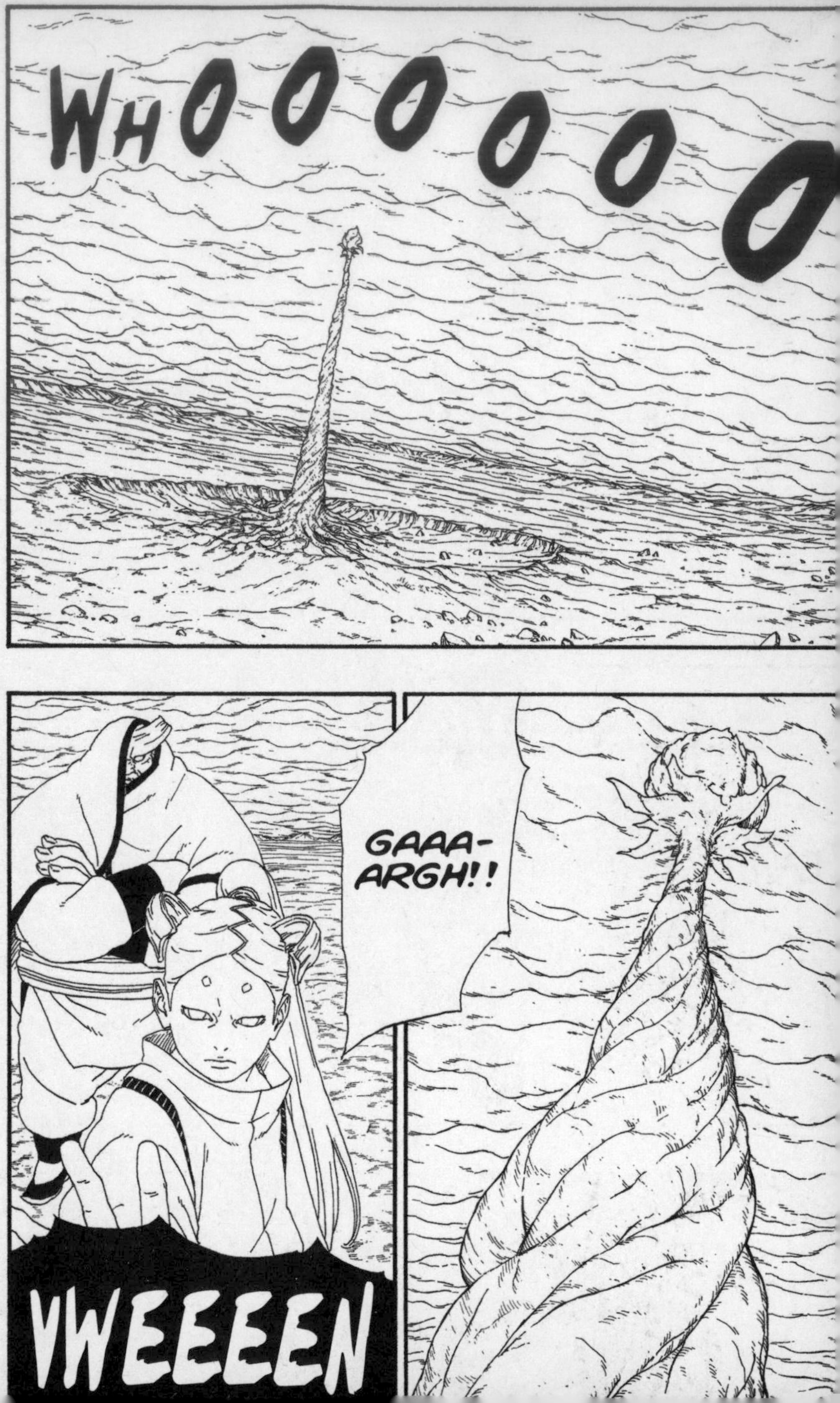
WHOOOOOO
GAAA-ARGH!!
VWEEEEN

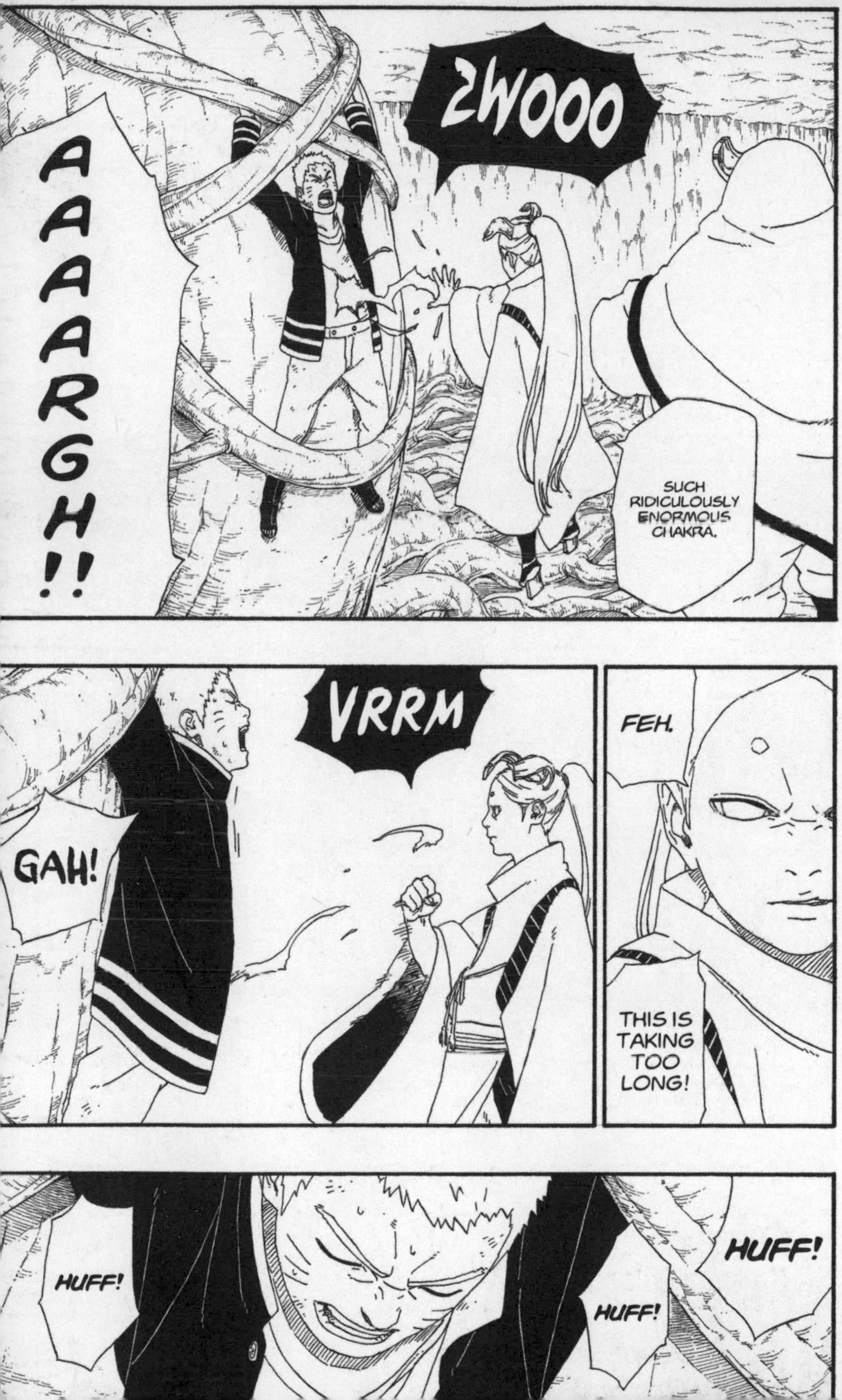
SWOOO
SUCH RIDICULOUSLY ENORMOUS CHAKRA.
AAAARGH!!
FEH.
THIS IS TAKING TOO LONG!
VRRM
GAH!
HUFF!
HUFF!
HUFF!

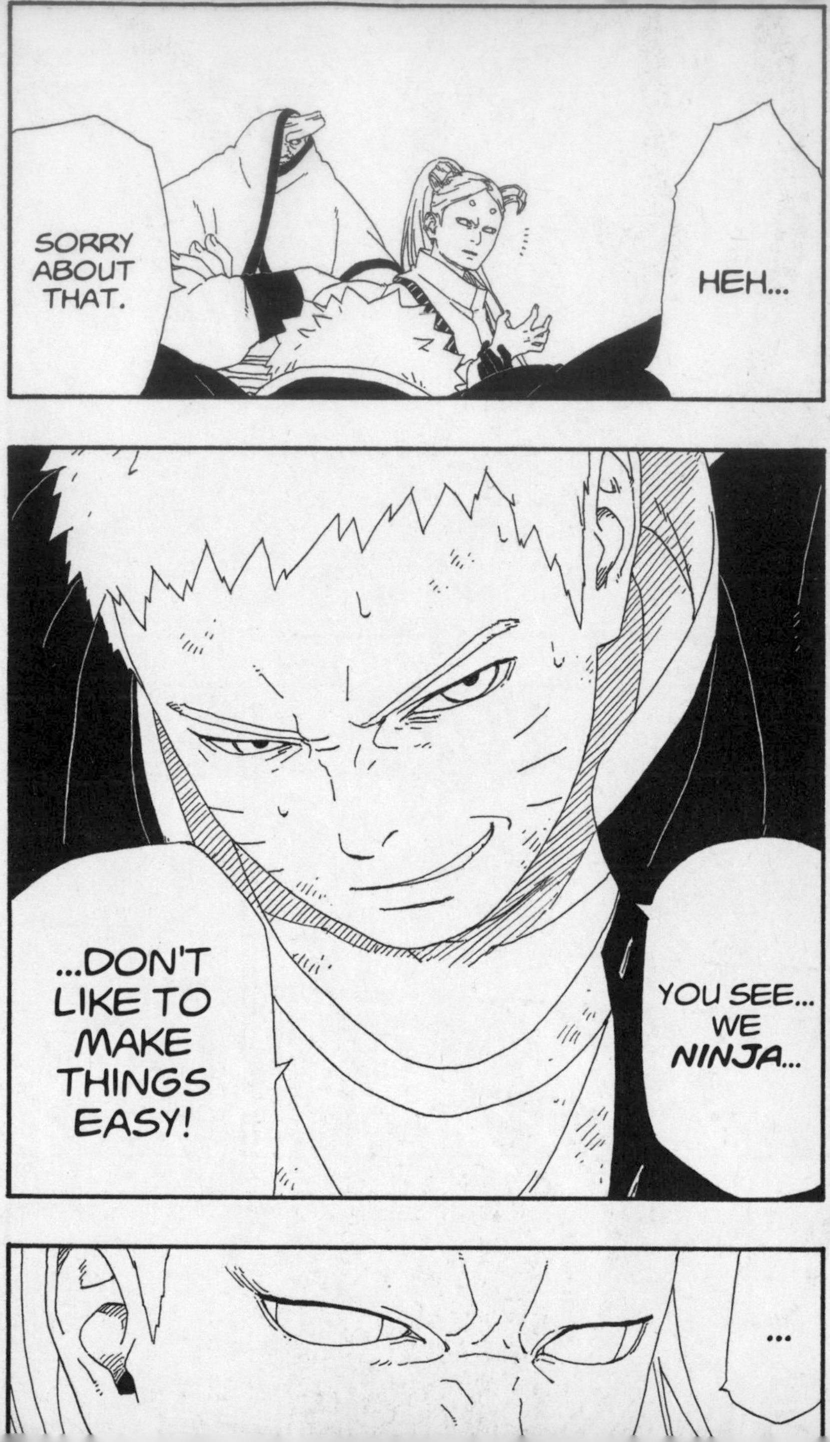
HEH...
SORRY ABOUT THAT.
YOU SEE... WE NINJA...
...DON'T LIKE TO MAKE THINGS EASY!
...

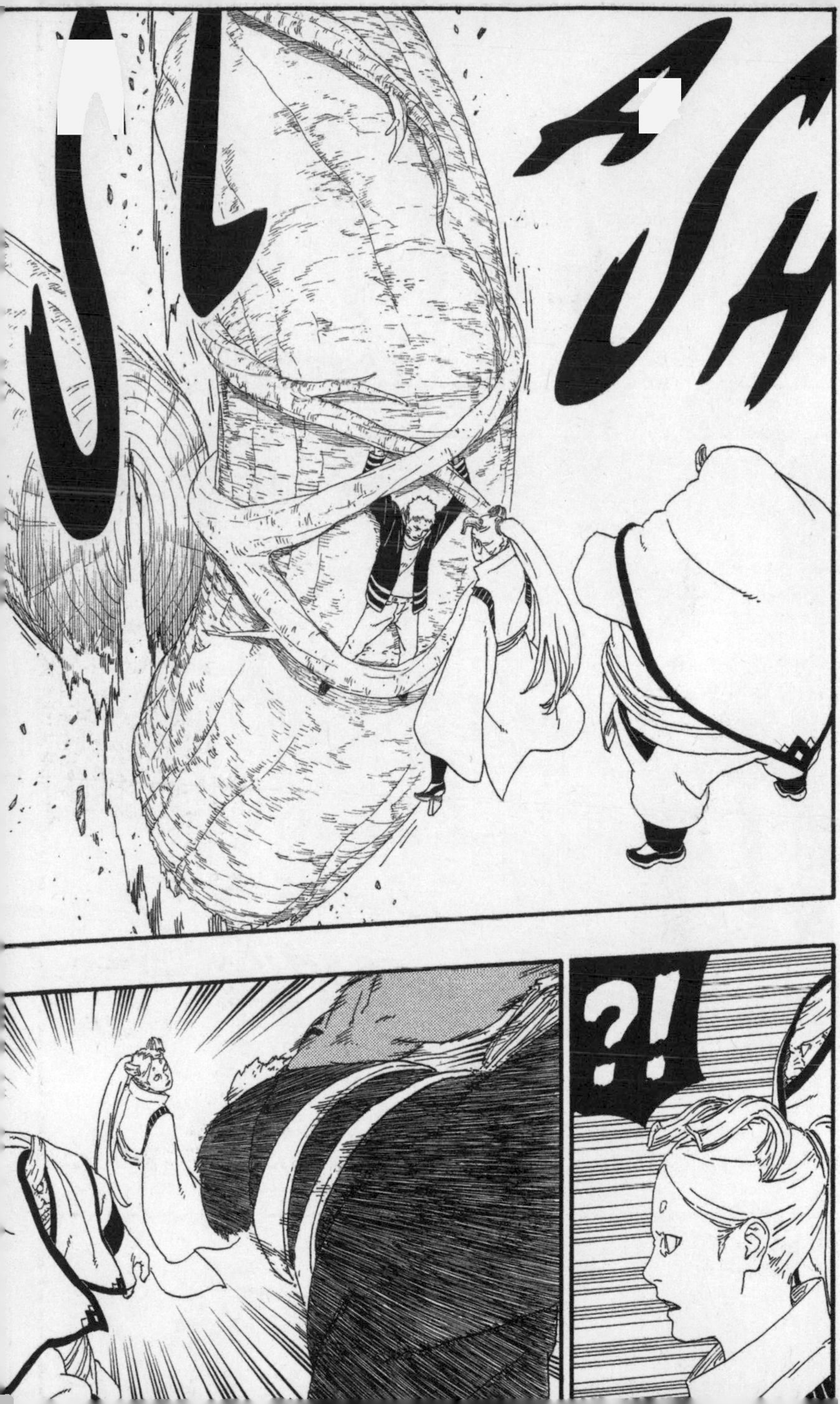
?!

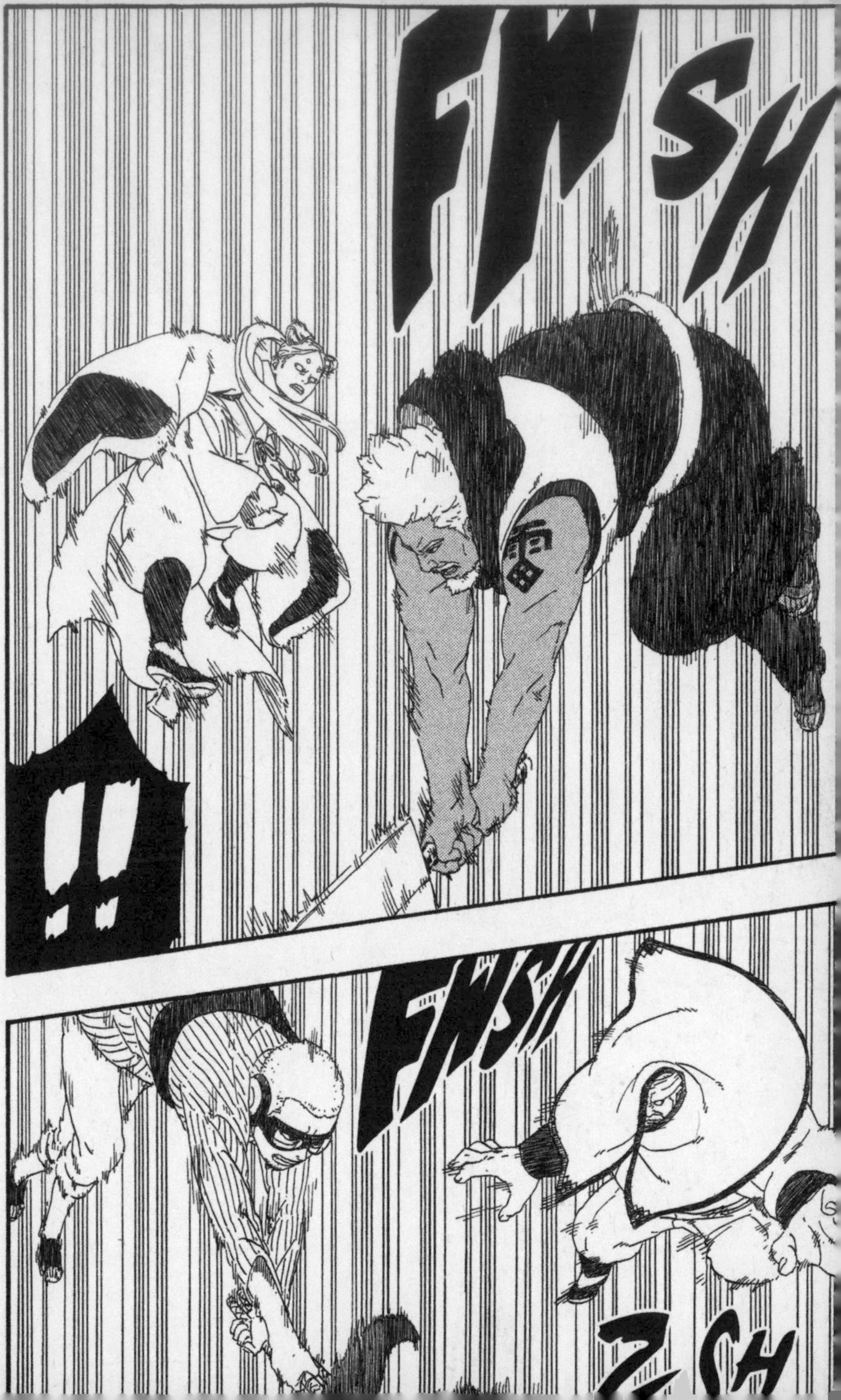
FWSH
!!
FWSH
ZSH

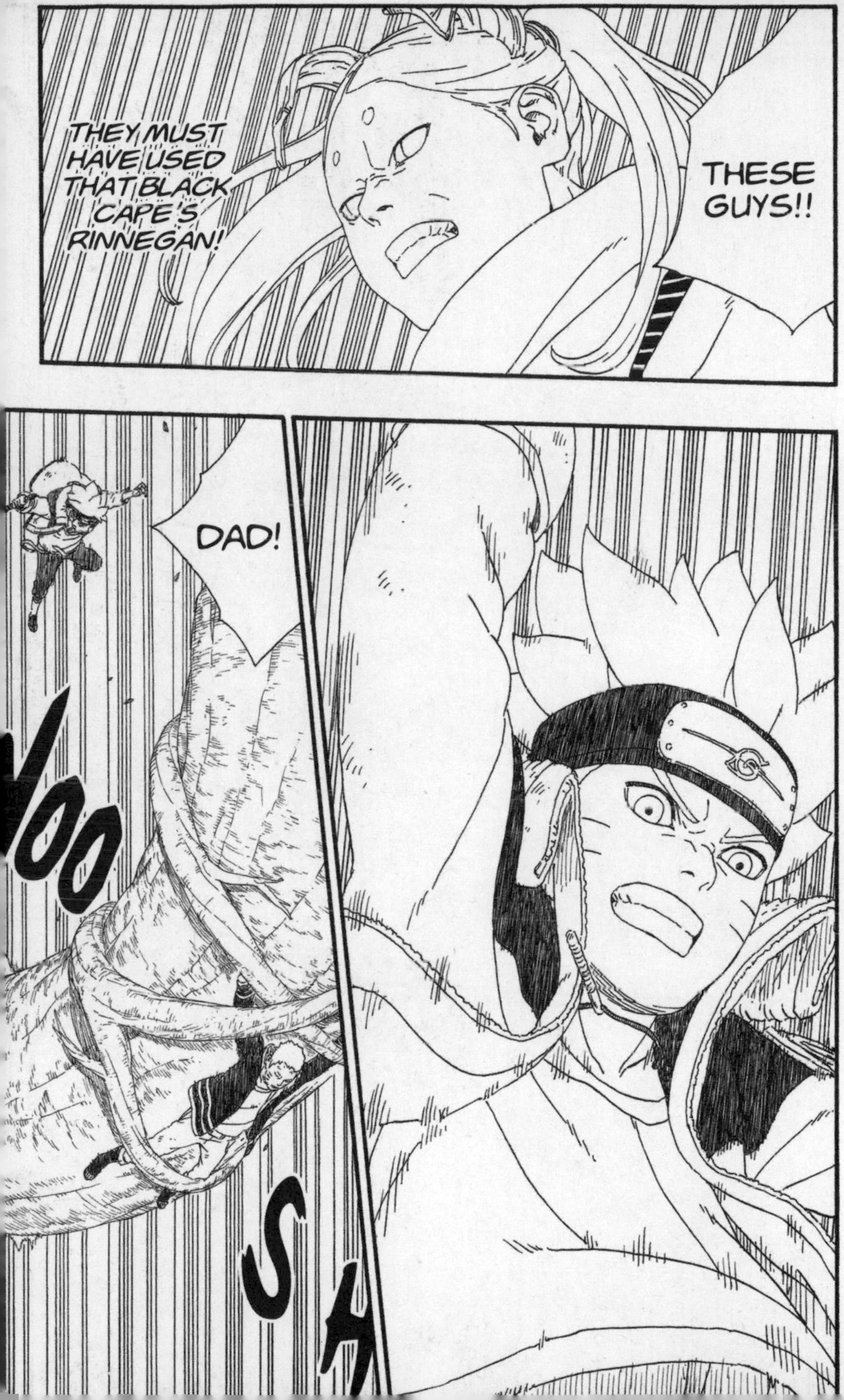
THESE GUYS!!
THEY MUST HAVE USED THAT BLACK CAPE'S RINNEGAN!
SH
DAD!

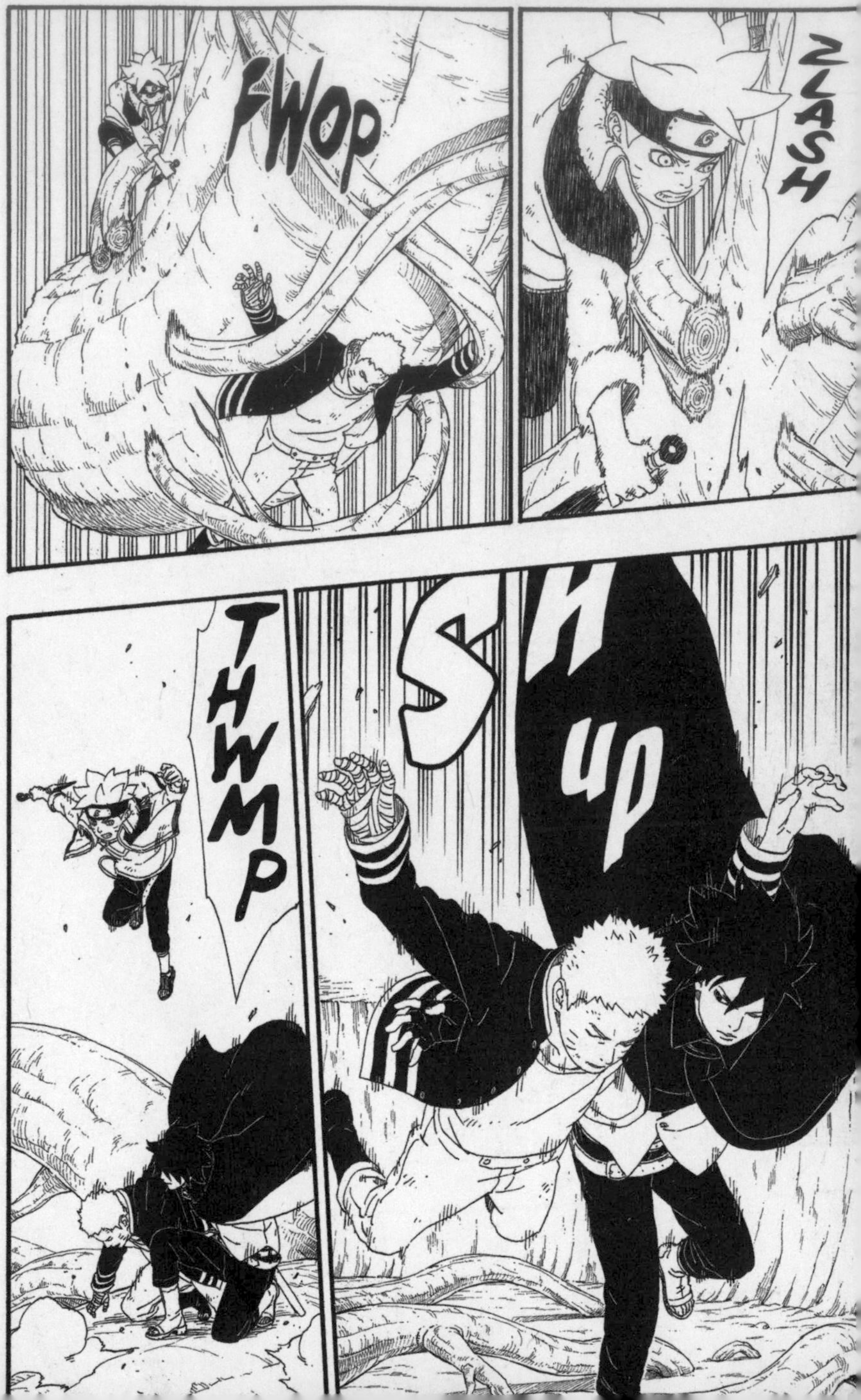
ZLASH
FWOP
SHUP
THWMP

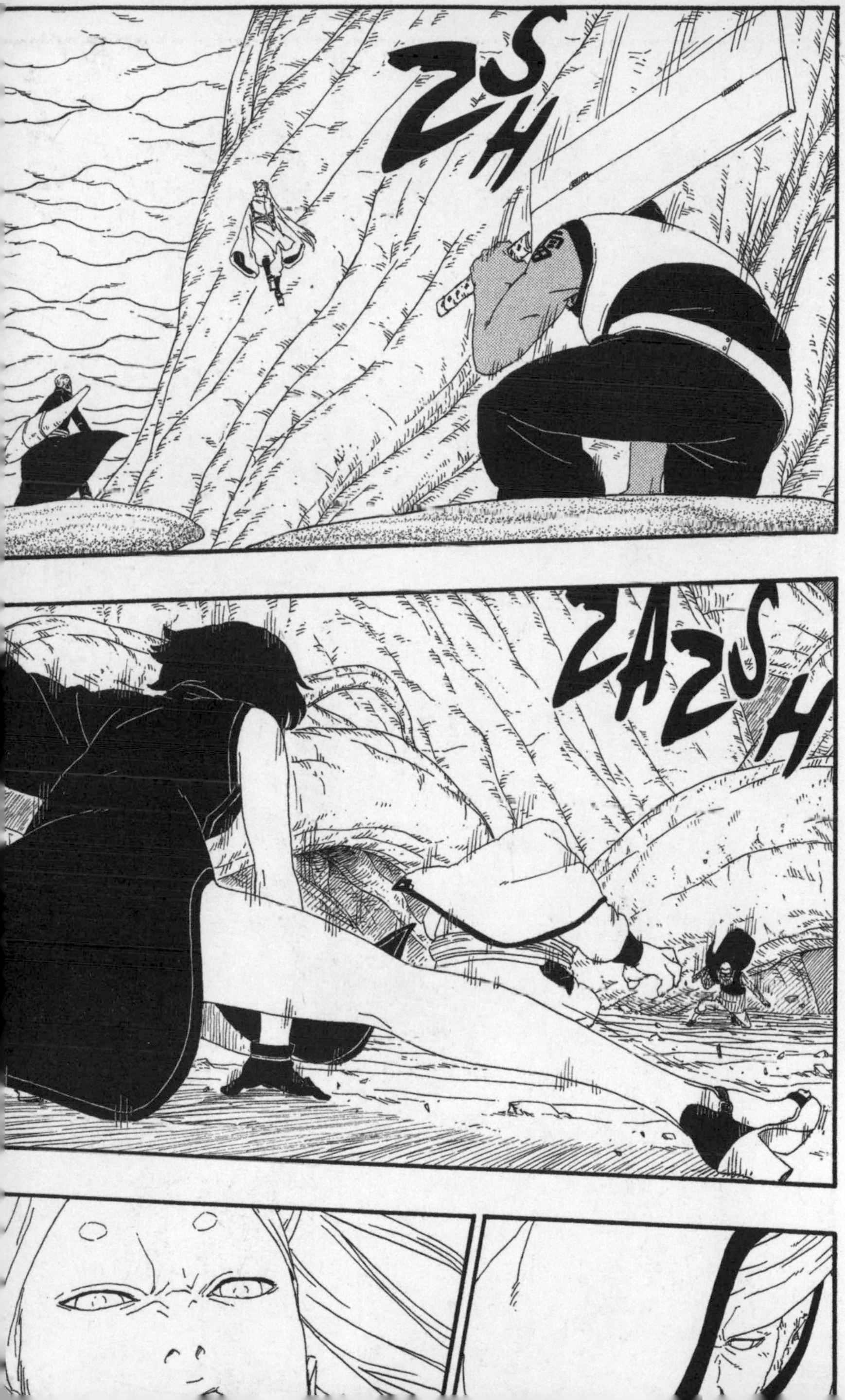
ZSH
ZASH

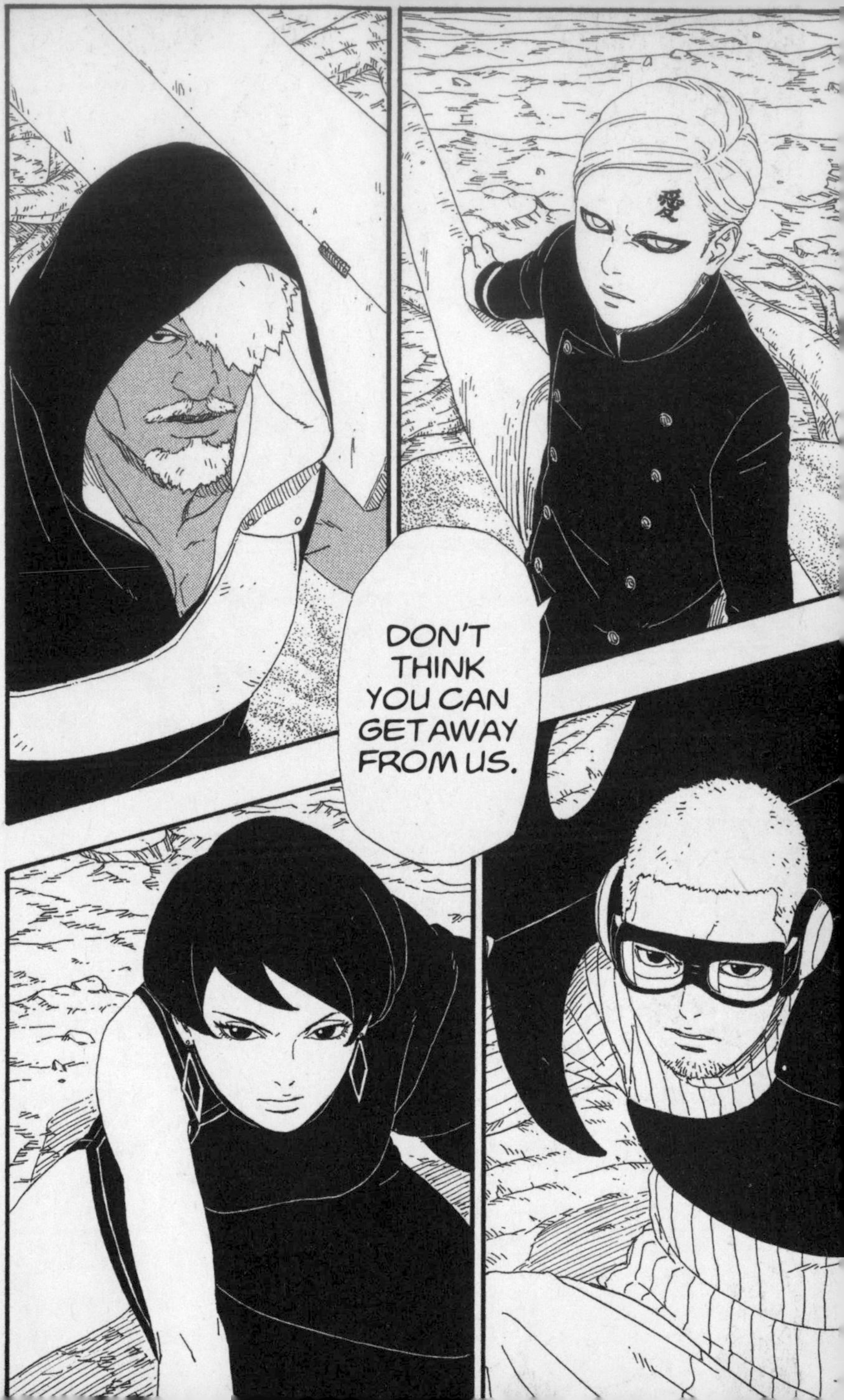
DON'T THINK YOU CAN GETAWAY FROM US.

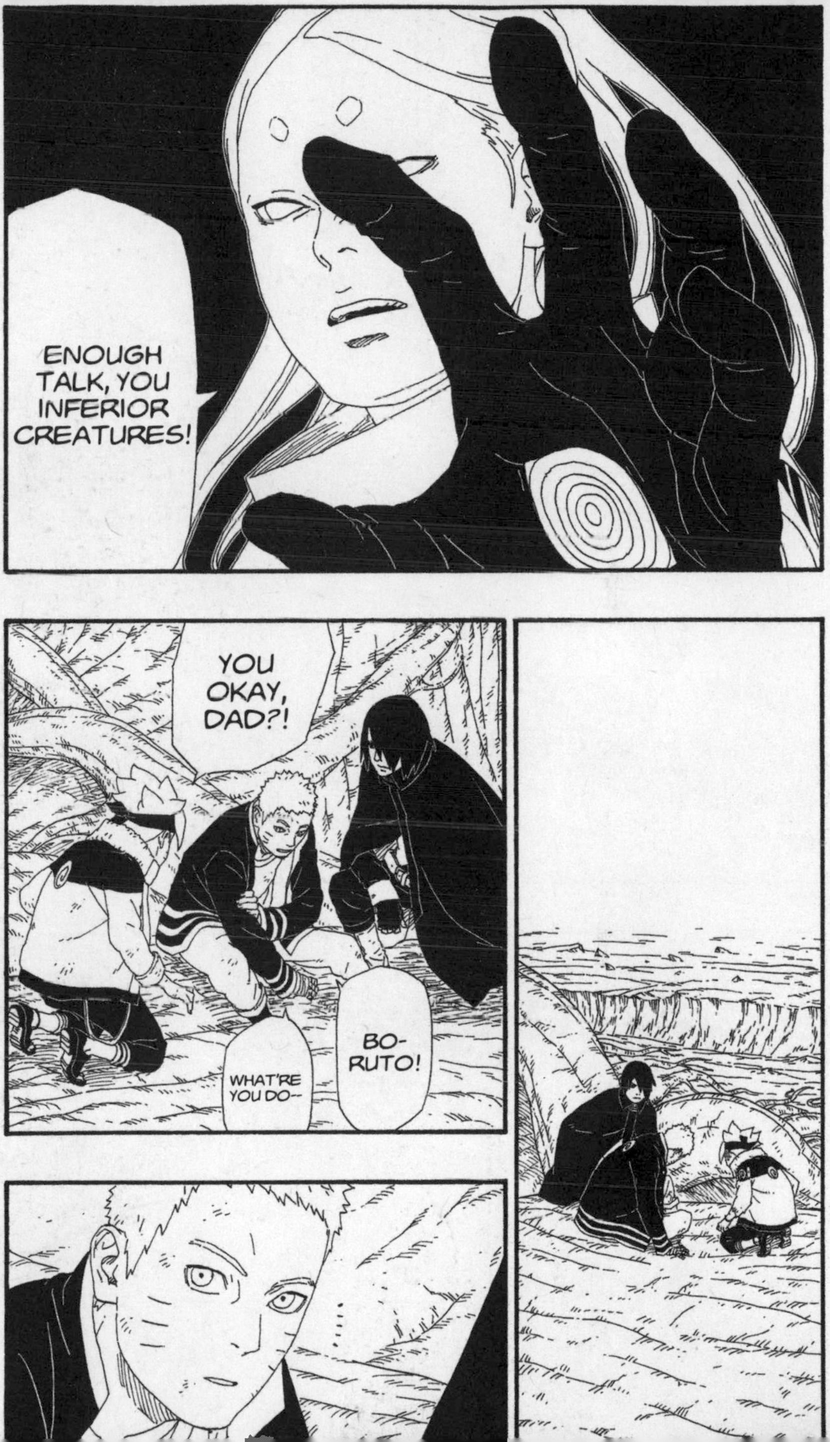
ENOUGH TALK, YOU INFERIOR CREATURES!
YOU OKAY, DAD?!
BO-RUTO!
WHAT'RE YOU DO--
...

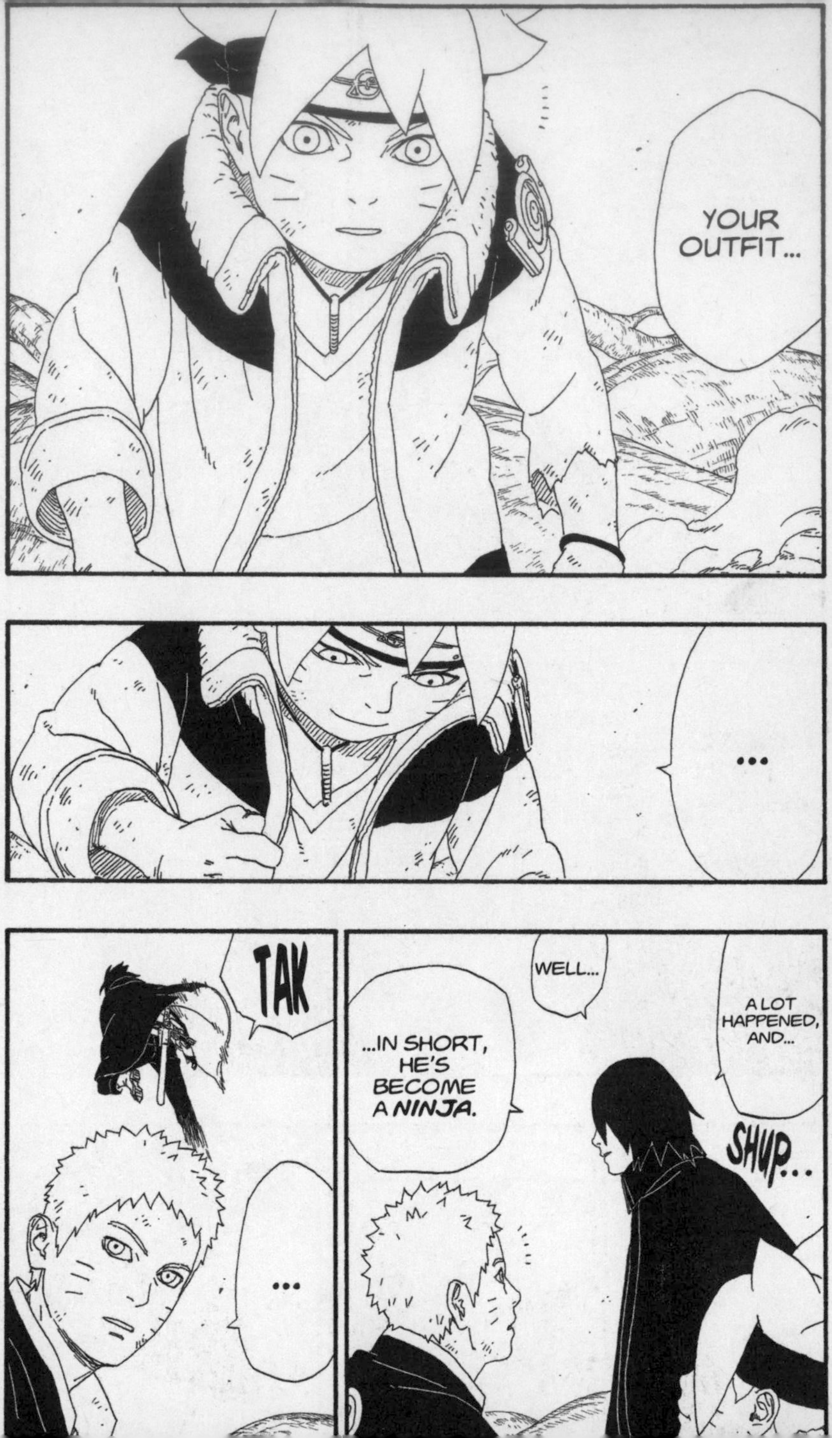
YOUR OUTFIT...
...
A LOT HAPPENED, AND...
WELL...
...IN SHORT, HE'S BECOME A NINJA.
SHUP...
TAK
...

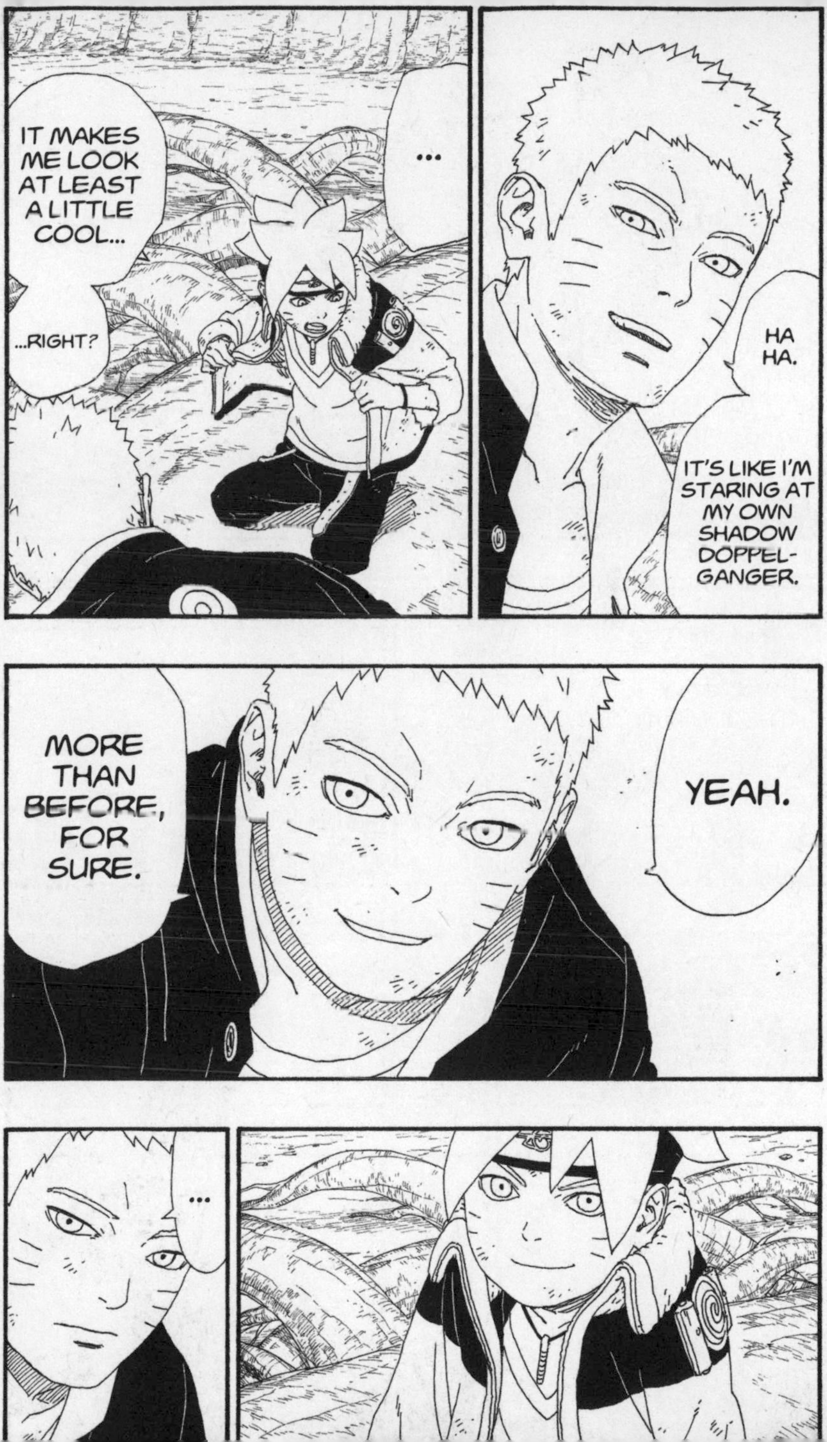
HA HA.
IT'S LIKE I'M STARING AT MY OWN SHADOW DOPPEL-GANGER.
...
IT MAKES ME LOOK AT LEAST A LITTLE COOL...
...RIGHT?
YEAH.
MORE THAN BEFORE, FOR SURE.
...

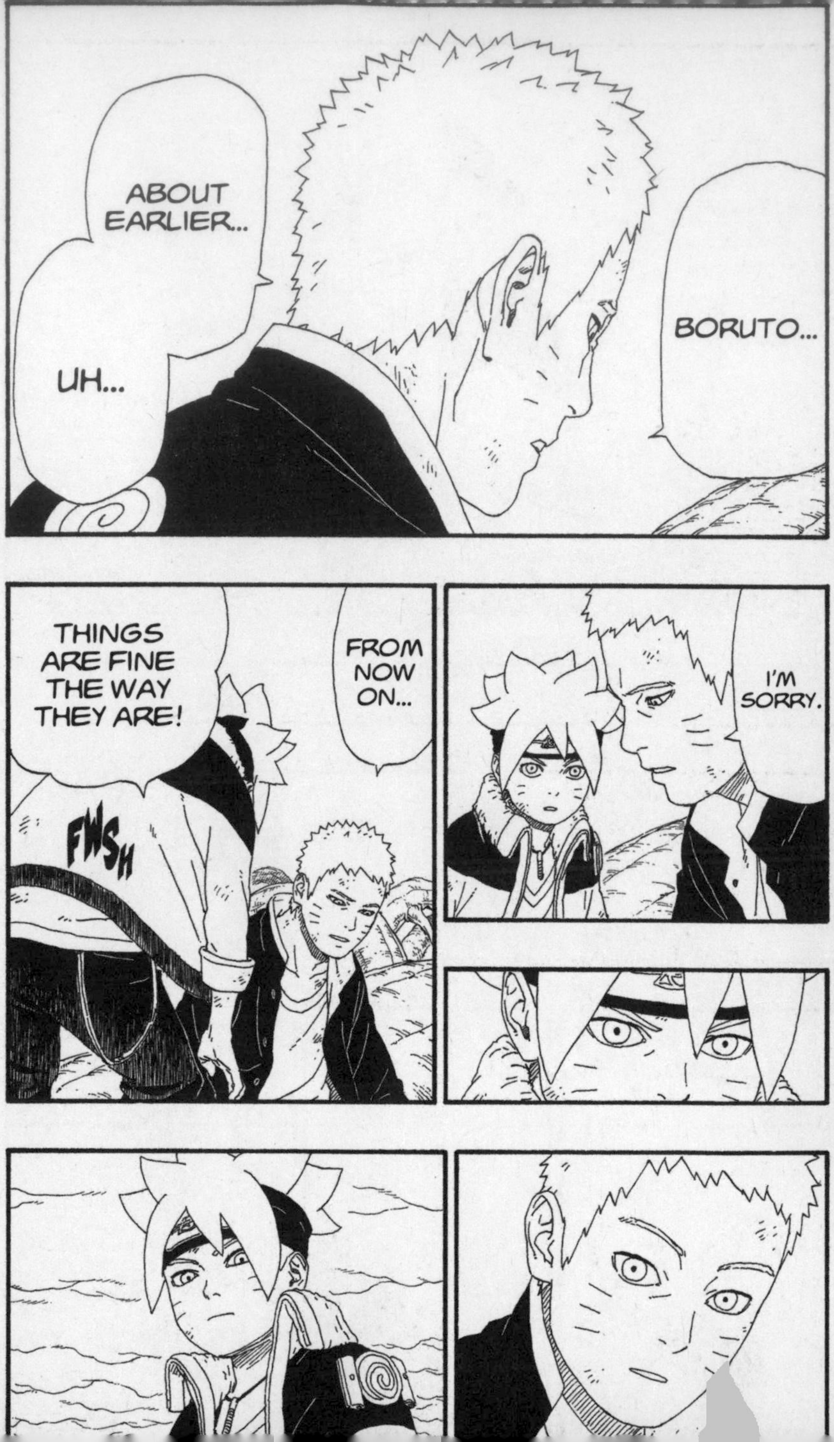
BORUTO...
ABOUT EARLIER...
UH...
I'M SORRY.
FROM NOW ON...
THINGS ARE FINE THE WAY THEY ARE!
FWSH

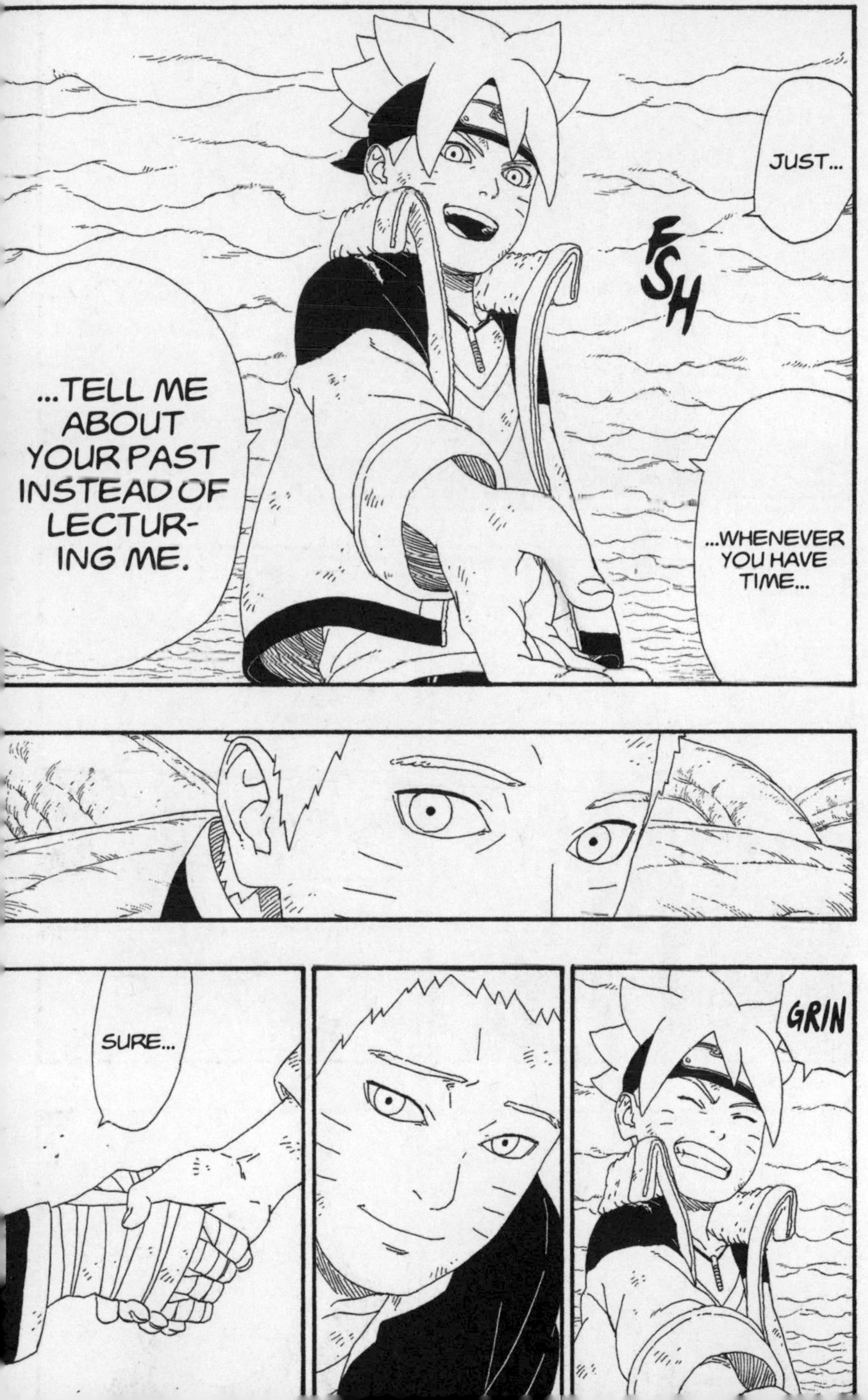
JUST...
FSH
...WHENEVER YOU HAVE TIME...
...TELL ME ABOUT YOUR PAST INSTEAD OF LECTURING ME.
GRIN
SURE...

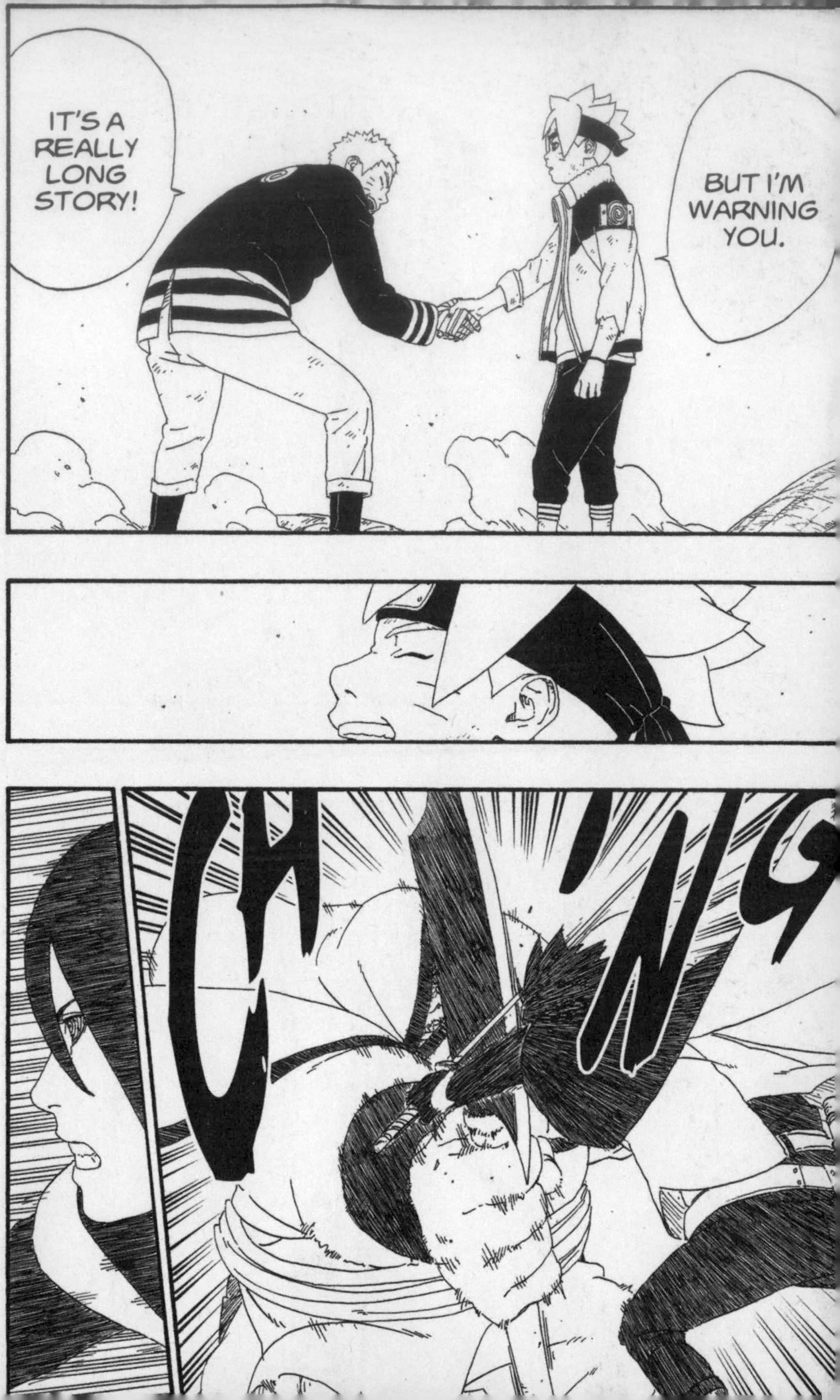
BUT I'M WARNING YOU.
IT'S A REALLY LONG STORY!

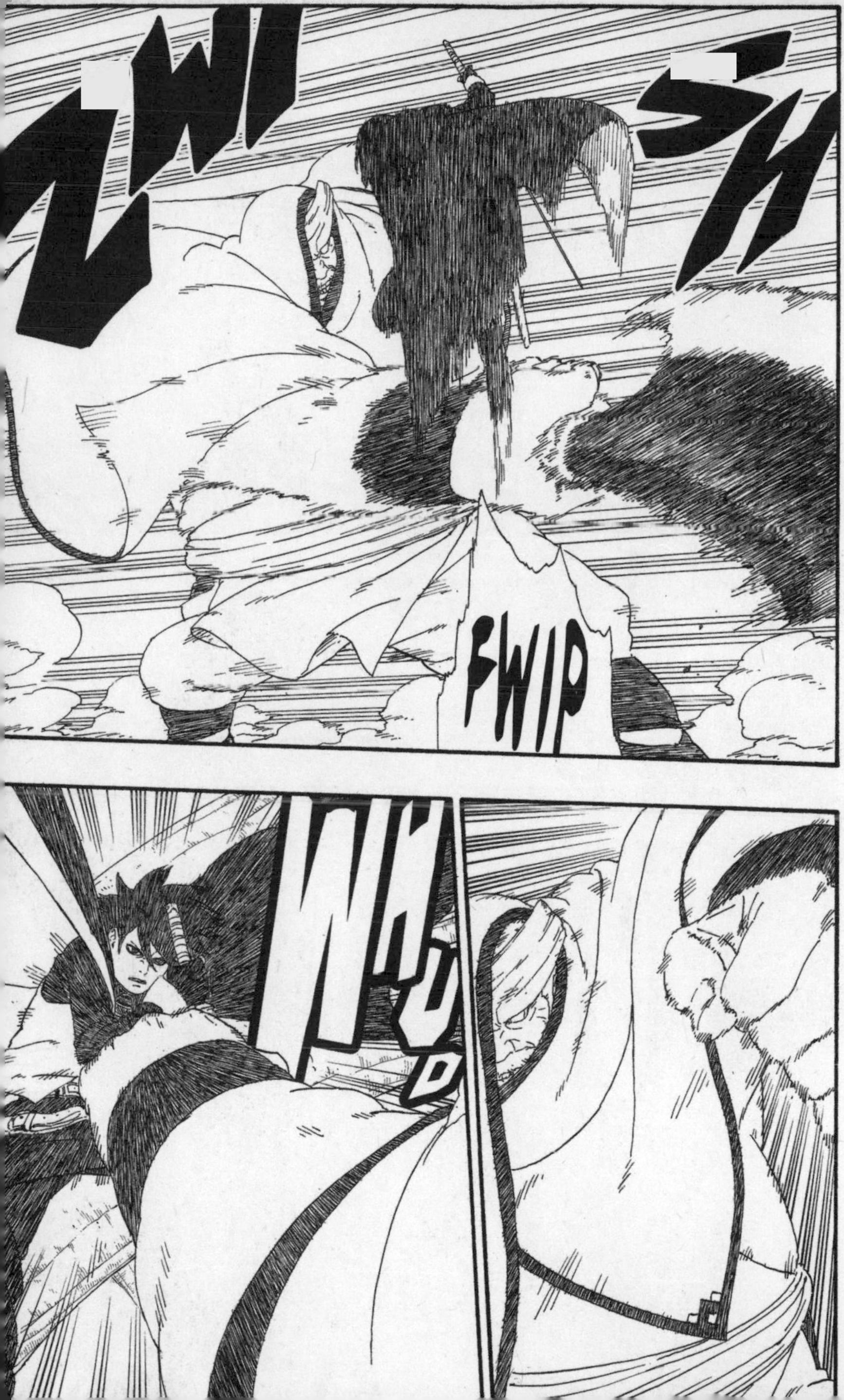
ZWISH
FWIP
WHUD

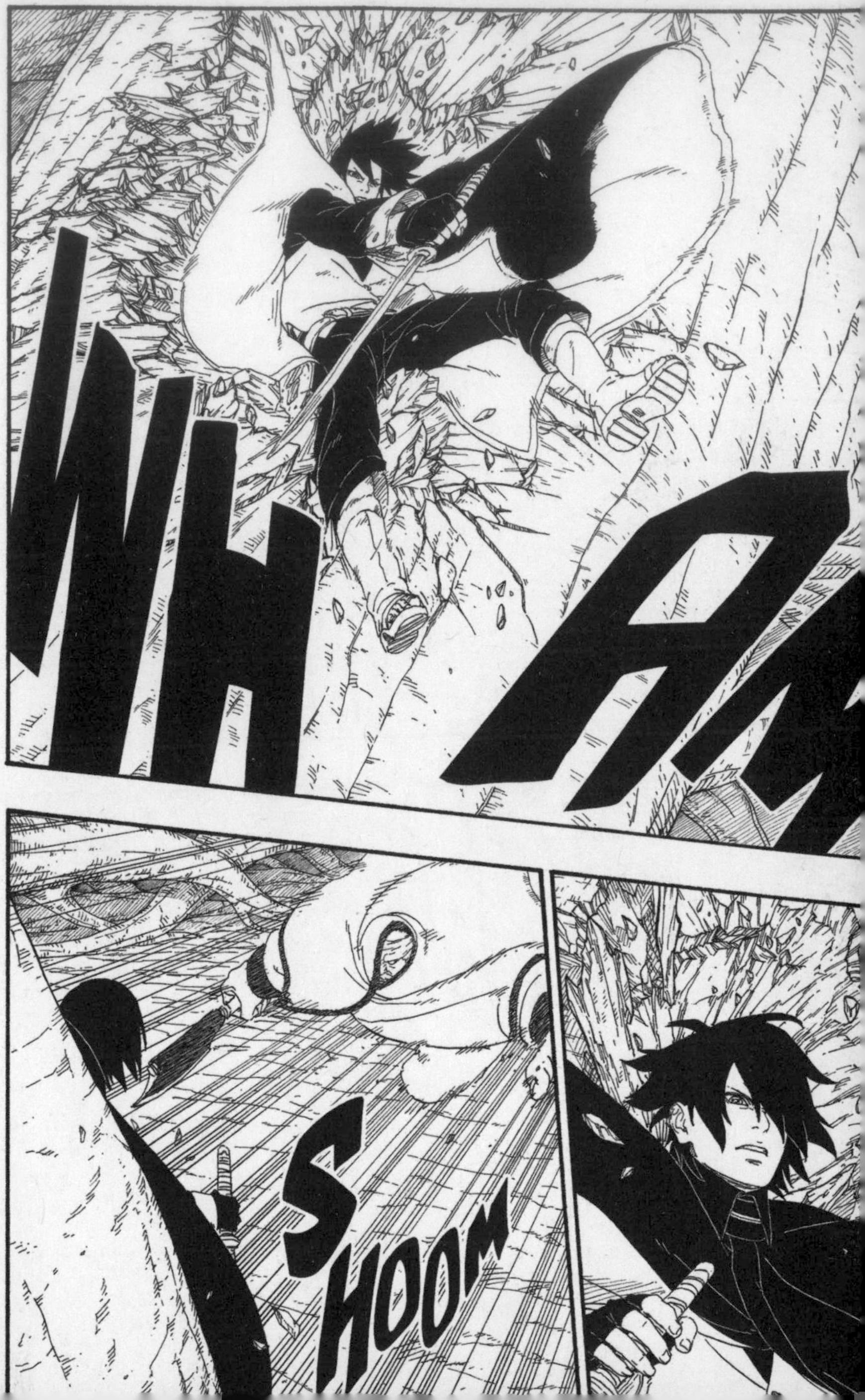
WHA
SHOOM

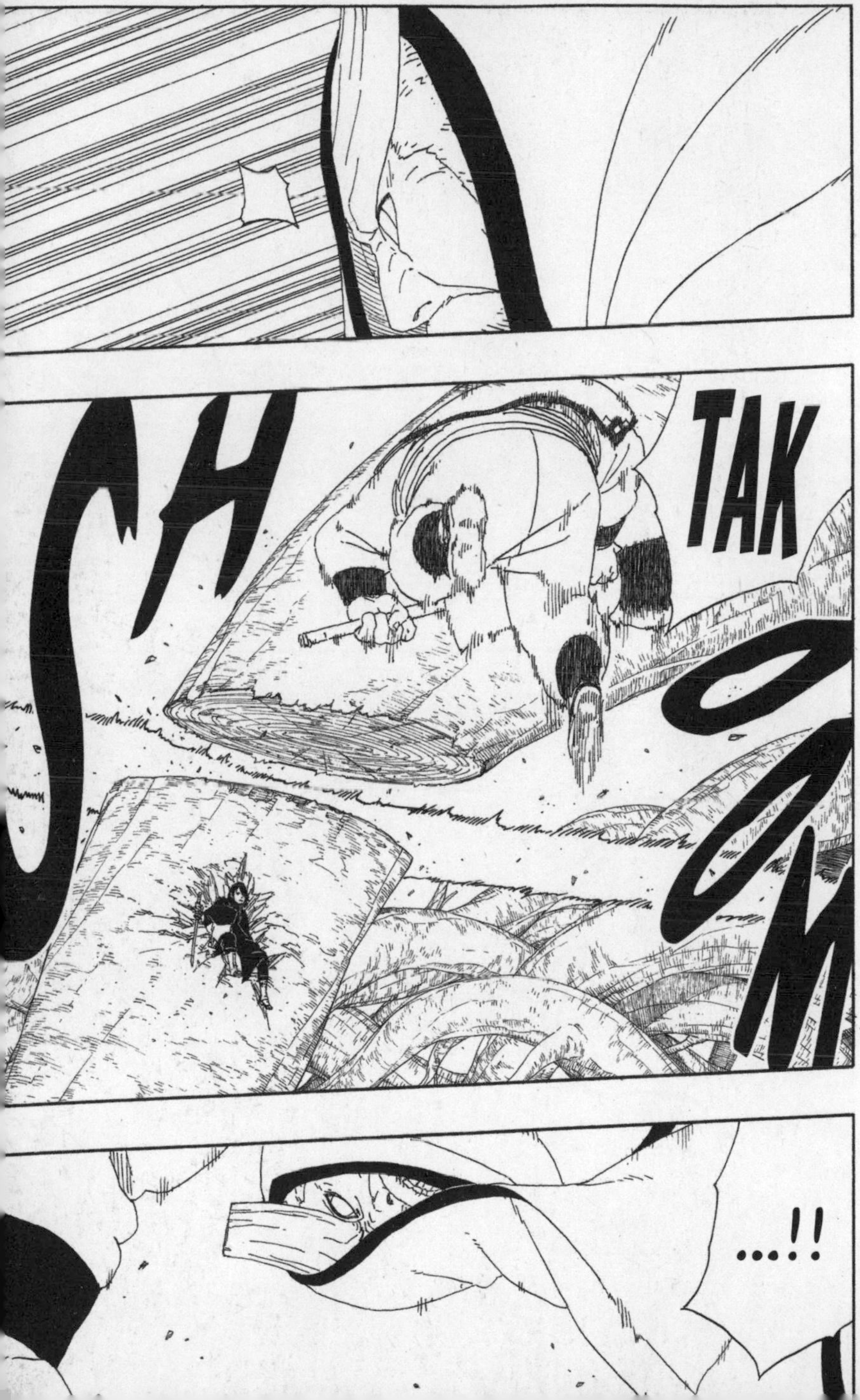
TAK
...!!

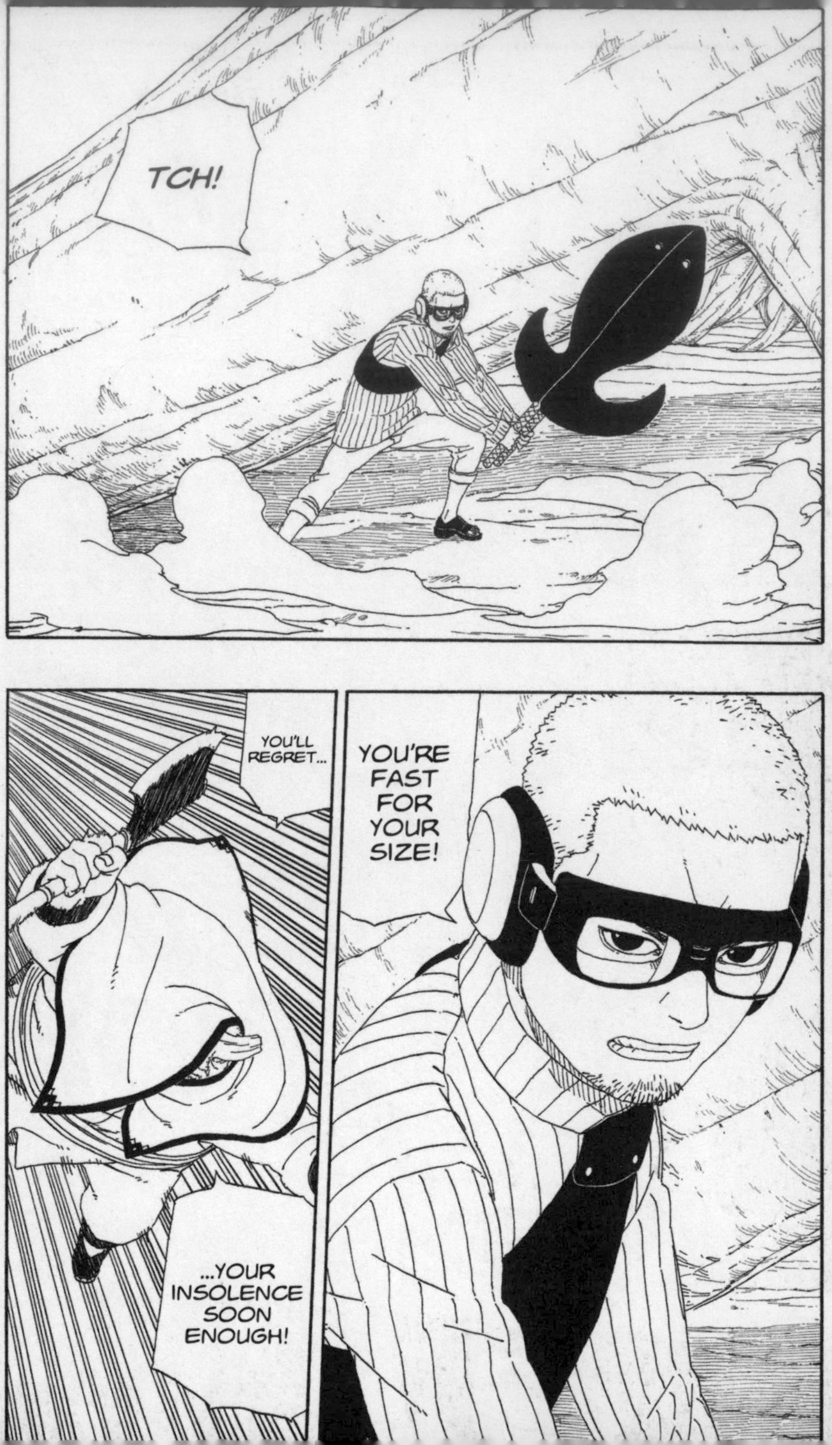
TCH!
YOU'RE FAST FOR YOUR SIZE!
YOU'LL REGRET...
...YOUR INSOLENCE SOON ENOUGH!

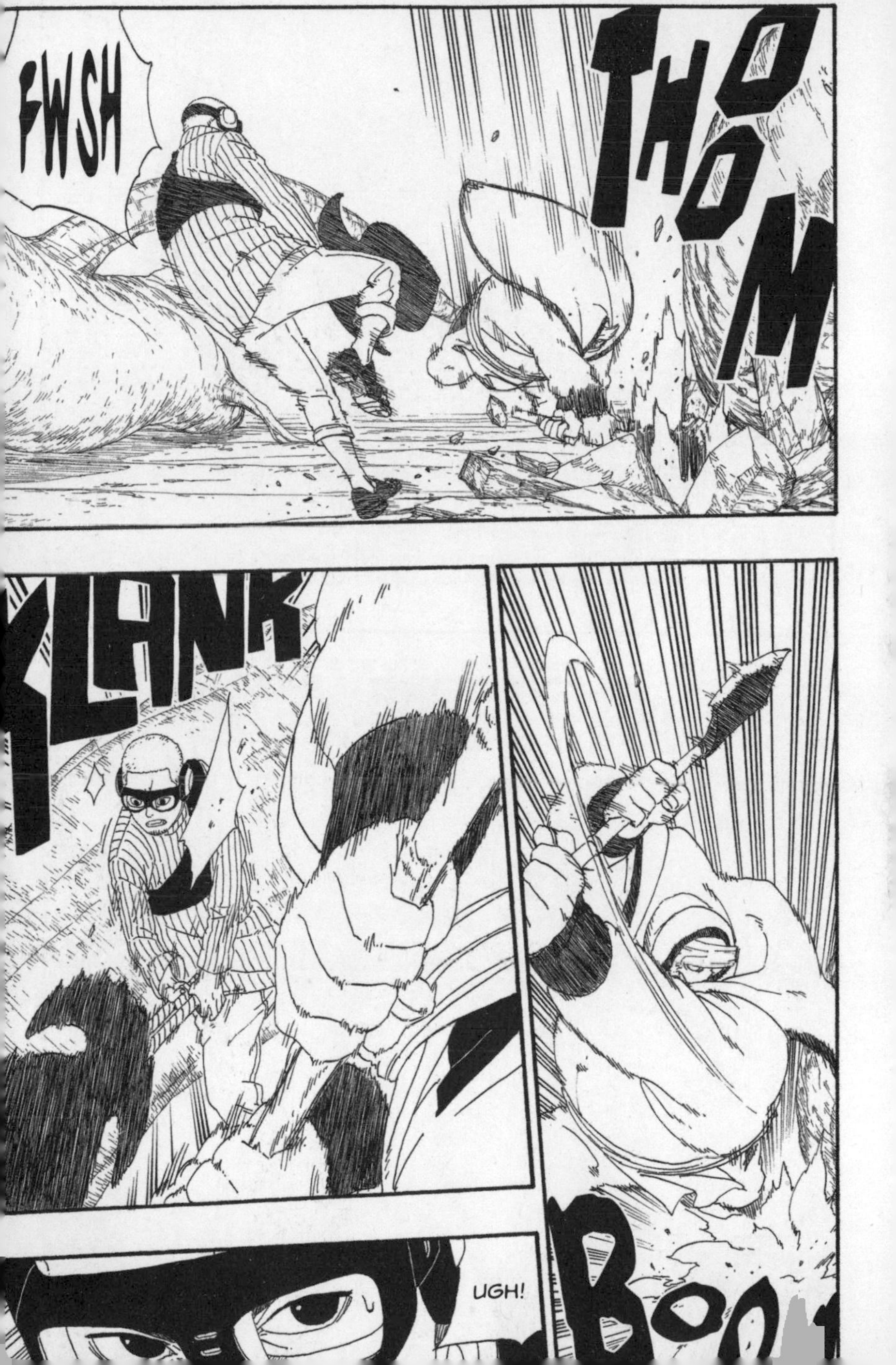
THOOM
FWSH
BOO
KLANK
UGH!

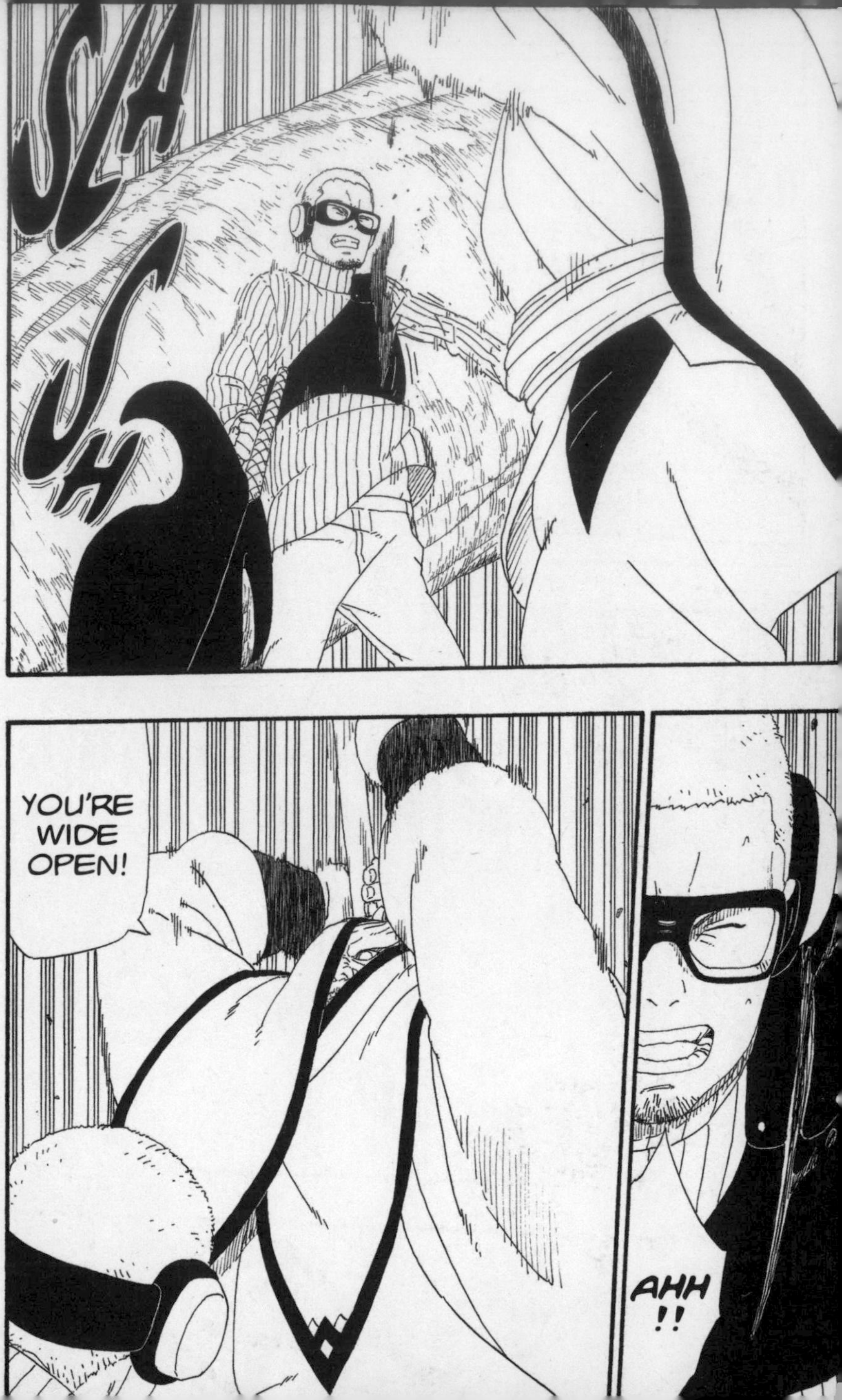
SLASH
AHH!!
YOU'RE WIDE OPEN!

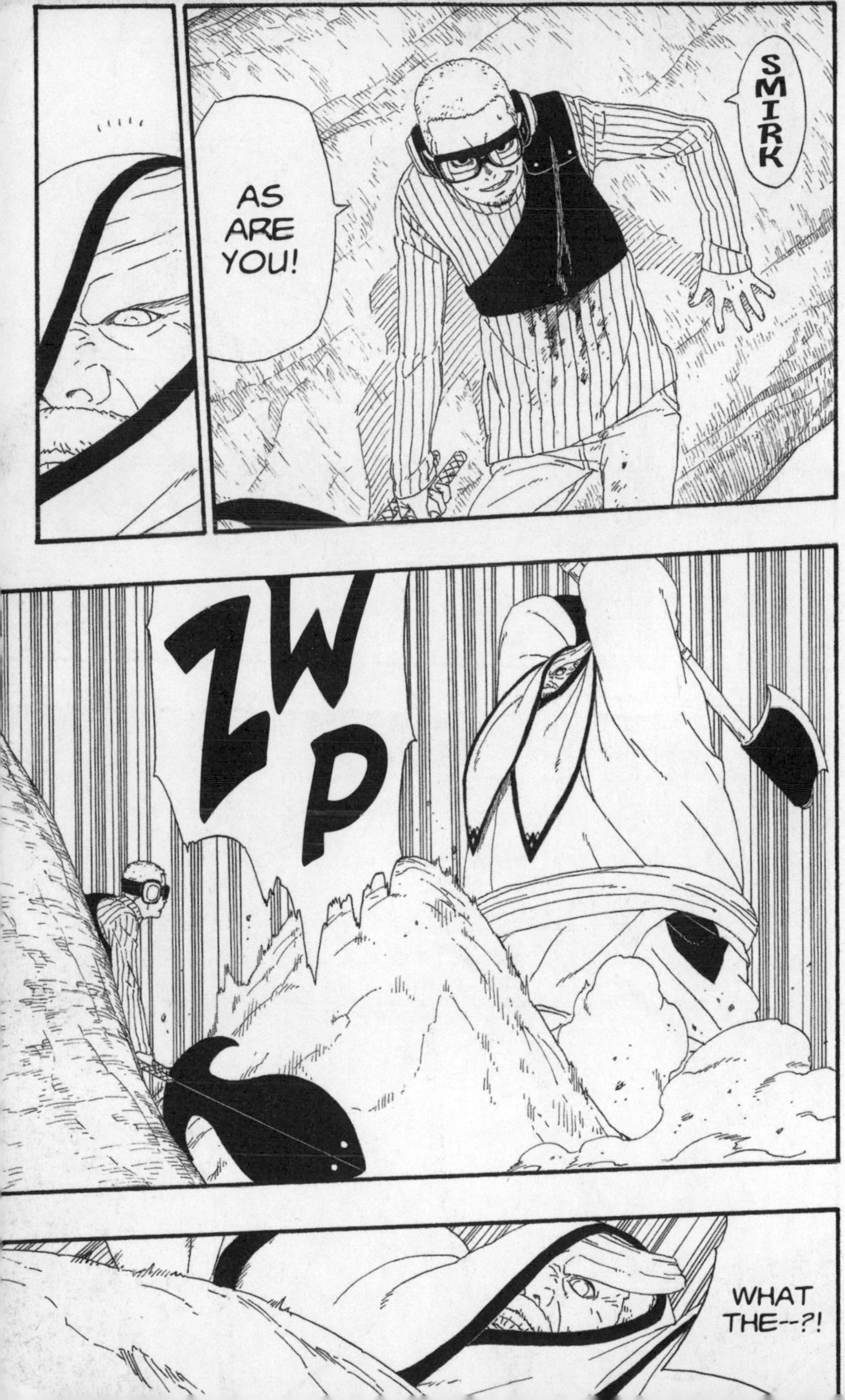
SMIRK
AS ARE YOU!
ZWP
WHAT THE--?!

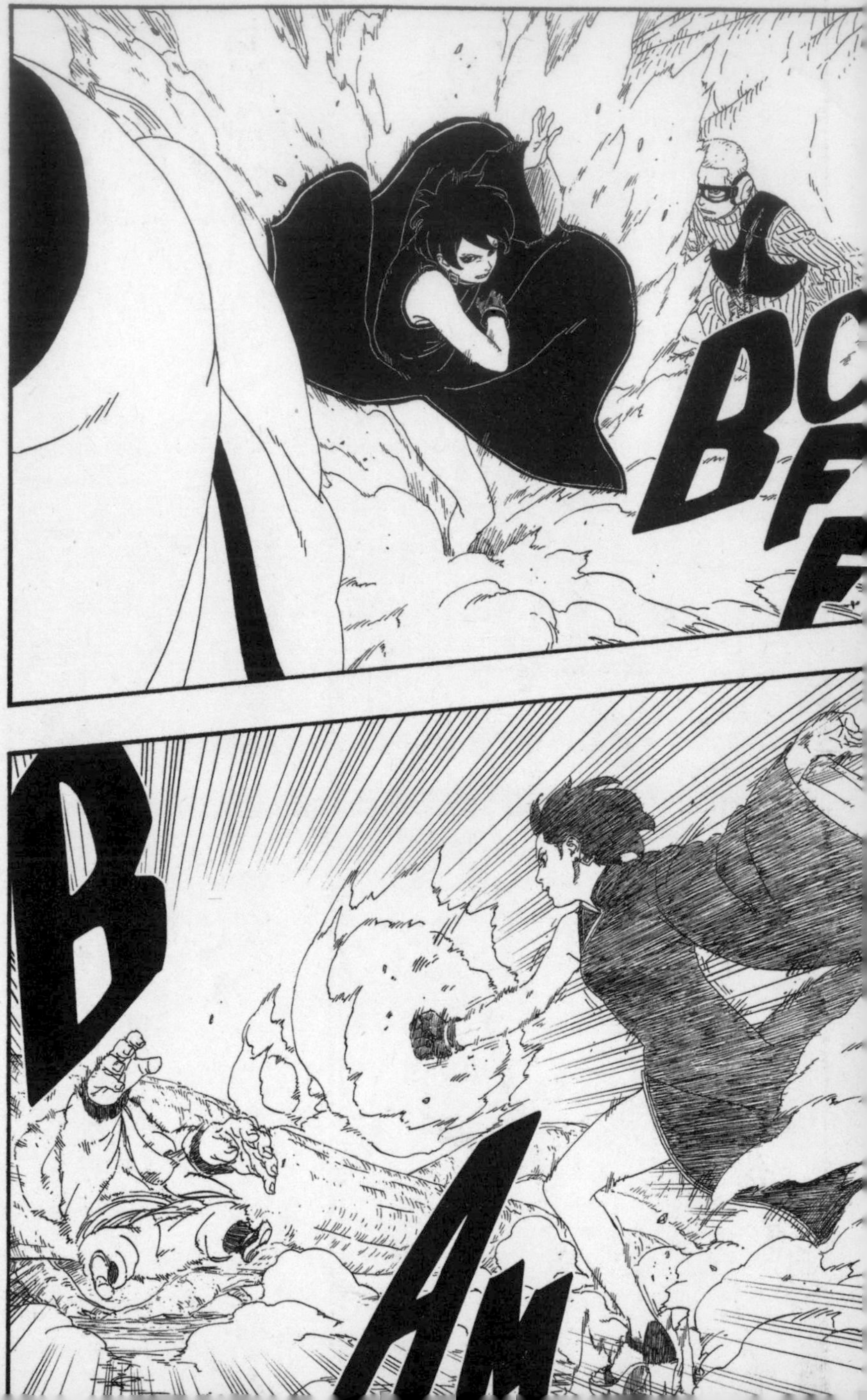
BOFF
BAM

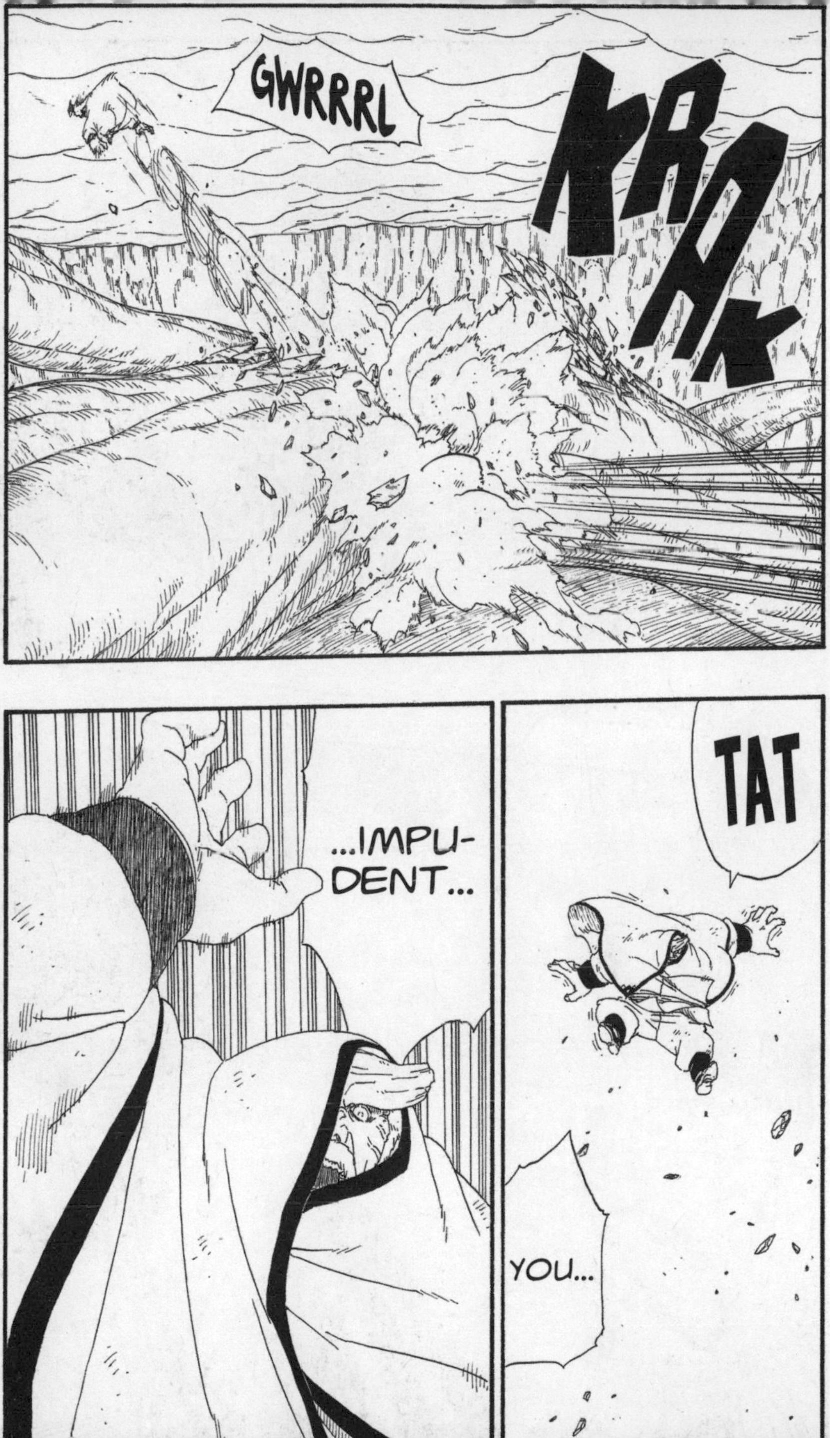
KRAAK
GWRRRL
TAT
YOU...
...IMPU-
DENT...

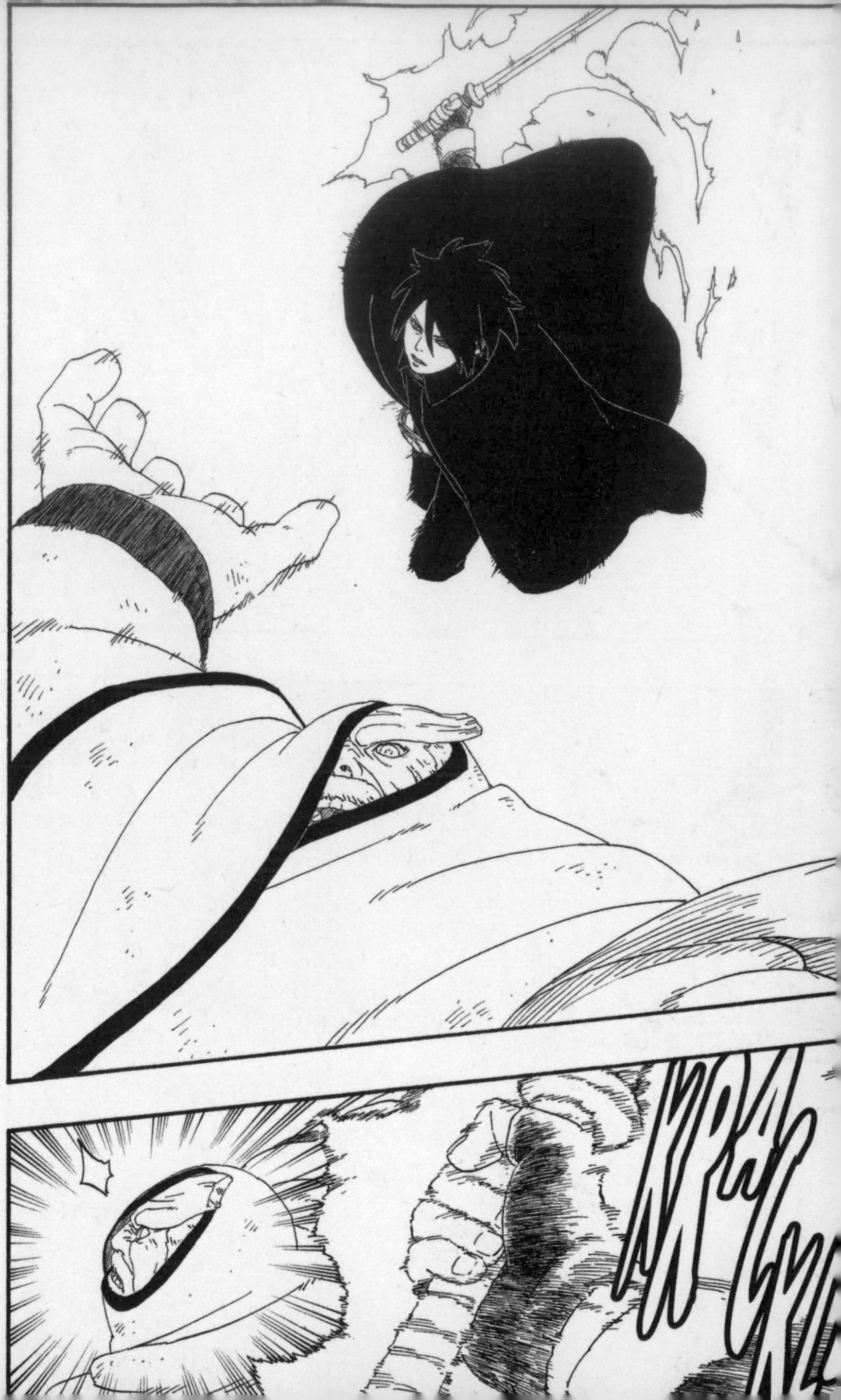

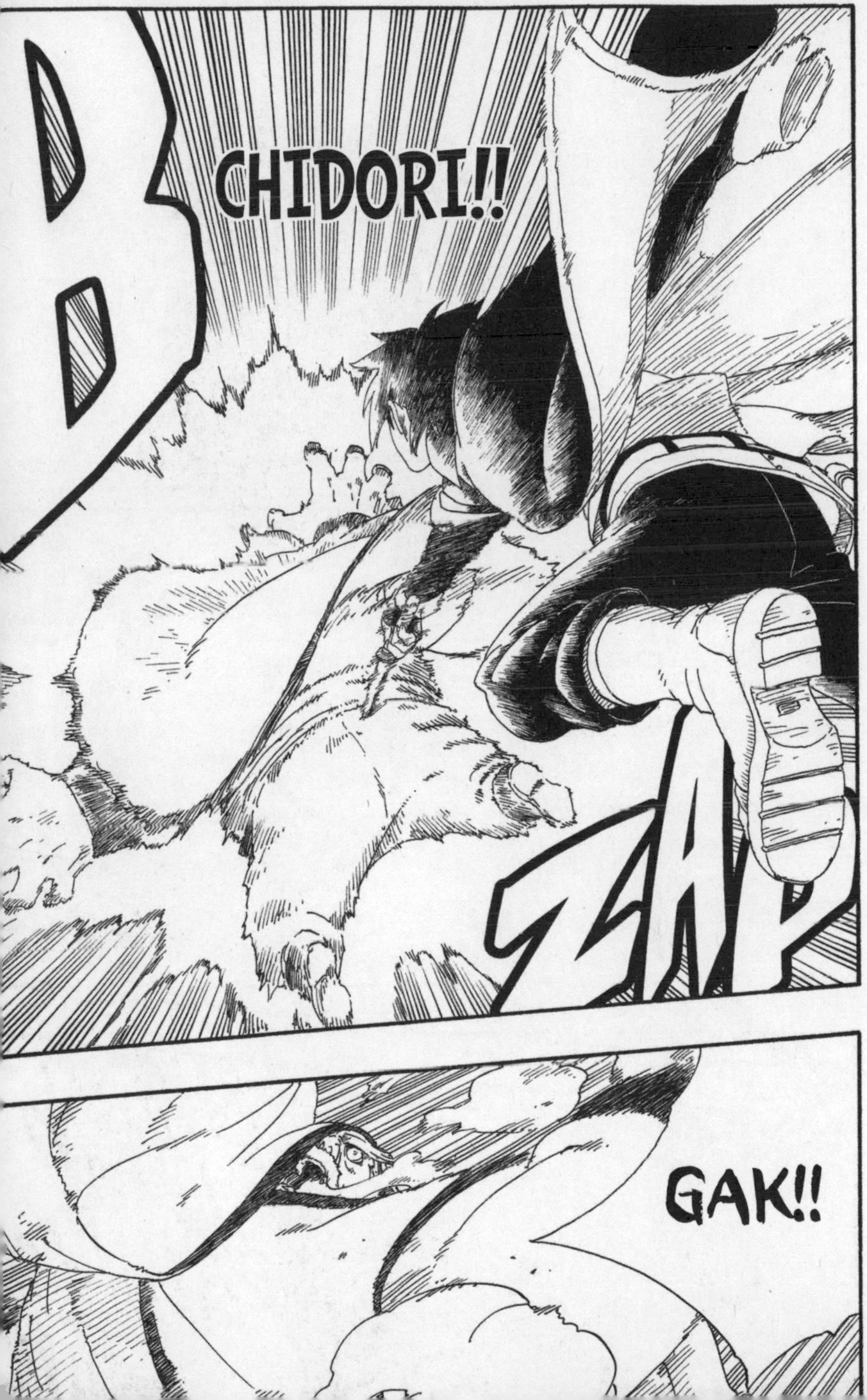
CHIDORI!!
ZAP
GAK!!

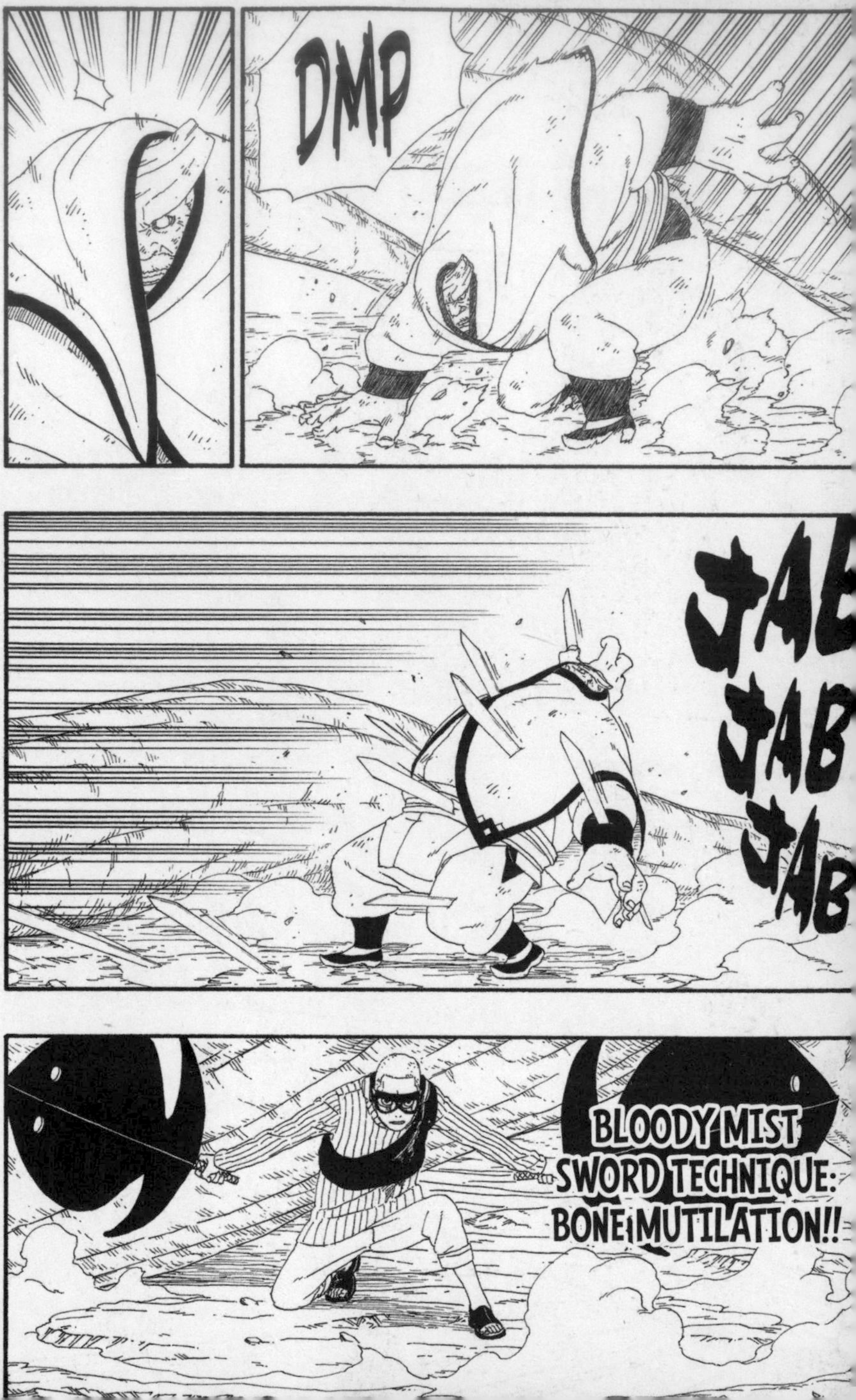
DMP
JAB JAB JAB
BLOODY MIST SWORD TECHNIQUE: BONE MUTILATION!!

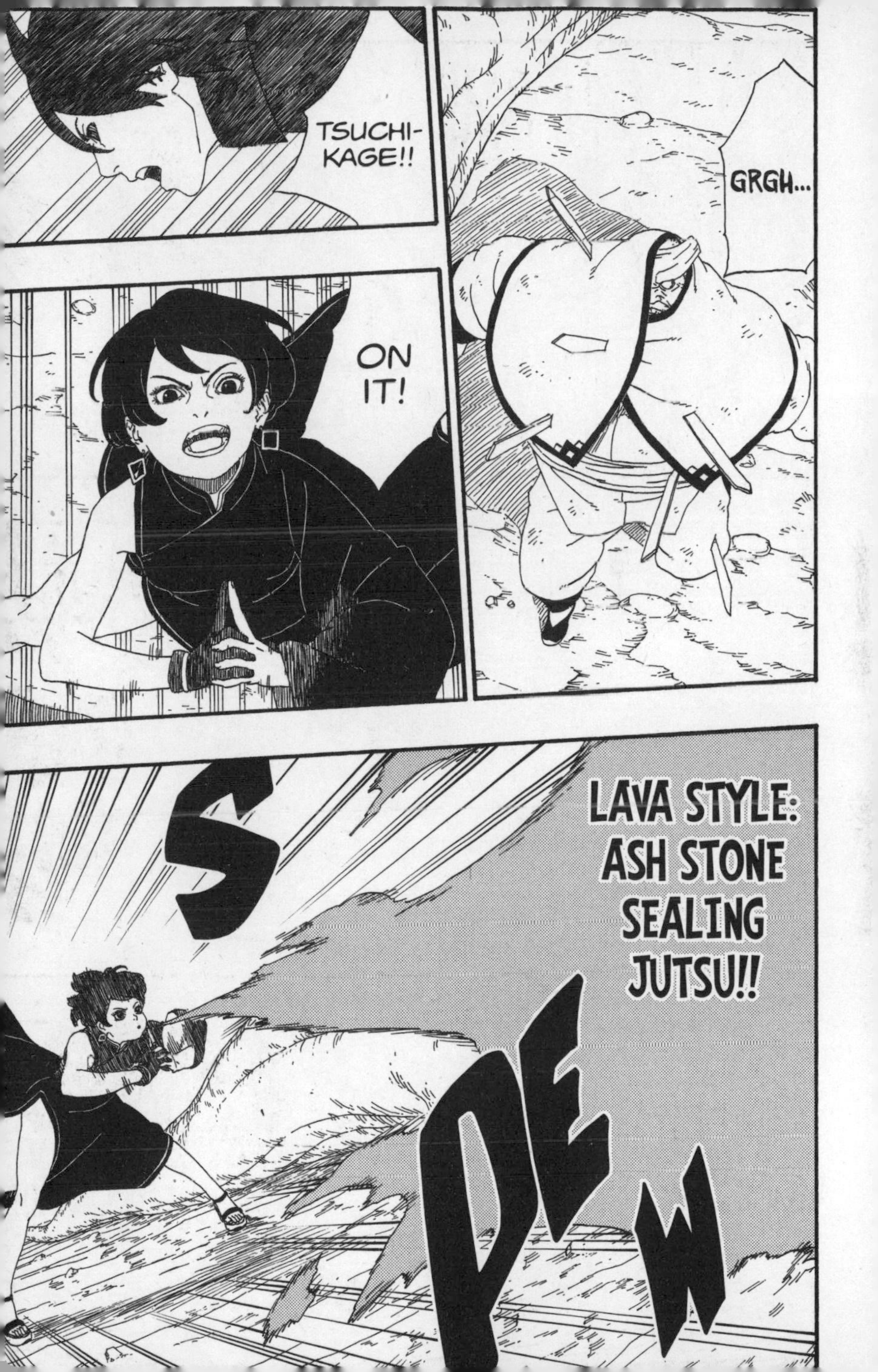
GRGH...
TSUCHI-KAGE!!
ON IT!
LAVA STYLE: ASH STONE SEALING JUTSU!!
PEW

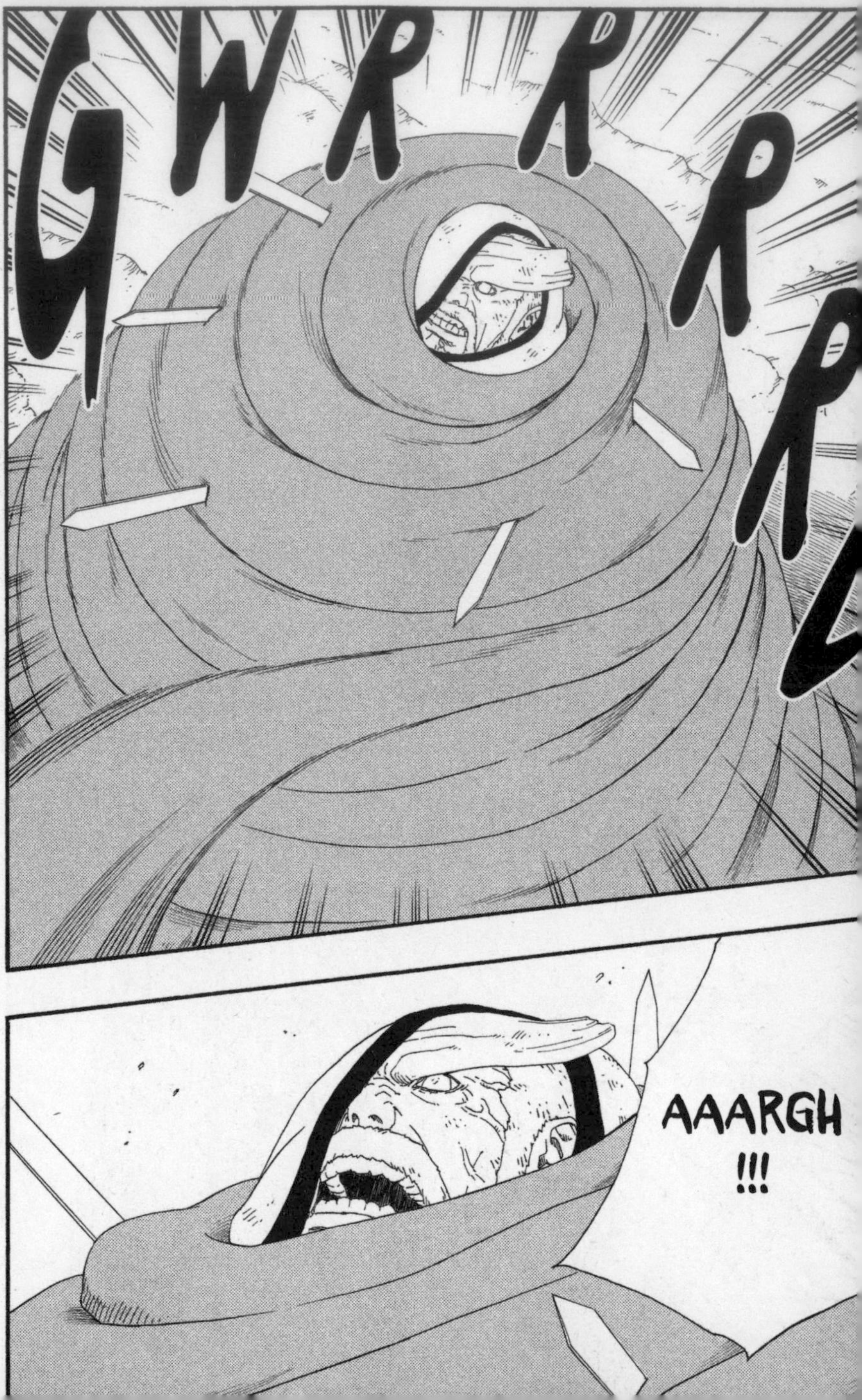
GWRRRR
AAARGH
!!!

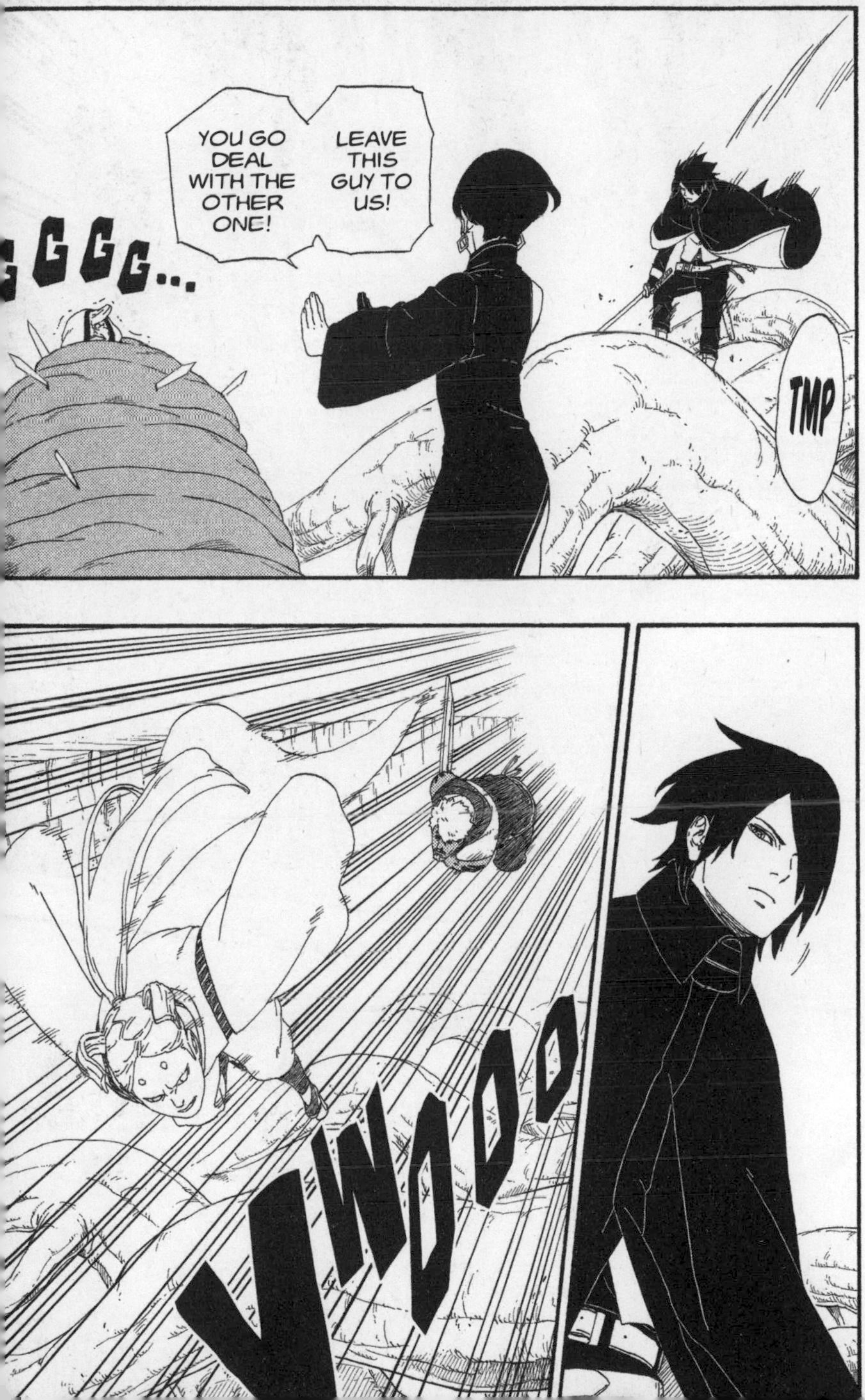
LEAVE THIS GUY TO US!
YOU GO DEAL WITH THE OTHER ONE!
TMP
GGGG...
VWOOO

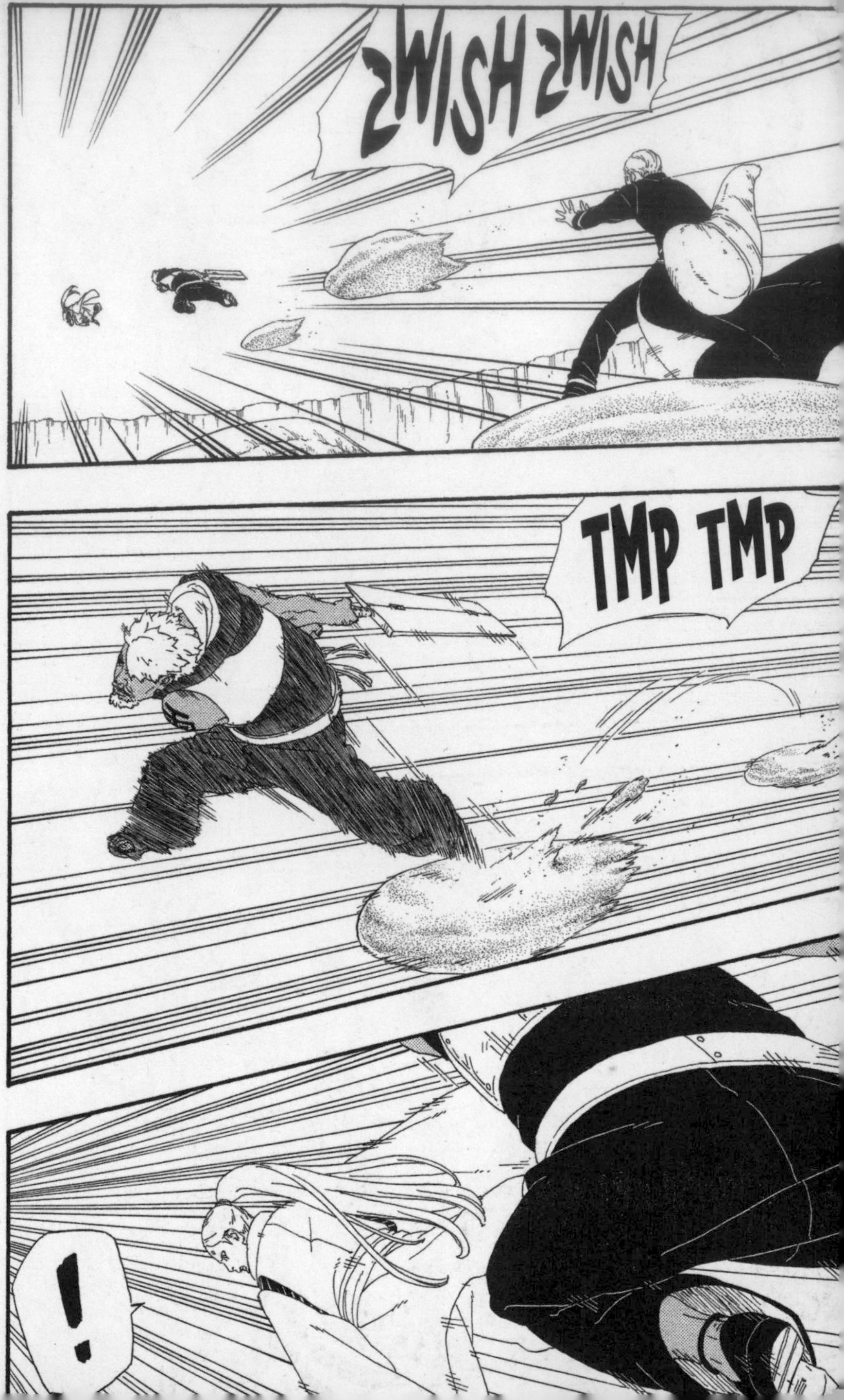
SWISH SWISH
TMP TMP
!

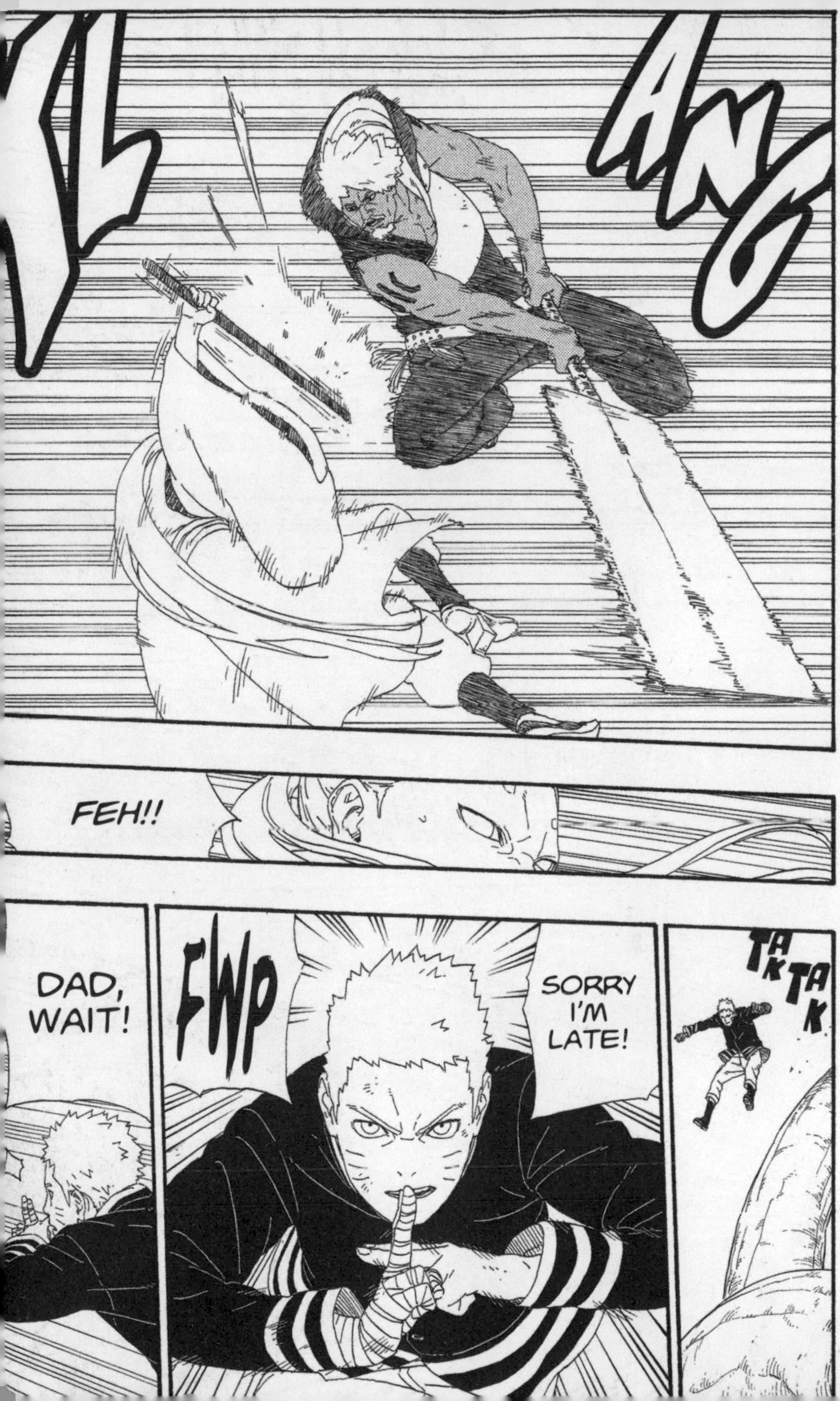
KLANG
FEH!!
TAK TAK
SORRY I'M LATE!
FWP
DAD, WAIT!

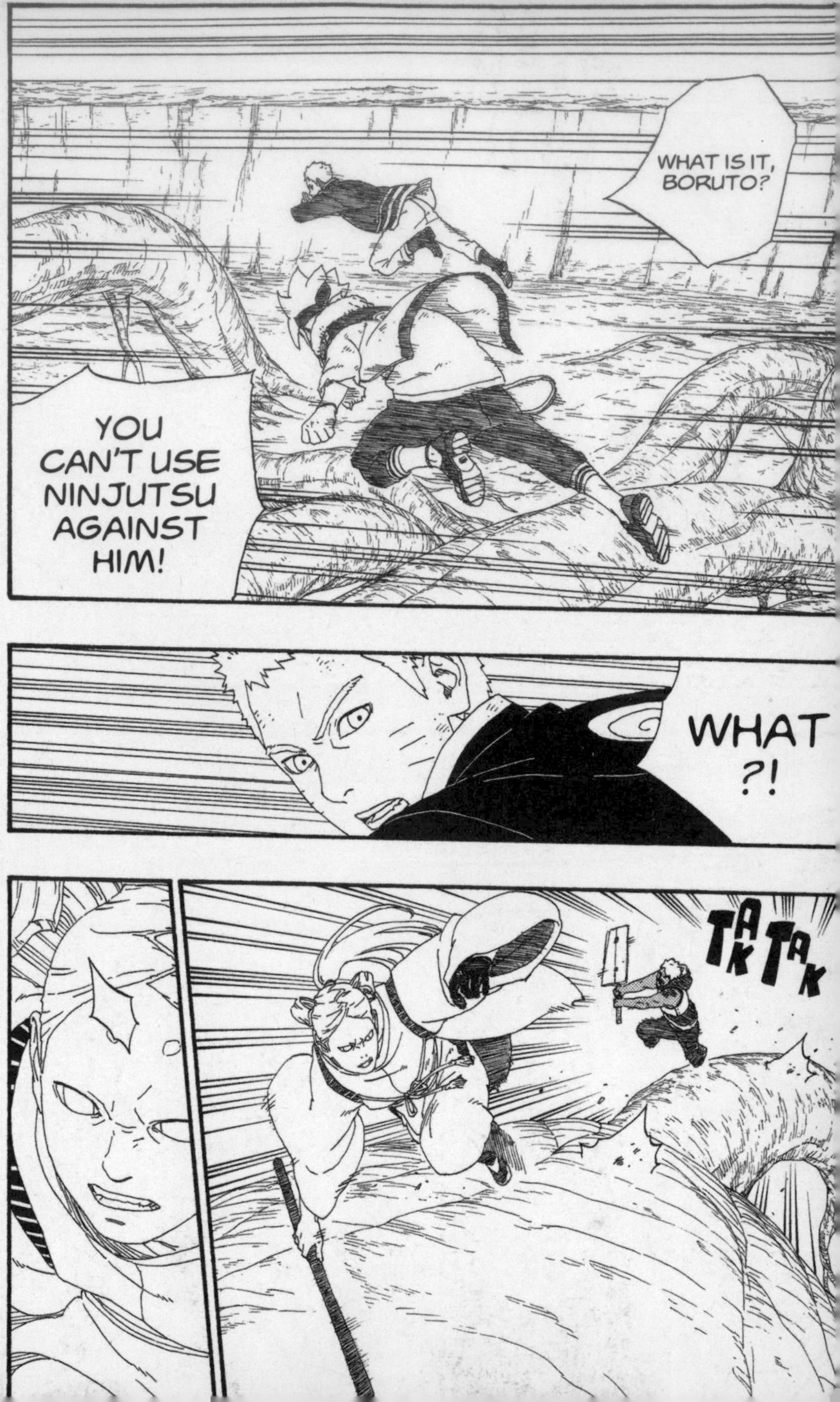
WHAT IS IT, BORUTO?
YOU CAN'T USE NINJUTSU AGAINST HIM!
WHAT?!
TAK TAK

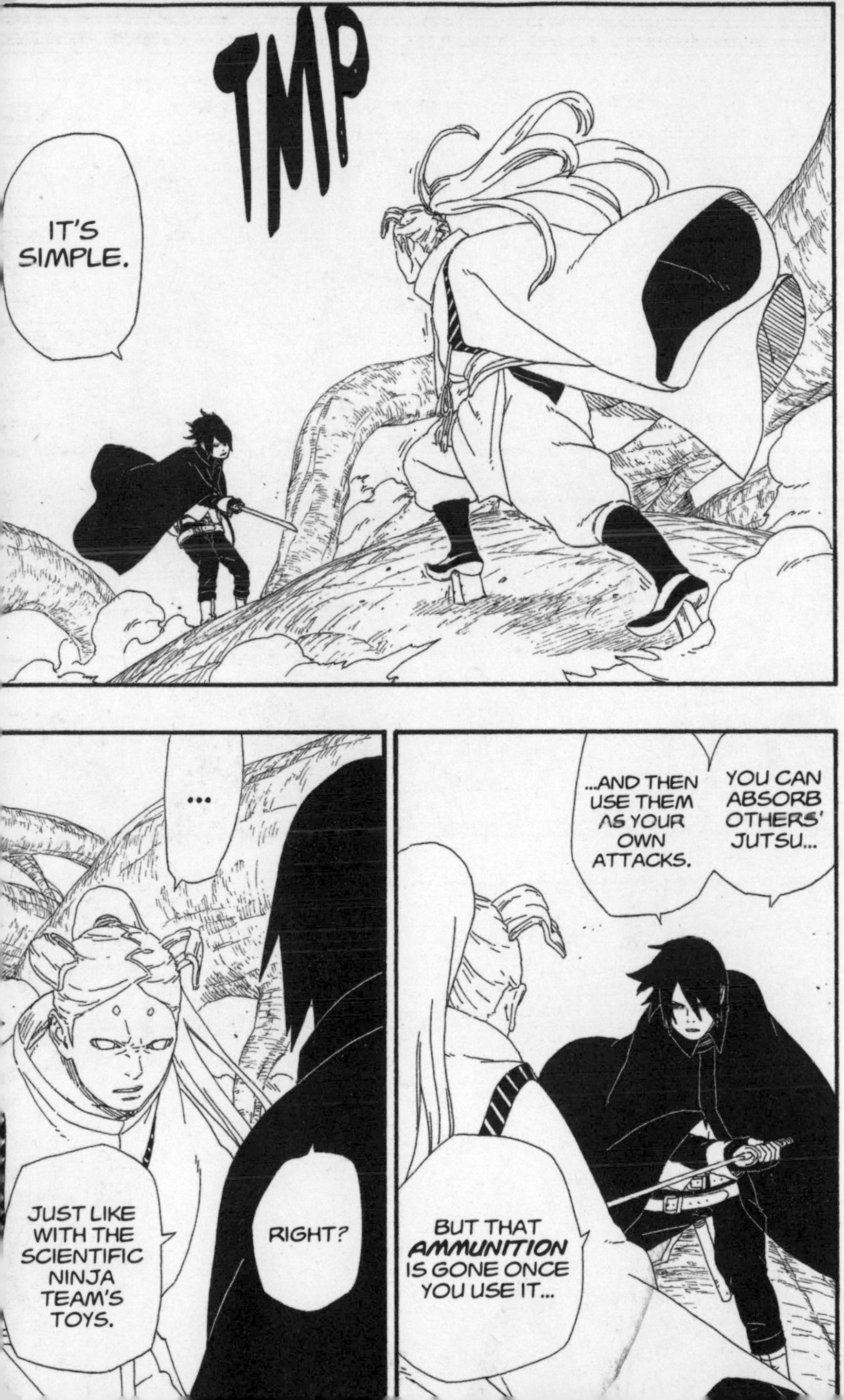
TMP
IT'S SIMPLE.
YOU CAN ABSORB OTHERS' JUTSU...
...AND THEN USE THEM AS YOUR OWN ATTACKS.
BUT THAT *AMMUNITION* IS GONE ONCE YOU USE IT...
...
RIGHT?
JUST LIKE WITH THE SCIENTIFIC NINJA TEAM'S TOYS.

THAT MAKES IT EASY.

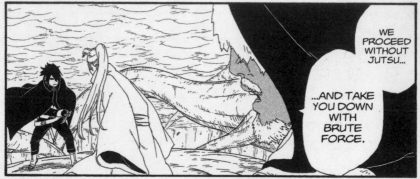

WE PROCEED WITHOUT JUTSU...

...AND TAKE YOU DOWN WITH BRUTE FORCE.

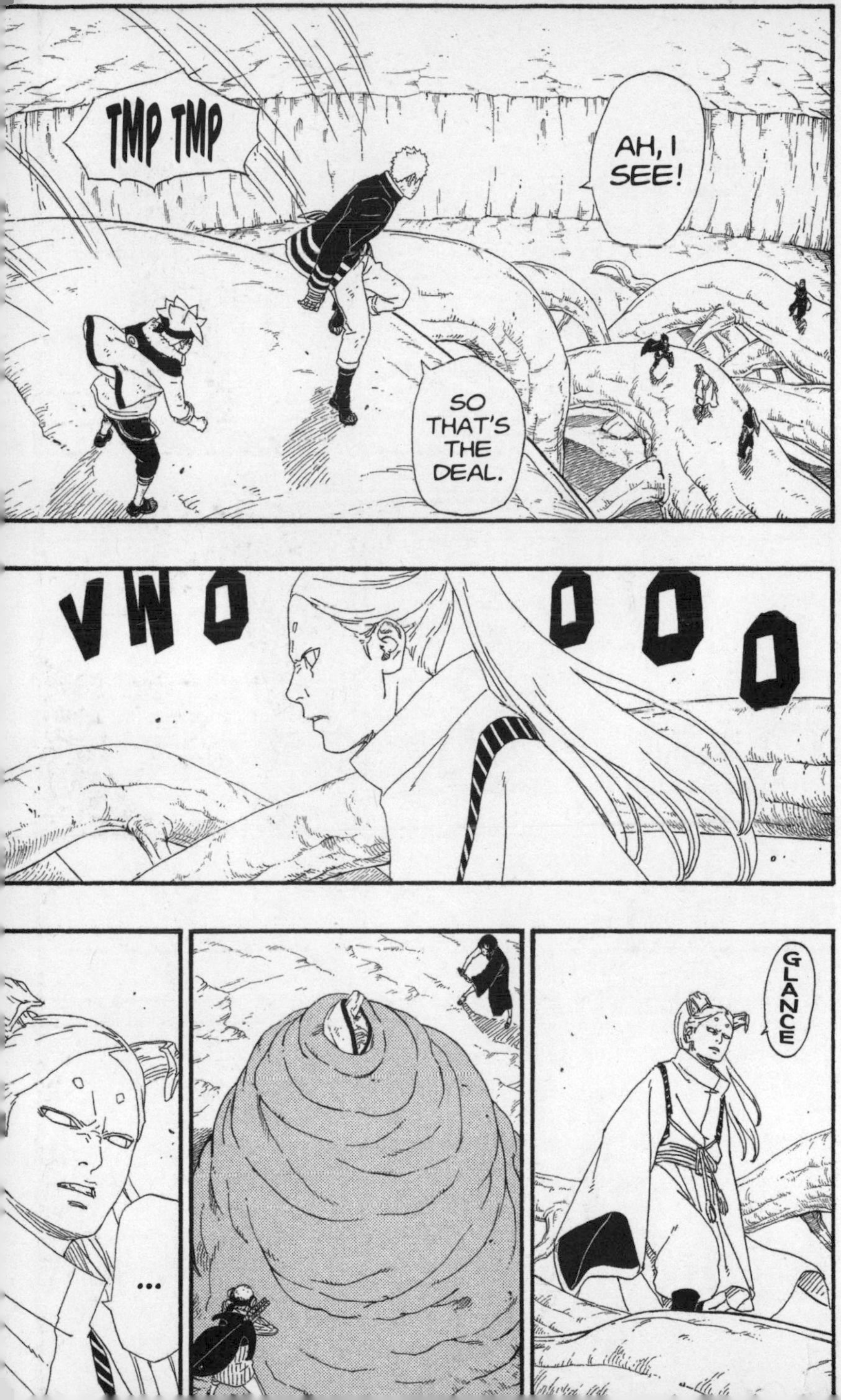
AH, I SEE!
TMP TMP
SO THAT'S THE DEAL.
VWOOOO
GLANCE
...

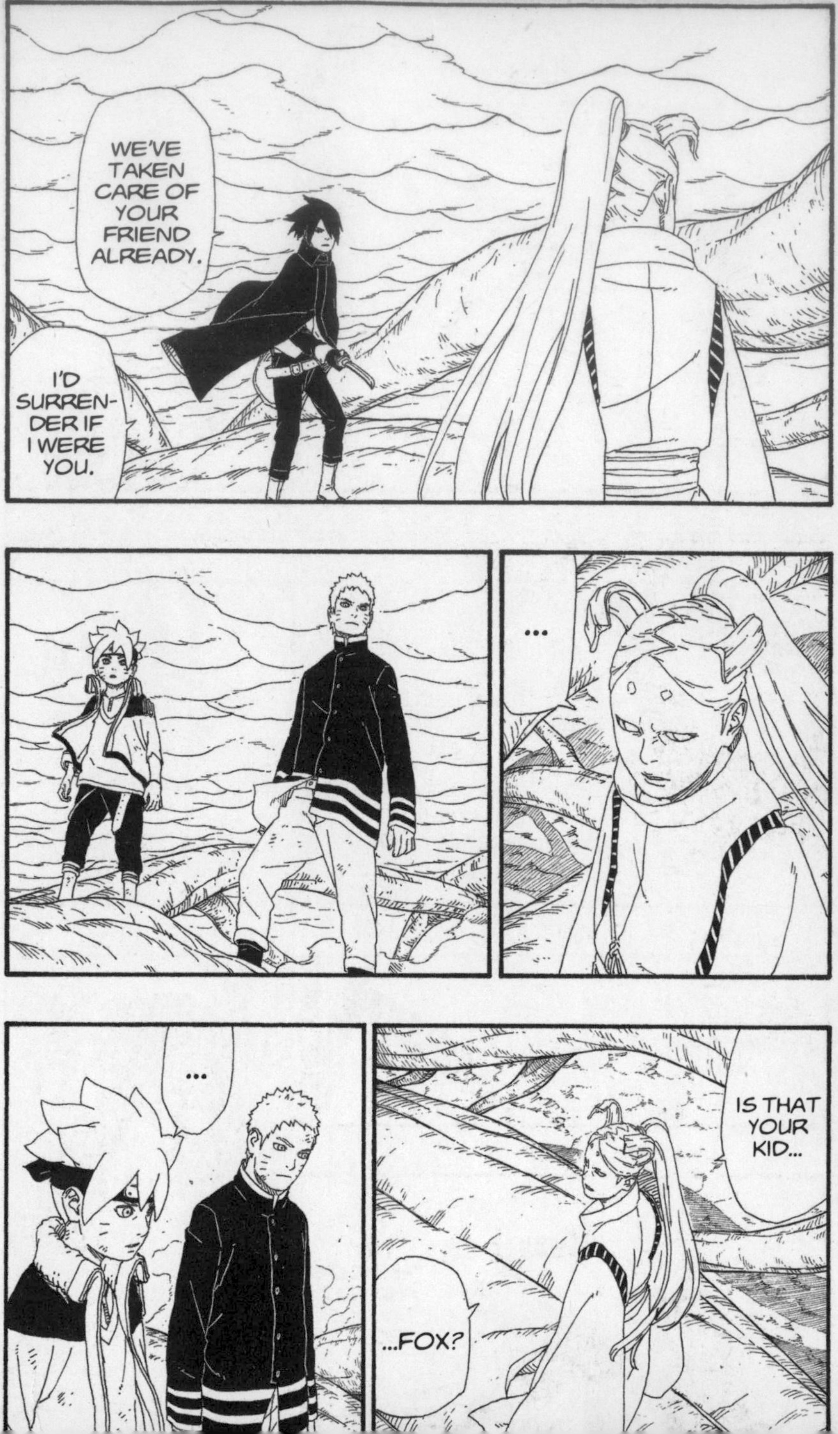
WE'VE TAKEN CARE OF YOUR FRIEND ALREADY.
I'D SURREN-DER IF I WERE YOU.
...
IS THAT YOUR KID...
...FOX?
...

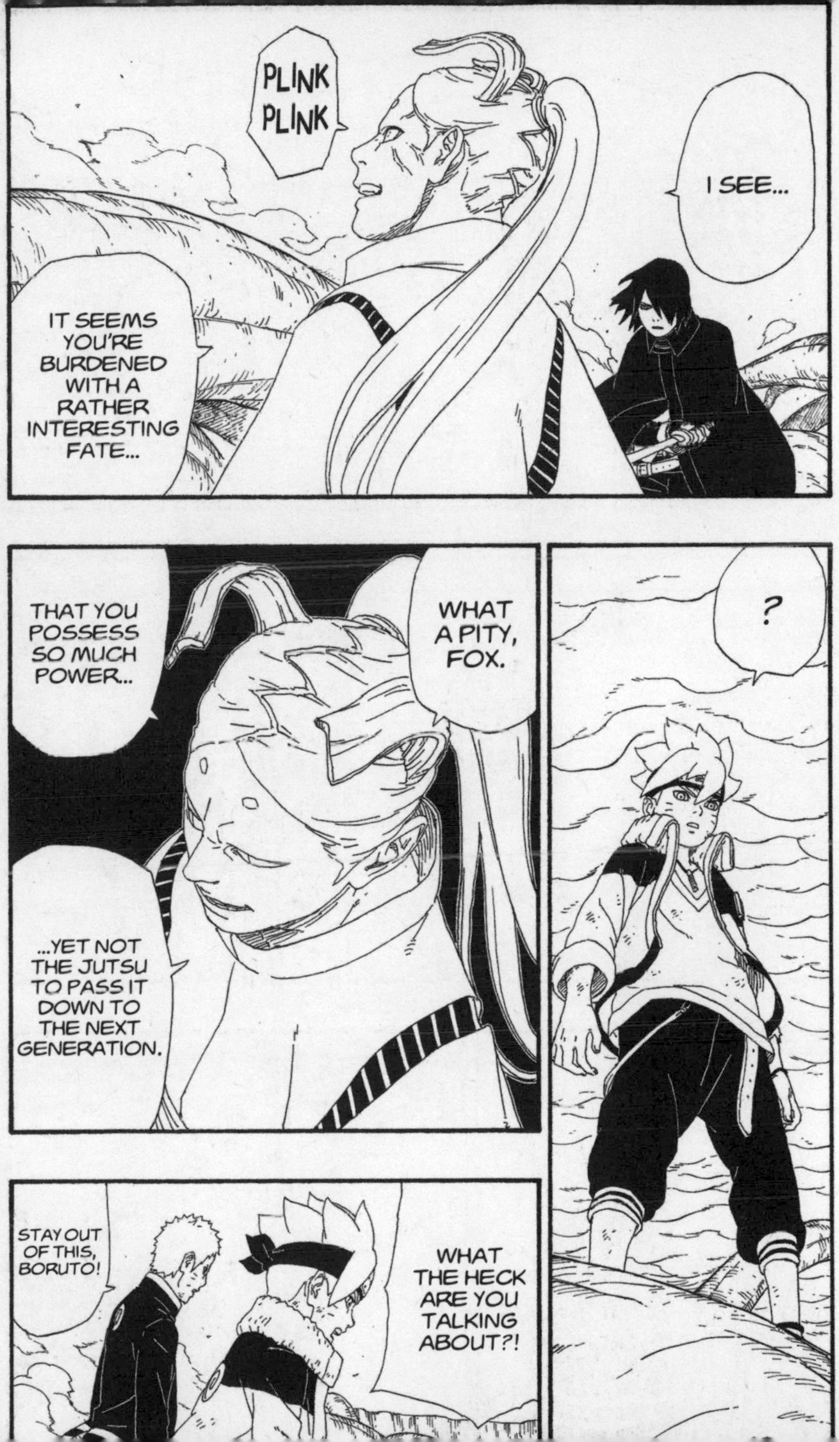
I SEE...
PLINK PLINK
IT SEEMS YOU'RE BURDENED WITH A RATHER INTERESTING FATE...
?
WHAT A PITY, FOX.
THAT YOU POSSESS SO MUCH POWER...
...YET NOT THE JUTSU TO PASS IT DOWN TO THE NEXT GENERATION.
WHAT THE HECK ARE YOU TALKING ABOUT?!
STAY OUT OF THIS, BORUTO!

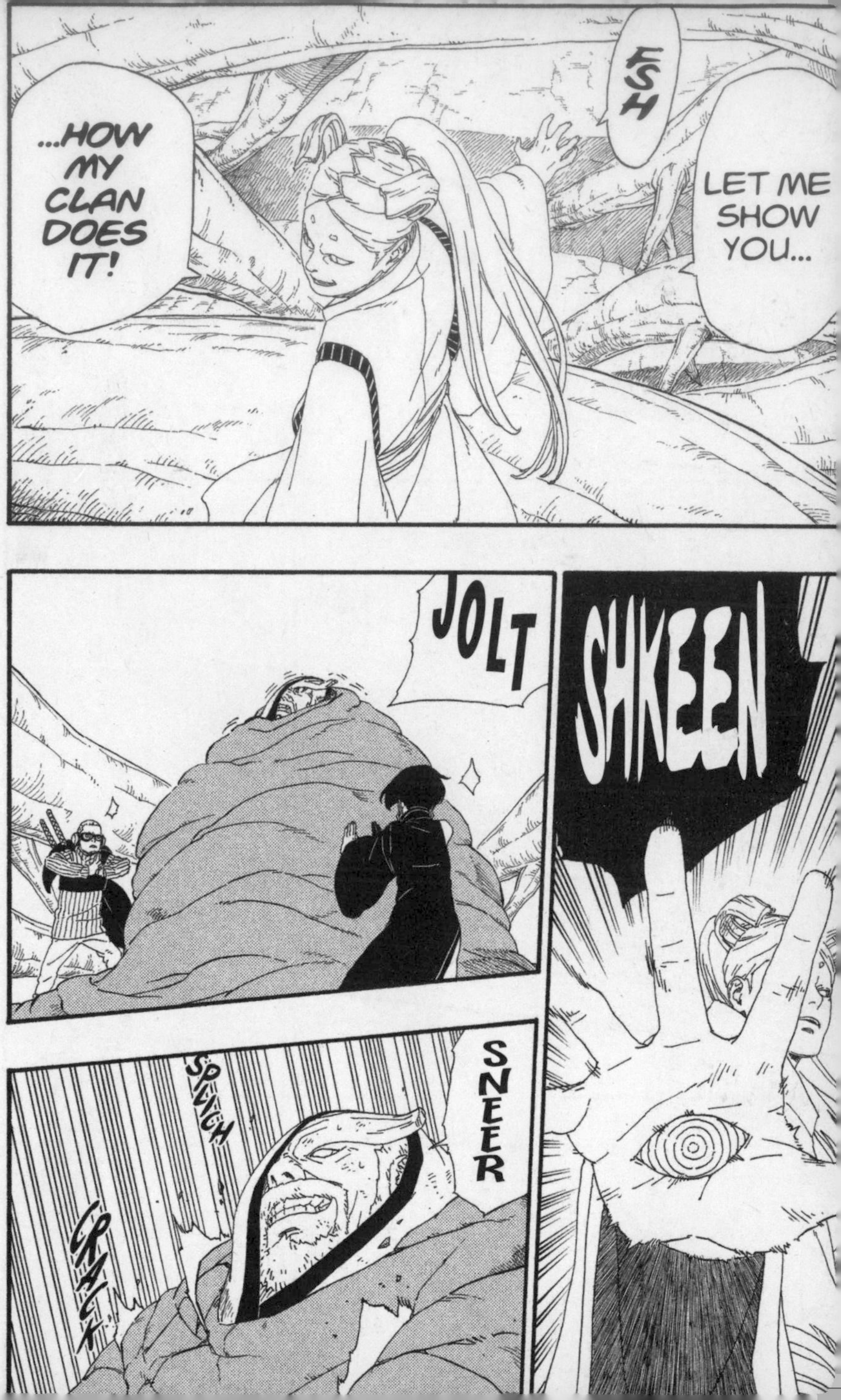
LET ME SHOW YOU...
FSH
...HOW MY CLAN DOES IT!
SHKEEN
JOLT
SNEER
SPLICH
CRACK

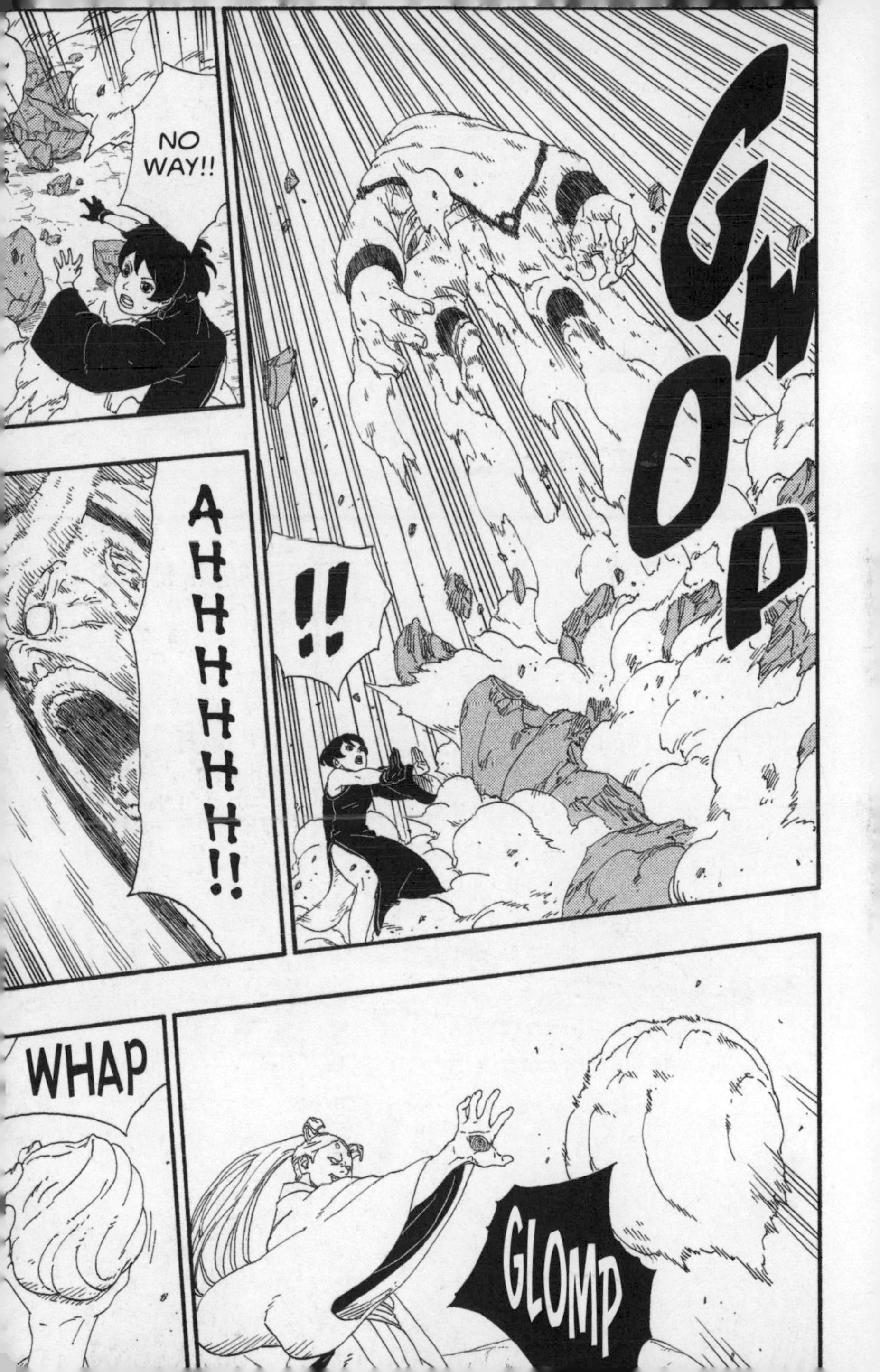

GWOOP
!!
NO WAY!!
AHHHHHH!!
GLOMP
WHAP

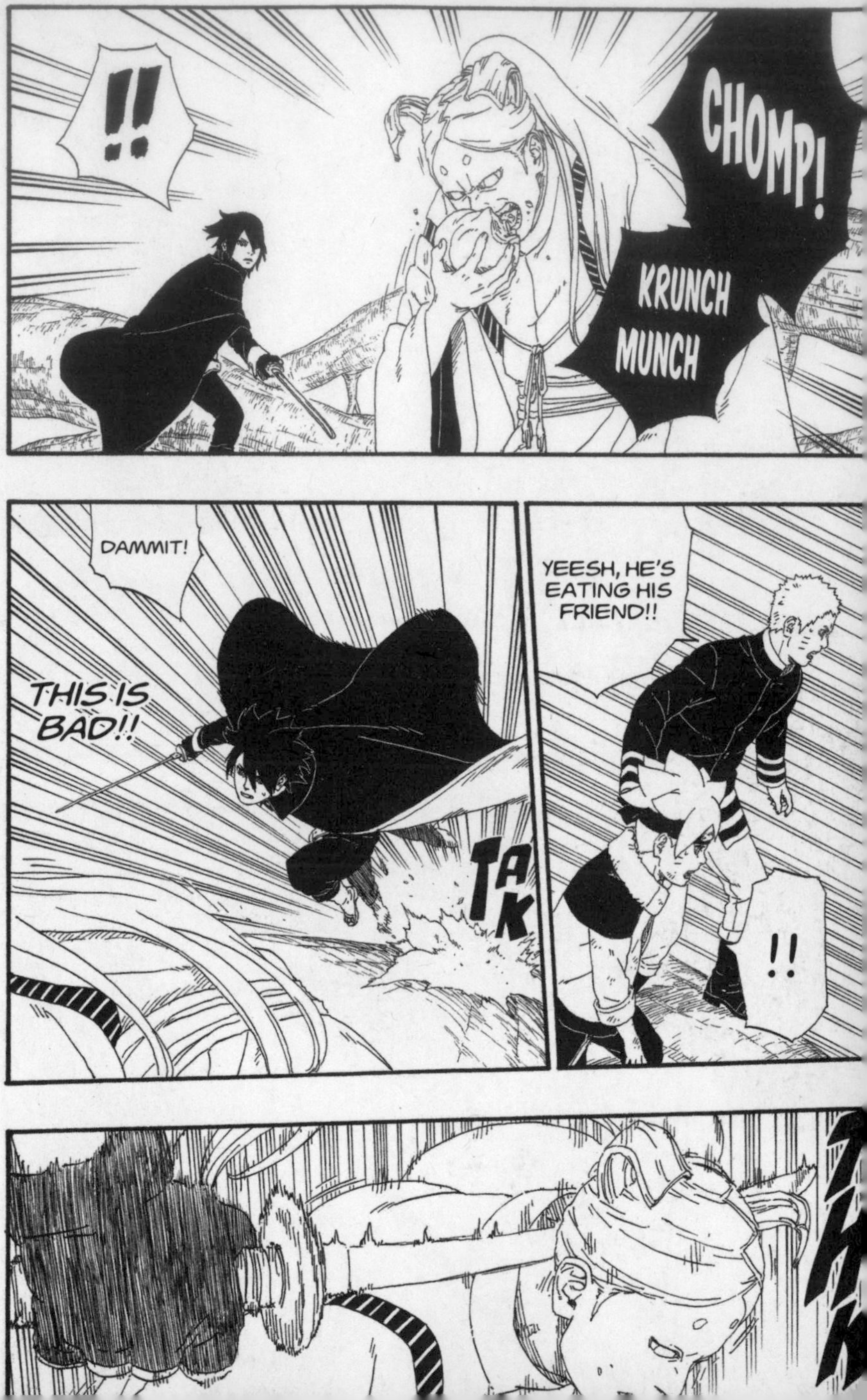
CHOMP!
KRUNCH MUNCH
!!
YEESH, HE'S EATING HIS FRIEND!!
!!
DAMMIT!
THIS IS BAD!!
TAK

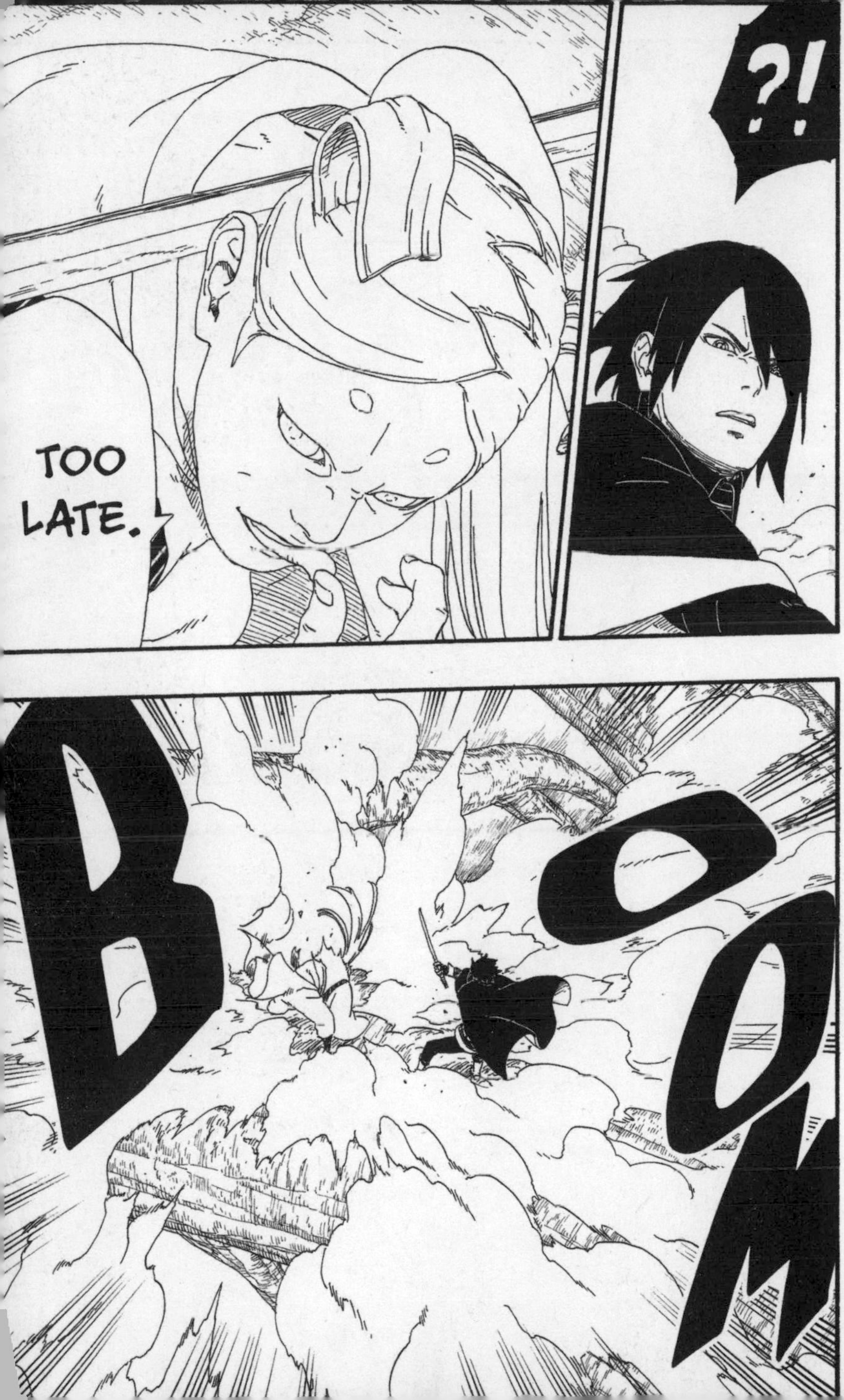
?!
TOO LATE.
BOOM

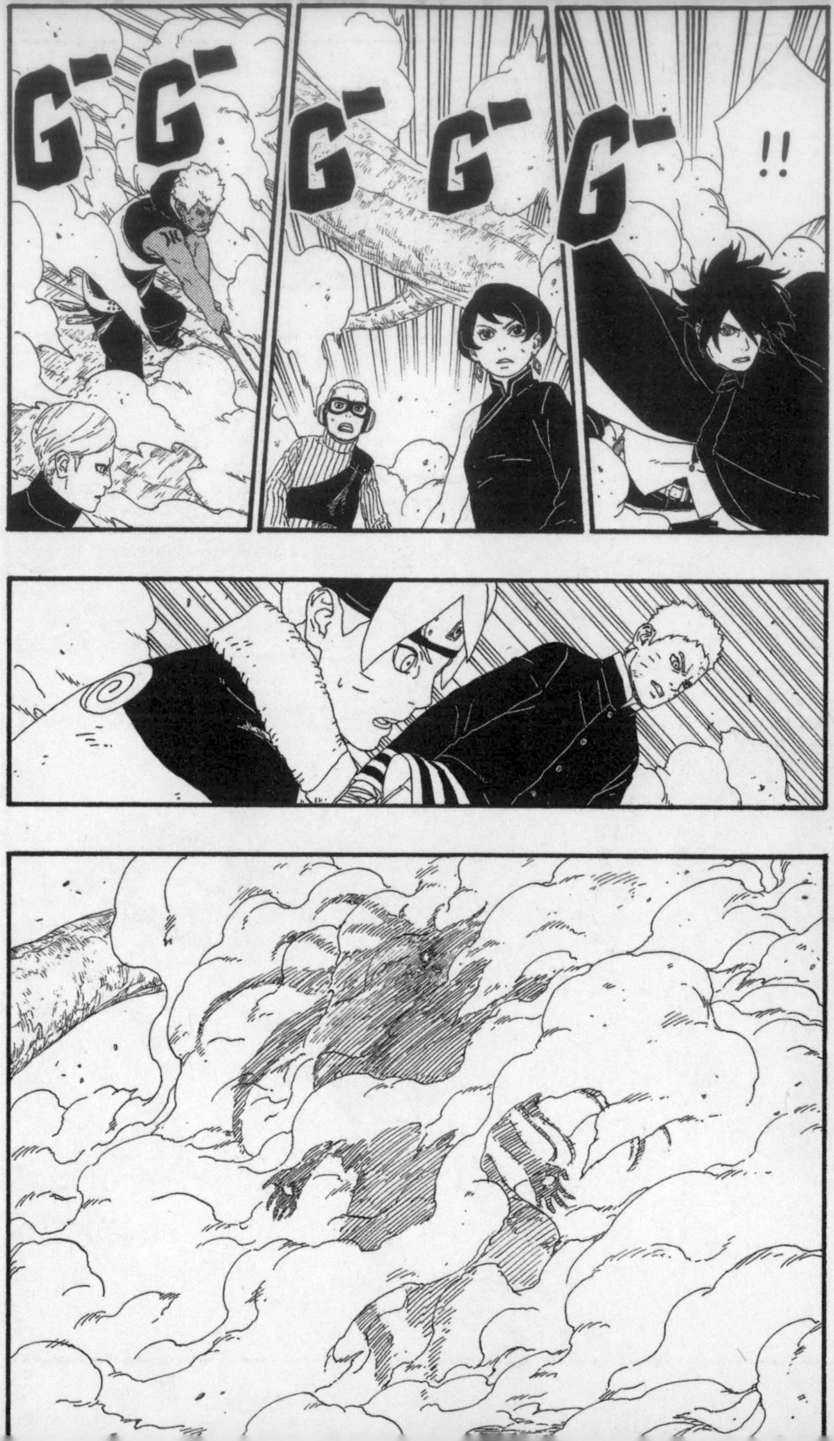
G-
!!
G- G-
G- G-

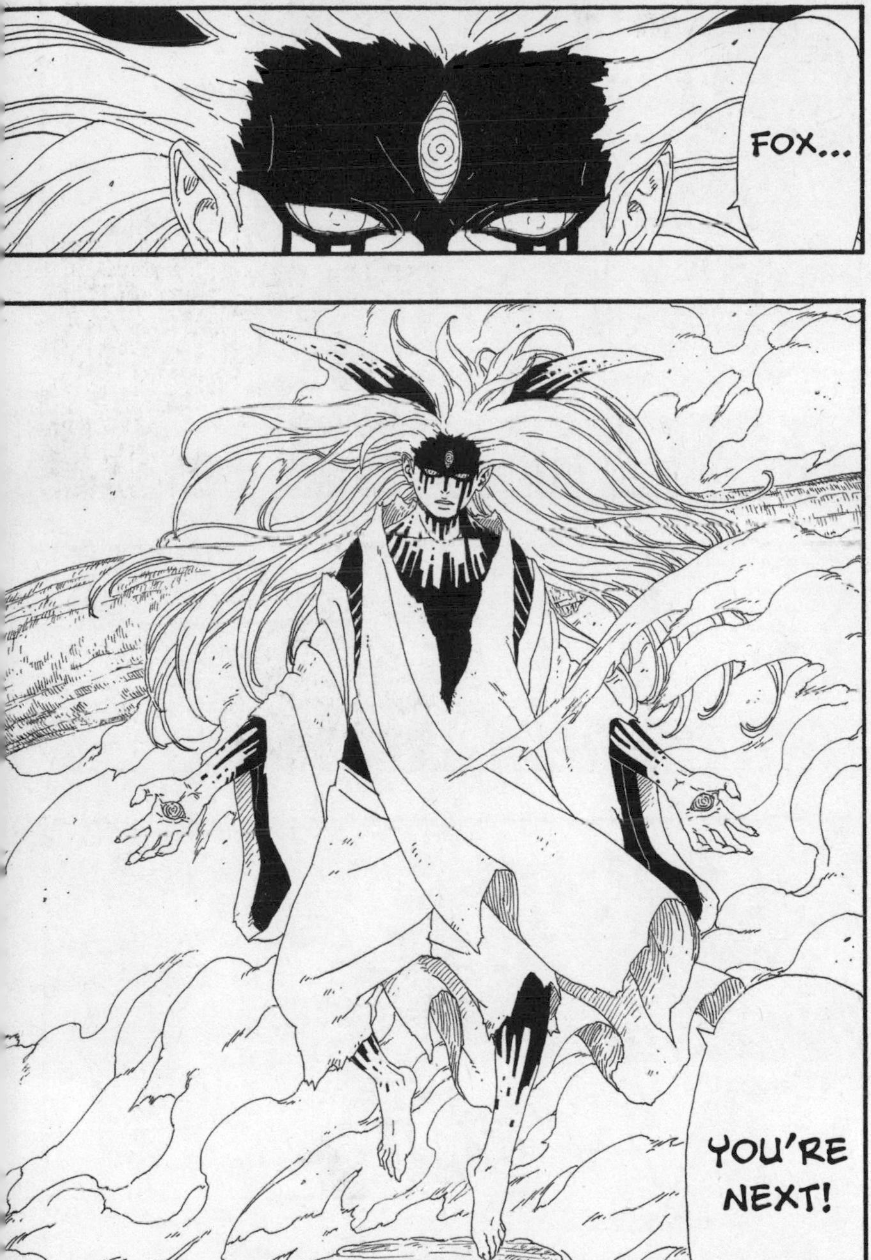
FOX...
YOU'RE NEXT!

BORU-FANS!!!

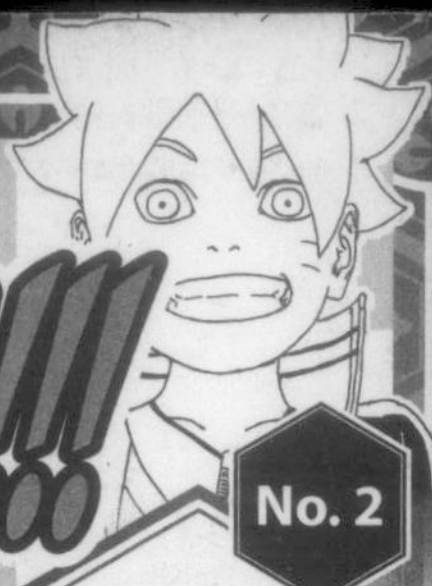

No. 2

Now, this round's *Boruto* Fan Cluster, abbreviated *Boru*-fans!!!, will be introducing Sand's new generation!! We'll reveal new intel that *Boruto* fans must not miss!!

Graphic novel edition!!

Introducing Boruto's Rivals

Boruto hasn't fought them yet, but the Sand trio are pretty formidable!!

SHINKI

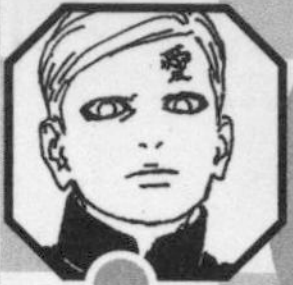

Even among the new generation shouldering the Sand Village's future, his abilities surpass the rest. He skillfully manipulates sand and iron sand, and I'd like him to become a leader who will steer the village.

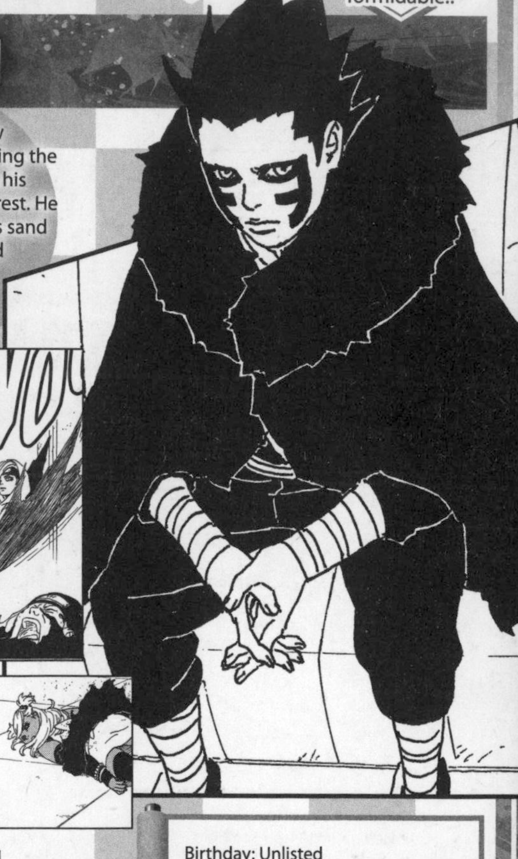

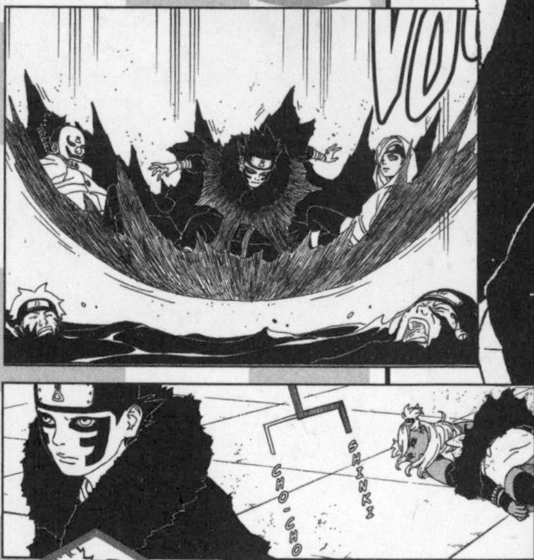
SHINKI
CHO-CHO

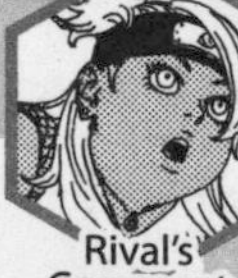

Rival's Comment

He's pretty good to've defeated me!

I wish he were a bit more handsome though.

Birthday: Unlisted
Favorite food: Gizzards, stewed offal
Food dislikes: Natto
Hobbies: Gardening, embroidery

Yodo

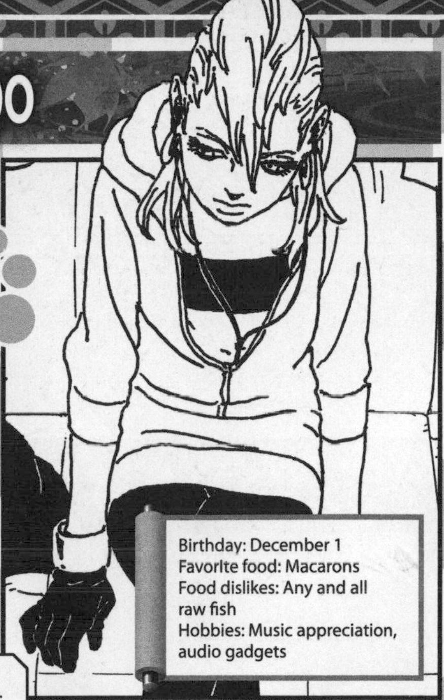

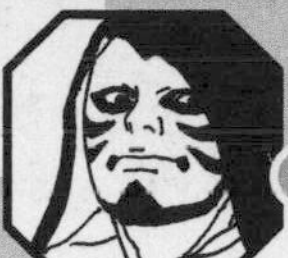

She's got talent. I'll admit that, but she's always listening to music on those earbuds… Listen to us adults now and then, will ya!

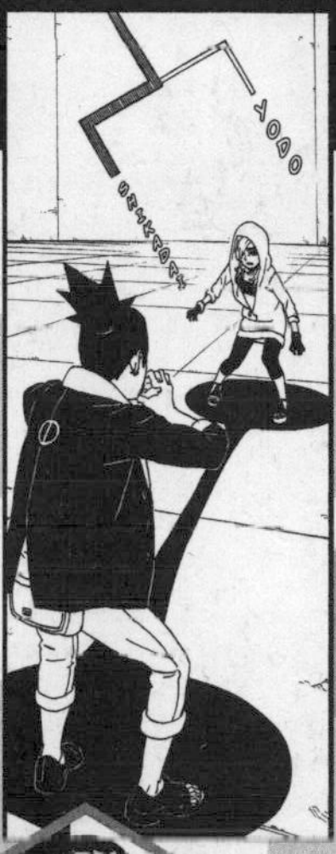
YODO

Birthday: December 1
Favorite food: Macarons
Food dislikes: Any and all raw fish
Hobbies: Music appreciation, audio gadgets

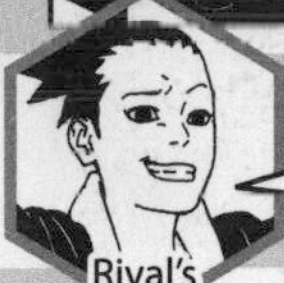

Rival's Comment

I happened to win this time, but who knows about next time?

It's such a bother…

Araya

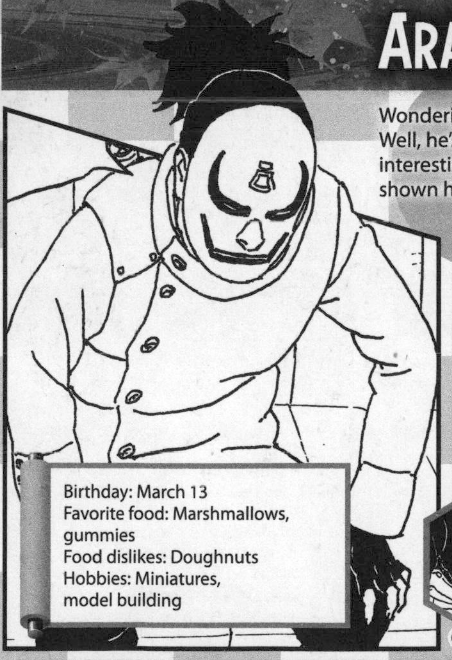

Wondering about that mask? Well, he's actually quite an interesting guy. He hasn't shown his full hand yet.

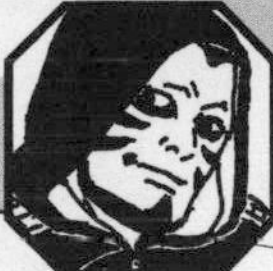

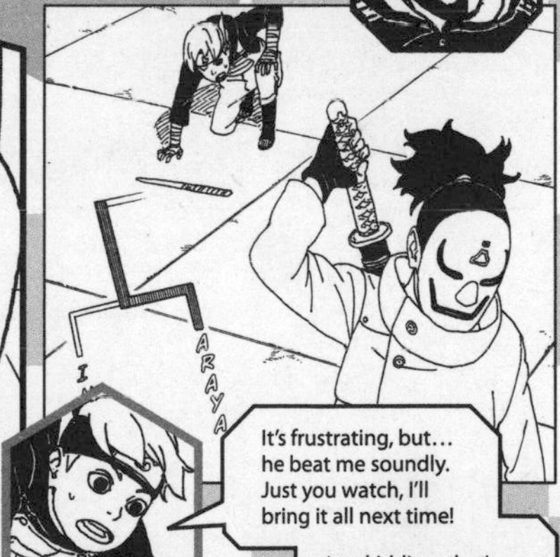
ARAYA

Birthday: March 13
Favorite food: Marshmallows, gummies
Food dislikes: Doughnuts
Hobbies: Miniatures, model building

Rival's Comment

It's frustrating, but… he beat me soundly. Just you watch, I'll bring it all next time!

Just kidding, that's not my style.

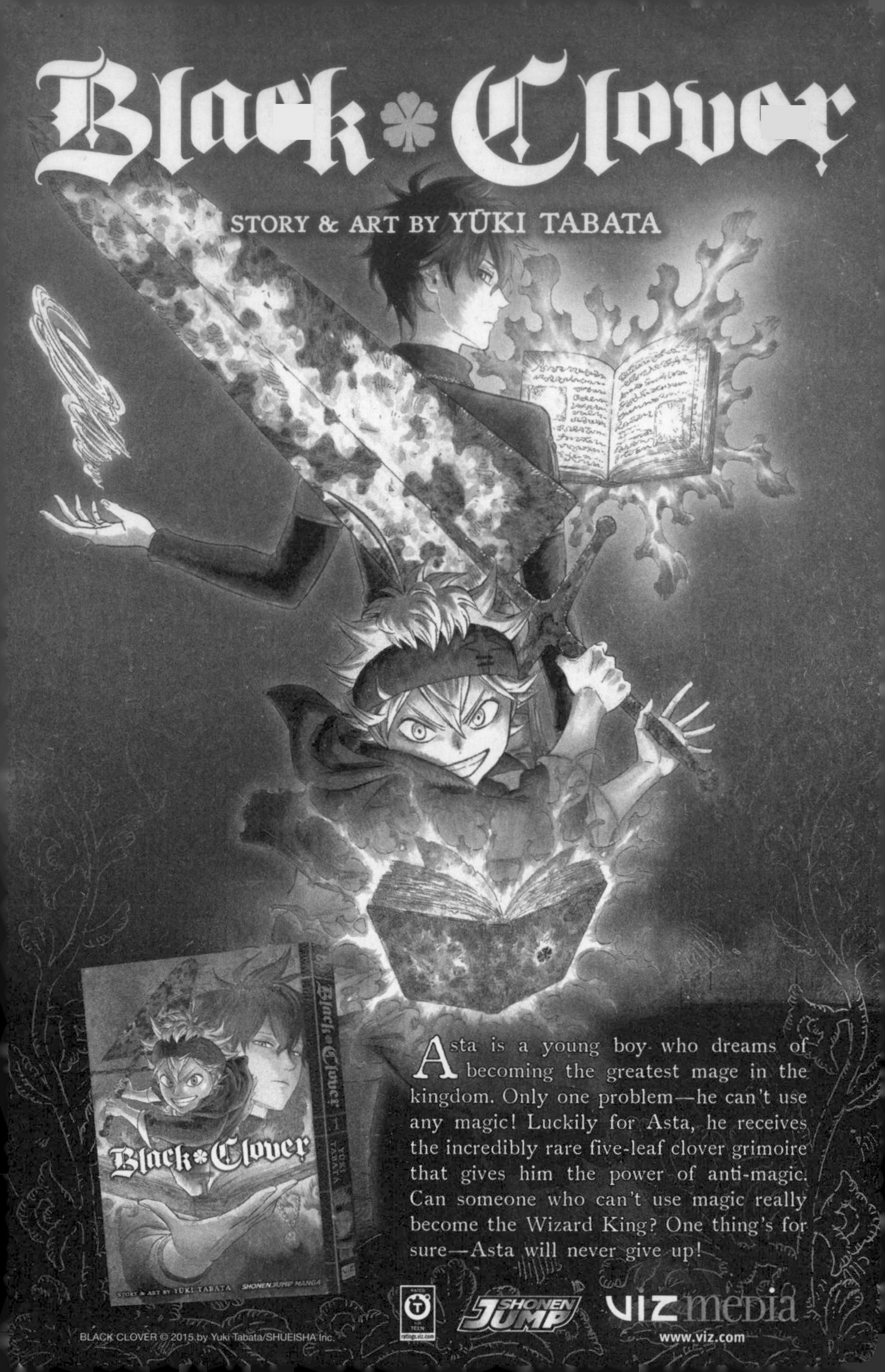
Black Clover
STORY & ART BY YŪKI TABATA
Black Clover
1
YŪKI TABATA
STORY & ART BY YŪKI TABATA
SHONEN JUMP MANGA
Asta is a young boy who dreams of becoming the greatest mage in the kingdom. Only one problem—he can't use any magic! Luckily for Asta, he receives the incredibly rare five-leaf clover grimoire that gives him the power of anti-magic. Can someone who can't use magic really become the Wizard King? One thing's for sure—Asta will never give up!
RATED T FOR TEEN
ratings.viz.com
SHONEN JUMP
VIZ media
www.viz.com
BLACK CLOVER © 2015 by Yuki Tabata/SHUEISHA Inc.

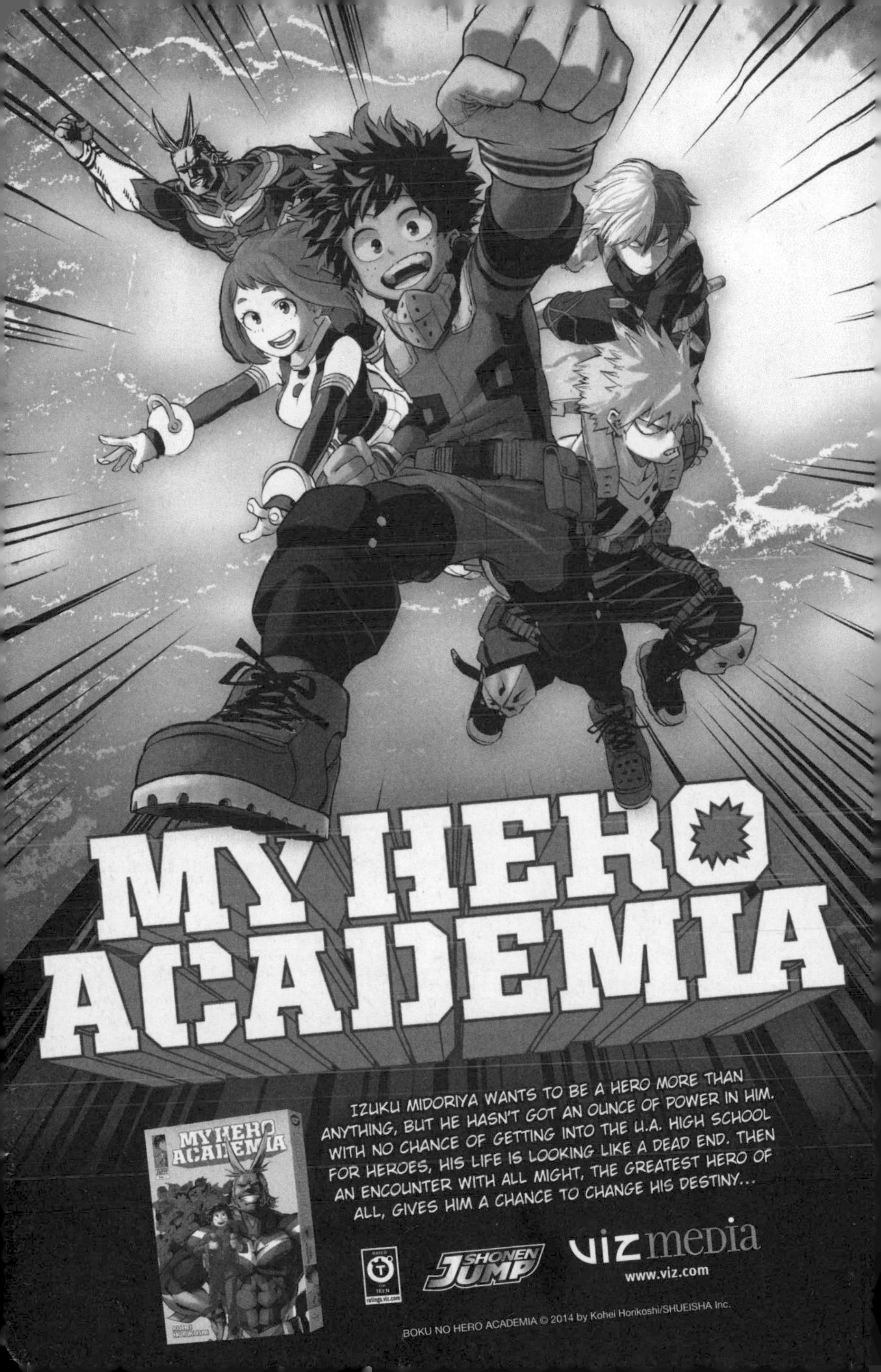
MY HERO ACADEMIA
IZUKU MIDORIYA WANTS TO BE A HERO MORE THAN ANYTHING, BUT HE HASN'T GOT AN OUNCE OF POWER IN HIM. WITH NO CHANCE OF GETTING INTO THE U.A. HIGH SCHOOL FOR HEROES, HIS LIFE IS LOOKING LIKE A DEAD END. THEN AN ENCOUNTER WITH ALL MIGHT, THE GREATEST HERO OF ALL, GIVES HIM A CHANCE TO CHANGE HIS DESTINY...
MY HERO ACADEMIA
SHONEN JUMP
VIZ media
www.viz.com
BOKU NO HERO ACADEMIA © 2014 by Kohei Horikoshi/SHUEISHA Inc.

YOU'RE READING
IN THE
WRONG DIRECTION!!

WHOOPS! Guess what? You're starting at the wrong end of the comic!

...It's true! In keeping with the original Japanese format, **Boruto** is meant to be read from right to left, starting in the upper-right corner.

Unlike English, which is read from left to right, Japanese is read from right to left, meaning that action, sound effects and word-balloon order are completely reversed... something which can make readers unfamiliar with Japanese feel pretty backwards themselves. For this reason, manga or Japanese comics published in the U.S. in English have sometimes been published "flopped"—that is, printed in exact reverse order, as though seen from the other side of a mirror.

By flopping pages, U.S. publishers can avoid confusing readers, but the compromise is not without its downside. For one thing, a character in a flopped manga series who once wore in the original Japanese version a T-shirt emblazoned with "M A Y" (as in "the merry month of") now wears one which reads "Y A M"! Additionally, many manga creators in Japan are themselves unhappy with the process, as some feel the mirror-imaging of their art alters their original intentions.

We are proud to bring you **Boruto** in the original unflopped format. Turn to the other side of the book and let the ninjutsu begin...!

—Editor